MAN-HUNTERS OF THE OLD WEST
2

MAN-HUNTERS
OF THE OLD WEST

VOLUME 2

ROBERT K. DeARMENT

UNIVERSITY OF OKLAHOMA PRESS : NORMAN

Library of Congress Cataloging-in-Publication Data

Names: DeArment, Robert K., 1925– author.
Title: Man-hunters of the Old West, volume 2 / Robert K. DeArment.
Description: Norman : University of Oklahoma Press, 2017. |
Includes bibliographical references and index.
Identifiers: LCCN 2016034602 | ISBN 978-0-8061-5911-9
(hardcover : alk. paper)
Subjects: LCSH: Bounty hunters—West (U.S.)—Biography. |
Peace officers—West (U.S.)—Biography. | Frontier and pioneer
life—West (U.S.) | West (U.S.)—Biography.
Classification: LCC F596 .D386 2017 | DDC 978/.020922 [B] —dc23
LC record available at https://lccn.loc.gov/2016034602

The paper in this book meets the guidelines for permanence and
durability of the Committee on Production Guidelines for
Book Longevity of the Council on Library Resources, Inc. ∞

1 2 3 4 5 6 7 8 9 10

Contents

Illustrations

Preface

In 2016 I published *Man-Hunters of the Old West*, sketches of eight notable outlaw trackers of the American frontier: Jim Hume, Dave Cook, M. F. Leech, Jack Duncan, Scott Davis, W. H. H. Llewellyn, Perry Mallon, and Charlie Siringo. These are all interesting characters, but aware that there are many more fascinating figures who played significant roles in running down frontier felons, I have written a second volume. Readers will find within these pages accounts of the remarkable careers of eight other western man-hunters whose lives ranged from 1810 until 1967: Harry Love of California, Tom Tobin of Colorado, Granville Stuart of Montana, Harry Morse of California, Bass Reeves of Indian and Oklahoma Territories, John Hughes of Texas, and Frank Norfleet, a Texas native who spent several years and his life savings pursuing a criminal gang from one end of North America to the other.

Life on the frontier was rough and at times brutal, and as readers will see, early man-hunters were especially calloused. Two such man-hunters from the early period, Harry Love and Tom Tobin, after tracking their quarries to remote hideouts and killing them, cut off the heads of the gang leaders, a gruesome act done not out of savagery, but to enable the man-hunters to return with positive evidence that they had indeed eliminated the wanted criminals.

These felon-hunters, like the vigilante organizations that preceded them, sometimes administered summary justice—hanging of their captured prey on the spot—when they believed the established court system was failing them. Rancher Granville Stuart, honored as "Mr. Montana," participated in this brand of law enforcement.

The eight depicted in this volume had widely divergent backgrounds, ranging from easterners Love and Morse, who both arrived in California as crew members on oceangoing ships, to Reeves, born into slavery in the antebellum South. In erudition they ranged from Tobin (who was illiterate), to Stuart (who authored a two-volume history of his life in the West and was commissioned to write a history of Montana), to Norfleet (who wrote or cowrote two books about his man-hunting adventures). Many, such as Morse, Reeves, Garrett, and Hughes, were career officers of the law. Norfleet was unique in being a private citizen turned dedicated nemesis of con artists.

Included in this volume are the stories of two man-hunters whose remarkable careers have been credited, one legitimately, the other dubiously, as forming the basis for the Lone Ranger, the fictional hero of popular comic books, movies, and television.

Of them all, Pat Garrett is no doubt the best remembered today because of the outlaw he hunted down and killed. Billy the Kid has been cemented into the collective memory of the general populace deeper than any of the eight man-hunters whose adventures are related here.

As in my first man-hunter book, I must take this opportunity to express my gratitude to those who followed the trails of these fascinating men before me. Providing much of the information herein recited, several of whom read pertinent chapters and provided useful comments, are my friends and astute chroniclers of California outlaw history: Bill Secrest and John Boessenecker, whose books contain a wealth of information about Harry Love and Harry Morse; James F. Perkins, biographer of Tom Tobin; Charles F. Price, recorder of the lives of the Espinosas; my friend and the foremost authority on Bass Reeves, Art Burton; and two other decades-long friends and fellow Wild West buffs, Leon Metz and Chuck Parsons, authors of the definitive biographies of Pat Garrett and John Hughes respectively.

As I pointed out in the foreword to the first volume, twenty-first-century readers should be hesitant before adversely judging the actions of these men. Born and raised in a century when a large section of the country accepted the institution of slavery, an idea absolutely abhorrent to modern-day Americans, these men held firm convictions of what constitutes right and wrong, and were willing to risk their lives to see that right overcame wrong, that good vanquished evil. Their convictions were not always consistent with current views. They could condone or even praise vigilante activity, including lynching, convinced that it was necessary to maintain some semblance of order under the conditions in which they lived. God-fearing men and women would flock to see the severed heads of outlaws displayed in pickling jars by man-hunters like

Love or Tobin, who had been hired by the state or territory to hunt down and exterminate vicious killers of innocent settlers. Like all the other men whose lives are related here, beheaders like Love in California and Tobin in Colorado were almost universally praised at the time. And Stuart in Montana and Hughes in Texas either participated in or condoned the lynching of malefactors by the dozen and were exalted for it.

It was a vastly different world, a different time, but all eight of these men played significant and important roles in bringing a semblance of law and order out of chaos, paving the way in the American West for a better world in a later time.

MAN-HUNTERS OF THE OLD WEST
2

— *1* —

HENRY "HARRY" LOVE
1810–1868

It appearing satisfactory by the within affidavits that Capt. Harry Love has captured the notorious Robber, Joaquin, I therefore believe him entitled to the reward of $1000 offered for his capture.

John Bigler, governor of California

One of the earliest to gain fame on the American western frontier as a fearless, sometimes brutal hunter of wanted men was an adventurer from New England with an incongruous last name, one that normally connoted tenderness and affection: Harry Love. Born in Vermont in 1810,[1] Love was christened Henry by his parents, but he preferred the name Harry, which he used throughout his life.[2]

The descendent of a reputedly notable American pioneering family—his paternal grandfather was a Revolutionary War veteran, and his mother was related to hero of that war Ethan Allen—Harry Love received only a rudimentary education as a youth. Still a young boy when his mother died and his father remarried, he could not accept what he called his stepmother's "petty tyranny," and he ran off to pursue a life at sea.[3]

Although the documentation of it is scant, he would later spin fanciful tales of his nautical career, stories which were picked up and promulgated by early chroniclers. One such storyteller wrote that after sailing out as a cabin boy on a West Indies–bound vessel, he discovered he was on a pirate ship, but his "exploits on the Spanish Main he would only allude to vaguely in after years." Over his "piratical life he studiously threw the veil of taciturnity."[4]

Although he evidently grew up at sea, and may even have spent some time as a Mississippi River keelboatman, an assertion by later writers that

Henry "Harry" Love. Courtesy of Santa Cruz Public Libraries (LH-0592).

he captained an ocean vessel at the age of fifteen is difficult to accept.[5] Other reports, originating perhaps with Love himself, had him serving as a scout and a warrior in conflicts as widespread as the Blackhawk War of 1832 in the upper Midwest, the 1835–42 Seminole War in Florida, and the Texas War of Independence in 1836, but reliable sources have not confirmed these claims, and it is doubtful that any are true.[6] Love was still a seaman as late as 1839, when he first visited California aboard a ship.[7] With the outbreak of war with Mexico in 1846, however, he definitely left the sea, as his service in that conflict is well documented.

Texans won their independence from Mexico in 1836. When, nine years later, Texas was accepted into the American union of states, many Mexicans felt that a vast expanse north of the Rio Grande had been stolen from them by the United States, and war clouds darkened over the U.S.-Mexican border. In 1845 General Zachary Taylor and a 3,500-man army were dispatched to the area to protect inhabitants from raids across the river.

Harry Love was in the port city of Mobile, Alabama, in early May 1846, courting a young lady with whom he was enamored, when news was received that a large Mexican military force had attacked an American patrol in South Texas, killing sixteen men and capturing the rest. Notices quickly appeared in Mobile, requesting military enlistees to go to the relief of Americans in the area. Harry Love, ever the adventurer, temporarily left his light-of-love to answer the call, signing up for a six-month tour of duty. His company, under Captain Robert Desha, moved to New Orleans, Louisiana, where a local paper greeted them: "Yesterday a company of seventy-six fine, noble-looking fellows from Mobile arrived in this city [and] marched down to the U. S. Barracks, all in excellent spirits."[8]

By May 13 Captain Desha's company and two others, encamped at Point Isabel, Texas—a supply depot that Zachary Taylor had established near the mouth of the Rio Grande—were welcomed by the general himself. For the next three months the new recruits performed routine garrison tasks, sentry duty, and uneventful patrol duty, while enduring torrid heat, swarms of mosquitoes, and bouts of dysentery and tropical fever. The death toll from disease was horrific; of the 754 Alabama volunteers, only 324 survived. Altogether an estimated 1,500 Americans died in this campaign, none of them from enemy action.[9] Harry Love apparently weathered this sad period successfully. The only significant change for him during this tour of duty was his promotion on July 2 to "fourth sergeant."[10]

Having signed up to fight Mexicans but finding no enemy to engage, the volunteers grew increasingly disgruntled, and desertions became a problem. In August, General Taylor ordered the volunteer companies back to their points of enlistment, and they disbanded.

Returning to Mobile, Love was struck with another disappointment, one not unique for servicemen. While he was off to the wars, his girl-friend had dumped him, perhaps for another not-so-patriotic suitor. "Alas for human constancy," wrote an acquaintance. "Harry, in a fit of misanthropic disgust, returned to the army, and throughout the war performed the most reckless feats of bravery. He never became entirely cured of his disappointment, which seemed to have taken a hold of his heart that neither time nor the instigation of common sense could entirely eradicate."[11] Love did not reenlist in the army, but took advantage of a general order issued on July 10, 1846, announcing that early volunteers would be welcomed as civilian employees of the army.[12] For seventy-five dollars a month he signed on as a courier for Captain William Chapman of the U.S. Army Quartermaster Department stationed at Matamoros, and it was in this capacity that he distinguished himself over the next year and a half in the Mexican War and beyond.[13]

As a mounted courier, astride one horse and leading another packed with military dispatches, mail, and newspapers, Love rode across northern Mexico, western Texas, and southern New Mexico. The country he traversed in Mexico was especially desolate and dangerous, infested with bandits and hostile Indians. During this time Love had many narrow escapes, including a particularly harrowing one in September 1848, which was recounted in a Matamoros newspaper. He had delivered dispatches at Chihuahua and was returning to Fort Brown, accompanied by a traveler named William Sherman, when the pair was attacked one evening by a Comanche war party. He and Sherman quit the trail and hid out in the mountains overnight. When in the morning it appeared that the hostiles had departed, the two men resumed the trail, but the Comanches found them again. Taking up a defensive position on the banks of an arroyo, with a stream swollen by recent rains at their back, Love and Sherman opened fire at the onrushing Indians. Spotting one whose elaborate headdress identified him as the leader, Love toppled him from his mount with a well-aimed shot. The charge was halted as the other Indians reined up and circled their fallen chieftain, providing the two white men an opportunity to escape across the rushing stream. Love and his two horses made it to the other side successfully, but Sherman's mount, weakened by a wound received in the previous day's action, floundered and was lost. Love saved Sherman from a similar fate by roping him, cowboy-style, and pulling him across. Sherman climbed up on Love's second horse, and the two men made a clean getaway from the leaderless Comanche warriors. By this experience, commented the newspaper's editor, Love had "proved himself a good and faithful soldier, and one of the most trustworthy and fearless express riders on this line."[14]

Stories of this and other adventures that Love experienced as a dispatch rider during these years were recounted in local papers and were picked up and republished throughout the West. He began seeing his name preceded by the designation "Captain," which was bestowed on him as a measure of respect for his prowess in a dangerous undertaking.

One of his most ardent admirers in the Matamoros area was Helen Chapman, the wife of Love's boss. In letters to her mother, Helen gushed about the brave young frontiersman whom she described as "a perfect specimen of the Border Dandy, browned by exposure to wind and weather, of magnificent physical proportions, and altogether bearing himself with a dashing easy kind of grace that would astonish you." She was shocked when the local paper reported that Love had been slain in Mexico, but when the report was later proven false, her relief was palpable: "We had heard he had been murdered and the joy of his safe return was boundless."[15] In another letter a few months later she described her meeting with Love, who was back from one of his adventurous trips:

> Last Sunday while on my way to prayer meeting in Brownsville, I discovered . . . our dashing and favorite express rider, Harry Love. . . .
> I wish I could picture him to your vision, as he came dashing down the street, well mounted as he always is, sitting his horse as if he were a part of the noble animal he rides, his long black curls flowing in the wind, his chest thrown out, his expression cool, frank and resolute, his saber and spurs clashing, his clothes torn by the

chaparral and covered with dust, one of Colt's revolvers, a six shooter, fastened to his side and an additional brace of pistols in his holsters. These are his usual accouterments.[16]

News of the discovery of gold in California swept the nation in 1849, and gold fever was as exciting in such remote outposts as the settlements along the Texas Gulf Coast as it was in New England. Perhaps it was inevitable that an ambitious and adventurous fellow like Harry Love, approaching his fortieth year, would see the goldfields of California as his last opportunity to strike it rich. His superior, William Chapman, now an army major, recognized the signs that his ace dispatch rider, tempted by stories of fabulous fortunes being made in California, was preparing to pull up stakes and head westward. Concerned with ways to utilize the Rio Grande to greater advantage for the U.S. Army and aware of Love's maritime experience, Chapman developed a plan to keep him longer. He christened a keelboat the *Harry Love*, made Love its captain, and assigned him the duty of traversing the upper reaches of the Rio Grande with supplies for the various army posts. The ploy worked. Love postponed his departure for California, happily took to the waters again, and over the next year created another legend for himself as the heroic skipper of a Rio Grande keelboat.[17]

Standing at the bow of his keelboat, Love certainly was a memorable figure. Second Lieutenant Egbert Viele, who worked with him during this period, described Love to his wife: "Six feet three, and stalwart and robust in proportion, as bold and intrepid as a lion, with a voice of thunder, and a mild blue eye, which softened the otherwise fierce aspect of his rough, sun-burnt face, which was half-concealed by a flowing black beard and a heavy mustache."[18]

Finally, in September 1850, Love could resist the pull of the California goldfields no longer. Bidding his Texas friends *adios*, he set out for the new El Dorado to make his fortune. He crossed northern Mexico and caught a coastal steamship bound for San Francisco, arriving on December 11 to find a burgeoning city vastly changed from the one he had visited eleven years before. Little is known of his activities during the first years of his California stay, but it is evident that he, like most fortune seekers, met with little success in his search for gold. He moved around, probably seeking opportunities for work more suited to his experience. He almost joined a prospecting expedition into the Gila River region in 1852, but the project fell through.[19]

In addition to fortune seekers, the California gold rush region was inundated in the early fifties with criminals of all types and nationalities, coming from other sections of the United States, Mexico, Central and South America, and as far away as Europe and Australia. Murder and robbery were rampant during these years in California, and a crime committed in 1852 proved to be the initial event leading to Harry Love's fame as a California man-hunter.

Brothers Allen and John Ruddle had joined the rush to California in 1849 and, after achieving little success at prospecting, had invested in farmland along the Merced River in Mariposa County. On the morning of April 25, 1852, Allen set out for Stockton in an ox-drawn wagon to purchase furniture for the new homestead he shared with John and their families. What transpired after he had gone about two miles was related succinctly in a letter dated April 29, which was published first in the *Stockton Journal* and later in other California newspapers:

> A young man named Allen B. Ruddle, who was driving a wagon to Stockton for supplies, was found dead on the road on Monday last, having been shot through the head and breast. He had about four hundred dollars in his possession when he left home, of which he was robbed. The deceased leaves an aged father, mother, brothers and sisters to mourn his untimely end. . . . There is good reason for supposing that the murder was perpetrated by Spaniards.[20]

Mexican outlaws Joaquin Murrieta, his brother-in-law Reyes Feliz, and Pedro Gonzales had been seen in the area immediately before Ruddle's murder and were suspected of that crime as well as the murder of another man on the Stockton Road three weeks earlier. When the Ruddle family offered a sizeable reward for the apprehension of the killers, man-hunters, including Harry Love, took up the trail.[21]

While dispatch riding in Texas, Love had come to know and despise the Mexican bandits who preyed on travelers crossing the desolate expanses in which he operated, but encumbered by his official duties, he had never assumed the role of man-hunter during that period. Now, free from responsibility to anyone other than himself, he eagerly grasped the opportunity to hunt murderous bandidos and perhaps make some money in the process. So began the career of the first famous man-hunter in California's history.

For weeks Love and his companion (whose identity has never been discovered by historians), following the distinctive hoofprints of a particular horse, trailed their quarry through the San Joaquin Valley, past Tulare Lake, and over the Tehachapi Mountains. In early June they rode into Los Angeles and lost the trail in the myriad tracks of horses. By means of discreet inquiries, they learned that Gonzalez had been there, but had gone on to San Buenaventura, an isolated community northwest of Los Angeles.[22]

On or about June 16 the two man-hunters confronted Gonzalez in a San Buenaventura roadhouse and, after a brief exchange of gunfire in which no one was hit, took him into custody. They—on horseback—then escorted their prisoner—on foot—back toward Los Angeles. On June 18 Love and his sidekick appeared in a Los Angeles justice of the peace courtroom without Gonzalez but with an explanation in the form of a prepared affidavit:

> The prisoner being on foot, complained of fatigue and made several ineffectual efforts to escape. When about 8 miles this side of the river he complained of thirst and pointing to a ravine near at hand told his conductors that there was plenty of water a little way up. Accordingly [Love] dismounted and proceeded with the man til they came to a small clump of bushes, when the prisoner darted forward into them and would have made his escape—Mr. L's boots and spurs preventing him from giving chase—but the latter, in endeavoring to knock him down with his pistol, accidently [*sic*] discharged it and shot him through the head, killing him instantly.[23]

Whether Harry Love shot Pedro Gonzales to death accidentally, as he claimed, or deliberately, as is quite possible, will never be known, but the act has been recognized as "the first serious blow" to be struck against the outlaw chieftain Joaquin Murrieta and his murderous followers.[24]

One of the killers believed responsible for the murder of Allen Ruddle had been dispatched by bullet, but there is no evidence that Harry Love ever received any reward money for hunting him down. For the next year he was apparently out of the man-hunting business, even as the depredations by Mexican bandidos, most of them led by the increasingly notorious Joaquin Murrieta gang, continued. Then, in April 1853, the California state legislature in session at Benicia received an extraordinary petition. Signed by 127 prominent residents of Mariposa County, the scene of many crimes attributed to the notorious Joaquin Gang, the petition contended that local law enforcement was unable to handle the crime wave in that area and requested passage of a special act "authorizing some discreet, prudent person to organize a company of twenty or twenty-five good horsemen, well-armed and equipped [and to be] called the 'California Rangers'" in order to bring down Joaquin Murrieta and his outlaw gang.

Before the legislature took any action in response to this petition, another was received, this one signed by one hundred Mariposa County ranchers and miners. It also urged the establishment of a ranger force to be armed, equipped, and paid by the state, and it strongly recommended Harry Love be given command of the unit. This second petition was personally delivered to the assembly by Love himself.[25]

On May 17, 1853, the legislature passed an act creating the California Rangers, with Harry Love as their captain, and Governor John Bigler signed it into law. It authorized the formation of a company, not to exceed twenty men, for service of three months, unless earlier disbanded. Each enlistee was to be paid $150 a month, but was required to furnish his own horse, weapons, equipment, and provisions. Although it was clear from the outset that this ranger force was established for the sole purpose of eliminating the Joaquin Gang of outlaws, what was not clear was the identity of "Joaquin." The bill referred to a "gang of robbers commanded by the five Joaquins. . . . Joaquin Muriati [*sic*], Joaquin Ocomorenia, Joaquin Valenzuela, Joaquin Botellier [*sic*], and Joaquin Carrillo, and their banded associates."[26] If this array of Joaquin targets did not confuse Love and his rangers, it certainly has puzzled newsmen and historians for years. As an editor at the time commented rather facetiously:

> It is possible that THE Joaquin is included in the above enumeration, but if so, his identity is destroyed and with it all the notoriety he has acquired. A dangerous name is "Joaquin" and all who bear it must need to keep a sharp lookout, especially during the period of service of the twenty mounted Rangers. The legal proprietors of

some of the respectable names outlawed by the Legislature should petition for a rebaptism.[27]

A more serious editorial comment regarding Love and his rangers had previously appeared in a Stockton paper: "Col. [sic] Harry Love, who has been authorized by the legislature to raise a company for the capture of Joaquin and his gang, passed through this city yesterday. An important power has been delegated to the gentleman and we hope that he will exercise it with vigor, yet with determination."[28]

Actually, the chieftain of the gang responsible for most of the depredations was one man, Joaquin Murrieta, and the other Joaquins either were aliases he had used at one time or another or applied to gang members who had adopted the well-publicized first name of their leader. Ranger Captain Harry Love may have sorted out this Joaquin name confusion before he took to the field with his company, for he focused on running down Murrieta from the first.

To help him in selection of ranger company men, he conferred with William J. Howard, a Mexican War veteran who, arriving in California in 1849, had done well with mining ventures. The owner of a large horse ranch in Mariposa County, Howard was familiar with the well-seasoned fighting men Love sought to enlist. He aided in that selection and also offered Love the use of his ranch as headquarters for the company.[29]

Chosen as first lieutenant of the company was Patrick Edward Connor, who had served with the Texas Volunteers in the Mexican War. Charles Bludworth and George W. Evans were second lieutenants. John Nuttall and William T. Henderson were appointed commissary officers, and Dr. S. K. Piggott was made company surgeon. Filling out the ranks as privates were an assortment of men from various occupations, all of them toughened by frontier life. Some were veterans of the Mexican and Indian Wars and others were gunfighters, survivors of deadly pistol encounters. Many officers and privates were conversant in the Spanish language, an attribute that would prove especially expedient in dealing with the Hispanic populations, both lawful and unlawful, which they would be confronting.[30]

Once his rangers were assembled in late May, Captain Love led the company out in his historic manhunt. For more than a month he and his men explored the San Joaquin Valley and Sierra foothills, searching for leads to the gang's current location. They checked out Mexican mining camps and stock herders' villages, arrested several suspects they believed had aided and abetted the Joaquin bandits, and recovered a number of stolen horses. Information derived from interrogation led them on across the Coast Ranges to Mission San Jose, where Murrieta was said to visit occasionally. There Love made his first notable arrest on July 10, when his rangers collared Jesus Feliz, a known confederate and relative by marriage of the gang leader.

After an intensive interrogation of Feliz, Love took his prisoner and company fifty miles south to San Juan Bautista, from where he dispatched a report to the governor on July 12, 1853:

> To his Excellency Govr Bigler
>
> Sir: I leave this place this night for the mountains. I have arrested a Mexican, Jesus, a brother in law of Joaquin's. He says he will take & show us to Joaquin if we will release him. I will try him a while to see what it will end in. There appears to be quite a number of horse thieves hid in the mountains back of this place and between here and the Tulare Valley. I hope I may make him useful to me in hunting them out. We get a few stray stock ever [*sic*] few days but nothing of importance has occurred.
>
> Your Obedient Servant
>
> Harry Love, Capt Cala Rangers[31]

Why Feliz, a hardened criminal, assisted his captors in their quest for his former partners in crime can only be surmised. He may have been tortured or enticed by promises of a share in the reward. He may have tired of the frenetic outlaw life, especially after seeing two of his brothers die violently, or he may have simply opted for gut spilling in return for leniency in coming court action. In any event, Love took him along on the hunt, and the information he provided proved essential to the California Rangers' ultimate success.

With provisions for an eighteen-day foray, Love's men spread the word at San Juan Bautista that they were heading off on a scout down the coast. This was deliberate subterfuge intended to foil the passing of their actual plans to Joaquin by any pueblo residents in league with the bandits.

Love led his rangers into the Salinas Valley and stopped in the afternoon, evidently to spend the night. But when darkness fell, he had them break camp, mount up, and make a forced march along the San Benito

River to Panoche Pass in a remote section of the Coast Ranges. He set up camp there and sent out scouting patrols looking for signs of the Murrieta band.

Not one to sit in camp and wait for his men to report, Love, with Feliz in tow, took charge of a scouting party himself. Following his nose, his trailing instincts, and perhaps suggestions from Feliz, he led the patrol southward for some twenty miles. On July 20 he came on a deep canyon where Mexican mustang hunters were encamped with a herd of several hundred horses. Brands on some of the animals made it clear that not all were wild mustangs, and Love suspected the herd included horses stolen from ranches on the coast. Without alerting the Mexicans to his presence, he headed back to his own encampment for reinforcements. The next day he returned with his entire ranger company and rode directly into the camp. While the Mexicans, some of whom were probably Murrieta gang members, silently glowered, he and his men examined the suspect horses and confiscated eight that they believed had been stolen. After telling the mustangers he was taking the horses to San Juan Bautista for positive identification, Love departed with his rangers.

Believing this incursion would send the mustang hunters straight to Murrieta to warn him that lawmen were hot on his trail, Love made camp about ten miles away from the canyon and waited three days, allowing the mustangers ample time to round up their horses and move out. On July 24 he and his rangers returned to an empty canyon. Tracks revealed that the mustangers had moved their herd westward, down the canyon. Convinced that his ploy had worked and the mustang hunters would lead him straight to Murrieta, Love rested his men the remainder of that day and evening in preparation for what was likely to be an exciting day on the morrow.

At two o'clock in the morning on July 25 the rangers moved down the canyon to the valley below. Dawn was breaking when they spotted smoke from a campfire some three miles ahead. Love and his men rode hard toward this site and got within four hundred yards before they were discovered. Startled cries rudely awakened the Mexicans—a mixture of mustangers and Murrieta gang members—as the rangers thundered into the camp. Pandemonium reigned. Most of the mustang hunters ran for their horses, while the bandidos went for their guns.

The mounted rangers herded those fleeing back into the camp at gunpoint. There, all were subjected to a barrage of questions as Love and his rangers endeavored to separate the wheat from the chaff. One man, "a handsome, long-haired, fair-complected young Mexican of about twenty-three," standing beside his horse at the edge of a deep arroyo, stepped forward and said, "Talk to me. I am the leader of this band."[32]

Ranger Bill Byrnes reined up at this point, took one look at the man, and recognized him as the one they sought. "This is Joaquin, boys!" he shouted. "We have got him at last!"[33] Hearing this, one of the bandit chieftain's followers, later identified as Bernardino "Three-Fingered Jack" Garcia, pulled out a pistol and triggered off two rounds, directing his fire at the ranger captain. One bullet grazed Love's head and made a new part in his hair while the other missed entirely. An immediate answering salvo of nine shots fired by Charlie Bludworth, Bill Henderson, and two other rangers riddled the body of Three-Fingered Jack. To make sure he was dead, Bill Byrnes and Love each pumped a round into his head.

Garcia had lived only seconds after shooting at Love, but if his intention was to divert the rangers' attention from his leader and give Murrieta a chance to escape, he was successful, at least for a few moments. Before the rangers could grab him, Murrieta vaulted onto his horse and, riding bareback, dropped down the embankment to the creek below and raced off along the arroyo floor. Henderson, the closest ranger to the fleeing bandido, emptied the other barrel of his shotgun at him, but his horse shied, causing him to miss. Dropping the scattergun, Henderson spurred his horse in pursuit. At full gallop, he fired his six-shooter, hitting Joaquin's mount in the leg, but the animal continued on. A second pistol shot dropped the animal, but Murrieta sprang to his feet and ran off down the canyon.

Ranger John White rode along the rim of the arroyo, firing his rifle at the wanted gang leader as Henderson continued his six-shooter fusillade. The long-sought bandit chieftain finally pitched forward into the creek with three bullets in his back. When the rangers reached Murrieta, he muttered his last words: "*No tira mas. Yo soy muerte.*" ("Don't shoot any more. I am dead.")[34]

While Love, Byrnes, Bludworth, Henderson, and White had been busy with Murrieta and Garcia, other rangers had been trying to round up the rest of Joaquin's gang. Two had been killed in brief gunfights and two others, Antonio Lopez and Jose Maria Ochoa, had been captured, but most escaped. A thorough search was made in the camp for stolen loot, but nothing of any great value was found.[35] When Love interrogated the prisoners, Lopez, a big, tough-looking older man, glared defiance and refused to answer any questions, but Ochoa, much younger and less hardened, was cooperative. He had come to California from Mexico with Murrieta, he said, but denied having committed any robberies. Most importantly, after a sad look at the dead body the rangers had dragged from the canyon, he confirmed that it was indeed Joaquin Murrieta.

Captain Love, now faced with the problem of proving he and his rangers had successfully carried out their assigned mission, did what he had to do, an act which was commonly performed in the early West to prove the death of a wanted fugitive: he had his men cut off the head of the bandit Joaquin.[36] In addition, he had them sever the head and deformed hand of Three-Fingered Jack to prove that Joaquin's lieutenant had also been dispatched. Aware that in the midsummer heat these grisly artifacts would deteriorate quickly, he handed them over to Bill Byrnes and a new recruit named John Sylvester with instructions to hurry to Fort Miller, about a hundred miles distant, and preserve the trophies in alcohol.[37]

Anxious to continue his pursuit of the scattered gang members, Love decided to take the cooperative prisoner Ochoa along to provide help, but the truculent attitude exhibited by Lopez convinced him that this tough hombre could only cause trouble, so he turned Lopez over to Byrnes and Sylvester with instructions to escort him to Fort Miller along with the heads and three-fingered hand.

With the grizzly trophies wrapped in a gunnysack and firmly secured behind Byrnes's saddle and Lopez tied to a horse, the two rangers set off. Attempting to cross the dangerous slough between Tulare Lake and the San Joaquin River, they lost their prisoner. Lopez's horse stepped in a hole and thrashed around in panic, and horse and rider disappeared in the swamp. Taking a longer route, the two rangers crossed the San Joaquin on a ferry operated by Samuel A. Bishop, to whom they explained their mission and displayed the gruesome trophies that were already starting to putrefy. It so happened that Bishop was well supplied with spirits, and he offered help. He produced an empty liquor keg into which the heads and hand were placed and covered with red-eye whiskey from a forty-gallon barrel. The keg was then secured to the back of a hired mule provided by the ferryman, and Byrnes and Sylvester continued on to Fort Miller. There, it was found that the head of Three-Fingered Jack was so badly deformed by the bullets that had killed him and by decomposition that it was useless for identification purposes, and so it was buried. The head of Joaquin and the hand of Garcia were retained in glass jars of alcohol so they could be viewed.[38]

Meanwhile, after burying the bodies of the outlaws killed in the raid on Joaquin's camp, Love, accompanied by his informants Feliz and Ochoa, led his company after the fleeing bandidos. Finding that they had scattered in different directions, he abandoned the chase and turned toward Fort Miller, arriving there only a day after Byrnes and Sylvester.

The first public notice of Love's achievement appeared in the form of a letter to the *San Joaquin Republican*, with an appended note regarding the weather, explaining Love's concern about the preservation of his severed heads:

> I hasten to inform you of the death of Joaquin, the robber, who has been such a curse in the country for some time. Captain Byrnes, one of the Rangers, and Mr. Sylvester arrived here yesterday evening with the heads of Joaquin and one of his band, whom they captured at a place called Singing River, about 140 miles from here. The remainder of the party are expected here this evening with two prisoners. . . . The weather is very warm—thermometer 115 degrees in the shade.[39]

When the news spread, political foes of Governor Bigler attempted to throw cold water on his coup in appointing Harry Love as captain of the rangers, who had had quick success in ridding the state of a notorious bandit chieftain. Joaquin was still alive, they claimed, and the head in the bottle was that of another Mexican Love had killed and decapitated to gain the reward. To disprove these tales, Love spent the next few weeks running down people who had known Murrieta and could identify him from the bottled head he carried. Typical was Pedro Monka's deposition: "I do solemly [*sic*] swear that the head Capt. Harry Love has is the head of Joaquin Muriati [*sic*]. I have known him for eighteen years."[40]

At a hearing held by a Mariposa County justice of the peace on August 5, eighteen citizens signed a document averring that Jose Ochoa, a prisoner taken in the ranger raid, knew Joaquin Murrieta well and was a member of his gang. They also were in full agreement that the head in the bottle was that of the notorious gang leader. This document was copied and added to the pile of testimonials Love had collected in preparation for his presentation to the governor in confirmation of his claim.[41]

Confident that his sworn depositions would still any remaining doubts about Joaquin's demise, Love made an appointment with the governor to deliver his final report. On the way to the state capital he read a piece in a San Francisco paper that must have made his blood boil:

> It affords some amusement to our citizens to read the various accounts of the capture and decapitation of "the notorious Joaquin Murieta [sic]." The humbug is so transparent that it is surprising any sensible person can be imposed upon by the statements of the affair which have appeared in the prints. A few weeks ago a party of native Californians and Sonoreans [sic] started for the Tulare Valley for the expressed purpose of running mustangs. Three of the party have returned and report that they were attacked by a party of Americans and that the balance of their party, four in number, had been killed; that Joaquin Valenzuela, one of them, was killed as he was endeavoring to escape and that his head was cut off by his captors and held as a trophy.[42]

Although angered, Love did not react overtly to this report. However, it so infuriated one of his rangers, John Nuttall, that he composed a furious response:

> As I [was] one of the [rangers that] pursued and captured a bloody wretch whose enormous and bloody deeds have justly alarmed the fears of the whole community, it is perhaps demanded of me that I should make a brief reply to . . . an insidious attack . . . prompted either by the most inexcusable ignorance of the effect of such a fabrication, or for the more wicked purpose of screening that infamous band who are still prowling at liberty, and who, for aught the public knows, have themselves . . . instigated the writing of the letter to which this is a reply.[43]

Meeting with Love on August 27, Governor Bigler scanned the documents the ranger captain presented and wrote the following to add to the file: "It appearing satisfactory by the within affidavits that Capt. Harry

Love has captured the notorious Robber, Joaquin, I therefore believe him entitled to the reward of $1000 offered for his capture." He signed and dated the document and then jotted an addendum, below which he had Love sign: "This certifies that Joaquin could not have been taken alive and delivered to the authorities as he was mounted & endeavoring to make his escape when shot on my orders."[44]

Authorization was then given to pay each of the rangers $450 for their three-month service, as well as their share of the $1,000 reward. Some members of the state legislature favored passage of a measure granting the rangers an additional $5,000 for their work, pointing out rightly that one thousand dollars divided equally among twenty-one men amounted to less than fifty dollars for each, hardly a decent reward for the hardships and dangers they had endured and the good work they had accomplished, but the measure was unsuccessful. Love and others lobbied to renew the ranger commission, but that too failed, and on August 28 the company was officially disbanded.

For the next few months Harry Love, basking in his hard-earned statewide celebrity, used his macabre trophies to solidify that fame. Together with former rangers Bill Henderson and Jim Norton, he toured the state, exhibiting the head and hand and giving talks about the expedition to capture Joaquin. The Sacramento exhibition's opening was advertised in the local paper:

> Joaquin's Head—We would respectfully inform the citizens of Sacramento and surrounding country that the head of Joaquin Muriatta, the renowned robber and bandit, whose depredations were so numerous last winter, and who with part of his band was captured by Capt. Harry Love and his rangers . . . on the 24th July last, will be exhibited this day at Vincent Taylor's Saloon. As there has been considerable doubts as to his being the genuine Joaquin, we have taken considerable pains to procure affidavits from persons who knew him in different parts of the State. Anyone wishing to see such affidavits can do so by [examining] true copies of the sundry affidavits now on file at the Comptroller's office in Benicia.[45]

For those who might not wish to visit the saloon personally to view the exhibits, a reporter for the paper described them:

The head of the noted murderer is preserved in a glass jar whose convex sides have the effect of magnifying the features into an unnatural expression. . . . A profusion of jet black hair falls below its ears, while the sightless orbs indicate them to have been possessed at one time of a flashing lustre. . . . Accompanying this bloody trophy is a right hand, containing three fingers and a thumb, believed to have belonged to Manuel [sic] Garcia, otherwise called "Three Fingered Jack."[46]

The article explained that the rangers' goals in arranging the exhibition were, first, to obtain additional affidavits of authenticity, second, to satisfy a natural public curiosity about "the most celebrated and infamous outlaw of his age," and last, to strike fear in the hearts of those members of Joaquin's band that were still at large or any others who might be tempted to go down that evil road.

From Sacramento, Love and his friends moved on to Marysville, where a reporter interviewing Love got the distinct impression that "the object of the exhibition [was] simply to let it become fully known and established that the much dreaded assassin and robber is at last captured and slain."[47]

Within a month the former rangers took their exhibits to a succession of mining towns and added many affidavits from people who claimed to have known Joaquin and recognized his head in the jar. The local newspapers generally welcomed the exhibitions, but an occasional naysayer agreed with the views of the editor of the *San Francisco Herald*, who grumbled: "Let this head and hand . . . disappear from the public gaze. Their being hawked about in this fashion can but minister to a depraved curiosity, which should by all means be discountenanced in a civilized community."[48]

Some Hispanics objected to the head of one of their kind being displayed in public, and a few, possibly aiders and abettors of the Joaquin gang, actually took action to disrupt the tour. When Love shipped the trophies ahead from San Andreas by stage, three Mexicans trailed behind and later stopped the coach and demanded the relics, but the driver talked them out of it. On successive nights shots were fired at the stagecoach carrying Joaquin's head in Tuolumne County, and there was speculation that remnant gang members were responsible.[49]

Love forwarded the packet of additional affidavits he had garnered on his tour to the state capital in the hope that they would help win passage of a bill under consideration by the legislature providing an additional appropriation for rangers. The measure did not pass in that session, but in November the former rangers received some great news from a totally unexpected source. Newspapers in San Francisco had reported some months before that Chinese residents of the city, having seen many of their countrymen killed and robbed by Joaquin's gang, had offered a reward of $5,000 for the capture of the bandit leader. This turned out to be a false rumor, but now, with the demise of Joaquin an established fact, the Chinese did manage to collect $1,000 and turned it over to the rangers in November 1853 as a token of their appreciation.[50]

In February 1854 the California state capital was transferred from Benicia to Sacramento. During the following months Harry Love spent much time at the new location, continuing his lobbying campaign to obtain just compensation for the rangers and himself. He stuck to his guns with the same tenacity he had shown as a man-hunter, and his persistence finally met with success. On May 15, 1854, Governor Bigler signed into law a bill awarding $5,000 to Captain Harry Love to be distributed among the members of the short-lived California Rangers. The editor of the *San Joaquin Republican* commented:

> We rejoice to learn that justice was done to [Captain Harry Love] by the Legislature and his claim against the State paid. It was through his courage and indomitable perseverance that the most infernal gang of rascals that ever infested any country was broken up. The vote to which his claim was allowed is most complimentary to him. In the Assembly the vote stood: ayes 43; nays 22. In the Senate he received 21 out of 26 votes.[51]

Unquestionably, the elimination of Joaquin was the high point of Harry Love's adventurous and action-filled life. But having turned forty-four in the year 1854, he was no longer a single, carefree, risk-taking young man, unconcerned with family responsibilities or property of any appreciable value. It was time to settle down, marry, and make a more ordinary living. When he learned that a sawmill with 320 acres of land was for sale in the Zavante Valley, a few miles north of the coastal pueblo of Santa

Cruz, he purchased it. The place had special attractions for him. Not only would it provide him with an established business, it was close to the ocean, and he still delighted in breathing the salt air. Perhaps most of all, a neighboring woman, the mother of the man who sold him the sawmill, interested him.

Mary Swain Bennett was fifty-one, seven years older than Love. A native of Georgia, she had come to California with her husband, Vardamon, and their eight children in 1845 before the gold rush. When Vardamon died in 1849, he left an estate valued at $150,000, mainly consisting of a great expanse of Mexican land-grant property he had acquired.[52]

Mary was not physically attractive. Six feet tall and weighing more than two hundred pounds, she was, in the words of an acquaintance, "unmistakably the head of the family—a large, powerful woman, uncultivated, but well-meaning and very industrious."[53] Harry Love was not particularly handsome either. As his biographer has pointed out,

> The attraction must have been mutual, but in a practical rather than a physical sense—both were large, unattractive people, but had qualities or assets that could be useful to each other. . . . Harry was famous throughout the state as a Texas border hero and the conqueror of Murrieta. A strapping six-footer, he was everything Mary's previous husband was not—a strong, successful, no-nonsense type who could protect a woman and her family in this rough-edged pioneer country. Plus, she needed a man to represent her in a male-dominated society. . . . She was constantly involved in land deals, squatter troubles, and legal squabbles in a time when women were not taken seriously in such matters. She needed a strong man to intimidate the court judges, squatters, and lawyers with whom she was continually involved. . . .
>
> To Harry the woman . . . represented stability in a frontier environment. . . . Large, rough, and a hard worker [Mary] was always on the move. She was quite charming when necessary—friendly and fond of joking when it suited her purposes. Better still, she owned property.[54]

It is ironic that the name Love, which Harry proudly bore and bestowed on Mary, apparently was absent as a term of passionate affection. In Monterey on May 31, 1854, they were united in a marriage that was more a business arrangement than a romantic union. There was no honeymoon. Two days after the wedding, Love, all alone, departed on a trip that would last three months.

On the first leg of a trip back east, he took passage on a steamer bound for Panama. He crossed the isthmus to an eastern port, taking a new railroad line that was under construction for part of the crossing. Then he boarded a steamship for New York City, arriving there on June 23, three weeks after leaving San Francisco.

It is not known why Love chose to travel back east without his bride so soon after his marriage. Perhaps it was part of a prenuptial agreement that Mary would finance this trip he had long desired but could never afford. He undoubtedly wanted to see his family, but it has also been suggested that perhaps he had journeyed east on another lobbying mission, to seek a commission in one of the new cavalry regiments being organized.[55] If this speculation is true, his efforts were unsuccessful, for after several weeks in the eastern country, he returned to California by the same route, arriving on the last day of August without any army commission.

Although Harry Love was still newsworthy in California during this period, notice of his marriage was extremely slow to reach the papers. Three and a half months after the event the editor of the *Columbia Gazette* made the belated announcement in his edition of September 16, 1854, together with an admonition taken from Charles Dickens's *Pickwick Papers*: "Captain Harry Love, the destroyer of the famous bandit Joaquin, turned Benedict just before his departure for the Atlantic States. He 'weakened' to the charms of Miss [*sic*] Mary Bennett, of Santa Clara. Poor fellow, we only hope that some fine day he may not find himself discussing the wisdom of the remark of the elder Weller to his son Samivel, to 'beware of the vidders.'" Unfortunately for Harry Love, the cautionary remark, probably injected in jest, turned out to be remarkably prophetic. After becoming entangled with Mary, the rest of Love's life took a downward course until his violent death at the hands of another of Mary's suitors.

His woes were not only matrimonial; they were professional, financial, political, and personal as well. Shortly after his marriage, he found that his sawmill was not the dependable source of income he had expected. Although California's continued explosive expansion created a heavy demand for building lumber, he discovered that his water-powered mill could not compete with other steam-driven mills. This problem was resolved by an act of God when heavy rains in the winter of 1861–62 caused floods, one of which completely carried away Love's sawmill.[56] He began working his acreage but had no aptitude for farming. In addition, he suffered severe financial setbacks from fires. One, in May 1864, reduced his personal dwelling, the tool house, and all their contents to ashes. Another, three years later, destroyed his entire crop of newly cut hay valued at six hundred dollars.[57] Although he had no real political ambitions, he surrendered to the prodding of friends in 1867 and ran for the office of justice of the peace of his township. Because of the celebrity he had attained only a dozen or so years before, he felt he had a good chance of winning, but he suffered another blow when he finished fourth in a list of seven candidates.[58]

As he wrestled with these misfortunes, Love received little or no help from his wife, an individual he had come to recognize as very manipulative and controlling. By marrying Mary he had expected to share ownership in her many property holdings, but she had refused to relinquish sole possession. The two lived separately; shortly after their marriage she had taken up residence in Santa Cruz, seven miles from the home Harry had purchased. But she used his time and assets to assist her and her grown offspring in the many legal entanglements to which they were prone. A possible reconciliation in this odd marriage was not helped by a story whispered around Santa Cruz that Mary had murdered her first husband.[59]

After living a dozen years with this acrimonious relationship, Mary evidently decided she had squeezed every possible benefit from her current husband and filed for divorce. In August 1866 Harry was served with a summons requiring him to appear in court for a divorce hearing. Harry used the fact that Mary's request was filed in Santa Clara County rather than Santa Cruz County, where Harry lived, to delay proceedings by requesting a change of venue to the closer location. It was more than a year before the case finally came to trial in October 1867.

Mary alleged in her complaint that Harry had not lived with her, acknowledged her as his wife, or provided for any of her needs since June 1864. In a written statement Harry denied all allegations. After numerous witnesses testified as to the veracity or lack thereof in these conflicting accounts, the judge, while recognizing the rancorous history of the marriage, saw no grounds for granting a divorce and dismissed the action, assessing Mary for the court costs.[60]

Harry made one last attempt to rescue this ill-fated marriage. In December 1867 he sold all his property in Zavante Valley, packed up a wagon, and moved to Mary's residence in Santa Clara, where he received a cool reception, but Mary allowed him to stow his few belongings in her barn, sleep there, and work on her farm.

Any hope for reconciliation evaporated, however, when in April 1868 Mary hired a young man as a handyman to help her around the house. His name was Christian Eiversen, but he preferred to be called Fred. Harry watched with grinding teeth as the strapping young fellow helped propel Mary's increasingly corpulent body into and out of her buggy and attended to her every wish. Well aware that her open display of affection for Eiversen was intended to hurt him, Love found his anger compounded when she spread the falsehood that Harry had beaten her and that she had hired Eiversen to protect herself from her husband's vicious assaults.

This highly charged situation came to a head on the morning of Saturday, June 27, 1868, when Love, armed with a double-barreled shotgun, pistol, and sheath knife, went to a new home Mary was having built in Santa Clara for a showdown with Eiversen. There he learned from Calvin Russell, a carpenter working on the house, that Mary and her handyman had gone to San Jose but were expected back later that day. Taking a stand at the gate, Love waited.

Like almost everyone else in Santa Clara, Cal Russell was aware of the acrimonious Love marriage. Watching the glowering old frontiersman at the gate with a shotgun cradled in his arm, Russell guessed Love's deadly purpose. Hoping to defuse the situation, he approached Love and invited him into the house to share his noonday meal, but Love declined, mumbling something about having to wait there until "that man Fred" showed up so he could "walk over his dead body." When Russell persisted, saying he needed some help with a job at the house, Love "ripped out a great oath" that frightened the carpenter, who then retreated.[61]

Clementhia Bennett, one of Mary's daughters, who had been asked by her mother to keep an eye on the place while she was gone, arrived at the house midmorning. When at about noon she saw her mother's buggy approaching, she came out, hurried past Love, who politely opened the gate for her, and ran to warn Mary and Eiversen of the menacing figure waiting.

The words were barely out of her mouth when Mary saw her husband step from behind the gate with a shotgun at the ready. She screamed, "There he comes! There he comes!"

Eiversen dropped the reins and jumped out of the buggy.

"He will shoot you!" Mary yelled. But the young man had his pistol out and strode toward Love. Eiversen was still some distance away when Love, in his eagerness to down the hated handyman, turned loose one barrel of his shotgun. A few pellets struck Eiversen in the face, but he raised his pistol, fired two shots that missed, and marched resolutely forward.

Love emptied the other barrel of his shotgun, also missing, and then pulled his handgun and fired two shots, one of which struck Eiversen in the arm. But still the young man came on.

Reaching the fence, he leaned over and fired point-blank at Love, hitting him with a bullet in the upper part of his right arm, smashing the bone. With a roar of pain, Love raised his empty shotgun with his left arm and swung it in one last futile effort to down his adversary. Blood streaming from his wound, he then staggered into the house. Eiversen leaped over the fence and pursued him. Catching up inside the building, he slammed his pistol over Love's head, knocking him to the floor. When the old man struggled to rise, Eiversen struck him another blow with the gun before Russell and J. L. Duff, a painter, jumped in to separate the two.

Bleeding from superficial wounds to his face and arm, Eiversen finally stepped back and watched as Russell and Duff carried Love, now in shock and jabbering incoherently, out of the empty house and placed him on the ground, where they did their best to stem the blood gushing from his arm.

A doctor was summoned, but it was more than an hour before medical assistance arrived in the persons of doctors Whipple and Caldwell. Love's wound was later described by Caldwell as an "orifus [*sic*] where the ball entered breaking the Humorus . . . about two or three inches below the shoulder joint." The arm bone was shattered into fragments. Although noting the damage to Love's head by Eiversen's pistol, the doctors concentrated on the immediate problem, the bullet-blasted arm.

They decided the arm could not possibly be saved and that amputation at the shoulder socket was necessary. Doctor L. R. Robinson, who arrived about an hour later, agreed. To anesthetize Love before the surgery, the doctors administered chloroform, but it never seemed to attain full effect, for his ravings continued throughout the process. Shortly after they sewed up the wound, a combination of shock, chloroform overdose, and loss of blood took the life of Harry Love. He was fifty-eight years old.[62]

A coroner's inquest held at the scene of the shooting concluded that Eiversen had shot and ultimately killed Love in self-defense. Immediately after being cleared of any criminal responsibility in the tragic affair, Eiversen disappeared and was never seen in those parts again.

Newspapers covered the story, but sparsely, for in the fourteen years since he had been lionized in the press for his feat in hunting down, killing, and beheading the infamous Joaquin, the luster had faded from his name. One San Francisco paper gave the news of his death little space, noting that Love was a member of the Society of California Pioneers, but omitted mention of the capture of Joaquin. His death received only two sentences in the *Visalia Delta*: "Harry Love, an old resident of California and well known to many persons in this county, died at the residence of Mrs. Love, near Santa Clara, on the 23 ult [*sic*]. He got into an altercation with a German employee, when they exchanged several shots, Love receiving his death wound."[63]

As successful as he had been as a mariner, scout, express rider, and man-hunting ranger captain, Harry Love had been a complete bust as a businessman. His entire estate at his death amounted to only $382.50, a sum almost entirely eaten up by the bills from the three physicians who treated him and amputated his arm, charging one hundred dollars apiece. Debts he had accumulated for years were never repaid.[64]

He was buried in an unmarked grave in the Santa Clara City Cemetery (now called Mission City Memorial Park).[65]

Mary Bennett Love did not survive her deceased husband very long. She continued to eat like a horse and, despite admonitions from her children, grew increasingly and obscenely obese. She was living with daughter Catherine in December 1868, only six months after Harry's passing, when Catherine warned her that if she did not stop gorging herself she would weigh four hundred pounds. On December 19 Mary looked up from her crocheting, said, "There now, you see, I never did get to weigh 400 pounds," and toppled over dead.[66]

Harry Love is remembered as the man who hunted down and killed one of the West's worst outlaws; his wife's claim to fame must be that she never weighed four hundred pounds.

— 2 —

THOMAS TATE "TOM" TOBIN
1823–1904

Tobin gained his great reputation as a trail man by his uncanny ability to detect and follow "sign." [He] could track a grasshopper through sagebrush.

Edgar Hewett

Called an "American adventurer, tracker, trapper, mountain man, guide, U.S. Army scout, and occasional bounty hunter,"[1] Tom Tobin is remembered today for one outstanding accomplishment: his role in the tracking down and killing of Felipe Espinosa, leader of the most murderous criminal outfit in Colorado's sanguinary history. Tobin was undoubtedly a colorful figure of the western frontier. Born in Saint Louis in 1823,[2] he was the son of Irish immigrant Bartholomew Tobin and Sarah Tate Autobees, a widowed Delaware Indian. Sarah had several children from her previous marriage, one of whom, Charles Autobees, would figure prominently in the life of Tom Tobin.

In the 1800s youngsters assumed adult responsibilities early in life. Teenaged girls routinely married and had children; boys of the same age went out into the world to seek fortune and adventure. Charles Autobees, Tom Tobin's half brother, was only sixteen when he left his Missouri home and family in 1828 to trap beaver on the western frontier. Beaver hats had been fashionable for men in Europe for many years, and by the early decades of the nineteenth century, the incessant demand for beaver pelts almost led to the animal's extinction. The resultant demand, which exceeded supply, meant high prices for trappers who could locate and harvest the remaining beavers, and young Autobees, a skilled woodsman and hunter even at sixteen, leaped at the opportunity for riches. Returning home on

Thomas Tate "Tom" Tobin. Courtesy of O. T. Davis Collection (Scan no. 10047139), History Colorado.

a visit nine years later, he was a twenty-five-year-old veteran mountain man with an abundance of stirring frontier tales, stories that Tom Tobin absorbed with rapt wonder. When Charles returned to the West, his half brother, still in his early teens, was at his side.

Tobin struck the frontier in 1837. He would be there for the next sixty-seven years, the rest of his eventful life. He would come to know and share adventures with such celebrated western frontier figures as Charles Bent and his brothers,[3] Ceran St. Vrain,[4] John C. Frémont,[5] Kit Carson,[6] and Uncle Dick Wootton.[7] He would become an expert on the topography, flora, and fauna of the Rocky Mountains as well as the habits and customs of the region's earlier inhabitants, Hispanics and Indians, both the peaceable and the hostile. He would gain respect as an intelligent, fearless, highly competent scout and tracker, a reputation that led directly to his selection as the man to hunt down and capture the most vicious gang of assassins ever to terrorize the West.

During their first years together on the frontier, Tobin and Autobees headquartered at Bent's Fort in southeastern Colorado. Although it was called a fort because of its surrounding stockade, it was not a military garrison but a trading post that the Bent brothers (Charles, William, Robert, and George) constructed in 1833 for commerce with the Indian tribes. As the only permanent Anglo settlement between Missouri and the Mexican pueblos, Bent's Fort became a major stopping point on the Santa Fe Trail during the massive westward movement of the following years. Tobin and Autobees hunted, trapped, and (employed by the Bent brothers) delivered supplies and whiskey to other hunters and trappers in the region in return for animal pelts. They made regular stops at Forts Lupton and Jackson, rival establishments near Denver, and the towns of El Pueblo in Colorado and Don Fernando de Taos in territory under Mexico's control. To sell their pelts and purchase additional supplies, they made annual trips as far east as Saint Louis.

In the early 1840s the partners changed their base of operations from Bent's Fort to Simeon Turley's store, mill, and distillery at Arroyo Hondo, a little settlement a dozen miles north of the two-century-old pueblo of Don Fernando de Taos (whose lengthy name was shortened by rendezvousing mountain men to simply "Taos"). They delivered supplies from the store and whiskey from the distillery to trappers throughout the region in exchange for furs, and then took the pelts to Saint Louis to trade for replenishment goods for Turley's store.[8]

This was the same type of work they had been doing for the Bents, but the half brothers, like the mountain men and other virile, unattached Americans, were drawn to the Taos area by a powerful magnet: the numerous attractive young Mexican girls who resided there. Many Anglos found wives in Taos: Charles Bent married Maria Jaranillo in 1835, Kit Carson later married Maria's younger sister, and Charles Autobees also married a Taos girl with whom he fathered a brood of children.[9]

As for Tom Tobin, he was enchanted with Taos and its surrounding country long before it became a part of an American state and its residents began calling it "the Land of Enchantment," and he learned to speak the Spanish language fluently. He was especially captivated by the charms of a teenaged girl named Maria Pascuala Bernal. In 1844 he became a naturalized Mexican citizen and joined the Roman Catholic Church so that he could wed Maria. When they married on November 3 he was twenty-one; she was fifteen.[10] Sadly, their first child, a boy named Jose Narcisco, born in September 1848, was blind.[11]

Tension building in these years between the United States and Mexico burst into open warfare in the spring of 1846. This conflict was fought mainly along the Rio Grande border by U.S. and Mexican military units until General Winfield Scott landed an expeditionary force at Vera Cruz in March 1847 and captured Mexico City in September. But one bloody affair took place far north in the Taos area and involved Tom Tobin.

Following the declaration of war by the U.S. Congress on May 13, 1846, General S. W. Kearny led a force of 1,750 men from Fort Leavenworth, Kansas, to Santa Fe. The Mexican military had retreated to Chihuahua, and he captured the city unopposed. With no opposing army remaining in New Mexico, Kearny appointed Charles Bent of Taos as provisional governor of the newly acquired territory. Kearny then left Colonel Sterling Price and a small contingent at Santa Fe and led his remaining troops westward to protect California. But some Hispanics and Native Indians, outraged by the invasion and conquest of their land by gringos, plotted revenge. On the morning of January 19, 1847, a rebel band led by Pablo Montoyo, who called himself "the Santa Anna of the North," and Tomas "Tomacito" Romero, a Pueblo Indian, attacked Charles Bent's undefended Taos home and shot the acting governor full of arrows and bullets. Bent was dying but still alive when Romero "raked a bow-string over his scalp, pulling away his gray hair in a glistening sheath, . . . cut as cleanly with the tight cord as it would have [been] with a knife."[12] This horrific deed was performed before the eyes of Bent's wife and children. Five other prominent figures were in the house, and the assassins killed them all: Bent's brother-in-law, Pablo Jaramillo; Taos County sheriff Stephen Lee; Judge Cornelio Vigil; attorney J. W. Leal; and Narcisco Beaubien, the nineteen-year-old son and heir of Charles Beaubien.[13]

While bands of rebels intent on murdering every gringo they could find roamed the streets of Taos, an American named Charles Town escaped and raced for Santa Fe, stopping briefly at Arroyo Hondo to warn Simeon Turley and his employees of the rebellion. Turley, certain that he was respected by the region's inhabitants of all ethnicities, could not believe the insurgents would target his facility, but at the urging of his men he finally came up with a plan of action. He sent Autobees to Santa Fe for military assistance while he and the eight remaining men began preparing a defense. Selecting the distillery as a redoubt, they erected a make-shift barricade around the building and boarded up its windows, leaving only shooting ports, then took their posts and waited.

Early on the morning of January 20 a force of some five hundred Mexicans and Indians appeared on the slopes surrounding Arroyo Hondo. A leader, waving a white flag, summoned Turley for a confab. He came out and was informed that they had killed all the Americans in Taos and intended to do the same at the distillery, but if Turley would surrender without necessitating a fight, his life would be spared. When Turley flatly rejected this offer and returned to his building, the battle began. Extremely uneven from the start, nine defenders against a force of five hundred, growing ever larger as more Indians arrived, the fight raged on throughout that day and night and into the next day.

About dusk of the second day some attackers slipped down to the mill and set it ablaze. The defenders, running low on ammunition and with their stronghold threatened by a fire in the adjacent building, held a council of war and agreed that their only hope was a desperate escape under cover of darkness. When they ran out of the distillery, some in groups, some singly, many were cut down by rebel rifle fire, but Turley, Antoine LeBlanc, John Albert, and Tom Tobin made it into the woods.

Turley and LeBlanc were later run down and killed. The only survivors of the siege at Turley's Mill were John Albert and Tom Tobin, who successfully escaped. In the dead of winter forty-year-old Albert walked 140 miles to Pueblo.[14] Tobin, a much younger man at twenty-three, hoofed the hundred miles to Santa Fe.[15]

When Charles Town, Autobees, and Tobin alerted him of the rebellion, Colonel Price led three hundred cavalrymen and a volunteer civilian force of sixty-five (including Autobees and Tobin) in a march to Taos. On the way they encountered the rebel coalition that had besieged Turley's mill and, in a sharp engagement, killed many and routed the rest. At Taos the insurgents, fearful of the American force, took refuge in the pueblo's church, but Colonel Price ignored church-sanctuary tradition and breached the thick adobe walls with his cannon. Before the fighting was over, some 150 rebels had been slain and about four hundred captured, but only seven Americans were killed.[16] There were a few more skirmishes with other rebel bands, but in practical terms, Price's victory at Taos ended the revolt. In March 1847 General Winfield Scott mounted an amphibious assault on Vera Cruz, Mexico, and then easily captured the capital, Mexico City, a triumph leading to the signing of the Treaty of Guadalupe Hidalgo on February 2, 1848.[17]

After the war Tom Tobin continued his frontiersman's life, trading, trapping, and hunting. When bands of Utes attacked travelers on the Santa Fe Trail in 1849, he gained fame as an Indian fighter, most notably at the battle of El Cerro de Olla.[18]

By 1850 Tobin was attempting to live the more conventional life of a husband and father. He moved his wife and infant son to a farmhouse he had built in Colorado, just over the line from Taos County, New Mexico. There he raised crops, which he sold at the military camp that Colonel William Gilpin had established near Bent's Fort. He and Maria Pascuala also raised children; over the next twenty years their son Narciso gained four sisters and a brother. Not letting his duties as a farmer, husband, and father interfere entirely with his love of adventure, Tobin from time to time accepted assignments as scout and dispatch rider for Colonel Gilpin.

In the early 1850s explorer Edward Fitzgerald Beale was beginning his ambitious project of surveying and building the most expeditious road to California. Beale had first gained renown by bringing the first gold samples to the eastern states from California, thus setting off the gold rush of 1849. His trail across the country would become the route of the first transcontinental railroad, and in the next century, the famous U.S. Route 66. Kit Carson had scouted and guided for Beale on previous expeditions, but being unavailable at the time, Carson recommended Tom Tobin for the project. Beale was not disappointed, later saying that Tobin was almost equal to Carson for "bravery, dexterity with his rifle, and skill in mountain life."[19]

Gilpin and Beale both advised other frontier military officers that Tobin possessed excellent scouting abilities, and throughout the 1850s he had all the employment he could handle. During this period he scouted with others he had known from earlier days, including Charles Autobees and Kit Carson as well as celebrated scouts William F. "Buffalo Bill" Cody and James Butler "Wild Bill" Hickok. He and Autobees helped build a military fort in the area, which was first called Fort Massachusetts, but later Fort Garland. By the decade's end Tobin was well established as a quietly disposed, peaceable rancher with substantial holdings, including real estate worth $2,000 and personal property valued at $3,000.[20]

A chain of events beginning in late 1862 propelled Tom Tobin onto the roster of celebrated man-hunters. In mid-December members of a Hispanic family set out on a career of outlawry, leading ultimately to their infamy as the "Bloody Espinosas," which resulted in the murders of dozens as well as Tobin's greatest fame.

The central figure in this development was Felipe Nerio Espinosa, who was born in northern New Mexico in 1827.[21] His younger brothers, Jose Vivian, Juan Antonio, and Francisco, followed and were later joined in the household by Jose Vincente, an adopted nephew. The two Joses, brother and nephew, would join Felipe on his path into violent outlawry.[22]

What exactly triggered the bloody Espinosa rampage has never been determined with certainty, but several explanations have been offered. According to some family members, the Espinosas originally came from Vera Cruz, Mexico, and six members of the family living in that town were killed when American gunships shelled the area during the invasion of 1847. Felipe's killing spree, they believed, was in retaliation for this atrocity, but they did not explain why he waited sixteen years to exact revenge. Others assert that Felipe was outraged because the American government ignored a Mexican land grant claim by the family and offer as proof a letter he reportedly sent to Colorado governor John Evans, saying he was prepared to kill six hundred gringos, including the governor, if he and his followers were not granted amnesty and given five thousand acres in Conejos County. Still others say that the Virgin Mary appeared to Felipe in a vision and directed him to kill one hundred Americans for every family member killed during the war with Mexico.[23] Martin Edward Martinez, a direct descendent of the Espinosas, contends that his extensive research indicates that Felipe sought revenge for atrocities, including murder, committed by U.S. troops against Mexicans in Colorado and New Mexico.[24]

A provision of the treaty ending the Mexican War guaranteed property rights to Mexican nationals living in the new American territories, including land grants, acquired under the Mexican rule, but unscrupulous land grabbers moved in after the war and manipulated the legal system to steal much of the property from the rightful owners. Unquestionably, many Hispanics, including the Espinosas, bitterly resented this.

In 1858 Felipe Espinosa, twenty-six years old and married to Maria Hurtado, moved with his extended family from New Mexico to settle in San Rafael, Conejos County, Colorado. Whether driven by poverty and a desperate effort to provide sustenance for the family or avarice and hatred of Anglos, Felipe and his brother, Jose Vivian, were soon sneak-thieving goods from wagon trains on the Santa Fe Trail. To avoid suspicion falling on them, they committed these crimes far from their home and escaped legal interference for four years.

Growing bolder, in mid-December 1862 they donned masks and stopped a wagon at gunpoint on the road from Santa Fe to Galisteo, New Mexico. Although the driver was Hispanic, they brutalized him with the type of savagery that soon made them notorious. They tied him under the wagon tongue with his face just above the ground and whipped up the horses. "The man was pulled for miles, his head plowing through every bump in the path. By the time the wagon was finally spotted and stopped, the driver was within an inch of his life, his face a bloody pulp."[25]

The teamster survived and had his revenge for this atrocity. A resident of Conejos County, Colorado, he recognized the thieves despite the masks they wore. The goods stolen from the wagon were destined for a store owned by a priest in Galisteo. When he heard the driver's story and learned the identity of the robbers, the priest immediately relayed this information to the American military. In due course Captain E. Wayne Eaton, in command at Fort Garland, received an order to arrest the suspects.

The first attempt to apprehend the lawless Espinosas came at a particularly inauspicious time, when rumors were rampant that a Mexican insurrection was brewing. So when on January 16, 1863, Second Lieutenant Nicholas Hodt led a ten-man squad of soldiers out from Fort Garland for the San Rafael home of the Espinosas, he was especially cautious. Deputy United States Marshal George Austin, who had encountered resistance while attempting to make arrests of rebellious suspects in the town the previous week, accompanied the detail.

In an effort to forestall any violent confrontation, Lieutenant Hodt had selected Mexican enlisted men for the mission, but this seemed to make no difference to the Espinosas, for the soldiers were met on arrival with gunfire and, remarkably, a rain of arrows. Before the clash ended with the retreat of the Espinosas, Corporal Decedero Abeyta was dead, Deputy Marshal Austin suffered a broken leg, and Lieutenant Hodt had a minor head wound. Infuriated by their comrade's death, the soldiers took out their anger on the Espinosa home, stripping it of all valuables and leaving it a shambles.

Deputy Marshal Austin, in his report of the action, identified Felipe and Jose Vivian Espinosa and one other Hispanic man, Jesus Sanchez, as the instigators of the clash and the murderers of Abeyta. A fifty-dollar reward notice was posted for the apprehension and delivery of the three, "dead or alive."[26] After the dustup at San Raphael, no more was heard of Jesus Sanchez, but the names of the Espinosa brothers would fill newspaper columns for months to come.

On March 16, 1863, they attacked millwright Franklin Bruce in the Wet Mountains, fired a bullet point-blank into his forehead, and slashed a cross on his chest.[27] Two days later the body of sawmill worker Henry Harkens was found ten miles south of Colorado City. Stabbed twice in the chest and shot in the forehead, his head had been "split open from the top to the mouth . . . and two pieces of skull and his brains lay on the ground."[28] A twenty-one-day lull in the killings followed, not coincidentally because the period coincided with Holy Week, and Felipe Espinosa, deeply religious, evidently did not believe that murder, even the murder of hated Anglos, was an appropriate activity for this time. Then on April 8 two young prospectors, Jacob Binkley and Abram Shoup, were unfortunate enough to encounter the Espinosa brothers at their South Park campsite. Binkley was shot in the back and had his pockets turned inside out. Shoup was stabbed four times in the chest, and his head was terribly mutilated.[29] Days later the murderers slew mail-station operator J. D. Addleman and ransacked his house southeast of Wilkerson Pass. A paper reported that he was shot "with two balls through the heart, but what seems more horrible, those fiends incarnate, seem to have worried their victim as the cat does the mouse before killing him."[30]

On April 25 a man named Bill Carter, walking down the road from Montgomery to his home at Fairplay, met Felipe and Jose Vivian Espinosa on horseback. One of them immediately raised his rifle and shot Carter in the chest, killing him instantly. They then stripped his body of his overcoat and valuables, hacked his head savagely with an axe, and threw his body into a snowbank. They were completing their brutal work when a man named Metcalf appeared on the road in an ox-drawn wagon and was also shot.[31] His butchered body would have joined Carter's in the snowbank but for a most fortunate circumstance. Metcalf had just picked up his mail from the post office at Montgomery and stuffed the thick packet into his left breast pocket. The murderer's bullet passed through his coat and the papers but stopped short of his body, just giving Metcalf a bruise. Frightened by the gunshot, the smell of Carter's blood, and their driver's sudden collapse, the oxen bolted, and the wagon, bouncing and careening, flew past the killers, who fired another ineffectual shot at Metcalf.[32]

His fortuitous escape from death was not only important for Metcalf; it also had significant consequence for the assassins. As the only living witness to have seen the perpetrators of these heinous crimes, he could dispel some previously held erroneous suspicions about their identity. Many were certain that hostile Indians were responsible for the murders, while others believed Confederate sympathizers in the bloody Civil War, then in progress, were committing the crimes. Metcalf's experience, however, proved that two Mexicans were the killers.

While word of the latest developments spread throughout the Anglo settlements, the Espinosas struck again, adding two more victims to their macabre list. On April 27 miners Fred Lehman and Sol Seyga were riding on horseback down the Denver-to-Fairplay road when a bullet from a hidden assassin hit Seyga in the chest, killing him instantly. Another shot struck Lehman in the arm, but he pulled a pistol and engaged his attackers in a gun battle before receiving a fatal wound. The murderers hacked the heads of Lehman and Seyga into bloody pulp, stripped the bodies, and stole the horses. Before leaving they ripped a paper collar from Lehman's body, scribbled a message on it in Spanish about wreaking vengeance upon Americans as a sacrifice to the Virgin Mary, and pinned it to a tree.

An editorial in the May 7, 1863, edition of Denver's *Weekly Commonwealth* summed up the feelings of most of the area's Anglo residents. It called for the organization of a "Vigilance Committee or secret police . . . to detect and punish the thieves and murderers" loose in the area: "If these robbers have any organization it is secret, permitting them to appear in the community as good citizens, and the only way to ferret them out is for all honest men to band together and spare neither vigilance nor rigor in punishing, whenever they can be caught [as] was done in San Francisco, in Denver, and many other localities in the West."

Several hastily formed parties searched for the killers. One party chased a man they suspected of being one of the killers for miles before catching him. They would have lynched him but for the timely intervention of a highly respected clergyman who vouched for the man and gained his release. Another innocent individual, not so fortunate, was captured by a vigilante party and summarily hanged.[33]

A better-planned and -executed search for the killers was led by Captain John McCannon from the California Gulch mining camp, high in Lake County.[34] After a long trek over the mountains, his posse struck the trail of the murderers, leading from the site of their latest slayings, and they followed it for several days. On May 9 they came upon the outlaw camp on Oil Creek, about twenty miles from Canon City. In an exchange of gunfire Jose Vivian Espinosa was killed, but Felipe escaped, together with his teenaged nephew Jose Vincente.[35]

A correspondent by the name of Dornick who wrote for Denver's *Weekly Commonwealth* was in Canon City when McCannon's party arrived with the news and relayed it to his paper, where it appeared under the headline, GLORIOUS NEWS! THE MYSTERIOUS MURDERS UNRAVELED AT LAST. Along with details of the short gun battle, Dornick included conclusive evidence that the suspects who had been attacked were indeed the wanted assassins. Among the effects found at the campsite was a memorandum book, believed to have been taken from Lehman, containing notes written in Spanish by the killers stating that they had killed many Americans and intended to kill more. The name Espinosa appeared several times in the notes, said Dornick, providing solid proof that the outlaw brothers were in fact the culprits. He concluded by praising McCannon and his volunteers, "who have so persistently followed them up and taken so active a part in ridding the Territory of these demon foes . . . whose career of crime will form one of the most terrible epochs in the annals of Colorado."[36]

As summer passed without another murder attributed to the brutal Espinosas, many residents of the South Park region concluded that Felipe, perhaps chastened by the death of his brother, had fled to Mexico. Actually, Jose Vivian's death had only intensified Felipe's hatred of Anglos, but finding South Park too hot for him, he had merely changed locations, removing with his youthful nephew to familiar Conejos County, almost two hundred miles southwest. Only three weeks after the Oil Creek debacle, he killed another American, a fisherman named William Smith, not far from his family home at San Rafael. He and the nephew may have killed others after the South Park murder spree. Tom Tobin thought so, and several Colorado historians have placed the total number of victims that summer as high as eleven.[37]

In late August, Felipe rode boldly up to the office of Lafayette Head, the Indian agent at Conejos, with a handful of letters he wanted delivered. One, addressed to Colorado governor John Evans, the contents of which were later disclosed in a newspaper report, was especially interesting. Its substance was that, having already killed twenty-two men, his "bravery" deserved an "honorable amnesty," and if he was not pardoned by the governor and his property restored, he would "commence a war of extermination against Mexican and American citizens of that section of the Territory, wherever he could strike them."[38]

If this audacious entreaty ever reached the desk of the governor, it was ignored, and within weeks Felipe renewed his war of vengeance. On October 10 grocer Leander Philbrook was driving a mule-drawn buggy on the tortuous road from Trinidad to Costilla with a single passenger, Maria Dolores Sanches. As he entered a canyon leading down to Fort

Garland, Felipe and his young nephew opened fire with rifles from a hidden site and killed one of the mules. Philbrook, armed with a pistol, exchanged ineffectual shots with his attackers before running up the opposite side of the canyon with the woman. The Espinosas came down, killed the other mule, ransacked and set fire to the buggy, and then pursued the fleeing pair. Unable to maintain her companion's frantic pace, Maria Sanches slipped into a crevice among the boulders and hid. Philbrook continued along the canyon, keeping to the high ground. After trudging nearly twelve miles, ever fearful that his assailants would catch up with him, he reached Fort Garland and related his harrowing tale to Lieutenant Colonel Samuel F. Tappan.

Meanwhile Maria was going through a dreadful ordeal. When a wagon appeared on the road, she left her place of concealment to beg the driver, Pedro Garcia, for help. She was still relating her story when the Espinosas reappeared, grabbed her, and ordered Garcia on with the ominous threat: "Go ahead, and if this woman is found dead, you can tell the people that the Espinosas of the Conejos killed her!"[39] The Espinosas raped the woman, tied her up, and left to search for Philbrook. When they were gone, the plucky female freed herself by chewing her bonds and escaped back up the side of the canyon. There she remained hidden until morning, when she set out on the trek to Fort Garland.

After hearing Philbrook's story, Colonel Tappan dispatched a squad of soldiers at first light to look for Maria. They met her on the road and brought her back to the fort.[40] The colonel, convinced by this latest outrage that the Espinosas must be stopped immediately at all costs, believed he knew the man who could track them down and end their fiendish acts. That man was Tom Tobin.

In 1863 Tobin was forty years old, living quietly on his farm with his wife and children, but when he answered the colonel's request to lead a manhunt for the killers, he looked every inch the mountain man he had once been. He wore a fringed buckskin coat and a bead-worked waistcoat. Moccasins covered his feet, and on his head was a feathered cap of bear fur. An 1851 Colt Navy revolver was at his waist in a holster fashioned from the rump and tail of a buffalo, and in his hand he carried a four-and-a-half-foot-long, sixteen-pound, .53-calibre Hawken rifle, with "ten notches filed into the barrel in front of the caplock, one for each man—

red, white and Hispano" whom he had killed. Dangling from his neck was a leather disc attached to percussion caps for the Hawken, which made it possible for him to load, cap, and fire the single-shot rifle in seconds.[41]

Tobin's size was hardly imposing. According to his biographer he stood about five feet seven inches tall and weighed about 140 pounds. His hair was jet black, his eyes blue, and his complexion "swarthy." To another historian he was "markedly unhandsome, even homely, and his heavily modeled features had a somewhat Indian cast, causing many to believe he was a half-breed, which in fact he was."[42]

Doctor Edgar Hewett, who knew Tobin in later years and was well acquainted with his record, wrote, "Tobin gained his great reputation as a trail man by his uncanny ability to detect and follow 'sign.' He could track a grasshopper through sagebrush. Those who had seen him trailing told me that he always took the most likely starting point, swung round and round in ever widening circles until he cut 'sign,' then clung to his 'sign' until his quarry was overtaken." Sometimes he would dismount and get down on his hands and knees on the ground, "following 'sign' that was imperceptible to less acute eyes."[43]

The matter of a reward offered for the capture of the Espinosas would become a bone of contention later, but Tobin would always claim that reward had not been a consideration for him when he accepted the task of going after these dangerous killers, as he "thought it the duty of all citizens to rid the country of all such characters as quick as possible."[44]

When Colonel Tappan briefed him at Fort Garland, Tobin expressed some doubt that the two who assaulted Philbrook and Sanches were indeed the Espinosas. The colonel told him to talk to Maria. "I questioned the woman carefully," Tobin recollected. "She said she knew they were Espinosas because she heard them tell Pedro Garcia who they were." When she told Tobin what they had done to her, he readily agreed to hunt down the vicious pair, but he wanted to go alone.

The colonel rejected this idea, telling Tobin that soldiers were needed for his protection. Officer and scout argued the point until Lieutenant Horace W. Baldwin, Tappan's adjutant, indicated his eagerness to participate in the hunt. Tobin liked and respected Baldwin and finally agreed to be accompanied by the lieutenant and a squad of men. He did insist on the inclusion of one more member of the party: Juan Montoya, a teenaged Mexican boy, whom Tobin needed to "lead my horse while I tracked the assassins."[45]

On the morning of October 12 Tobin, along with Montoya, a civilian scout from the fort named Loren Jenks, Lieutenant Baldwin, and fifteen First Colorado Cavalry enlisted men, left Fort Garland on horseback to hunt the Espinosas. They started at the scene of the attack on Philbrook's wagon. Amazingly, the outlaws, certainly aware that their latest victims had escaped to Fort Garland and that troops would be out in search of them, defiantly remained in the area. Tobin quickly picked up their trail and, as he related the story years later, spotted the brothers a couple of times, but the outlaws got away in the woods before anyone could get a clear shot at them.[46] They camped that night, and on the second day they came across tracks that Tobin recognized as having been made by Ute Indians, but Jenks and some of the cavalrymen, certain they had been left by the fugitives, followed them, became lost from the main group, and consequently had no part in the final act of the unfolding drama.[47]

The reduced party followed Tobin on, hunting by day and camping at night. On October 15, the fourth day of the search, they followed a creek down Veta Mountain until midmorning, when they came across the tracks of a pair of oxen. Closely scrutinizing the tracks, Tobin concluded—apparently using his sixth sense, for he didn't say how he knew—that the oxen were being driven by the criminals he sought. Tracking them, he found where the fugitives had released one of the animals, keeping the other, he believed, to butcher at their camp. Now convinced that he was close to his prey, he wanted to continue stealthily on foot, taking only the Mexican boy, so he sent Baldwin and his soldiers off with the horses. Two soldiers remonstrated, saying they wanted to stick with Tobin and be in on the kill, and both Baldwin and Tobin nodded their approval. Later, a third trooper joined them.

In his account Tobin said the trail was difficult to follow in the dense woods, often with no sign other than broken twigs. He finally came to a clearing, where he could see some magpies circling an area he was sure held the outlaw camp. He stated, "I told the soldiers not to speak [and] if I raised my hand to squat down and cock their guns but not to fire unless I told them to. I took a step or two . . . and saw the head of one of the assassins."[48]

The man he saw was Felipe Espinosa. He sat across a small fire from his nephew, young Jose Vincente. As Tobin watched, Felipe got up, strode over to the hanging carcass of the ox they had butchered, carved off a steak, and returned to his resting place. Suddenly, with the intuitive sense of danger inherent in the wild animals he resembled, he leaped to his feet, grasped a revolver, and spun around toward Tobin.[49] "Before he turned around fairly," said Tobin, "I fired and hit him in the side; he bellowed like a bull and cried out, 'Jesus, favor me,' and cried to his companion, 'Escape. I am killed.'"[50]

As Vincente ran from the clearing toward the dense tree growth, Tobin shouted for the soldiers to fire. All three missed him. Tobin then performed the lightning reload-and-shoot feat for which he was famous: "I tipped my powder horn into my rifle, dropped a bullet from my mouth into the muzzle . . . while I was capping it. I drew my gun up and fired at first sight and broke his back above his hips."[51]

Tobin ran first toward Felipe, who, clutching his pistol, was crawling away. "Do you know me?" Tobin demanded, evidently wanting to be sure the murderer knew who bested him before dying. Felipe, still showing fight, fired a last shot at the approaching cavalrymen. He missed and they riddled his body with bullets. "I then caught him by the hair," said Tobin, "drew his head back over a fallen tree and cut it off. I sent [Montoya] to cut off the head of the other fellow. He cut it off and brought it to me."[52]

While the cavalrymen gathered up the effects of the now-headless outlaws, including their weapons and the articles stolen from Maria Sanches, Tobin dumped the severed heads of Felipe and Jose Vincente into a gunnysack. The decapitated bodies were left where they fell.

The party's separate elements rejoined and made camp for the night. The next morning Lieutenant Baldwin led his triumphant unit back to Fort Garland. Tobin described that memorable day in an interview thirty-two years later:

I rode up in front of the Commanding Officer's quarters and called for Col. Tappan. I rolled the assassins [*sic*] heads out of the sack at Col. Tappan's feet. I said, "Here, Col., I have accomplished what you wished. This head is Espinosa's. The other is his companion's head and there is no mistake made." Lieut. Baldwin spoke, "Yes, Col., there is no mistake, for I have this diary and letters and papers to show that they were the assassins. The diary showed that they had killed twenty-two up to the date the first Espinosa was killed. . . . There was about thirty killed altogether.[53]

Kit Carson III, the grandson of two notable frontiersman, Christopher "Kit" Carson on his father's side (for whom he was named), and Tom Tobin on his mother's side, remembered hearing the story slightly differently from his Grandpa Tobin:

> When grandpa got back to Fort Garland he found that Colonel Tappan and some other officers were out horseback riding with their wives. He didn't say anything; just stood around with his gunnysack, waiting.
>
> After a while the riding party came back and somebody told the colonel Tom Tobin was waiting to see him. So he sent for grandpa, and when he came into the room, he asked, "Any luck, Tom?" Grandpa said, "So-so," and he held the gunnysack upside down and rolled the two heads out on the floor and the ladies screamed and grandpa said the colonel himself turned kind of green.[54]

If Colonel Tappan was sickened by the sight of the severed heads, he recovered quickly, for the next day he issued a long order congratulating his men for ridding the territory of the predators who had terrorized the populace for months.[55]

Tom Tobin basked in the glory of the praise heaped upon him by the colonel and the region's newspapers in the following days and carried his feat as a badge of honor for the rest of his life, knowing that his trailing skill had been absolutely essential to accomplishing the assigned mission. Although Colonel Tappan told Tobin he had seen a newspaper report saying that Governor Evans had offered a $2,500 reward for the capture of the Espinosas,[56] he had accepted the job without promise of payment or reward and returned home to work his farm, making no effort to put in a claim at that time.

The year 1863 was memorable for Tobin in a way quite different from his notable man-hunting achievement, for he became a father that year—twice. Early that year he had purchased a twenty-three-year-old female Navajo slave named Dominga from Mexicans, presumably to perform housework in the Tobin home. But she performed other functions as well, for she was soon impregnated by her owner. Tobin's wife, also pregnant at the time, delivered on October 23 a baby girl who was christened Maria Pascuala Tobin, after her mother. Two months later, on December 31, the slave girl, who had been baptized as Maria Dominga, gave birth to another baby girl and named her Maria Catarina Tobin. Thus in 1863 three more Marias entered into the Tobin household.[57]

As he grew older things turned increasingly sour for Tom Tobin. He gradually lost the physical and mental attributes distinguishing him as an outstanding mountain man and scout. His judgment may have suffered also, for while hunting in 1876 when he was fifty-three, he unheedingly approached a den of bear cubs, something he would have avoided in earlier days, and was severely mauled by the mother of the cubs.

Then in 1888 he went berserk and almost lost his life. Since the early days when Kit Carson and Tom Tobin had scouted together, their families had remained close. William "Billy" Carson, Kit's oldest son, married Tom's daughter Pascualita and settled near the Tobin farm.[58] When Tom learned that Billy, while drunk, had beaten Pascuala, he flew into a mindless rage and attacked his son-in-law with a pistol and a knife. Carson, reacting, pulled a revolver and shot the old man in the groin, almost killing him.[59]

Two years before this episode Maria Pascuala, Tom's wife of forty-two years, had died at the age of fifty-seven. Still depressed by her passing, suffering from his bear-inflicted wounds, and unable to work his farm, Tobin began selling off his property as his health and spirits declined rapidly. Seven months after his violent encounter with Billy Carson, in an effort to assuage his loneliness, he married a forty-year-old widow, Maria Rosa Quintana. Remarkably, although still almost illiterate, he then became interested in education and over the next few years helped open schools for Hispanic children and even served as president of the school board.[60]

Thirty years passed before anything was done about the $2,500 reward Governor Evans had reportedly offered for halting the Espinosa murder rampage. During those years Tom Tobin's financial condition had worsened along with his gradually deteriorating health. Then in April 1893 the Colorado General Assembly passed an appropriation of $1,000 "for the relief of Thomas T. Tobens [sic] in full payment for the killing of the Espinosa Brothers."[61]

Four years later John McCannon, who had led the posse that killed Jose Vivian, Felipe's brother, began his own lobbying effort. In January 1897 he wrote to his Lake County representative in the state legislature, Alex Whitney, reminding him of the dramatic events of 1863, the significant role he had played in bringing down the Espinosas, and the fact that Tobin had received reward money for his part and was seeking more. "I never put in a claim yet," McCannon wrote, "but I do now. I don't want such men as Tom Tobin paid for my work. . . . Tobin has no more right to that reward than you have." Claiming he had spent $125 of his own money on the expedition, he suggested that the *Rocky Mountain News*, which was always "in the habit of making a great hero of Tom Tobin," should interview Judge Wilbur F. Stone "to get the facts of the case."[62]

In its February 25, 1897, edition the *Rocky Mountain News* published this letter and Judge Stone's reply together with the recommended interview with the judge. The paper explained that during the Espinosa "reign of terror," Governor Evans had offered a large reward for the capture or death of the bandits, and this had been duly reported in the *News*, but all copies of that edition, together with many other records, had been swept away in the Cherry Creek flood of 1863. Appeals were made to legislatures for many years thereafter to appropriate funds for this reward, believed to be $2,500, but since all documentation of it had been destroyed, the amount was uncertain. Responding to McCannon's letter, Representative Whitney had introduced a bill for his relief, but the appropriations committee rejected it, citing the long time intervening and the inability to secure reliable data.

In his letter Judge Stone confirmed that he was well acquainted with those fateful events in 1863. At Canon City, when McCannon's posse returned from their Espinosa encounter, he and a "Mr. Hinsdale" had spent "nearly half the night" translating from Spanish to English the Espinosa memorandum book in which the brothers claimed to have killed so many Americans. The judge said he knew Tobin well, had personally visited the site where he killed the last Espinosas, and had seen the severed heads preserved in alcohol by the post surgeon at Fort Garland. He agreed with McCannon that without his organization, his "skillful trailing," and the killing of one Espinosa brother, "Tobin never would have found the other one." However, when interviewed by the *News* reporter, the judge seemed to contradict what he had written to McCannon, giving "as his firm belief that the Espinosas were killed by Tom Tobin and no one else."[63]

All of this back and forth between McCannon and Tobin and their advocates over the reward money availed nothing, but even as Tobin's fortunes declined, he still persisted in his plea for state or federal financial assistance. On December 26, 1901, he dictated a letter to United States senator George Laird Shoup, a brother of Abram Shoup, who had been brutally slain by the Espinosas. At the time of his brother's murder, George Shoup was a deputy U.S. marshal and a first lieutenant in the First Colorado Cavalry, and he had participated in the hunt for the killers. Learning a few years earlier that Tobin was experiencing hard times, Shoup had sent him $200 as an expression of "warm gratitude for his bravery and for his noble work in disposing of that arch fiend and desperado, Espinosa."[64]

Tobin, finding himself "beset by illness, poverty, and old age, bereft at last of his old-time stubborn self-sufficiency and silent pride," confessed in his letter to Senator Shoup that he was a "humble petitioner" whose times had "sadly changed." Now "78 years old, very feeble, always bed-ridden and almost blind," he said he was unable to maintain even the poor existence to which he had been reduced, and he was turning to the federal government for help. He reminded Senator Shoup that Governor Evans had promised to pay him $2,500 "for killing" the Espinosas, but only after "much petitioning and wrangling in several Colorado legislatures" did he receive a portion of the amount, $1,500. Tobin concluded with a plaintive plea: "I would ask you now, in these the hours of deepest misery after a long and eventful life, to help an old and broken-down man."[65]

Senator Shoup forwarded Tobin's appeal to Colorado senator Edward M. Teller with the notation, "If you will introduce a Bill for the relief of Mr. Tobens [sic] I will render all the assistance in my power to secure favorable action in the Committee on Pensions, of which I am a member." But there the matter died.[66]

Two and a half years later Tom Tobin also died. He passed away on May 15, 1904, and was buried beside his wife near Fort Garland.[67] In the more than four decades that had elapsed since he hunted down and killed the last of the murdering Espinosas, two generations had been born and had grown to adulthood in Colorado, and for the vast majority of them the names Tobin and Espinosa had no special meaning. In the exciting new century (which was exemplified by the famous Saint Louis World's Fair in the year of Tobin's death) the events of the 1800s, many of them brutal and sordid, were all ancient history. Many oldsters with memories of the state's frontier history recalled Tom Tobin as a ruthless and callous killer and beheader of outlaws, and he has been depicted that way in most references since.

Recent historians, however, have examined the man's life and found a much more complex individual. Charles F. Price, author of *Season of Terror*, the definitive history of the Espinosas, quotes John M. Francisco, who knew Tobin well, as saying the scout's "only fault was his recklessness in an Indian fight. While the enemy was in view he seemed to regard the battle as individually his own." Although noted for his savagery in combat and his almost rude reticence in common conversation,[68] Tobin was described by Edgar Hewett, another intimate, as "golden hearted."[69] He "was remembered as a warm and loving father and grandfather, especially by his grandson, Kit Carson III, whose reminiscences of Tobin are tinged with a deep fondness and admiration."[70] This man,

> who could inflict shame on his beloved wife by openly fathering a child with another woman, who could kill without thought or hesitation even when his victims were his own relatives by marriage, whom life on the raw edge of the frontier had hardened to an implacable toughness—this same man was also capable of such a tender sensitivity that as long as he was financially able, in fact for many years, he secretly contributed to the welfare of Felipe Espinosa's destitute widow, Maria Secundina, and her children. . . .
>
> As long as his own resources permitted, he sent food and money not only to Secundina and the children but also to the other members of the Hurtado family. . . . On May 23, 1872, Tom attended, by special invitation, the wedding of Maria Vincenta Espinosa, Felipe's daughter. He signed the wedding book as one of the honored witnesses. Clearly there was far more to Tom Tobin than the ruthless, self-absorbed and saturnine reticence many observers saw.[71]

One cannot study the careers of Tom Tobin and Harry Love without being struck by the remarkable similarities in their histories, the incredible parallels in significant events that shaped that record. Their beginnings, however, were as different as their careers were similar. Love was a New

Englander and Tobin a midwesterner. Tobin was only fourteen when he reached the frontier; Love, arriving a decade later, was thirty-six. Love was a big, powerful man; Tobin never intimidated anyone with his diminutive size.

These disparate characters first gained fame in the southwest during and after the Mexican War, Tobin in northern New Mexico and Love on the Texas border of that territory. But separated by ten years in time and more than a thousand miles in distance, each became the central figure in the dispatch of a notorious Mexican bandit and killer, thus firmly enshrining his name in frontier western history. In 1853 Love tracked down and killed Joaquin Murrieta, the most wanted outlaw in California, and a decade later Tobin did the same with Felipe Espinosa, the murderer terrorizing Colorado. To prove his accomplishment and collect any rewards offered, each man decapitated his prize and, for good measure, removed a trophy from the body of the leader's accomplice.

In the most ironic similarity of all, each survived numerous violent encounters with Indians and Mexican bandits without serious injury only to be struck later in life by a bullet fired in a domestic dispute.

— 3 —

GRANVILLE STUART
1834–1918

We do not advocate mob law or vigilante committees on general principles . . . but when the courts are impotent to deal out justice and check an evil, it is time for the community, over-ridden with law-breakers of whatever class, to rise in their might and suppress them. . . . The most speedy and safe cure is to hang them as fast as captured.

Mineral Argus, June 12, 1884

On the roster of memorable western frontier man-hunters, Granville Stuart stands out as the most unlikely. In his eighty-four eventful years, Granville Stuart was a prospector, miner, trader, merchant, entrepreneur, rancher, politician, diplomat, historian, and author. He contributed so much to his adopted state that he was dubbed "Mr. Montana." He was never a lawman of either the public or private variety, but for one brief period, in the summer of 1884, he led a band of riders in a campaign of outlaw elimination unmatched in the history of the West.

Born at Clarksburg, Harrison County, Virginia (later West Virginia), on August 27, 1834, the second son of Robert and Nancy C. Stuart, Granville moved westward with his parents and older brother, James, to a farm in Illinois and then to Muscatine, Iowa, where the boys grew up. Granville was fifteen and James seventeen when their father, upon learning of the gold discoveries in California, turned farm operations over to his sons and joined thousands of other fortune-seekers headed for the new El Dorado. He returned two years later without a fortune, but with great stories of the golden West. Within a year the boys had talked him into heading back to California and this time taking them with him.[1]

For a year the three Stuarts prospected around Sacramento with little success, and in 1853 the father returned to Iowa, leaving his two sons to continue the search for gold. Giving up on Sacramento, the brothers

Granville Stuart, 1868. Courtesy of WA Photos File, Beinecke Rare Book and Manuscript Library, Yale University (3724565).

moved to new boom camps at Yreka and the Klamath River Valley. In 1855 clashes between the Indians inhabiting that region and the newly arriving whites became increasingly frequent, developing into what have been called the Rogue River Wars. In February 1856 the Stuart brothers enlisted as three-dollars-a-day scouts in a unit of the California militia but saw no action in their month of service.[2]

In the spring of 1857 the brothers joined a party of nine others and headed back east for a family visit. In northern Utah, Granville became seriously ill and could not proceed. Eight of the party continued on while James and Rezin "Reece" Anderson, a close friend, remained behind to help care for him. For seven weeks Granville lay helpless in a feverish condition before finally recovering. His brother James was not a physician, but having an interest in the medical field, he had picked up some knowledge of its practice, and Granville always credited him for saving his life.[3]

This all took place in the summer of 1857, during the height of the so-called Mormon War, a confrontation between United States Army units and Mormon settlers in Utah in which armed conflict was often threatened but never occurred. But it added to the tension felt by those in the Stuart camp, who were already greatly concerned about Granville's condition. The Stuarts and Anderson finally decided to leave that country and travel north some three hundred miles to a place called Beaverhead Valley, where it was said the Indians were friendly, the winters moderate, and the game plentiful. In September they pulled out, unaware that they were heading for country where they would spend the rest of their lives, a place that would later be called Montana.

As they broke camp they were also unaware that, not too far away, one of the most notorious events in American history was taking place. Scores of westbound emigrants were being slaughtered by a band of Mormons and Indians in what is remembered as the Mountain Meadows Massacre. Granville would later write:

> Had we known on the eleventh day of September, 1857, . . . of the dreadful deed being done at Mountain meadows . . . , we would doubtless have traveled, without camping day or night, as long as our stock could go, in our desire to get as far away as we could in the shortest space of time. We did not hear of the massacre until June 26, 1858. When James, Anderson, [John E.] Ross, and I went to Fort Bridger, Utah, for supplies.[4]

In this new country the brothers Stuart and two men who had become attached to them, John Ross and Reese Anderson, lived in elk-skin lodges, hunted, and traded with members of the local tribes. In the spring of 1858 they moved to Deer Lodge Valley, where game was more plentiful, and they began prospecting again. Finding enough trace evidence to convince them that rich gold deposits were nearby, they named the nearby stream Gold Creek, but lacking the necessary tools and equipment for serious gold digging, they never profited from their discovery. Granville's letters home reporting the find are believed to be the spark igniting the great gold rush to Montana in the early 1860s, however, and contributed to the legendary status he would later achieve as Mr. Montana.

When the mining camp of Bannack sprang up in 1862, Granville Stuart moved from Gold Creek to the new boomtown and opened a butcher shop. That same year, on April 15, he took as his wife a twelve-year-old Indian girl named Awbonie Tookanka. Eleven children would be born to this union, nine of whom survived.[5]

As more rich gold deposits were discovered near Bannack, the town grew rapidly and, as in all boom camps, unsavory criminal types flocked in. "There were more desperadoes and lawless characters in Bannack the winter of 1862–63 than ever infested any other mining camp of its size. Murders, robberies and shooting scrapes were of frequent occurrence," Stuart would later write.

> These were dark days in Bannack; there was no safety for life or property only so far as each individual could, with his trusty rifle, protect his own. The respectable citizens far outnumbered the desperadoes, but having come from all corners of the earth, they were unacquainted and did not know whom to trust. On the other hand, the "Roughs" were organized and under the leadership of that accomplished villain, Henry Plummer.[6]

That "accomplished villain" Plummer had arrived in Bannack along with hordes of others. After he killed a desperado in a stand-up gunfight the following January and townsmen learned that he had worn a lawman's badge in a tough California boom camp, they touted him as the man to control the criminal element and elected him sheriff in May 1863. It was a bad mistake, for Plummer was a hardened criminal, and soon he was not controlling, but instead leading the outlaw element in a wave of robberies and murders. This triggered vigilante reaction and the hanging of many of the criminals, including Sheriff Henry Plummer.[7]

In the many accounts of Bannack's violent history, Granville Stuart is not mentioned as a member of the legendary vigilante organization that carried out the brutal but effective campaign of retribution. It is clear from his writings and the accounts of others, however, that while perhaps not actively participating, he fully endorsed and supported the vigilante actions. Of Bannack's residents in its tempestuous first days, an early Montana historian wrote:

> The leading men among this little band of pioneers were admirably qualified to grapple with the varied difficulties and dangers incident to their exposed situation. The brothers Stuart . . . were among the most enterprising and intelligent citizens of Montana. [To them the State will be forever] indebted for the predominance of those principles which saved the people from the bloody rule of assassins, robbers and wholesale murderers. . . . They were men bred in the hard school of labor. They brought their business habits and maxims with them, and put them rigidly into practice. Having heard of the lawlessness which characterized the Salmon River camps, they were on the alert for every suspicious arrival from that direction.[8]

It is abundantly clear that the vigilante campaign against outlaws conducted in the 1860s provided the template for Granville Stuart's war on outlaws twenty years later.

When prospector friends of the Stuarts discovered new gold deposits in Alder Gulch, a new rush developed. Virginia City sprang up and Granville was soon established there with a mercantile business, while James was leading expeditions into the Yellowstone country in the never-ending search for more gold.[9] Ever restless and in search of new and greater opportunities, Granville sold his business in 1865 and returned to Deer Lodge, where he opened a store and lumber yard.[10]

On September 26, 1873, James Stuart died, reportedly from a "liver ailment," at the Fort Peck Indian Agency. Of course, this came as a severe blow to Granville, as the two brothers were quite close, having shared many adventures together. Granville brought his brother's body back to Deer Lodge for interment.[11]

Granville Stuart had first entered the political arena in 1871, when he was elected to the territorial legislature and served as one of the thirteen members of the Montana Territorial Council, which met in Virginia City.[12] When he was reelected to the legislature in 1875, Stuart also became vice president of the Montana Historical Society, which he had been secretary of when it was first founded in 1865. The year 1875 was also notable for his receipt on August 31 of one of the first Winchester model 73 "One of a Thousand" rifles, which had his name engraved on a side plate. This model rifle was to become famous as "the gun that won the West."[13]

Samuel Thomas Hauser, a banker and longtime friend, induced him to take over as bookkeeper for the First National Bank of Helena, and this led to the most significant change in Stuart's multifaceted career. In the summer of 1879 he entered into a partnership in the cattle business with Hauser and Andrew Jackson Davis, a wealthy Montana liquor distiller.[14] With initial capital stock of $150,000 they established a ranch on public land in Lewis and Clark County, Montana, and called it the DHS, after the last-name initials of the owners. None had experience in the ranching business, but Stuart, who was a minor partner with an investment of $20,000 that he had borrowed from Hauser, was made superintendent and general manager with a residence at the ranch site.

His first order of business was the purchase of cattle to stock the range, and he tackled the chore with his usual alacrity. By January 1, 1880, he had purchased two thousand head of cattle at prices ranging from fourteen to seventeen dollars a head, and by the first of March he had contracts for an additional two thousand.[15]

He spent most of the spring of 1880 exploring the vast Montana prairie for the best cattle ranges.[16] In July he began hiring experienced trail drivers to bring cattle he had purchased to his selected grazing lands. For DHS Ranch's headquarters and his future home, he chose a location on Ford's Creek, twenty miles northeast of Lewistown and close to the foot of the Judith Mountains. There, assisted by his older sons, Jim's boys, Reece Anderson (still sticking with his old friend), and men he had hired, he built two log houses—one for the Stuarts and one for Anderson. Since Indians were still a threat in that remote area, the houses were connected "with a bastion like those used at the early trading posts." He fenced in a large corral and erected a log stable, a bunkhouse for cowboys, and a blacksmith shop.[17] By the first of October all the construction was completed, including some outlying range cabins, and about five thousand head of DHS cattle (branded simply with an H) and sixty horses were peacefully grazing on the selected rangeland.

While accomplishing all this, Stuart retained his position in the Montana Territorial Legislature, where he was gaining greater prominence and had been elected president of the Senate Council in 1883.

In the winter of 1880–81 Stuart first became aware of stock theft, the problem that would turn him into a noteworthy man-hunter; but the initial losses were caused by Indians, not white rustlers. When informed by his cowpunchers that Cree Indians from Canada were killing his cattle, Stuart took men and rode straight to the Cree encampment. There they found about fifty Indian men, women, and children as well as a white man claiming to be a Catholic priest. Stuart wasted little time in palaver:

> I called for their chief and an old Indian came out to meet me. Pointing to a frozen beef hide thrown against a pole, I asked for an explanation. The chief said his people were starving and game was scarce, that my cattle being on the range made the buffalo go away; that the priest told him that he had a right to kill the white man's cattle when his people were hungry. I asked him if he did not know his hunting grounds were in Canada and not south of the Missouri River. He . . . said they could find nothing to eat there. . . . I called for the priest . . . and asked him what right he had to come on our range and advise the killing of our cattle. His excuse was that the women and children were hungry. I discovered that they had killed three steers, one cow, and one yearling. I ordered the chief to round up their horse herd and then selected five ponies to reimburse me for the slaughtered cattle, then told the chief to leave the range at once. Some of the young Indians protested at my taking their ponies and became quite ugly. I called for the priest and in dealing with him was rather more emphatic, promising to hang him higher than Haman if he ever set foot on the range again. He and the Indians lost no time in getting north of the British line.[18]

The spring roundups of 1881 confirmed heavy losses of cattle to Indians. Stuart calculated that in two Montana counties alone, Indians killed three thousand head of cattle the previous winter, a loss of $60,000 for the ranchers.[19] To deal with this problem, cattlemen from the two counties met at Fort Benton in August 1881. Stuart, busy on his own roundup, was unable to attend, but sent a letter assuring his full support for any action his neighboring ranchers might take. Many cattlemen, convinced that the root of the problem was illegal whiskey sales to Indians, voted to employ more stock detectives and to post rewards ranging from $100 to $500 for the "apprehension and conviction of any person or persons selling, bartering, or giving whiskey to Indians on the ranges of stockmen, members of the association."[20]

At his roundup Stuart found that the H brand on some of his stock had been blotched or defaced. With the assent of his partners, he changed the H to DS. Since brand defacing was not practiced by Indians, he knew it was the work of whites. But he incorrectly attributed the few altered brands to some local settlers, unaware that this was the first sign he would soon be at war, not with Indians, but with organized bands of cattle and horse thieves, a war that would engage him completely.

For Montana cattlemen, the problem of brand defacing was exacerbated by the practice of mavericking, taking unbranded calves from the herds of the big stockmen, which Stuart adamantly opposed. He explained:

In the early range days the Texas system of everybody's placing his brand on every calf found unbranded on the range, without even trying to ascertain to whom the animal belonged, was in full vogue. From the first I took issue against this kind of business. It was only a step from "mavericking" to branding any cow without a brand and from that to changing brands. Cowboys permitted to brand promiscuously for a company soon found that they could as easily steal calves and brand for themselves. If we are to believe the stories that floated up from Texas to our range, a goodly number of big Texas outfits had their beginning without capital investment in anything save a branding iron. In the broad open country of the range a man's conscience is apt to become elastic. A strong stand against anything approaching cattle stealing must be taken if the industry is to survive.[21]

Other ranchers of the territory sharing Stuart's concern organized the Montana Stockgrowers Association. Its first meeting, held at Helena in August 1882, resulted in no actual cattle-theft policies, but with the passing of another year it became apparent that the problem was only worsening, and rustling became the major topic of discussion at the April 1883 meeting in Miles City. The stockmen, desirous to work within the law, voted to employ a stock detective in each county at the organization's expense to "track up rustlers and horse thieves and do all in his power to have them arrested and brought to trial." When put into effect, however, the plan made little difference. According to Stuart, "Our detectives pursued and brought back stolen property and caused the arrest of the thieves and we hired counsel to assist the county attorneys to prosecute them but all to no purpose. The thieves managed to evade the law and became bolder each season."[22]

Under Stuart's management twelve thousand head of shorthorn cattle were roaming the DHS range by the summer of 1883, and he was turning a nice profit for the company, but he was still unhappy. At the fall roundup his tally showed the loss of about 3 percent, most of which he attributed to rustling. Some of the shrinkage, he knew, was the work of minor independent ranchers who were augmenting their small cattle holdings by mavericking. Although he found some humor in this kind of rustling activity, Stuart nevertheless dealt with it sternly:

> Near our home ranch we discovered one rancher whose cows invariably had twin calves and frequently triplets, while the range cows in that vicinity were nearly all barren and would persist in hanging around this man's corral, envying his cows their numerous children and bawling and lamenting their own childless fate. This state of affairs continued until we were obliged to call around that way and threaten to hang the man if his cows had any more twins.[23]

It was not small ranchers that concerned Stuart, but rather large, well-organized bands of outlaws who came out of their hideouts in that wild and sparsely populated country to rustle cattle in great bunches. "These thieves," he said, "were splendidly organized and had established headquarters and had enough friends among the ranchers to enable them to carry on their work with perfect safety."[24]

When the Montana Stockgrowers Association met at Miles City in April 1884, the 429 attendees included prominent Dakota Territory stockmen Theodore Roosevelt and the Marquis de Morés.[25] All had suffered heavy losses from rustling and were primed to take drastic action against the thieves. As Stuart assures readers of his memoirs, these cattlemen were peaceable and law-abiding men, but their property, worth $35 million and scattered over seventy-five thousand square miles of wilderness, was under criminal attack. Since the civil laws and courts had been tried and found wanting, it was agreed at the meeting that the only recourse remaining to protect their industry was to make the penalty for stealing so severe that it would lose its attraction. Arguments raged over how this could be accomplished. Some members, mostly young hotheaded types like de Morés and Roosevelt, proposed wiping the country clean of outlaws with an army of cowboys. Surprisingly, Granville Stuart, who had already been formulating a similar plan in his own mind, argued against it.

> I openly opposed any such move and pointed out . . . that the "rus-tlers" were strongly fortified, each of their cabins being a miniature fortress. They were all armed with the most modern weapons and had an abundance of ammunition, and every man of them was a desperado and a dead shot. If we had a scrap with them the law was on the side of the "rustlers." A fight with them would result in the loss of many lives and those that were not killed would have to stand trial for murder in case they killed any of the "rustlers."[26]

After a heated debate in which Stuart was joined in his pacifying argu-ment by other older, more conservative members, the proposal for a declaration of war against the rustlers was tabled for the time being. After the meeting adjourned and the cattlemen returned to their respective ranches, Stuart checked with his informants, cowpunchers, stock detec-tives, settlers, and small ranchers who had special knowledge of the outlaws and their activities and found that the rustlers had heard that the cattle-men decided against a coordinated attack and, elated by the news, had relaxed their guard and celebrated with jubilant carousing.

Stuart had been waiting for this exact outcome. His unexpected con-ciliatory stance at the meeting had been a cover for his ulterior plans: first, to go on record as being against a bloody attack on the outlaws in order to quell possible later criticism of his actions, and second, to lull his quarry into a false sense of security in order to gain the advantage of a surprise assault.[27]

Two decades earlier he had watched and admired the secretiveness and success of the Bannack vigilantes in their attacks on the brigands plagu-ing them. Now, infuriated by loss of his cattle and horses, he found it necessary to employ the same strategy and methods against those he viewed as parasites in need of eradication.

MAN-HUNTERS OF THE OLD WEST

At least one Montana newspaper editor was in full agreement. The editor of the *Mineral Argus* of Maiden, Montana, opined:

From every side comes reports of horses being stolen, single and in bands. . . . It is high time some measures were taken to stop this nefarious business. Horses are stolen in one section of the territory and taken to another and sold for what can be obtained regardless of their value. The ease and grace with which horse thieves have escaped punishment, owing to the difficulty in securing witnesses and the distance from the seat of justice, seems to preclude all hope of stopping this species of rascality through the courts. We do not advocate mob law or vigilante committees on general principles— in fact it should be the last method of redressing any wrong—but when the courts are impotent to deal out justice and check an evil, it is time for the community, over-ridden with law-breakers of whatever class, to rise in their might and suppress them. . . . It is time a lesson should be taught this class of criminals, and the most speedy and safe cure is to hang them as fast as captured. An organization should be formed for this purpose without delay.[28]

A report in the same paper a few weeks later may have been the last straw for Stuart: "We have it from reliable sources that several head of cattle belonging to Granville Stuart were found dead . . . . Their carcasses all bearing evidence of being shot, excites serious apprehension, should the perpetrators be discovered."[29] Following the spring roundup, Stuart called a meeting at his home and presented his plans to cowmen of like disposition, stockgrowers association detectives, and gun-handy ranch hands. He envisioned a tightly knit organization of fighting men, numbering not much more than a dozen, to attack the outlaws.[30] Since the desperadoes were dispersed at various hideouts, the little army would be made up of squads, each unit targeting a particular outlaw chieftain and his minions, and each led by a man intimately familiar with that outlaw's haunts. Secrecy was to be preserved at all times to ensure a surprise attack and the greatest opportunity for success. Once a squad wiped out its assigned targets, members were to join another vigilante unit to strengthen it. If a squad faced an encampment of rustlers too numerous to attack, one member was to be sent for reinforcements while the others were to remain in hiding. With the Bannack vigilantes still in mind, Stuart directed that any outlaws not killed by gunfire were to be hanged on the spot. No prisoners were to be taken and later released by incompetent legal officials or rigged juries; this would be a war of vermin extermination, as necessary and virtuous as squashing bedbugs, lice, or cockroaches. He would personally be in charge of the entire operation, and his second in command would be William "Floppin' Bill" Cantrell, the DHS stock detective.[31]

In June 1884, even as Stuart was finalizing plans for his campaign, unexpected events brought an abrupt end to several outlaws on his death list. On the twenty-sixth of that month Narciss Lavardure and Joe Vardner stole seven horses from a herder on the Judith River. As they retreated, they ran into a tough cowboy named William Thompson, who killed Vardner with a well-aimed shot and captured his cohort. The next day a party of Stuart's vigilantes broke into a stable where Lavardure was being held and hanged him.[32]

By the first week of July Stuart's vigilantes were actively seeking outlaws on his list. On July 3 a squad caught Sam McKenzie, a notorious horse thief, with two stolen horses and suspended him from a cottonwood tree.[33]

Two hard cases on the list were Charles "Rattlesnake Jake" Fallon and Edward "Long-Haired" Owen. In riding his range, Stuart had encountered this pair, and their very appearance had left an indelible impression. "They were as tough looking characters as I have ever met," he remembered,

> especially Owen, who had long unkept [sic] black hair, small, shifty, greenish gray eyes and a cruel mouth. "Rattle Snake Jake," despite his bad sounding sobriquet, was not quite so evil looking as his pal, although he was far from having a prepossessing appearance. Both men were armed, each wearing two forty-four Colt revolvers and a hunting knife. When I rode into their camp, Fallon was sitting on a roll of blankets cleaning a Winchester rifle. Owen was reclining against a stump smoking and another Winchester lay on a coat within easy reach. Owen was self-possessed, almost insolent, "Rattle Snake Jake" was civil but nervously tinkered with the gun and kept his eyes on me all the time I was in the camp. I knew that they were a bad lot but had nothing to cause their arrest at that time, but [I] decided to keep an eye on them while they were on the range.[34]

Before one of Stuart's squads could corner these desperadoes and administer vigilante justice, they went into Lewistown to celebrate the Fourth of July. Not surprisingly, they got drunk and tried to tree the town. A battle erupted on the main street, and they killed one man before townsmen filled them full of lead. Examination of the bodies showed that Rattlesnake Jake had been hit nine times and Long-Haired Owen eleven.[35] Thanks to the citizens of Lewistown, Stuart could remove two names from his extermination list without any help from his vigilantes.

While Fallon and Owen were being gunned down in Lewistown, a party of Stuart's avengers was closing in on an outlaw hangout at the mouth of the Musselshell on the Missouri River. Only two listed outlaws were there, one was Billy Woods and the other was known as California Ed. When they were captured and grilled, both admitted to stealing ponies from the Indians but denied taking any stock from white men. They could not account, however, for twenty-six horses in their corral, all bearing nearby ranches' brands, or cattle hides with the brand of a local ranch, which were salted and stacked in the stable, awaiting shipment downriver. They were taken to a little grove of trees and summarily hanged.[36]

When another squad of Stuart's man-hunters approached the headquarters of two known horse thieves, "Red Mike" and "Brocky" Gallagher, they found their quarries gone. Following tracks of a herd of horses driven across the river, they caught up with the two and found, as they had suspected, that the horses in the herd were stolen. In his account Stuart merely states that both men pled guilty to horse stealing without further comment, but it can be surmised that his orders were obeyed and that Red Mike and Gallagher soon dangled from trees.[37]

At Bates Point on the Missouri, a man called "Old Man" James and his family made their ramshackle home in an abandoned woodyard. James, his two sons, and a nephew were in tight with an outlaw gang headed by a man known as Jack Stringer, or sometimes Stringer Jack. Having once met Stringer, Stuart found him several cuts above the scum with whom he associated and described him as "a tall handsome fellow, well educated, and of a pleasing personality. His distinguishing features were his piercing gray eyes, white even teeth, and a pleasant smile. He did not drink to excess, but was an inveterate gambler." A former buffalo hunter, he had turned to cattle rustling and horse theft when the buffalo were gone.[38]

Before dawn on the morning of July 8 a party of vigilantes, augmented by squad members who had completed other assignments, closed in on the James place. Stuart himself must have led this operation, for in his memoirs he describes in graphic detail what transpired while carefully avoiding the use of first-person pronouns:

Here was the favorite haunt of Jack Stringer. There was a log cabin and a stable with a large corral built of logs, connecting the two buildings. One hundred yards from the cabin in a wooded bottom was a tent constructed of poles and covered with three wagon sheets. At the cabin were old man James and his two sons, Frank Hanson and Bill Williams. Occupying the tent were Jack Stringer, Paddy Rose, Swift Bill, Dixie Burr,[39] Orvil Edwards, and Silas Nickerson.

[The] men were divided into three parties. Three guarded the tent, five surrounded the cabin and one was left behind with the saddle horses. They then waited for daylight. Old man James was the first to appear. He was ordered to open the corral and drive out the horses. This he did but refused to surrender, backed into the cabin and fired a shot from his rifle through a small port hole at the side of the door. This was followed by a volley from port holes all around the cabin and in an instant the whole party was in action.

Two of the vigilantes crawled up and set fire to the hay stack and the cabin. The men inside stationed themselves at port holes and kept up the fight until they were all killed or burned up. The cabin burned to the ground. The tent was near the river bank and almost surrounded by thick brush and it was easier to escape from it than to get out of the cabin. Stringer Jack crawled under the tent and reached a dense clump from which he made his last stand. Dixie Burr had his arm shattered with a rifle ball but jumped into an old dry well and remained until dark. Paddy Rose ran out of the tent, passed back of the [vigilantes] engaged at the cabin and concealed himself in a small washout and after dark made his escape. Nickerson, Edwards and Swift Bill reached the river bank and crawling along through the brush and under the bank, succeeded in passing above the men at the cabin and hid in some brush and drift wood. Orvil Edwards and Silas Nickerson were the only ones who escaped without wounds. After the fight at the cabin the [vigilantes] went down the river and spent the day looking for the men who had escaped but failed to find them.[40]

Dixie Burr joined up with Nickerson, Edwards, and Swift Bill the next day, and the four slapped together a rude raft and started down the river. Soldiers from Fort Maginnis spotted them, ordered them ashore, and turned them over to Deputy U.S. Marshal Samuel Fischel, but a Stuart squad intercepted Fischel and took his prisoners from him at gunpoint. Without admitting that he had personally witnessed what then happened, Stuart described the scene: "Nearby stood two log cabins close together. A log was placed between the cabins, the ends resting on the roofs, and the four men were hanged from the log. The cabins caught fire and were burned down and the bodies were cremated."[41]

Of the eleven felons gathered at the James encampment, ten had now been dispatched by Stuart's vigilantes: outlaw leader Jack Stringer by gunfire, five shot or burned to death in the James cabin, and four later hanged downriver. The sole escapee, Paddy Rose, made his way to Fort Benton, and wealthy relatives helped him slip into Canada.[42]

News of the raids was slow to reach the outside world. It was almost a month after the battle at Bates Point when reports from Helena were wired to periodicals around the country. An August 5 dispatch informed readers that a horse-stealing gang, "too large to be taken," was surrounded there, but would "be held until help comes. Hot times are expected." A few days later the story of the raid, headlined A DEADLY BATTLE, was told in admittedly "meagre details," concluding with the wholly unsubstantiated pronouncement that "fully fifty thieves were hanged or shot in the past month."[43]

The elimination of the gang at Bates Point culminated Granville Stuart's war on outlaws. His men recovered a total of 284 stolen horses and returned them to their rightful owners.[44] "The vigilantes disbanded and returned to their respective homes. This clean-up of horse thieves put a stop to horse and cattle stealing in Montana for many years," he said with obvious satisfaction.

But the cleanup was not accomplished without criticism. He and other cattlemen were accused of importing professional gunmen to drive settlers and sheepmen off the range. Stuart, in his memoirs, responded,

"There was not a grain of truth in this talk." Those taking part in the raid, he said, were "fourteen men who had stock on the range and who had suffered at the hands of the thieves." They hanged no one on suspicion or for a first offense, but only those "members of an organized band of thieves that for more than two years had evaded the law and robbed the range at will."[45]

The story of Granville Stuart's assault on the outlaws plaguing Montana has been recounted often in later books and magazine articles. Along the way the alliterative label of "Stuart's Stranglers" became attached to the man-hunters who carried out the mission and has since appeared in almost every recital of those dramatic events.

Although he received severe criticism in some quarters for his actions, Stuart showed no remorse for what he had done. His son-in-law recalled hearing a woman revile him for hanging thirty men. Tipping his hat to the lady, Stuart responded, "Yes, madam, and by God, I done it alone."[46]

The number of outlaws killed by Stuart's vigilantes has been a point of dispute ever since 1884, with the figure varying widely. Oscar Mueller states in a 1951 article, "The DHS raids were responsible for a minimum of 15 and a maximum of 18 during 1884."[47] Joseph Howard's 1943 book describes and refutes rumors of higher numbers: "Estimates of the number of men killed in the cleanup of horse thieves vary from 19 to 75. . . . The *Mineral Argus*, deploring wild rumors, thought even 17 was 'placing the number a little too high.'"[48]

Wallis Huidekoper, a son of one of the region's ranchers, wrote for the Montana Stockgrowers Association, "No authoritative information has ever been given, as the strictest secrecy has always prevailed." But, he continues, "Without mentioning names, suffice it to say that the men responsible . . . were a small group of cowmen of that strong and practical type who had already pioneered the west, quiet on speech and demeanor but quick to assume justifiable action when convinced of its need." He says,

> The real storm did break with terrible force, coming like an avalanche in a sudden, secret and terrible way with the lifeless bodies of well-known rustlers hanging from the limbs of cottonwood trees. . . . The entire action was swift and thorough and showed a master hand at organization. . . . Apparently there was a carefully prepared list of the prominent rustlers and these were put on the rope first,

with others following as evidence of their guilt appeared. . . . The deadly nature of this work, the secrecy of it, and the uncertainty of who might be next put such fear into the hearts of any remaining rustlers still alive that they soon quit the country and wholesale cattle and horse stealing became a thing of the past. . . . The work was done by a few range detectives and the quiet top hands of some of the larger outfits. The outlaws called them the "Stranglers" which they undoubtedly were. The total number of outlaws hung and shot in extreme eastern Montana and western Dakota was sixty-three.[49]

A writer for one of the "true" western magazines popular in the 1960s and '70s settled for nice even numbers: "The rustler stronghold had been broken in just 14 days by 14 determined men. A total of 28 rustlers had been hanged or shot."[50]

In his introduction to *U-Bet*, the memoirs of John R. Barrows, a cowboy who rode for the DHS during this period, Richard Roeder sums up the Stuart raids as

one of the more controversial episodes in Montana history. . . . This was a bloody affair. Barrows' account refers to thirteen victims. There were probably far more than that, but the true number of victims is not known. Unlike the Virginia City activities of twenty years earlier, the raids did not meet with uniform positive public reaction. Barrows did not participate in them, remaining back at the ranch to herd horses, and . . . afterward DHS employees who were part of the action were reluctant to talk about what took place. Barrows, who greatly admired Stuart, justified the raids as necessary to "restore security and order," [but later] referred to the raids as "criminal" and added that he had heard men talk "of atrocities that would make one's blood run cold."[51]

Although it was not universally condemned in nineteenth-century America as it is today, vigilantism was certainly not accepted in all quarters of the frontier West during the 1880s. Editorial comment about the Stuart raids in the surviving Montana papers was mixed, but tended to be supportive. Typical was an editorial in a Diamond City paper:

The severe measure adopted recently by the stockmen of eastern Meagher county to rid that section of horse thieves, is looked upon by them as a most disagreeable duty. But having for the past three years been subjected to great loss of stock . . . , and the civil law having entirely failed to bring a single thief to justice, and [aware] that there was a regular organized band of horse thieves in the county, they determined to break it up at all hazards, and the result shows how thoroughly they have done their work. Extravagant stories in regard to the details of this onset upon the most efficient and thoroughly organized band of thieves that has probably ever existed in the West, are being heralded far and near and Meagher county is getting up a notoriety that is not calculated to be of any benefit as an immigration card, as those seeking homes will regard the people of this section as a lawless community. [However] thieves will in the future steer clear of it. Mob law is certainly to be abhorred [but] we cannot censure [the ranchers for] summarily dealing out justice without waiting the inefficient, slow action of the law.[52]

A letter to the editor from James Fergus, a Montana rancher and close friend of Granville Stuart, also appeared in this issue of the paper. Fergus, wishing to clarify an earlier edition of the paper indicating that a "Mr. Fergus" had helped clean out the outlaw gang, pointed out that several Ferguses lived in the area, but since he was the oldest and best known, some might assume he was the one cited. He was sorry the assumption was untrue, he said, for only old age and ill health kept him from joining in the raids. Admitting that "men have been hung and shot in this so-called civilized country without due process of law," he recited a number of instances of recent outlaw crimes without law enforcement action and asked,

> Now what is to be done? We must either gather up what stock we have left and leave the country or gather up these desperadoes and put them where they will kill and steal no more; there is no alternative, and we choose the latter. It is now simply a state of war. Wars are often waged between peoples without provocation. Here we are waging war on thieves, bandits and desperadoes. . . .
>
> Now as the county don't protect us, the army don't protect us, there is no way left but to protect ourselves. . . . A history of this summer's raids on the horse and cattle thieves . . . would show as much good management, bravery and endurance as anything during the war for the Union, and that is saying a great deal. That fourteen

men should attack a blockhouse with port holes, defended by nearly as many armed men with heavy Spencer rifles . . . , kill a number of the thieves, wound several more, and get away without losing a single man or having one wounded, would be [praised] as an act of good generalship and bravery if it were not unlawful. But unlawful or not, necessity compels it. It has got to be done and will be, but others deserve the credit, not me.[53]

The contrary viewpoint was expressed in a Miles City editorial. When a member of the territorial legislature in a speech advocated resorting to lynch law, since the legal authorities were unable to cope with outlawry in thinly populated sections of the territory, the editor adamantly disagreed:

It is a shame and a disgrace . . . that any such utterances should emanate from the floor of the legislative council of Montana. There may be cases in which this summary way of disposing of suspected or even known thieves may be excused by peculiar circumstances, but as a principle it is radically wrong and never justified. If one man kills a thief on sight it is murder, but if ten men or a hundred men constitute themselves court, jury and executioners and hang a thief it is forsooth only "lynch law." . . . If the laws for the protection of property are inadequate, then [correct] the defects. If the penalty for the larceny of horses or cattle is too light, then let it be increased. If horse stealing should be punished by death, then let it be made a capital offense, but until then, it ill becomes a member of the legislature to advocate punishment in excess of law, and is an insult to law and order to advocate the methods of mobs who administer lynch law.[54]

The following year Stuart conducted another campaign against those preying on his stock, but his foes this time were not white outlaws but Indians. The problem originated following the Riel Rebellion in Canada in which several hundred Cree Indians revolted against the Canadian government. Defeated, they moved across the border and began preying on the Montana cattle herds.[55] A Fort Benton, Montana, newspaper described the problem: "Indians are raising Cain on the Judith ranges. . . . They have raided cabins, killed cattle and stolen horses, and have been so bold in their depredations that the settlers are arming for protection. . . . Sixty head of horses are known to have been stolen. . . . Granville

Stuart with fifteen men from that section, well mounted and armed, have gone after the Indians."[56]

On October 5, 1885, Stuart wired Chouteau County sheriff James McDevitt: "Ten Crows captured with 60 horses and sent to Crow Agency. . . . Go to Crow Agency and arrest these Indians and take them to Benton for trial. Will see if we can't put a stop to this business. Granville Stuart, Pres. Ter. Stock Commissioners."[57]

It is obvious from his actions at the time and from his later writings that Stuart did not harbor the same bitter animosity toward Indians, even those preying on his stock, as he did for white stock thieves. His wife being Indian and his many children having mixed blood may have been a factor, but he seemed to commiserate with the Indian plight because of the way whites had encroached on their lands. He harbored no such sympathy for white criminals.

Despite all of these problems, cattle ranching in Montana prospered during this period, and the DHS Cattle Company, under Stuart's management, was valued in 1885 at more than a million dollars. Recognizing his leadership as a ranch manager (and, no doubt, as an exterminator of horse and cattle thieves), his peers elected him president of the Montana Stockgrowers Association. A founding member of the Society of Montana Pioneers, established in 1885, he was made president of that organization the next year. In 1890 he assumed another presidency, that of the Montana Historical Society.

But beginning in 1886 ranching problems increased. A severe drought that summer followed by an unusually harsh winter devastated the cattle industry throughout the West. The 1887 roundups revealed a loss of 66 percent of DHS herds to winterkill, and the remaining stock was in deplorable condition. For cattlemen like Stuart, the scenes on the range were heart wrenching: "The ranges presented a tragic aspect. Along the streams and in the coulees everywhere were strewn the carcasses of dead cattle. Those that were left alive were poor and ragged in appearance, weak and easily mired in the mud holes. A business that had been fascinating for me before, suddenly became distasteful. I wanted no more of it. I never wanted to own another animal that I could not feed and shelter."[58] He remained at the DHS a couple more years, but his heart wasn't in the work, and in 1890 Granville Stuart left the ranching business.[59]

The hard blows continued throughout those mean years. In 1888 Awbonie, his wife and the mother of his nine children, died of puerperal fever. Two years later, on January 8, 1890, Granville, now fifty-five years old, remarried to Allis Belle Brown, a twenty-six-year-old schoolteacher at the DHS ranch.[60]

Still highly regarded in many influential circles, especially in the Democratic Party, he was not long without work. In 1891 he accepted an appointment as state land agent and personally selected some 600,000 acres of land granted to Montana by the federal government.

Following Grover Cleveland's election to the U.S. presidency in 1884, his fellow Democrat Samuel Hauser had been appointed governor of Montana Territory, and Stuart's longtime friend and business associate sat in the governor's chair during the late 1880s while Stuart struggled with the ranch. After four years out of the White House, Cleveland was elected again in 1892, and Hauser began lobbying for an appointment for Stuart, who held a position as lieutenant colonel in the Montana territorial militia, a ceremonial office providing no income. At Hauser's urging, in 1893 Cleveland appointed Stuart the envoy extraordinary and minister plenipotentiary to the republics of Uruguay and Paraguay. Thus the former miner and cattleman, whose sole qualification for such a position was his ability to speak Spanish, spent the next four years in South America.[61]

Of course, when Republican William McKinley succeeded Democrat Cleveland as president in 1897, Stuart was also replaced. He was sixty-two years old by this time and was content to retire with his wife, Allis, to a home in Silver Bow, Montana. He had kept a journal all those adventurous years of his life on the frontier, and with that as a basis began writing an autobiography. In 1916 he was commissioned to write a history of Montana, a project he was working on when he died of heart failure at the age of eighty-four on October 2, 1918. He was buried at Deer Lodge beside his brother James, who had passed away forty-five years earlier.

The Arthur H. Clark Company published Stuart's account of his frontier life in two volumes in 1925. Entitled *Forty Years on the Frontier as Seen in the Journals and Reminiscences of Granville Stuart, Gold-Miner, Trader, Merchant, Rancher and Politician* and edited by Paul C. Phillips, it has since become a standard source in any study of American western frontier history. Reviewing the book for the June 13, 1926, issue of the *New York Times*, Arthur Pound informed his readers that Stuart

> left a mass of diaries and memoirs, from which a judicious selection has been made by Paul C. Phillips, who has done excellently in correcting his principal's occasional lapses in dates. Still, despite the color and vigor of the present volume, the unpublished residue must contain much else of value. In such a rich mine as Granville Stuart, even the tailings should be worth rework at some time. As the incidents unfold themselves richly, the reader has the feeling somehow of buried treasure just around the corner, of things left unsaid for lack of space, even though they richly deserve telling. Still, lovers of frontier lore should be grateful for the salvaging of so many tales of high emprise which deserve a place in the folklore of America.

Because of his significant impact on the early history of the state, Granville Stuart is celebrated as "Mr. Montana," although his man-hunting expedition of 1884 and its reliance on the administration of hempen justice by Stuart's Stranglers remains as controversial today as it was at the time. During his remarkable life he pursued many professions, but unlike other famous man-hunters of the frontier West who dedicated their lives to the hunt for felons, Stuart's career in the business spanned only a few weeks. For cold-blooded determination and efficiency, however, he was never surpassed by any of his contemporaries.

— 4 —

HENRY NICHOLSON "HARRY" MORSE
1835–1912

> The thrilling history of Harry Morse is familiar to every citizen . . .
> of the entire State. His numberless encounters with desperadoes have
> been the theme upon which have been woven some of the most famous
> literature of the west.
>
> *San Francisco Morning Call,* November 5, 1894

At his birth on February 2, 1835, in New York City, the boy who would
gain fame chasing outlaws in California was christened Henry Nicholson
by his parents, Abraham Washington Morse and Charlotte E. (Speight)
Morse. But he preferred "Harry," and so it was as Harry N. Morse that
he was known throughout his career.[1]

He descended on his paternal side from a line of patriotic American
warriors; his great-grandfather fought in the French and Indian War,
his grandfather in the Revolution, and his father, as an eleven-year-old
drummer boy, in the War of 1812. Inheriting the adventurous nature of
his predecessors and with little schooling, at the tender age of ten Harry
set out to see the world. Large for his age, he signed on as an able-bodied
seaman on a ship bound for England. He would follow a seafaring voca-
tion for the next four years.[2]

Back in New York in February 1849, when all the talk was of the great
gold discovery in California, he caught the fever and worked his way to
California as a crewmember on the *Panama,* a ship bound for the one-
way trip around Cape Horn. Slowed by bad weather, heavy headwinds,
and layovers for repairs, the *Panama* took more than six months before
finally anchoring in San Francisco Bay on August 8, 1849.[3]

Fourteen years old and broke when he arrived in the new El Dorado,
Morse did kitchen work at five dollars a day to earn a grubstake before

Henry Nicholson "Harry" Morse. Courtesy of John Boessenecker collection.

attacking the mining district. Panning and gold digging in the mountains produced little pay dirt, and Morse soon decided his chances of striking it rich with pan and shovel were slim. Never daunted by adversity and with an eye always out for new opportunities, he returned to the port city, and with the little gold he had saved, he purchased several small boats and began a ferry service between the city and ships in the harbor.

For the next thirteen years he engaged in all sorts of occupations, always searching for a life's work, but as soon as he accumulated enough for an investment, he started a new business. He built and managed a hotel, conducted an express service between San Francisco and Oakland, and opened a grocery store.[4]

He was twenty when he met and began courting sixteen-year-old Virginia Elizabeth Heslep, the daughter of prominent San Francisco lawyer Augustus M. Heslep. They were married September 14, 1855, in Oakland.[5]

An incident in 1858, when Morse was running an express service across San Francisco Bay, clearly demonstrated that the ambitious young entrepreneur was also courageous and quick to act in an emergency. He was on the ferry crossing the bay one day, when a young boy of about twelve fell overboard. Quickly stripping off hat, shirt, and boots, Morse dove over the side, swam to the struggling boy, and brought him safely back, to the cheers of passengers and crew. One passenger was so impressed that he wrote an account of the experience for a San Francisco newspaper twenty years later. Even before the life-saving event, the passenger had taken notice of the young man as he sat on a horse-drawn wagon loaded with packages at the boat's bow. The article described him as clean-shaven, with a long, thin nose denoting shrewdness. His eyes were dark blue, "slightly inclined to gray, [and] looked fearlessly into your own when they were turned toward you. The square, finely cut jaw indicated great firmness of character. [It was a face] most people would take a second look at when meeting its owner for the first time. He was well known to all on board as a quiet, determined young fellow, who was always ready to fight for his friends, and as equally ready to forgive an enemy."[6] At the outbreak of the Civil War in 1861, Morse, a lifelong Republican and great admirer of President Abraham Lincoln (he later named one of his sons Lincoln), helped organize the Oakland Guard, the first military unit in Alameda County to support the Union cause. Enlisted as a corporal, he was soon promoted to first lieutenant and then to captain, a rank he held for four years.[7] He was an ardent supporter of the Union, ever ready to defend Lincoln, Republicanism, and Yankeedom with his fists. A newspaperman a decade later would recall that during the war "rough, brutal Southerners" would revile Unionists and "make themselves a terror to the community," but Harry Morse, a young man in the express business, was "afraid of nobody. More than one of those bullying secessionists felt the force of his powerful arm."[8]

Years later, after Morse had distinguished himself as an outstanding law enforcement officer and had been repeatedly elected to the sheriff's office on the Republican ticket, the editor of a Democratic-leaning Alameda County newspaper brought up an old secessionist charge that Morse, "young, athletic, and notoriously pugnacious," had been a "shoulder striker," as political bullies in those days were called, but "withal was considered the most decent of the fellows who were 'on the shoulder.'"[9] To this accusation, the editor of the Republican paper in Oakland responded that Morse "did knock down a man occasionally [but] never struck a man except for reviling the flag of his country, and cheering for the Southern army."[10]

As an officer in the Oakland Guard, Morse pursued Copperheads (as Southern sympathizers were called) and members of the rebellious secret society Knights of the Golden Circle. In 1863 he led a squad in a raid on a hangout of the subversive organization, arrested three members, and hustled them off to the military prison on Alcatraz Island. Reportedly, plans were discovered in the raid for taking over the California state government in the name of the Confederacy. When news of the assassination of President Lincoln reached the West Coast, riots erupted in San Francisco, and the Oakland Guard joined other militia units in restoring calm.[11]

Morse's work with the guard led to his appointment as deputy provost marshal for the county, which would in turn lead to his candidacy for sheriff. He was elected on September 2, 1863, easily defeating the Democratic candidate. At the age of twenty-nine, on March 7, 1864, he was sworn in to serve a two-year term as Alameda County sheriff.[12]

By pinning on a badge, Harry Morse found a career for which he was well fitted in temperament, intelligence, good judgment, and physical courage, but as he admitted himself, he was green to the business.[13] Central California counties in the 1860s were infested with scores of outlaws, mostly vaqueros of Mexican heritage, who would periodically leave their seemingly peaceful and mundane pursuits to follow charismatic leaders like Tiburcio Vasquez and Joaquin Murrieta in raids of plunder and murder, and Alameda County was no exception. But, as his biographer pointed out, Morse's world had been primarily confined to city streets and dwellings;

he knew little about the ranges and mountains of his county and even less about the investigation of crime and criminal apprehension. His knowledge of the language, customs, and habits of the vaqueros was negligible, and he lacked expertise with horses and weapons. He had used brawn to subdue unruly Copperheads, but fistic ability would be of small advantage against heavily armed outlaws on swift steeds who looked with scorn at the beardless young sheriff and mockingly nicknamed him *el Muchacho*, (the Boy).[14] Morse would later claim that, despite his admitted limitations, he pursued such brigands immediately after his initial election, and many later newspapermen and historical writers have followed his version of events. As early as 1872 the *San Francisco Chronicle*, in a lengthy account of his tenure as sheriff, stated that "from the very outset of his official career [Morse was known for his] shrewdness, energy, and high qualities of courage, coolness, and readiness of resources in the face of peril."[15]

But, actually, he made no real effort against the county's major outlaws during his first term in office, and in July 1865 he suffered severe embarrassment when, through his negligence, four lesser miscreants he had locked up in his jail escaped. He was celebrating the Fourth of July in San Francisco, his undersheriff was in San Leandro, and the calaboose was left unguarded, so four inmates used the opportunity to cut the bars of a window with a smuggled saw blade and took off.[16]

Despite this debacle, Alameda County voters reelected Morse overwhelmingly only two months later. This lopsided victory could not have been because of any great work he had accomplished his first two years, but was a result of the low regard voters held for the Democratic Party since it had supported secessionist Copperheads during the war years.[17] Given a second chance, Morse determined to make himself a top-notch lawman. He memorized faces, nicknames, habits, and descriptions of countless known outlaws; learned conversational Spanish and how to read, sign, and follow a track; became an expert horseman; practiced with handgun and rifle until he was deadly accurate with both; and began to develop informants to alert him to outlaw movements.[18]

He was still in his self-education program in May 1866, when one of the locals he was cultivating tipped him off regarding the movements of Eduardo Gallego, a fugitive cattle thief described by the *Alameda County Gazette* as "an old and hardened sinner," who boasted that no white man could ever take him.[19] Together with two other lawmen, Morse followed this lead for twelve days and more than a hundred miles, but lost his trail and returned home empty handed.

Disappointed, but still determined to capture Gallego, a month later Morse acted on another report of the rustler's hideout. Accompanied by the Swain brothers, George and David, he hurried to the site and stealthily approached the camp at dawn. About thirty armed vaqueros were readying their horses, preparing to leave. Spotting Gallego, Morse drew a bead on him and ordered him to raise his hands. George Swain, moving quickly, pressed a pistol to the startled outlaw's head and disarmed him. They handcuffed Gallego, tied him to his horse, and rode off with their prisoner before any of his compadres could interfere. This bold and daring piece of police work was lauded in the local press.[20]

In September Morse went after Narciso Bojorques, another hard case he described in a later account as "a reckless, devil-may-care sort of fellow." About nineteen, sturdily built, with muscles "like wire rope, [he was] easy and graceful in his movements, [with] the strength of a lion, and withal one of the best horseman in the country."[21] With a warrant from another county in hand, Morse rode twenty miles to the vicinity of Mission San Jose, where Bojorques had reportedly been sighted, and made inquiries at a trading post that confirmed Bojorques was camped nearby. He was, in fact, expected back again that evening. Morse stationed himself out of sight and waited.

As this was the first real bad man he had ever tackled, Morse was nervous as he waited for what could well be a violent confrontation. Confident he could handle the desperado with physical power, as he was young and strong, it would be another story if guns came into play. In his whole life Morse had never used weapons, but Bojorques was reputed to be an expert in their use.

It was dark when a lone horseman rode up. Wanting to get the outlaw off his mount and on his feet when he confronted him, Morse had earlier asked a young boy at the trading post to entice Bojorques to come inside when he appeared. The boy did as requested, but the desperado, reacting perhaps with the instinctive caution of the habitual criminal, refused to dismount. Morse's narrative continued:

> I came quickly forward from my hiding place, intending to seize the horse's bridle rein and give it a sudden jerk backward, thus setting the horse down on his haunches, and then to reach out, take Narciso

by the throat, and pull him off his horse to the ground. . . . But I never got him there. I [was] almost within reach of his horse's head, when Narciso . . . suddenly drew his horse back out of my reach and at the same time, with the rapidity of lightning, he drew his revolver, and cocking it, thrust it into my face. . . .

God! What a shock it gave me! Caught in my own trap and completely at the mercy of the desperado . . . who would [take] my life to make his escape! . . . I did not even have my pistol out. . . . I expected each instant to see the flash and feel the bullet crash through my flesh. . . .

Lord! How quick my mind worked! It occurred to me if I could only get my pistol out, cock and shoot it, no matter in what direction, the effect upon the desperado might be demoralizing, and if he hesitated a moment longer to shoot I could get the best of him. He did hesitate, and that saved my life.

In a swift movement, accelerated by desperation, Morse pulled his six-shooter, cocked the hammer, and without aiming, triggered off a round in the outlaw's general direction. Morse said the effect was "electric." The bullet missed, but Bojorques, dumbfounded by this bold move, screamed, "*No tiras!*" ("Don't shoot!"), and galloped off. Aiming this time, Morse fired another shot that struck the desperado in the arm and knocked him off his horse. Jumping up, he disappeared into the night. After an unsuccessful night hunting him on foot, Morse gathered a posse the next day for an organized search, which revealed nothing but bloodstains. The hunt went on for days, but Bojorques was not found.

For several months Morse looked for Bojorques but never captured him. A friend of the outlaw later told him the bullet he had fired that night struck the outlaw near the elbow, descended through his arm, and emerged in his hand, permanently crippling his fingers.[22]

The hunt for Bojorques was not entirely unsuccessful, however, because in checking out one of the outlaw's hideouts, Morse nabbed Augustin Avila, one of the escapees from his jail the previous year. Lodged in the county jail once more, he was later convicted of grand larceny and given a three-year prison term.[23]

The exciting combat between Bojorques and Morse profoundly affected the criminally inclined vaqueros of Alameda County. The way Morse had bravely confronted the outlaw mano a mano,[24] wounded him in a gunfight, and put him to flight like an injured animal drastically changed their attitude about the man. The derogatory epithet *el Muchacho* vanished from their vocabularies, replaced by *el Diablo* (the Devil).[25] Conversely, the outcome of the encounter with the fearsome Bojorques convinced Morse that many outlaws with frightening reputations were essentially cowards and would turn tail when confronted by a determined and courageous officer. After that, his work as sheriff improved noticeably.

The year 1867 was notable in several respects for Morse. He engaged in a grueling nine-hour chase after a horse thief over forty-five miles of rough, mountainous terrain, culminating in the return of the stolen mount and the thief.[26] Gang leader Joaquin Olivera was also caught that year, causing a local newspaper editor to marvel at Morse's success in nabbing "one of the most desperate ruffians and thieves in the region."[27]

In November 1867 Morse engaged in a gunfight strangely reminiscent of the previous year's Bojorques battle. A notorious ruffian named Narato Ponce was wanted for the murder of an inoffensive old man in a Hayward saloon. Morse investigated and began a search for the killer, but Ponce had disappeared. Then, late in the month, one of his informants tipped him off that on a certain night the fugitive would come down from his hideout in the hills for supplies. Morse and Oakland policeman John Conway set up a trap at a gate in the road that Ponce would pass. To make certain Ponce could not get by him, Morse positioned himself in the middle of the road beyond the gate and stationed Conway behind one of the haystacks flanking the road on either side. When Ponce appeared and leaned down from his horse to open the gate, Morse leaped to his feet with leveled shotgun and shouted, "Hands up!" In response, the outlaw whipped out his six-gun, triggered a shot at the dim figure in the road, and jerked his horse around to escape. The officers' return fire struck him, but he galloped off. To discern Ponce's direction of flight, Morse set the haystacks afire to light up the night, but to no avail. Ponce, like Bojorques, though badly wounded, escaped into the night.

Morse and Conway searched for hours but found no trace of Ponce in the dark. Local villagers helped them comb the area the next day. They found nothing but a bloody jacket, riddled with bullet and buckshot holes. Frustrated and angered by the escape of another murderer, temporarily at least, Morse alerted other lawmen to watch for Ponce and posted a notice of $500 reward for his capture.

Morse knew that Ponce, with his severe gunshot wounds, would need nursing help and someone to provide him with necessities until he recovered, but it was mid-December before he got a lead on such a person. A suspected cattle thief that he arrested blurted out that an old man had cared for the fugitive. Together with Conway and George Swain, Morse found and interrogated the old man and learned that Ponce was hiding in Pinole Valley. The lawmen went there immediately and began searching the adobe houses scattered throughout the canyon. As George Swain stepped from the bright sunshine into the darkness of one house, the glint of a gun caught his eye. He jumped back, pulled his own pistol, and shouted to Conway that he had found their fugitive. Conway, carrying a Spencer rifle, came running as Ponce emerged from the house and began firing. Both officers shot back, but in their excitement all three shooters missed. Ponce then turned tail and ran. Morse, on horseback some distance away, heard the gunfire and spurred his mount toward the sound. Stopped by a fence, he pulled his Henry rifle from the scabbard, dismounted, climbed over the obstacle, and ran to a creek running high with winter rains. Looking across, he spotted Ponce running along the opposite bank, searching for a likely place to cross.

"Stop and lay down your pistol!" Morse shouted, but Ponce ran on. Morse triggered four rounds from his Henry rifle at the running man, but missed every time. Conway, in pursuit of the fugitive, was more successful with his Spencer rifle, and one of his shots struck Ponce in the hand. Stopping his frantic running, Ponce evidently decided to go down fighting. He rested his pistol on his wounded arm and squinted through the sights at Morse across the creek. But no longer running, Ponce was now in the sights of Morse's rifle, and the sheriff squeezed his trigger before the outlaw could, slamming a .44-caliber slug into his body. Ponce keeled over and expired within moments. The killing was declared justifiable at an inquest, and local newspapers praised Morse highly. The *Oakland Daily News* opined that a thief was as likely to escape from Morse as a camel was to get through the eye of a needle.[28]

The murder of Morgan Leighton, an elderly and widely respected Alameda County rancher, by a young tough named Joe Newell set Sheriff Morse off on a long and arduous manhunt in September 1868. When learning of the murder, Morse, without waiting for county or state authorization, posted wanted notices for Newell with a full description. Acting on advice that Newell might have returned to the Mount Diablo coal mines, where he once worked, Morse and San Leandro constable Lewis C. "Lew" Morehouse combed that area, covering two hundred miles in four days without success.[29]

The search provided one valuable lead, however. Gilroy city marshal Billy Berger informed Morse that a man answering Newell's description had passed through town some days before. When suspicious local officers questioned him closely, he mentioned he was looking for work in Los Angeles County, far to the south. Acting on this slim bit of information, Morse rented a spring wagon drawn by a team of tough little mustangs, packed in supplies, and set out with Morehouse in mid-October on a forty-one-day manhunt that would cover twelve hundred miles.[30]

Realizing they were on a very cold scent, the officers questioned people along the route, asking if they recalled seeing a man answering Newell's description passing through, but few could remember one particular individual after almost three weeks. A few did remember, however, which convinced the man-hunters that they were on the right trail. They passed through a half-dozen California counties, crossed deserts, climbed mountains, and experienced cold nights and blistering days before arriving at Llano Verde in Los Angeles County. There they came across an innkeeper who remembered Newell well because the outlaw had ridden a little roan mare the entire way but had left the animal there to die when the poor animal finally gave out. The innkeeper told Morse that Newell had headed for the Soledad Canyon gold and copper mining camps. The lawmen went there, but they were disappointed to learn that Newell had moved on to Los Angeles. After four or five days fruitlessly searching that town, they concluded he had continued southward, and they followed. Morse was determined to nab him in Mexico if necessary.[31]

Stopping at a railroad construction site about twenty miles south of Los Angeles to see if Newell might have taken work there, Morse entered a tent that served as a kitchen and immediately spotted the man he had chased across half the length of California. Although the young fellow denied being Newell, claiming that his name was George Hartley, Morse arrested him. Only after he was sitting handcuffed between Morse and Morehouse in the wagon on the road back to Los Angeles did the prisoner break down and confess to being Newell and to the murder. The next morning Morse boarded a steamboat for San Francisco with his prisoner, while Morehouse started for home with the team.

A year later an atrocious mass murder was committed in neighboring San Joaquin County, horrifying Californians. Storekeeper Frank Medina, one employee, and three customers were brutally shot to death at Medina's establishment outside the village of Bellota. Suspicion immediately fell upon three men of bad reputation: two Hispanic men, Jesus Tejada and Ysidro Padilla, and an Indian, Antonio Garcia, all of whom had been seen near the store just before the killings. Reward notices were posted, and posses scoured the surrounding hills for weeks without success. Eventually the coldblooded murder of five men receded in the public consciousness, and the crime became just a part of California's violent history.[32]

But Sheriff Harry Morse, his eyes and ears always open for information that might help him apprehend a wanted man, quite accidentally got on the trail of Jesus Tejada, leader of the three murder suspects. After collaring a horse thief and recovering the stolen horse south of San Jose in May 1870, he decided it was too late in the day to start back for San Leandro, so he put his prisoner in a San Jose cell, left his horse and the recovered one in a livery stable, and registered in a hotel. Before retiring, he dropped into a Mexican *fonda* for a nightcap and was seated near two Hispanics in close conversation. Hearing the name Jesus Tejada mentioned, Morse strained to hear more. The man said he had seen and talked with Tejada a few days before in the Los Banos Canyon home of Jose Maria in Merced County. The outlaw, suffering from a severe foot strain, had slit his boot from toe to ankle to relieve the swelling and said he would remain there a month before heading for Mexico, never to return.

Morse returned to San Leandro, jailed his horse thief, returned the stolen horse to its owner, and began preparations for a manhunt. After obtaining a description of Tejada from Stockton authorities, he enlisted the ever-reliable Lew Morehouse, and to everyone's surprise, his thirteen-year-old son, George, to accompany him.[33]

Since he was well known in the country they would enter, Morse disguised himself. Wearing ragged clothes and a hat with a broad brim flapping around his ears, he donned green goggles and a fake gray beard and set out for the canyon, 140 miles distant, in an old wagon with Morehouse and the boy.

From San Luis Rancho they entered the canyon and located Maria's hut. Morse's disguise worked perfectly; passing himself off as a sheepherder looking for new grazing lands, he talked at length with men who had known him well in earlier days and none recognized him. Judicious inquiries interspersed in innocuous conversations informed him that Tejada and his gang, who were out somewhere, were expected back before night. Driving the wagon off to one side, Morse and his companions waited.

As dusk fell Morse heard the jangle of Mexican spurs and saw five riders approaching. As they drew closer, Morse looked the leader over carefully. He did not match the description given by the Stockton lawmen, but Morse's gaze focused on the man's boot, slit from toe to ankle, and he was sure he was looking at Tejada.

The riders pulled up at Maria's hovel and dismounted. Four hobbled their horses some distance away, while their leader remained at the hut. Watching them, Morse disclosed his plan of attack. While he hid in the rear of the wagon, his son would take the reins and, with Morehouse beside him, drive down the canyon. Stopping in front of Maria's hut, Morehouse was to alight and appear to adjust his harness while he stealthily drew his pistol. Morse would then rise up from the rear of the wagon and keep the surprised bandit covered with his rifle while Morehouse handcuffed him. Morse told his boy that if a fight ensued and he and Morehouse were disabled, he was to he was to flee with the wagon to San Luis Rancho for assistance.

All was going according to plan until Morse was struck with a feeling of foreboding and aborted the arrest attempt, perhaps reacting to the sixth sense that players in this cat-and-mouse game seemed to develop. He climbed down from the wagon without his rifle, walked past Tejada, and asked Maria for a drink of water. After sipping it, he bid everyone a friendly adios, joined Morehouse and his son on the seat of the wagon, and drove off.

Admitting later to being "chagrined" by his behavior, feeling even "cowardly," Morse explained in his account that he was troubled by a lingering doubt about the disparity between the Stockton officers' description of Tejada and the dangerous man he was about to confront. If the slit boot was just a coincidence, he could end up in a gunfight with a man he was not seeking at all. He explained to Morehouse his reason for the sudden change of plans, and his friend agreed that the description variance was troubling and that Morse had made the right decision.

Back home in San Leandro, Morse wrote the Stockton authorities, reminding them of the description of Tejada they had given him and relating how different it was from the man he had seen and believed to be the wanted fugitive. A return letter apologized for their error and confirmed that the man he had seen and described was indeed Tejada.

Now Morse hired a Mexican youth who was well acquainted with Tejada and who hated him for having shot his uncle some years before. He had the boy go into the canyon, see if Tejada was still there, and wire back his findings. When a confirming telegram arrived six days later, Morse and Morehouse departed at once for the canyon. George remained behind, as his father apparently believed the boy had been subjected to enough excitement for a thirteen-year-old.

At San Luis Rancho the officers met their Mexican informant, who told them that Tejada and his gang members slept in the open under a big oak tree near Jose Maria's hut, but they posted old Patricio Mancella as a lookout by the road to sound an alarm if suspicious strangers approached. Based on this information, Morse finalized details for their assault. It was simple, daring, bold, and extremely dangerous, perhaps foolhardy. He instructed his young accomplice to accompany the two officers to the mouth of the canyon that night and then leave them, return to the ranch, and wait for them until noon the next day. If they had not shown up by then, he was to summon help and go to their rescue. Under cover of darkness the two officers would proceed on foot, climb about two miles to get above Maria's hut, descend a ravine leading to the main canyon, and approach the outlaw gang from the unguarded higher elevation. Morse and Morehouse had difficulty making their way through the scrub growth, but the light of a full moon helped considerably. When they reached the end of the ravine, they found they were close to the corral and could make out the lay of the land they had seen on their earlier visit. They could see old Mancella asleep by the road. The plan, as Morse later explained it,

> was to run quickly by him and surprise the others in their sleep. I was to hold the gang under cover of my Winchester while Lew handcuffed Tejada. Then he was to march down the canyon while I covered the retreat. . . .

Soon the cocks commence to crow, announcing the approach of day. As the time for action came a strange feeling of dread came over me, but I quickly shook it off. . . . [When] it was light enough to make all things visible [we] made directly for old Patricio [who] awoke with a start [and] looked into the muzzle of a six-shooter. I stooped down and whispered in his ear that if he made the least noise we would blow the top of his head off.

All he said was "Bueno, senor," and fell back into his blankets again and covered up his head. We had captured the outpost and now for the main army.

"Now for the house, Lew," I said. "Run, boy, run!"

And we did run, too. In a second we were in the midst of the camp and got a cross-fire drop on them before they knew we were there. A quick, stern command from me for them to hold up their hands had a most magical effect, and brought every one of them into a sitting position, with each of them holding his hands high above his head. I told Tejada to get up and come to us. He seemed rather slow to obey, but a sharp "Pronto! Pronto! Senor!" and at the same time pointing the rifle directly at his head, had the desired effect, and we soon had him handcuffed and on his way down the canyon. As Lew withdrew with the prisoner, I walked slowly backward until I got out of pistol range. . . . In half an hour we were well clear of all danger and out of the canyon.

A nine-mile walk with their prisoner got them to the San Luis Rancho and a welcome reception from Luis and the rancheros living there. That same morning they started back to San Leandro with their prisoner. Camping at night, they kept Tejada shackled with heavy chains and took turns guarding him between some badly needed naps. When they reached Banta, which was on the line of the Central Pacific Railroad, Morse took his prisoner on by rail while Morehouse drove the team and wagon home. Morse arrived back on May 27. In no hurry to turn over to the lawmen of San Joaquin County a mass murderer whom they hadn't been able to catch themselves, or even provide a decent description for, he kept Tejada in the county jail for a week before finally delivering him to Stockton.[34] The Medina murders were committed in another county, out of Morse's jurisdiction, so he was not legally obligated to hunt for the killers, but his pursuit of Tejada, paying all his expenses with his own funds, was a clear indication of his complete dedication to eradication of murderous criminals at any cost in time, money, or even risk of life.

A sequel to the Tejada capture took Morse back to that outlaw-infested canyon for a third time. He contacted Santa Clara County sheriff Nick Harris and told him he knew the current whereabouts of Patricio Mancella, who was wanted in that county for burglary, and offered to guide him there. When Harris agreed, the two officers made the arrest without difficulty and soon had old Patricio behind bars.[35]

During the summer of 1870 two notorious bandit leaders, Tiburcio Vasquez and Juan Soto, completed prison sentences and returned to their former bailiwicks in Santa Clara and Monterey Counties. Morse, who kept track of such things, made note of their release in his notebooks. Soon he would play a major role in ending the bloody careers of both criminals.

If ever a villainous man looked the part, Juan Bautista Soto was that man. A California historian describes him as the most fearsome outlaw to ever roam the state's hills. Part Indian, he stood six feet two inches tall, weighed more than two hundred pounds, but was "powerful and as agile as a wildcat." He was singularly unpleasant in appearance, with "a thick underlip, narrow forehead, long coarse black hair, heavy brows beetling over violently crossed eyes, and a general expression of animal ferocity." Even his followers were said to fear his outbreaks of wild fury.[36]

On the night of January 10, 1871, three masked men invaded a store near the village of Sunol in Alameda County, terrifying the proprietor, Thomas Scott, and his wife and children. While looting the store, they shot to death a visitor, Otto Ludovisi. Sheriff Morse and a deputy, Ralph Faville, together with Santa Clara County sheriff Nick Harris, who happened to be in the vicinity, quickly came to the scene. For the next four days the officers searched the surrounding countryside for the outlaws without success. After questioning neighbors who had seen three suspicious characters in the area before the crime, Morse concluded that two of his prime suspects were Juan Soto and a longtime pal, Bartolo Sepulveda. When he notified officers in the surrounding counties that Soto and Sepulveda were wanted, word spread to the Hispanic community, and Sepulveda fled.

Aware that Alameda County folks were outraged by the senseless murder of Ludovisi, Morse worked diligently on the case for months. While searching every known outlaw hideout, he was not heard from for five weeks, and his family and friends feared for his life.

A break in the case came in May. Hearing a report that Soto and his outlaw gang were hiding out in Saucelito Valley, Sheriff Harris organized a posse to investigate and wired Morse, inviting him to go along. Morse quickly answered in the affirmative. Hopping a train for San Jose, he joined Harris, San Jose policeman Theodore C. "Sam" Winchell, and a posse of six well-mounted and armed local citizens.

None of them had ever been to Saucelito Valley or knew exactly where it was, and for several days they cautiously searched every mountain fastness they found. Finally, a sheepherder who was familiar with the valley agreed to lead them there on the condition that they would never reveal to the outlaws what he had done, for he was sure they would hunt him down and kill him if they found out.

Guided to the site, members of the posse looked down from a crest at five adobe buildings scattered in a valley, one of which the guide pointed out as the outlaws' headquarters. Morse and Harris formulated a plan of attack. They divided the posse into four teams, each of which would enter one of the other adobe dwellings and arrest its occupants to prevent them from alerting the outlaws. Then all would regroup to assault the believed headquarters.

Morse, packing a six-shooter, and Winchell, with a shotgun, approached the nearest building. A man working at the corral did not seem surprised to see the two armed Anglos, and when Morse, speaking Spanish, asked for a drink of water, the man politely invited them to follow him inside. Stepping into the main room of the adobe, Morse faced a half-dozen people seated at a table, one of whom he recognized immediately, a man with unforgettable ferocious features: Juan Soto.

Whipping out his pistol, Morse aimed it at the brigand's head and ordered: "*Manos arriba!*" ("Hands up!"). Soto remained immobile. Again Morse barked the command, and still the only reaction was a defiant stare. A third order, with a threat to shoot him where he sat, was met with the same look of malevolence. Morse reached around with his left hand, pulled handcuffs from his gun belt, and told Winchell to cuff Soto. The deputy took the cuffs but, paralyzed with fear, made no move to comply. Seeing the situation, Morse snapped, "Then cover him with your shotgun while I do it!" Winchell turned and bolted out the door.

Throughout this perilous confrontation, everyone in the tightly packed room with the exception of Morse had remained immobile. Winchell's flight changed all that. A large female on his right, whom Morse would later describe as "a muscular Mexican Amazon," seized his gun hand and pushed it up, as a man on his left grabbed his other arm. As Morse struggled to free himself, Soto leaped to his feet. He was wearing a long blue U.S. Army coat buttoned over two gun holsters. He worked feverishly to open the coat and get at his weapons.

With a strenuous effort Morse freed his right arm from the woman's grip and brought his six-shooter up again. But he did not pull the trigger. A small man had jumped or been pushed between him and Soto, and all he could see was Soto's ugly face. So he raised his pistol and shot at his only target, the gang leader's head. His aim was thrown off by the two grappling with him, however, and his bullet simply ripped the hat from the killer's head. Freeing himself from his cumbersome coat, Soto jerked out a pistol, but before he could cock and fire, Morse was out the door and racing for his rifle, which was in the scabbard on his horse. Soto was not far behind. Realizing the outlaw could shoot before he reached his horse, and not wanting to be shot in the back, Morse stopped running and turned to face his foe.

Sheriff Harris, alerted by the sound of gunfire, was still some distance off, but as an eyewitness to what then transpired, he best described one of the strangest gunfights of frontier history. Soto fired immediately at Morse.

> I thought Morse was surely hit, for his body went almost to the ground, but, quick as a flash, he sprang erect and fired. Soto, advancing with a bound, brought his pistol down to a level and fired again, and Morse [went] through the same maneuver as before. This was continued through three or four . . . rounds, and I firmly believed Morse was hit every time. The shots were fired in quick succession, Soto advancing on Morse every time he fired, with a leap or bound of six or eight feet, with pistol held above his head, landing on his feet, his body erect, bringing his weapon down on a level with Morse's breast, and then firing. After firing, he never moved until he cocked his pistol and was ready for another shot, when, tigerlike, he would spring at Morse again. Soto fired the first shot after they came out of the house and Morse returned every shot. There was about the same interval in time between each shot, Morse firing while Soto was cocking his pistol. Morse was retreating to his Henry

rifle, and Soto was pursuing until he received Morse's last shot, when he wavered like he was hit, and then ran into the house.[37]

Morse's last shot had hit Soto's six-gun, disabling the weapon. The force of the shot had driven Soto's pistol back into his face, momentarily stunning him. When he recovered and ran back to the adobe, Winchell, standing nearby, fired his shotgun at him, but the deputy was still shaking with fright and missed completely.

Sheriff Harris galloped up as Morse, his pistol now empty, ran to his horse and grabbed his rifle. Just then, two men emerged from the building. Harris took aim at one with his rifle, but Morse, recognizing the other man as Soto, pushed his barrel up before he could fire. Soto, a pistol in each hand, ran to his horse, but before he reached it, the animal was spooked by the gunfire and galloped off. Soto, followed by his companion, ran for another horse that was hobbled some distance away. Morse's shouted orders to stop went unheeded.

They were more than 150 yards away when Morse got Soto in his rifle sights and triggered off a round that struck the outlaw in the shoulder. Roaring with rage, he turned around and charged back. With a pistol in each hand and another in his belt, he evidently hoped to get within handgun range of the two tormenting lawmen. Harris snapped off a shot but missed. Soto was still more than a hundred yards away when Morse took careful aim again and fired; this bullet hit the outlaw directly in the forehead, tearing off the top of his head and killing him instantly.[38]

When the story of Harry Morse's spectacular gunfight with Juan Soto was reported in the California press, it further enhanced his reputation as the archenemy of outlaws. The acclaim expressed in a San Francisco newspaper was typical:

> [Sheriff Morse] has distinguished himself by one of the most daring and desperate acts that have ever been performed in the history of detective work on the Pacific Coast, and his own life has been preserved only by the manifestation of astonishing self-possession and presence of mind. It so happened that circumstances placed him in the focus of danger, out of reach of his companions, where he had to rely solely upon that steadfast courage and steadiness of nerve which have given him deserved celebrity among the foremost detective officers of the country. He had previously been through many

perilous adventures among the most desperate characters of California, but we suppose the hand-to-hand and long continued conflict with the chief of the brigands was the most exciting and desperate of all.[39]

Later that year Morse was required to perform his most distasteful duty as sheriff, an execution. Nine years had passed since the last hanging in the county, and Morse had to recover a scaffold from storage and erect it behind the courthouse to carry out the court-ordered hanging of convicted murderer Ramon Amador. However troublesome the execution was for Morse personally, he did his duty and did it well. The execution went off without a hitch.[40]

With Juan Soto gone, three major criminals, Procopio Bustamante, Bartolo Sepulveda, and Tiburcio Vasquez, remained loose in his area. After several unsuccessful trips into the mountains in search of these killers, he concluded he was unable to extract information about the brigands from the Mexican population because he was too well known. Finally, subscribing to the old adage, "it takes a thief to catch a thief," he looked up Alfonso Burnham (a former Soto cohort who, with Morse's assistance, had gone straight after serving time) and asked him to go into Monterey County to see what he could learn about the outlaws operating there. Grateful to Morse for straightening him out, the ex-con accepted the dangerous assignment. Posing as a fugitive on the run, Burnham nosed around Salinas, the seat of Monterey County, dropping discreet inquiries about some of the crooks he had known in prison. He learned that Vasquez and Bustamante were camped with an outlaw gang near the village of Sotoville and often rode into the town to carouse. To verify the report, Burnham went to Sotoville, where he met some of his former convict pals, who took him back to their camp. He spent a week there before he was sent into Salinas for supplies and was able to send a message to Morse, reporting his findings. Unfortunately, the sheriff was off on other business, and before he received Burnham's information and could take action, Vasquez and Bustamante had a falling out and went separate ways, and the opportunity to corral them was lost.[41]

A few months later chief of police Patrick Crowley of San Francisco wired Morse that Bustamante had been spotted in frequent visits to one of the city's brothels. Holding an outstanding warrant for the outlaw's arrest on a grand larceny charge, Morse, together with his old sidekick,

Lew Morehouse, crossed the bay to San Francisco. There he enlisted the help of two police detectives to establish surveillance of the bagnio. After an all-night vigil failed to produce a sign of Bustamante, Morse learned that the outlaw had been inside the house all along. Perhaps on a hunch emanating from his long experience chasing desperate felons, Morse had the other officers enter the brothel from the front entrance while he approached from the rear. Bustamante was eating breakfast when he heard a commotion at the front, as several prostitutes attempted to keep the officers from entering. He leaped to his feet and was reaching for a pistol when Morse's strong left hand closed on his throat. He felt the cold muzzle of a six-shooter in his ear and heard the quiet voice of the man he had once vowed could never take him alive: "Put up your hands, Procopio. You're my man."[42]

Morse and Morehouse conveyed their prisoner back across the bay and lodged him in the San Leandro jail that same morning. The arrest of California's most notorious outlaw of the time was big news on the West Coast. Local newspaper accounts were picked up and reprinted in dailies across the country, and for the first time Harry Morse became nationally known.

Paying particular attention to this reportage was E. Z. C. Judson, who, under the pen name Ned Buntline, was turning out a prodigious number of blood-and-thunder stories for the popular dime novels of the time. Buntline's fictional accounts of the derring-do of such frontier figures as William F. Cody, James Butler Hickok, and Martha Canary were largely responsible for establishing their sobriquets, Buffalo Bill, Wild Bill, and Calamity Jane, which remain household names even today. Always seeking new heroes and villains, Buntline ripped off another fabricated account. Entitled "Red Dick, the Tiger of California," the story's leading characters were Sheriff Morse as the hero and Procopio Bustamante as the villain.

In April 1872 Bustamante was tried in Alameda County on a grand larceny charge for the theft of a cow. A jury deliberated only fifteen minutes before finding him guilty, and a judge sentenced him to seven years at San Quentin. The *San Jose Mercury* complained that Bustamante was doubtless guilty of crimes ranging from petit larceny to murder and that it was "absurd" that he could only be convicted "of stealing a $75 cow." In response the *Alameda County Gazette* stated that the man was convicted of the only crime he ever committed in Sheriff Morse's county and suggested that if officers of other counties were as diligent as Morse, the desperado could be locked up for the rest of his life.[43]

Not only were newspaper editors and Ned Buntline taking note of Sheriff Morse's determined effort to rid California of some of its most murderous outlaws, the California legislature passed a bill in March 1872 authorizing payment of $2,000 to reimburse Morse for his personal time and expenses incurred in tracking down Jesus Tejada and Juan Soto. Before passage of the measure, several state senators had risen to applaud the Alameda County sheriff. Senator W. W. Pendergast declared that Morse had accomplished more "by his personal courage, coolness, skill and bravery to clear the state of a band of desperadoes and outlaws" than any other man. Senator Edward Tomkins was also fulsome in his praise, saying no other man in California was more widely or favorably known than Harry Morse: "Under circumstances where other men shrink he has gone forward, until today he is the best known and . . . conceded to be, the best sheriff in the state."[44]

The year 1873 was marked by disruption and change for the Morse family. The electorate voted to move the county seat from San Leandro to Oakland, which necessitated a relocation of their home. The new house in Oakland reflected Morse's growing affluence. Built in the Victorian style on eleven acres of land, it had fourteen rooms and a carriage house. Harry and Virginia would live there for the rest of their lives.[45]

Another major change was much more troublesome. Morse's son George, now seventeen years old, was exhibiting the rebelliousness that characterizes many teenagers. In the hope of straightening him out, Morse enrolled George in McClure's California Military Academy in Oakland, but academy officials, having no more success with the obstreperous youngster than his father, soon expelled the boy for insubordination. But then it got worse. Shortly after George was kicked out of school, a tremendous fire swept through the buildings, destroying the academy. Former cadets claimed they had heard George threaten to burn the place down before he was expelled, and he was arrested on suspicion of arson. Having spent most of his adult life chasing down lawbreakers, Harry Morse was appalled that his son was suspected of a major crime. When other academy cadets came forward to testify that George was a habitual braggart, the charges were dropped, but George's misbehavior would plague Harry Morse for years to come.[46]

As for his professional career, it had been successful for sure, but he still had some loose ends. Although Morse had disposed of Soto by gunshot and Bustamante by prison sentence, Sepulveda and Vasquez still remained on his most wanted list. To his amazement, on March 20, 1873, after two years as a fugitive wanted for robbery and murder, Sepulveda walked into Morse's office and surrendered, claiming he could prove in court that he was innocent of those crimes.

Convinced of the man's guilt, Morse worked diligently over the next four months, building a case against Sepulveda, but he suffered a major setback. His key witness, Tom Scott, owner of the store where the crime was committed, was not available to testify, having departed California. Morse still thought he had a strong circumstantial case against Sepulveda, though. After a lengthy, vigorously fought trial, he was pleased when the jury found the defendant guilty of first-degree murder and the judge sentenced Sepulveda to death by hanging, the mandated punishment for first-degree murder at that time. Sepulveda's attorney moved for a new trial, basing his appeal on the mostly circumstantial evidence presented by the prosecution. After long deliberation, the judge granted the request. The second trial, conducted in June 1874, again resulted in a guilty verdict, but the criminal code had since been changed, authorizing jury discretion in sentencing, and this jury gave Sepulveda a life term.[47]

Sheriff Morse, who had always prided himself on never losing a prisoner in his personal custody, suffered the embarrassment of losing one while escorting Sepulveda and two others to San Quentin on August 5, 1874. He had his three prisoners manacled together on the ferry crossing the bay to San Francisco, where a prison launch would take them on to the prison, when one of them, Charles Edwards, complained that the cuffs were cutting his wrists, and Morse loosened the shackles. When the boat reached the dock, Edwards slipped out of the cuffs, leaped ashore, and disappeared into the crowd waiting to board for the return trip. This was the only prisoner that Morse ever lost, but he was scolded nonetheless by the *Oakland Tribune:* "Sheriff Morse needs a lesson occasionally, like the rest of us. He is not infallible. There was no sort of sense in his trying to escort a murderer and two highway robbers to San Quentin without assistance."[48]

With Soto dead and Sepulveda joining Bustamante in San Quentin, only Vasquez, who now assumed the mantle of California's most-sought-after desperado, remained as Morse's special target. In 1873 Vasquez headed a gang of ten cutthroats in plundering raids throughout central California, which included the looting of a store and hotel and the slaughter of three innocent bystanders in the village of Tres Pinos. A posse pursued the brigands all the way to Los Angeles County, but the outlaws escaped after a brief gunfight. The 1873 raids culminated the day after Christmas with an attack on Kingston in Fresno County, where the bandits robbed two stores, a hotel, and thirty-five residents.

Since California still lacked a state police force, legislators who were outraged by these atrocities met with the governor on January 2, 1874, to request the formation of a special posse to hunt down, capture, or kill Vasquez and his followers and promised to fund the enterprise. Governor Newton Booth agreed; in the following days he offered a reward for Vasquez—$3,000 alive, $2,000 dead—and named Sheriff Harry Morse to head the special posse. The legislature, as promised, passed a bill authorizing the expenditure of $15,000 for the operation. Calling Morse to Sacramento, the governor directed him to lead a thirty-man posse in a sweep of the central California counties with the goal of capturing or killing Vasquez and everyone known to have ridden with him. When Morse disagreed, insisting that his experience had shown that much smaller parties were more effective in manhunts, a compromise was reached; Morse was to head up a posse of eight men, all of his choosing.

For his second-in-command Morse chose San Joaquin County sheriff Tom Cunningham, a reliable officer, and filled out his posse with Ralph Faville and A. J. McDavid, personal friends he knew would follow his direction without argument; Fresno County deputy sheriff Harry Thomas and former Santa Clara County sheriff Ambrose Calderwood, two officers with intimate knowledge of Vasquez's gang members; A. B. Henderson, a reporter for the *San Francisco Chronicle* (a choice he would later regret); his son George (simply to keep a close eye on his wayward boy); and as a five-dollar-a-day guide, Ramon Romero, who was a surprising selection. Once sentenced to hang for stabbing a man to death in a quarrel over a woman, Romero had later been acquitted and freed. Convicted of knifing another man, he had served ten years in prison. Morse ignored this background and valued his assistance because he knew

Romero had ridden with Vasquez and other gang members and knew their hideouts.[49]

The next two months were spent preparing for the hunt and waiting for spring rains to provide plenty of grass for his horses. On March 9 he set out with his posse. His selection of a newspaper reporter to accompany the posse soon provided his critics with fodder. Santa Clara sheriff John H. Adams, a rival for the appointment as posse leader and for the opportunity to gain acclaim by nailing Vasquez, fed information to the *San Jose Mercury* that Henderson's reports of Morse's movements were alerting Vasquez and allowing him to avoid capture. "When Morse went south, Vasquez went north, and vice versa."

After quoting these allegations in his paper, the editor of the *San Francisco Chronicle* appended his own logical comment: "All this may or may not be true. If true, why has not the editor of the *Mercury* or his informants, made the facts and the whereabouts of Vasquez known to Morse, and so aided in the capture of the bandit? Morse is making a great effort to bring the outlaw to justice, and it is but a sorry spirit which can incite nothing better than cavil at the method in which in which he has proceeded. We fear there is too much jealousy among the sheriffs."[50]

Once Morse and his posse had chased Vasquez and his followers all the way south to Los Angeles County, the "jealousy among the sheriffs" that had been alluded to was exacerbated by dispatches from newsman Henderson. He criticized Sheriff Billy Rowland for his lack of cooperation with Morse, basing his charge on Rowland's rejection when Morse asked for his help raiding the home of a character called Greek George, where Vasquez was reportedly holed up. Rowland had scoffed at the suggestion, saying Greek George could not possibly be harboring the notorious outlaw, and Morse, relying on Rowland's better knowledge of local residents, gave up on the idea. To Morse's dismay, the reporter in the posse ended up handicapping the venture in two ways: the bandits, alerted to Morse's every movement by Henderson's dispatches, had been able to keep one or more jumps ahead of the posse, and the newsman's criticism of Rowland had angered the Los Angeles sheriff and contributed to his unwillingness to help.

By late April Morse and his posse had been in the saddle for six weeks. Tired and frustrated after trailing the outlaw band all the way to Los Angeles County with no success, and aware that some members of his posse were restless and anxious to return to their normal pursuits, Morse decided to head back home.

Upon his return, he learned that the governor had increased the bounty on Vasquez to $8,000 alive and $6,000 dead, a sure indication of how badly the desperado was wanted. Morse was preparing to conduct another expedition after the fugitive when the news broke that Sheriff Rowland had made the arrest. To Morse's consternation, a posse organized by Rowland had closed in on Greek George's place, and after a brief gunfight, had wounded and collared Vasquez.[51]

If Morse suspected Rowland of duplicity—after all, he had rejected Morse's earlier request for help and then acted on his information to capture Vasquez and reap the reward and acclaim that would follow—there was no indication of it in a laudatory letter Morse sent to the Los Angeles sheriff:

Friend Rowland:

Allow me to congratulate you on your success in the capture of Vasquez, and the masterly manner in which it was done. No one rejoices more than I do at your success, although I should like to have been in at the last. . . . The boys of my party all join in sending their respects, and are . . . only sorry that we were not fortunate enough to effect the capture. . . . If there is anything that I can do to assist you in this part of the country, please call upon me; I will be ever ready to respond.[52]

In his official report to Governor Booth, Morse leveled some criticism at the Santa Clara County officers for having a "feeling of jealousy toward myself and party, and [making] known my whereabouts and plans through the public prints, and thereby making it difficult for us to do our work properly." But again he heaped praise on Sheriff Rowland and his deputies. He emphasized in his report, however, the hardship the posse had suffered while having a significant effect on California outlawry. "Through heavy rains, never resting, always on the go," they had spent sixty-one days in the saddle. He said,

We rode 2,720 miles, searching the southern part of the state from the San Joaquin River to the sea coast, and, although we did not succeed in catching our man, yet we did the state a good service [by breaking] up many dens of reputed murderers and thieves in places where officers had never ventured to go before. . . . We deserve credit for the thoroughness of our search. Had we not been out, Vasquez would still have been at liberty. At least Vasquez told me so himself. He told me that the only thing that kept him about Los Angeles was the fear of meeting my party.[53]

In January 1875 Tiburcio Vasquez was tried at San Jose for murder, convicted, and sentenced to death by hanging. Harry Morse was on hand when the sentence was carried out in March. Sheriff Adams, putting aside any animosity he may have still felt for Morse, invited him to climb the steps of the scaffold to join former sheriff Nick Harris and other prominent lawmen who had hunted the notorious outlaw. Morse found Vasquez's demeanor remarkable: "He did not wince or flicker an eyelash. Perhaps because he had eluded the dark angel so many times, he was willing to meet her at last. He swung quietly out into eternity and died almost instantly."[54]

With the last of the miscreants from Morse's personal most wanted list gone, he focused on the second echelon of brigands. Believing Clodoveo Chavez, a top Vasquez lieutenant with a $2,000 bounty on his head, had assumed leadership of the gang, Morse concentrated on him first and laid out a plan for his capture in a letter to Governor Booth. With two dependable associates, Tom Cunningham and Harry Thomas, he intended to search the mountains where he believed Chavez was hiding, offering all the reward money to anyone who could lead him to the outlaw's lair. He and his fellow officers would be satisfied simply with the capture of the bandit.[55] Morse did lead a foray into an area Chavez had been known to frequent, but before they could corner him, he fled to Arizona, where later that year two cowboys killed him, cut off his head, and took it to California to collect the reward.[56]

In addition to his failure to capture Vasquez and Chavez, Morse had other problems during this period. There were worries about his son George and, for the first time, concern about his reelection as sheriff. Over a twelve-year period he had won election six times by wide margins; the political game had not been a concern. But as political ramifications of the Civil War receded in the public mind, Republican Party dominance receded as well, and in 1875 he faced a serious challenge for the sheriff's office. The Democrat opposing him was Thomas O'Neal, and surprisingly, there was an independent candidate, an old friend and outlaw-hunting compadre, Lewis Morehouse. The September election was a squeaker, with Morse receiving 2,091 votes, O'Neal, 2,080, and Morehouse, 1,242. Clearly, without Morehead's candidacy Morse would have won easily, but with only eleven votes separating the top candidates, O'Neal demanded a recount. When this was undertaken, Morse's margin of victory increased to thirty-eight, and he was officially reelected, but he got the message: thereafter, every election would be a battle that he might lose.

In 1876 Joe Newell, the man Morse had hunted down and arrested for murder, who had escaped the hangman's noose and received a lesser sentence for manslaughter, reappeared in Alameda County. After his release from prison in 1873, Newell, trouble-prone as ever, had knifed a man, and when his victim survived, had gotten off with another light sentence. Once again Morse had escorted him to the penitentiary. One would think two terms in San Quentin might change Joe Newell, or at least convince him that Sheriff Morse's county was unhealthy for him and that he should try another, but not being very smart, Newell came right back to Alameda County upon his second release. It wasn't long before he again tangled with Morse.

As he related the incident later, Morse said he was walking through the tough section of Livermore one dark night, rounding up witnesses for the next day's court session, when there was a flash and a sharp pistol report before a bullet whizzed by his head. Pulling his pistol, he ran toward where he had seen the flash and found Newell and another ex-con named Hays. Demanding to know who fired the shot, he was met with denials by both. Snapping, "You lie, you scoundrel," Morse seized Newell by the throat, threw him to the ground, and fell on him, driving his knees into the man's stomach. Hays skipped out while Morse "gave Newell a good thrashing and then preached him a good moral lecture." A few months later Newell tangled with Pio Ochoa, an hombre just as tough and murderous as he but a little faster on the draw. When Newell went for his gun, Ochoa whipped out his pistol, and Newell paid for his indiscretion with his life.[57]

Seeing the direction politics had taken, and too proud to risk defeat at the polls, Morse chose not to seek an eighth term as sheriff in 1877 and threw his support to Jerry Tyrel, his undersheriff.[58] Tyrel was elected, and on March 3, 1878, after fourteen tempestuous years in office, Morse turned over the office and jail keys to his successor. That last day was marked with a simple ceremony during which his officers presented him with a splendid mesquite cane, its solid-gold head suitably inscribed and adorned with large, polished gold quartz stones.[59]

Soon after being relieved of the pressures of the sheriff's office, Morse journeyed back east to see his family in the land of his origins. It was just short of three decades since he had left New York to seek his fortune in California, and it must have been an emotional experience for him.

On his return, officials from an Oakland bank asked him to investigate an unresolved case of fraud. A year earlier a swindler had used a forged property deed to fleece the bank of $4,000. Detectives working on the case had given up, and the bank's directors, aware of Morse's reputation for determination and persistence in man-hunting, hoped he could do better. Beginning with only the crook's description and aliases, Morse followed the year-old trail through several California counties for only a few months before nabbing the suspect in Stockton.[60]

Well-rewarded financially by the bank for his excellent work, Morse realized there was money to be made in the detective business, a profession at which he was proficient and which he enjoyed, so in July 1878 he founded the Morse Detective Agency, with offices in Oakland and San Francisco. Seeing that businesses in crime-ridden San Francisco needed burglary, theft, and fire protection, he changed the name of his organization in 1882 to the Harry N. Morse Detective Agency and Patrol System and hired a force of private officers to provide this service. Patterned after the city police force, this organization was manned by uniformed personnel working six-hour nightly shifts, supervised by a captain, a lieutenant, and two sergeants. By 1888 he had expanded the patrol operation to Oakland and employed sixty men including plainclothes detectives.[61]

As sheriff he had been committed to high standards of conduct, and Morse tried hard to maintain these high standards in the work of his detective agency. He refused to accept divorce cases, which were as lucrative a mainstay of the detective business then as they are now. His advertisements claimed that the agency hired only reputable detectives who abjured rewards, because "working for reward for the detection of crime is no less despicable than the crime itself. No man, or set of men, can faithfully and justly pursue an investigation under the stimulus of what is in effect a bribe."[62]

Major cases for private detective Morse differed greatly from the arduous manhunts that characterized his days as sheriff, which had often led to deadly, heart-pounding, confrontations with murderous brigands. Two cases dealing with corruption in San Francisco, which were essentially political in nature, filled the city's newspapers for weeks. The first implicated Mayor Andrew J. Bryant and his underlings in a nefarious scheme to profit immensely by manipulating funding for the widening of Dupont Street, an important thoroughfare. Hired by attorneys for a property owner who suspected skullduggery, Morse's detectives investigated and were able to reveal machinations at the highest levels of city government. The affair brought Morse into direct contention with Captain Isaiah Lees, chief of detectives in the San Francisco police department, whom Mayor Bryant introduced into the case to refute Morse's allegations. The feud between the two lawmen continued for the rest of their lives.[63] The evidence developed by the Morse agency ruined Bryant's political career, but his battery of lawyers saved him from criminal conviction and a prison sentence. He died mysteriously a few years later in a plunge off a ferry into San Francisco Bay.[64]

The second major scandal involving Morse and his agency, involving the workings of what the newspapers labeled the Harkins opium ring, began in 1882 when the collector of customs at San Francisco suspected that a large-scale opium-smuggling operation was in progress at the port and requested aid from Washington to investigate. Probing by Joseph F. Evans, a treasury special agent, confirmed initial suspicions and pointed to involvement by wealthy landowner James Harkins. Seeing a big case brewing, more than he could handle alone, Evans requested Washington's permission to engage the Morse agency for help. Permission was granted to offer Morse and one assistant six dollars a day to proceed with the investigation. Although this was less than his usual fee, Morse knew that success in the case would put another feather in his cap and accepted the terms.[65]

Morse and his operative, John Gamage, began with surveillance of Harkins and suspected smugglers Joseph Goetz and brothers James and Henry Kennedy. After five months they had uncovered sufficient evidence to bring charges against the initial suspects as well as three customs officers, a U.S. Secret Service agent, a deputy U.S. marshal, and the federal officer responsible for investigating counterfeiting and smuggling in the district. Although he lacked proof, Morse believed all were protected by political ties to those as high up as both U.S. senators from California. That political clout enabled Harkins to thwart indictment efforts, as Evans bluntly reported: "Captain Morse states that this is the most difficult case he ever had, that the persons employed are so mixed up in local politics as to almost defy exposure."[66] Evans, however, with backing by the treasury secretary, had all federal employees involved in suspected smuggling activity fired, including twenty customs officers and the deputy U.S. marshal.

Continued investigation by Morse turned up evidence that U.S. circuit court commissioner Joseph F. O'Beirne had accepted a $1,200 bribe to throw the case against Harkins and company out of court. Acting on information that Harkins and William Gaffey, his brother-in-law and fellow smuggling conspirator, had had a violent argument over an old debt, Morse and Evans offered Gaffey and his pal John Hicks, a cashiered customs official, a deal: they would drop charges against Gaffey and return Hicks to his former position in return for their testimony against Harkins and O'Beirne on bribery charges. The offer was accepted and the suspects were indicted, but their trial in August 1883 resulted in a hung jury.[67]

It took four years for a new trial, but during that time the work done by Morse and Evans had its effect. With a bribery charge hanging over his head, Commissioner O'Beirne had been removed from office. Exposed by the investigators, the Harkins opium ring was in disarray, and customs duties collected at the port doubled. At a second trial in November 1887, a broken and chastened Joseph O'Beirne confessed to taking Harkins's bribe. Harkins was convicted, but the jury, because of his age and ill health, recommended "extreme mercy" in his sentencing. Responding to that plea, the judge fined Harkins $2,500 and gave him a year in prison, a very lenient sentence considering the seriousness of his crime. For his testimony, O'Beirne was not prosecuted.[68]

Morse's success in the Dupont Street fraud and the Harkins opium ring cases ensured his reputation as the foremost private detective on the Pacific Coast. Even as he aged and no longer spent long days in the saddle in pursuit of felons, Morse would play a central role in the apprehension of California's most notorious outlaw, a stagecoach robber whose daring, audacity, and openly expressed contempt for pursuing lawmen won him national publicity and even admiration. The bandit's name was Charles E. Boles.

For eight years Boles had singlehandedly held up California stages coaches, leaving in his wake scornful notes in rhyme, signed with the alias Black Bart, to exasperate investigating officers. Born in England about 1829, Charles Boles was brought to the United States as an infant and raised in New York.[69] Like Harry Morse and thousands of other adventurous young men, he joined the gold rush to California, and like most of the others, was disappointed when he did not find his fortune in the diggings. He left for the Midwest, where his family had settled, and he married and started a family. At the outbreak of the Civil War he enlisted as a private and served honorably in the Illinois volunteer infantry of the Union army. He fought in seventeen battles, was wounded twice, and received several promotions, including a battlefield commission to first lieutenant. Mustered out, he returned to his family in Iowa. But even after his former fruitless prospecting efforts in California, he was still afflicted with gold fever, and on May 1, 1867, set out for the new mining camps of Montana. His wife and children would never see him again.[70]

When digging in Montana proved no better for making a fortune than California, Boles decided his gold fever could be cured quicker and easier by mining the contents of Wells Fargo express boxes and the U.S. mail. He returned to the golden state and began his career as a highwayman.

His first recorded holdup on July 26, 1875, was of the Sonora-to-Milton coach carrying ten passengers and a Wells Fargo treasure box containing a few hundred dollars. Wearing a flour sack with eyeholes cut in it over his head, Boles stopped the coach with a leveled shotgun. "Please throw down the box," he politely asked John Shine, the driver. When he complied, the robber, with equal equanimity, requested the mail sacks. A female passenger in the coach tossed out her purse, but Boles returned it, saying with great magnanimity, "Keep it, madam. I don't need your money. I only want Wells Fargo's." Returning his attention to the driver, he called out, "If he makes a move, give him a volley, boys!" Shine looked at the bushes siding the road, discerned what he thought were the barrels of rifles pointed in his direction, and made no aggressive move. When the sack-headed robber ordered him to drive on, he quickly complied. The robber stopped a following coach, but when the driver said he had no treasure box or mail, he was ordered on. Later the two drivers met and returned to the scene of the holdup to find that the "rifle barrels" were just sticks protruding from the bushes.[71]

Over the next eight years Boles, acting alone, would commit no less than twenty-seven more stagecoach robberies. His modus operandi never varied. Clad in a linen duster to conceal his body shape and with a flour sack over his head to hide his features, he would suddenly appear, brandishing a shotgun, as a coach slowed on an upgrade and demand the treasure box and mail. He never harmed or robbed the passengers or fired his weapon. (He would later claim that his shotgun was not even loaded.) As his notoriety as the so-called lone bandit increased, he began leaving taunting notes, written in rhyme, at the scenes of his robberies, a practice that infuriated lawmen but endeared him to sensation-loving newsmen. His most famous composition read:

I've labored long and hard
For honor and for riches,
But on my corns too long you've tread
You fine-haired sons of bitches.

The bits of doggerel were signed "Black Bart, the Po8." Thereafter he was known as Black Bart, the poetic bandit.[72]

If Black Bart had labored hard and long for honor and for riches, James Hume, a crack detective for Wells, Fargo & Company, had labored just as hard for eight years to collar him. Finally, after Bart's twenty-sixth successful holdup on June 23, 1883, Hume, completely frustrated in his hunt, called on the other widely celebrated California detective, Harry Morse, to devote all of his time to the task of identifying and arresting the pestiferous highwayman.[73]

For months Morse worked on the case. He studied the history of the lone bandit's holdups, their location and timing, and the testimonies of the drivers and passengers with regard to his demeanor. He got nowhere, except to satisfy himself that, unlike other stagecoach robbers, toughs who hid out in the hills, Black Bart lived in San Francisco as an ordinary citizen and ventured forth to pull off another holdup when he required funds. Morse waited for the bandit to pull off his next heist, hoping to arrive quickly on the scene and perhaps find a clue leading to an arrest. His big break came on November 3, 1883, when Black Bart committed his twenty-seventh and last stage holdup. Strangely, it was at almost the exact spot where he had pulled off his first stagecoach robbery eight years before. This time the coach, driven by Reason E. McConnell, carried no passengers, but did have registered mail and gold treasure valued at more than $4,000 in the Wells Fargo strongbox.

Nineteen-year-old James Rolleri had been riding up on the boot with McConnell, but shortly before the robbery, having been told that deer were frequently seen in that area, had grabbed his rifle and dropped off the coach to see if he could shoot one and provide some venison for his family.[74] McConnell was hardly startled when he saw the hooded, shotgun-toting figure in the middle of the road, for as a driver of long experience, he had frequently been held up before—three times in 1876 alone—and instantly recognized that it was Black Bart.[75]

Uncharacteristically nervous and devoid of his usual polite manner, Bart demanded to know the whereabouts of the other man he had seen beside the driver. Not wanting to endanger the young man's life be saying he was deer hunting and therefore armed, McConnell replied that the other fellow had gotten down to look for some missing cattle. Evidently satisfied with this response, Bart turned his attention to the strongbox, which was bolted to the coach. He ordered McConnell to unhitch the horses and lead them on up the hill while he went to work on the box with a sledgehammer.

Once atop the grade, McConnell spotted Rolleri, a hundred yards away, and waved him over. When the youth joined him, the driver grabbed the rifle and snapped off a quick shot at the robber. He missed, jacked in another round, fired again, and missed again. Young Rolleri snatched back his rifle and shot once at Bart, who was by this time in full flight, carrying the stolen gold and mail. He missed, too, and the robber disappeared into the underbrush.

Wells Fargo detective John N. Thacker received notice of the holdup and hurried to the site. He was joined there by Calaveras County sheriff Ben Thorn at the head of a party from Copperopolis, which included McConnell and Jimmy Rolleri. Unable to trail the bandit very far because, as usual, he had escaped on foot, they did find a derby hat he had lost while running from the rifle fire. Continuing in in the direction he had fled, they stumbled on his hastily deserted camp. It contained a number of articles including paper bags from an Angels Camp grocery, flour sacks bearing Stockton and Sonora logos, a leather case for opera glasses (but not the glasses themselves), three soiled linen cuffs, a razor, a magnifying glass, a belt, and a buckshot-laden handkerchief.[76]

When he received the items in his San Francisco office, Wells Fargo special officer Hume kept the hat and glasses case for his operatives to investigate for ownership and turned the handkerchief over to Morse, who thought he detected something important in the silk crepe bit of cloth. On one corner he saw a barely visible identifying laundry mark, which he read under his own magnifying glass as "F.X.o.7." That single clue would lead Harry Morse to his quarry within the next few days.

He started out to canvas the laundries of San Francisco to see if he could locate one that would recognize that mark. It was a daunting task, for by his count there were ninety-one laundering facilities in the city.[77] He also realized he might be wasting his time, for although he believed that Black Bart resided in the city, the robber might have had the handkerchief laundered in any number of other locations. But with his usual determination, he tackled the job. A mere nine days after the holdup, he struck pay dirt. At a laundry on Bush Street the owner, Thomas C. Ware, recognized the markings as those of a mining man named C. E. Bolton and provided his description and address. Assuming the role of an investor in mines, Morse arranged for a meeting with Bolton and for the first time set eyes on the man who had baffled Wells Fargo detectives and California law officers for eight years. Struck by Bolton's appearance, Morse later described him to a newspaper reporter:

> He was elegantly dressed and came sauntering along carrying a little cane. He wore a natty little derby hat, a diamond pin, a large diamond ring on his little finger, and a heavy gold watch and chain. He was about five feet, eight inches in height, straight as an arrow, broad-shouldered, with deep sunken, bright blue eyes, high cheek bones, and a large handsome grey mustache and imperial; the rest of his face was shaven clean. One would have taken him for a gentleman who had made a fortune and was enjoying it, rather than a highwayman. He looked anything but a stage robber.[78]

Stepping up to the dandy, Morse introduced himself as a mining man named Hamilton. Having heard that the gentleman he addressed was knowledgeable in that field, he asked if he would accompany him to his office to discuss mining matters with him and his associate. Bolton agreed, and the two men, chatting amiably, walked to the corner of California and Sansome Streets, where Bolton found himself in the office of James Hume, chief of detectives for Wells Fargo. There the conversation quickly changed from mining to stagecoach robbery, a subject of which Bolton claimed complete ignorance. As the interrogation grew more intense, the suspect became increasingly agitated and "great beads of perspiration stood out on his forehead." But he did agree to go to his lodgings with Hume and "Hamilton."

There the detectives found another handkerchief, shirts, and cuffs with the telltale markings that had led Morse to Bolton, as well as a letter written by Bolton with handwriting matching the notes left by Black Bart. Bolton was then informed that he was suspected of being the notorious stage robber. He was taken to the city jail and held overnight. In the morning Hume and Captain Appleton W. Stone of the San Francisco police took the suspect to the scene of the recent robbery, where T. P. Martin, a hunter, positively identified him as a man he had seen in the area just prior to the robbery. Stage driver McConnell said he could not identify the suspect because of the flour sack mask Black Bart wore, but the voice sounded the same. Hume had to return to the city on business, but Morse and Sheriff Ben Thorn joined Stone to continue the investigation.

That night Morse spent some time alone with the suspect in a cell at the San Andreas jail, going over the damning evidence they had found. Morse explained that if Bolton pleaded guilty to the single latest crime, he would save the county a great deal of time and expense and likely receive a light sentence. If, on the other hand, he forced the investigating officers to develop evidence linking him to all the previous robberies and he was convicted, he would undoubtedly receive a life sentence. Morse was a good salesman as well as a detective, and Charles E. Boles, alias C. E. Bolton, alias Black Bart, chose the former of the two alternatives.[79]

When Boles led Morse and other officers to the place where he had hidden the loot from the last holdup, Morse fired off a telegram to Hume: "Black Bart throws up the sponge. Stone, Thorn, and myself have recovered all the stolen treasure. Inform Thacker."[80]

Within days Boles appeared in court, waived bail, and entered a plea of guilty to the recent robbery. The next day he again pled guilty, waived the right to trial by jury, and as promised by Harry Morse, was rewarded for his guilty plea and assistance in recovery of the stolen gold by receiving a lenient sentence of six years.[81]

The capture and conviction of Black Bart solidified Harry Morse's reputation as one of the preeminent lawmen of California, but it did not endear him to other outstanding officers of the state, in particular Jim Hume and Ben Thorn, both of whom questioned his widely publicized version of the investigation and Black Bart's subsequent confession. Thorn was especially vociferous in his condemnation, claiming that Morse hogged the glory of the capture and tried to get all the reward money.

Probably for political reasons, the *San Francisco Examiner* took up this theme. The *Call* had printed Morse's account in full and defended him. In the end, the Wells Fargo reward money (which was probably of greater concern to the rivals than any perceived glory) was divided between Morse and Thorn, with each receiving $228.75. In addition, the company granted Morse $99.50 in expenses and reimbursed him $20, which he had given laundryman Ware. The company paid $105 to the driver, McConnell; $20 to the hunter, T. P. Martin; and $100 to Captain Stone to cover his expenses.[82]

Harry Morse was not only becoming famous; his detective business was prospering, so he was becoming wealthy, and he began investing in mining properties. But coincident with this prosperity was the dark cloud of his wayward son George. Ever since his only surviving boy had shown rebellious signs and errant behavior, Morse had tried to straighten him out, first by enrolling him in a military academy, and when that turned out badly, by taking him along on a dangerous man-hunting expedition in the hope that the excitement might lead him to follow in his father's footsteps and pursue a law enforcement career. That effort had also failed, and as George grew to manhood, his aberrant behavior did not change.

George was nineteen when he married a young girl, and over the next few years he fathered three children. But his wife, unable to abide his rowdy, often-violent conduct, divorced him after only five years. He married again, this time to a widow named Annie Nightingill. While working as a plumber he suffered a blow to the head, which apparently aggravated an old injury, for thereafter be became even more violent, once beating a stepson so severely that the boy was bedridden for a week. George developed a fascination with guns, went about armed, and often pulled the weapon on those with whom he had dealings. He finally was arrested on an insanity charge. Called to testify, Morse said he had broken off contact with his son and had not spoken to him for three or four years. While admitting that George was not of sound mind, he did not believe he was insane. It was finally ruled that the young man was not insane but suffering from delusions, and after promising not to cause any more trouble, he was released. The entire affair, of course, was very painful for Morse.[83] Estranged from his parents and divorced by his second wife, George continued on his erratic way until his tragic end in 1904, when a fourteen-year-old boy he had abused got hold of George's pistol and shot him dead.[84]

Because of his long campaigns to capture fugitives of Mexican heritage such as Jesus Tejada, Juan Soto, Narato Ponce, and Tiburcio Vasquez, Harry Morse's enemies sometimes accused him of racial bigotry. But the vigorous efforts he put forth on behalf of another Mexican, his old friend and posse guide Ramon Romero, belies that charge. There was no doubt that Romero was a violent man; he was imprisoned for stabbing a man to death. Although he had a record of stabbing men, in every case he had claimed he was fighting in defense of a woman. Morse, understanding the culture from whence his friend sprang, honored that defense. In 1889, believing that after twelve years of incarceration Romero had been punished enough, he and Sheriff Tom Cunningham began a campaign to secure his release. After lobbying three different California governors over nine years, the two old lawmen finally succeeded in achieving Romero's release in 1898. An overjoyed Romero told a reporter, "Thank God I am free, and I thank Sheriff Cunningham and Mr. Morse. If I have five millions dollars I would give it all to them and not think it enough for what they have done for me."[85]

His efforts on behalf of Romero were not the only evidence of Morse's lack of racial bias. As his biographer, John Boessenecker, astutely points out, Morse would be branded a bigot today for his use of the politically incorrect term "greaser" when referring to Hispanics, but he was actually "far more open-minded than most Californians. Morse had deep respect for and understanding of the language, customs and culture of the Spanish-speaking people. He counted numerous Hispanics as friends; his personal attorney for many years was a Californio, R. M. F. Soto. It was bandidos that he disliked, not Hispanics. Harry Morse judged men by their deeds, not by the color of their skin."[86]

Morse always claimed in his detective agency advertisements that he did not work for rewards and hired only men of the highest personal character. However, he deviated from his own boasted doctrine on both counts when the train-robbing crime spree of Chris Evans and John Sontag hit the headlines in 1892. Wells Fargo and the Southern Pacific Railroad both pronounced the bandits to be the most dangerous criminals on the Pacific Coast and offered a $10,000 reward for their apprehension.

Morse decided to go after that huge reward and, aware of the great danger any man-hunter would face when approaching this pair of quick-triggered outlaws, employed two men of the same ilk for the job, men fast with a gun. Tom Burns, an ex-convict from Visalia, had two attributes: he had known Evans for years, and he carried a reputation as a gunfighter, perhaps because of his unusual manner of packing his shooting iron. His six-shooter was attached to his belt by a device that allowed him to go into action by simply swiveling the weapon up and firing from the hip while his adversary was drawing from a holster or pocket. Working with Burns would be Sam Black of San Diego, a Civil War veteran reputed to have killed several outlaws while wearing a badge in Texas.

Posing as woodcutters, Burns and Black lived for months in a cabin near Camp Badger, high in the mountains of Tulare County, where the train robbers were believed to be hiding. Rumors or useful bits of information picked up from inhabitants of the area, some of whom were obviously aiding the fugitives, were forwarded to Morse. In May 1893 the outlaws grew suspicious of Black and sent word by one the locals that he must leave or be killed, a warning he ignored.

Shortly thereafter the Morse operatives, while walking back from Camp Badger to their cabin, were met by a hail of gunfire from shotguns wielded by Evans and Sontag. Burns escaped unhurt, but Black, struck with ten buckshot, crawled into the cabin and returned fire until the assailants withdrew. He survived, but facing a long recovery, took no further part in the campaign to capture or kill Evans and Sontag.[87]

Burns remained, however, and was a member of the posse, led by U.S. Marshal George E. Gard,[88] that shot up Evans and Sontag a few weeks later, leading to their arrest by Tulare County deputies.[89] The man-hunters who ended the Evans and Sontag crime wave were praised in the press, but when it came to reward money distribution, their behavior was far from laudable. With the exception of Marshal Gard, who refused any share in the money, everyone involved in the pursuit and capture wanted a piece of the pie.

Since both Morse agency operatives figured prominently in the chase—Sam Black was severely wounded in a gunfight with the fugitives, and Tom Burns was a member of Gard's posse—Morse demanded a share of the reward, claiming that information provided by his operatives led directly to the capture of the outlaws.[90]

A judge, apparently reasoning that there were two outlaws and two apprehensions by two separate groups of officers, ruled that the reward money should be equally divided between the two parties of lawmen. For the apprehension of Evans by the Tulare County deputies, the judge awarded $5,000 to Sheriff Eugene Kay to be divvied out as he saw fit. The other $5,000 was divided among the members of Gard's posse, with the marshal and Fred Jackson (who lost a leg in the posse's gunfight with the outlaws) receiving $1,500 each, and Burns and Fresno County deputy sheriff Hiram Rapelje getting $1,000 apiece.[91]

But this judicial decision was not accepted in good grace. Marshal Gard had publicly announced that he wanted no part of the reward and deplored the judge's ruling, saying a larger portion should have gone to poor one-legged Fred Jackson. He also thought no reward money should go to the Tulare County officers, who took the outlaws into custody after they had been wounded and rendered helpless by his posse, comparing them to one who picks up and claims a fallen quail after another hunter shoots it down.[92]

Deputy Sheriff George Witty, who had made the official arrest of Sontag after the outlaw was shot up by the Gard posse, first agreed that those doing the shooting deserved the reward, but two years later he changed his mind and sued Wells Fargo and the Southern Pacific, claiming that his efforts in the case had been inadequately rewarded. On the night of October 9, 1895, the dispute culminated in gunplay between Witty and Burns. Following court hearings on the suit in Los Angeles, and some liberal saloon libation, the two were returning by train to Visalia when the argument was renewed on the rear platform. There was a scuffle and a gunshot before both fell off the moving train and were injured. Witty also had a bullet wound in his arm, but no charges were filed. On December 11, 1896, a judge denied Witty's claim and assessed him court costs.[93]

Harry Morse, evidently missing the excitement of his sheriff days, made a bid to return to that office. Although he was a lifelong Republican, by 1894 he had become so disenchanted with the GOP because of corruption within its California leadership that he threw his hat in the ring for sheriff as a nonpartisan. The People's Party, a different reformist group, ran another candidate, splitting the disaffected Republican vote, and Morse finished a dismal fourth at the polls.[94] Never one to be disheartened by adversity, he would take three more cracks at political office. In January 1901 the Republicans nominated him for mayor of Oakland. Honored by the selection and grateful for the opportunity to clean up the some of the venality in the city administration, he accepted, but he soon realized that at the age of sixty-six he lacked the vitality to run both his detective agency and the city, and he regretfully declined the nomination. When Vice President Theodore Roosevelt took office as president following the assassination of William McKinley that year, Morse sought appointment as U.S. marshal for Northern California. He received strong support—endorsing petitions were signed by five justices of the California Supreme Court and all the judges of the Alameda County Superior Court— but Roosevelt, perhaps believing Morse too old for the position, chose another candidate. In 1904 Morse sought political office for the last time, accepting the nominations of both the Democratic and independent parties for election to the county board of supervisors, but he was defeated.[95]

The people of San Francisco were shocked in April 1895 by the discovery of the bodies of two young women in the Emanuel Baptist Church in the city's Mission District. One was found in a storage shed, the other in the belfry of the church. Both were partially nude and had been raped and brutally murdered. Twenty-four-year-old Theodore Durrant, a church-going medical student and California National Guard member, was quickly arrested and charged with the double homicide. The city's newspapers soon sensationalized the case as the crime of the century and called the accused the "Beast in the Belfry." Other papers picked it up, and the story ran on front pages across the nation.

Durrant maintained his innocence, but within days it became evident that chief of detectives Isaiah Lees was building a strong case against him. Durrant's attorneys, unable to cope with what appeared to be overwhelming circumstantial evidence against their client, turned to Harry Morse for help. "Captain Morse was not inclined to touch the case at first," Jules

Callundan, one of his associates, explained to a reporter. "He spent a week looking into it. When he became convinced that the young man was not guilty, he went in as a matter of business and justice."[96] Durrant and his family were not well-off and could not afford services such as the Morse agency, so Morse waived his fee and worked for nothing.

Perhaps his motivation was more than just a belief in Durrant's innocence. The case may have reminded him of the trial of Bartolo Sepulveda twenty-two years earlier. Although Morse had been convinced of the man's guilt and had developed seemingly incontrovertible evidence against him, Sepulveda was proven innocent and exonerated in 1885 after barely escaping the gallows and spending twelve years in prison. Or maybe he just saw the Durrant case as an opportunity to go head to head against—and perhaps defeat and humiliate—Isaiah Lees, the man who had been his enemy since the Dupont Street fraud affair sixteen years before. In any event, he labored diligently for months to counter Lees's prodigious evidence, but in the end he could not. A jury, given the case on November 2, 1895, deliberated only twenty minutes before bringing in a conviction for first-degree murder. Appeals going all the way to the U.S. Supreme Court were denied, and Theodore Durrant was hanged at San Quentin in 1898.[97]

Harry Morse's last big case was the mysterious death of Jane Lathrop Stanford, the wife of railroad mogul and Stanford University founder Leland Stanford. On January 14, 1905, Mrs. Stanford drank some Poland Springs mineral water and became quite ill. Fearful that she had been poisoned, she had the mineral water tested and found that it contained strychnine. Her alarmed husband called on the Morse agency to look into the matter. Morse went to work, assisted by Jules J. Callundan—his most trusted employee, who had risen in thirty years of service from office boy to captain to general manager. Elizabeth Richmond, a recently employed maid who had handed Mrs. Stanford the tainted drink, became their prime suspect. Under intensive interrogation by the detectives, she adamantly denied any culpability, however, and without additional evidence, the Stanford's only option was the woman's dismissal.

Word leaked out that someone had tried to murder the wife of one of the most important personages in California, and newspapers leaped on the story. In an effort to quiet the press and avoid unwelcome attention for the Stanford family, both Morse and Callundan falsely assured reporters that their investigation had shown there was no poisoning attempt on

Mrs. Stanford's life. But Jane Stanford knew better. Emotionally distraught by the affair, she heeded her doctors' advice and departed on what she hoped would be a rehabilitating trip to Hawaii, telling inquiring newsmen that the trip was to recuperate from a severe cold and an attack of tonsillitis.[98]

Only nine days after her arrival in Honolulu, Mrs. Stanford complained of an upset stomach and swallowed a spoonful of bicarbonate of soda from a bottle she brought from the mainland. Her jaw soon locked, then she was wracked by convulsions and she quickly died. Detective Callundan embarked for Hawaii at once. After investigating, he reported to Morse that he believed Mrs. Stanford was murdered, probably by Elizabeth Richmond, who had placed strychnine in the medicine bottles. But the former servant had departed for her native England and could not be reached, and the death of one of the most prominent socialites of turn-of-the-century America still remains an unresolved mystery.[99]

The earthquake and fire that devastated San Francisco in April 1906 destroyed the offices of the Morse agency in that city and brought an abrupt end to Harry Morse's detective career. Too old and infirm to rebuild the agency himself, he turned management over to Callundan, who promised to pay him half of the firm's profits.[100]

Morse was hit with another blow only a year after the terrible disaster of 1906. On May 23, 1907, his wife of fifty-two years passed away. During all of his exciting, highly publicized, years, it was quiet, seldom-mentioned Virginia who had maintained his home, raised his children, and sweated out his sometimes long absences, never knowing if, any day, she might hear he had been killed by one of the murderous bandits he pursued. And she had shared with him the heartbreaking history of their firstborn, their wayward son George. Like many active, professionally successful husbands, Harry Morse never realized how much he leaned on his wife for support until she was no longer there. To assuage his mourning and get to know some of his progeny better, he took two trips to Europe, the first in October 1907 with grandson Harry de la Montanya, and the second in the summer of 1908 with granddaughter Blanche Kenna.[101]

In November 1911 Morse suffered a paralyzing stroke. Although bedridden and helpless, his indomitable spirit drove him to draw breath for two more months. Finally, on the night of January 12, 1912, the old man-hunter died in his sleep. He was buried with full military honors and laid to rest in a Mountain View Cemetery plot he had long before purchased, joining Virginia, their deceased children, and his and Virginia's parents.

Accolades for the extraordinary life of Harry Morse filled the pages of California papers after his death, but no tribute could be more accurate than two that had been penned back in the 1880s: D. S. Richardson had written in the *Overland Monthly*, "The audacity of the man and the rapidity of his movements bewildered the outlaws. No one could tell when he was safe or where he might be free from the searching eye of the tireless official, who seemed to know everything and be everywhere at the same time."[102] And Charles Howard Shinn stated, "He was brave, and feared nothing on earth, except to do wrong; never had an enemy, even among the many desperate men whom he brought to justice, although he passed through numerous serious shooting episodes."[103]

—5—

BASS REEVES
1838–1910

> Although Bass was not a killer by nature, his job was that of a man
> hunter. He was fascinated by the hunt which was so unpredictable that
> it drew on his every skill and sometimes his intuition.
>
> Paul L. Brady

Bass Reeves was remarkably different from almost every other man-
hunter of the Old West. He was born a slave and grew into adulthood
in the antebellum South. Freed by the Emancipation Proclamation of
January 1, 1863, he compiled an incredible record as a stalker and capturer
of dangerous felons who infested Indian Territory in the late nineteenth
century. Because of lingering race prejudice and the fact that he did not
look like the widely held perception of a dauntless western lawman, he
and his deeds remained unpublicized and unknown to the general public
until recent years.[1]

Born in July 1838 in Crawford County, Arkansas,[2] the son of a fifteen-
year-old girl named Pearlalee, who was one of a number of slaves owned
by William Steele Reeves,[3] the boy was given the first name Bass to honor
his grandfather Basse Washington, and as was the custom, he adopted
his master's surname, Reeves.[4]

In 1846, when Bass was eight years old, the Reeves clan that included
the families of William S. Reeves and of his son, George Robertson Reeves,
loaded up their belongings and all their slaves in thirty wagons and moved
from Arkansas to Grayson County in North Texas, just across the Red
River from Indian Territory.

Over the following decade Bass grew into a strapping young man, 180
pounds and six feet, two.[5] Impressed by not only the size and obvious

Bass Reeves. Courtesy of Wikimedia Commons.

strength of his young slave but also his intelligence, ambition, and willingness to learn, William Reeves removed Bass from the cotton fields and made him his personal servant. Always close to his master, the young man had an opportunity to learn skills other slaves were denied—the use of firearms, for instance. Soon aware that his young slave had extraordinary talent with both rifle and pistol, William Reeves began entering Bass in shooting contests, which he invariably won. He even allowed him to practice the fast draw with a handgun until he "could draw and shoot from the hip with great speed and accuracy if necessary, but he favored the slower, even more accurate, method of taking his time, planting himself solidly, and drawing 'a bead as fine as a spider's web on a frosty morning.'"[6]

When the Civil War erupted, William Reeves turned his black "companion" over to his son, George Robertson Reeves, who took Bass along with him when he raised a cavalry company for the Confederacy.[7] During the war George Reeves rose in rank to colonel and led his men in many battles with his "body servant" always at his side, but Bass never respected and accepted this "master" as he had George's father. One night a bitter dispute over a card game brought an abrupt end to their association. According to Bass Reeves's daughter, Alice Spahn, the army officer so enraged her father that he "laid him out cold with his fist and then made a run for the Indian Territory, north across the Red River, with the hue and cry of 'runaway nigger' hounding him until the Emancipation."[8]

This incident is the first indication of a major flaw in the character of Bass Reeves. Obviously intelligent, he had to know that for a black slave to strike his owner—a Confederate army officer in wartime, no less—was an unforgivable offense that would be met with severe punishment, possibly death. But he allowed his quick temper to overpower his judgment. This fault would become evident on at least two later occasions and almost ruin what would otherwise be a most notable career as a law enforcement officer.

Bass escaped to Indian Territory after his contretemps with George Reeves because, having been raised in Grayson County, Texas, adjacent to "the Nations," he was familiar with the country across the Red River and the people who lived there. He was one of many black people who headed for Indian Territory, both as fugitive slaves before emancipation and later after they had been freed. The two races, black and Indian, got along well together, sharing a deep resentment for mistreatment by whites, and there were many interracial marriages and biracial children. Law-breaking white men also drifted into the Nations, and Indian Territory soon became a haven for criminals of all colors, red, black and white.

While living in the Nations, Bass Reeves gained an intimate knowledge of various tribes' customs and became proficient in several of their languages, an expertise which served him well in his later career as a lawman patrolling the territory. In about 1864 he took a wife, a fourteen-year-old black girl named Jennie,[9] and started a family of his own. Unable to find enough work in the Nations to support a family, by 1870 he had established residence in Crawford County, Arkansas, where he was employed as a farm laborer. Together with Jennie and four children, three girls and a boy, aged six months to six years, he lived in a small house in Van Buren.[10]

He was in his early thirties when he ventured into law enforcement, a profession that would become his life's work. In 1871 the United States district court for western Arkansas, which included Indian Territory, was moved from Van Buren to Fort Smith, closer to the territorial border. Several deputy United States marshals from Van Buren remembered that their neighbor Bass Reeves had extensive knowledge of the land and inhabitants of Indian Territory and also possessed exceptional tracking ability, and they began using him in their posses. Reeves took to the work immediately.[11]

Each nation within Indian Territory had its own laws as well as an organization of mounted policemen known as the Light-Horse to enforce them. But since lawbreakers easily evaded arrest by slipping from one nation into another, the Light-Horse had great difficulty catching felons. It became the responsibility of the deputy U.S. marshals working out of the district court at Fort Smith to bring a semblance of order to the Nations. Judge William Story presided over the Fort Smith court for the first few years, but when lawlessness had not abated and more than a hundred murders were committed in the Indian Territory during his short tenure, he resigned to avoid discharge or possible impeachment.

On March 19, 1875, a no-nonsense jurist named Isaac Charles Parker was appointed to replace the discredited William Story.[12] When Judge Parker announced that he intended to bring order out of chaos in the troublesome territory and ordered U.S. Marshal James F. Fagan to hire two hundred deputy U.S. marshals to help him do it, Bass Reeves was one of the first to apply.

But any ambition Reeves entertained of becoming a deputy U.S. marshal was greatly jeopardized that year, when his violent temper got him into serious legal trouble. Details of the case have been elusive, but as it was reported in the *Van Buren Press*, he was arrested and charged with assault with intent to kill. When a jury acquitted him in September,[13] Marshal Fagan and Judge Parker accepted him, and he became one of the first of his race to hold the position of deputy United States marshal.

Evidently it proved difficult to locate two hundred qualified men who were willing to take on this dangerous job; records show that only forty or fifty deputies were employed at one time. For those few who did enlist, the job was challenging; it came with responsibility for apprehending felons in western Arkansas and all of Indian Territory (present-day Oklahoma), a total area of seventy-four thousand square miles, which was the largest federal court district in terms of area in United States history.[14]

Because of his race, Bass Reeves was an anomaly among applicants for the deputy marshal position. He was also a newcomer to law enforcement, and since federal law mandated that a deputy marshal take at least one other man with him into the field,[15] he went on early assignments as a posse member under the direction of an experienced officer. Over the next few years he backed up Deputy Marshals Robert J. Topping, Jacob T. Ayres, and James H. Mershon.

Born the same year as Bass Reeves (and Judge Parker), a Kentuckian of French descent, Mershon epitomized the ambiguity regarding slavery that was prevalent in border states such as Kentucky. In the Civil War he had fought on both sides, first for the Confederacy and then for the Union. In his fifteen years working as a deputy marshal out of Judge Parker's court, he proved to be a most able officer, one devoid of the racial bigotry held by some of the other officers, particularly Confederate army veterans. After Reeves served his posse apprenticeship, he and Mershon often teamed up in roundups of suspected felons.[16] A typical report of their work together appeared in the *Arkansas Gazette* of July 4, 1884:

> Deputy United States Marshals J. H. Mershon and Bass Reeves came in late this evening from the Chickasaw country with twelve prisoners. . . . Ed McCurry of the number is badly wounded in the groin, having been shot while resisting arrest near Tishomingo, about three weeks ago. The officers had some rough experience on the trip. A man named Webb, charged with murder, engaged them in a running fight and was fatally wounded, dying the next day. One Hamilton, a full-blooded Chickasaw, also resisted arrest, and in the fight Mershon's horse fell . . . , bruising the officer up badly. Hamilton was wounded, but escaped into the woods where it is reported he has since died.

Other papers provided additional details of this expedition, including one that named the prisoners, the charge against each, and interestingly, the diversity of their racial heritage. It was abundantly clear that the two deputy marshals who rounded them up, one white and one black, were obviously unbiased regarding race. Two prisoners were white, five were

Indians, and five were black.[17] "Webb" and "Hamilton," the names given for the murder suspects who resisted arrest and were shot by the officers, were no doubt aliases, for Hamilton was an Indian, "a full-blooded Chickasaw," and Webb, according to Reeves, was Mexican.

Relating this capture to a newsman some years later, Reeves said it was he who killed Webb, at the same time praising the outlaw for his courage: "The bravest man I ever saw was Jim Webb, a Mexican that I killed in 1884. . . . I got in between him and his horse. He stepped out into the open and 500 yards away and commenced shooting with his Winchester. Before I could drop off my horse his first shot cut a button off my coat and [his] second cut my bridle rein in two. I . . . grabbed my Winchester and shot twice. He dropped and when I picked him up I found that my two bullets had struck within a half inch of each other."[18]

Reeves, usually taciturn when describing his experiences, was voluble in providing details of this long-distance gunfight to D. C. Gideon, an early Indian Territory historian who recorded the account in 1901. When Reeves approached the dying man, he saw that Webb had a pistol in his hand and ordered him to throw it aside. Webb obeyed, saying, "Give me your hand, Bass. . . . You are a brave man. I want you to accept my revolver and scabbard as a present. . . . Take it, for with it I have killed eleven men, four of them in Indian Territory, and I expected you to make the twelfth."[19]

According to Reeves's biographer Paul L. Brady, this was not Bass's first deadly encounter with Jim Webb. Several years earlier Webb and fellow outlaw Frank Smith had come up against Reeves and Deputy Marshal Floyd Wilson with guns drawn, but when Webb's attention was diverted for a second, Reeves "knocked Webb's gun away, wrapped his left arm around the outlaw's throat, drew his own gun with his right hand," and rammed it into Webb, who meekly surrendered. Smith fired two wild shots at Reeves, missing both. While controlling Webb with his left arm, Bass fired, dropping Smith to the ground with a mortal wound. On the way back to headquarters, Smith died and was buried "without ceremony."[20]

While in a posse led by Deputy Marshal J. F. "Bud" Ledbetter, Reeves reportedly dropped another outlaw with a remarkable long-distance shot. The posse had cornered its quarry but was held off for an entire afternoon by the fugitive's ineffectual expenditure of much ammunition. Daylight was fading when the desperado made a run for it. At a distance later calculated to be a quarter-mile, Reeves dropped the man with a rifle bullet through the neck.[21]

Many newspaper reports of felon killings attributed to Reeves cannot be verified in the contemporary records. A 1908 laudatory review of his exploits as a lawman, for instance, included a wild tale of his encounter with two outlaw brothers named Brunter, who ambushed Reeves and held him at gunpoint. The article claimed he remained cool and engaged them in conversation, and when they dropped their guard for only an instant, he whipped out his pistol and shot one of them to death before he could react. The other brother fired three errant shots at Reeves before he was felled by a blow to the head from Bass's six-gun.[22]

However, this story may have originated with an account of an 1884 shootout appearing in an Indian Territory newspaper. After announcing the arrival at Fort Smith of "Bass Reeves, one of the best marshals on the force," with ten prisoners, the paper related how Reeves had sent "one man where he won't fool with other people's horses." The story went that he had warrants for two men, Frank Buck and John Bruner, but lacked their descriptions. Coming upon a suspicious pair, he joined their camp but kept a wary eye out. When Bruner stealthily pulled his pistol, Reeves grabbed it, pulled his own, and shot Buck as he was drawing.[23]

Other unverifiable stories come from the recollections of old-timers, such as this account by a Creek Nation resident in Indian Territory days:

> [Reeves] went after two mean Negroes [and he knew] if he didn't kill them they would kill him, for it would be impossible to bring them back alive. When he found them, they were lying under a tree asleep, but . . . one awakened and got up. Reeves started talking to him and gave him a letter to read. By that time the other was up. When the first had read the letter Reeves told him to let the other one read it. When he turned to give the letter to the other one, Reeves shot him and [then] the second [one] before he could draw. That looks like a cold-blooded murder to us now but it was really quick thinking and bravery.[24]

The *Fort Smith Weekly Elevator* of September 5, 1884, noted Reeves's return from the Nations with a wagon loaded with fifteen prisoners on charges ranging from murder to introducing liquor into Indian Territory. One of the prisoners wanted for murder was Chub Moore, a Chickasaw

Indian charged with leading a mob that had lynched a black man believed to have raped a white woman.[25] Reeves arrested him on August 7 after the suspect was shot in the thigh by posse member Frank Pierce. The wound was serious, and Moore lay in the wagon during the 265-mile journey to Fort Smith. When the party arrived on September 1, doctors attending Moore found that gangrene had set in and that amputation was necessary.[26]

The selection of Frank Pierce for his posse, whether by Reeves or a higher authority, was ill advised, for the man was nothing but trouble. Soon after the posse's arrival at Fort Smith, Pierce disappeared. "Frank Pierce, who shot Chub Moore, turned out to be a notorious horse-thief, and fled the country to avoid arrest," the *Fort Smith Weekly Elevator* of September 5 informed its readers. A newspaper report several weeks later had him involved in more gunplay: "Frank Pearce [*sic*] is getting quite a reputation in the Chickasaw Nation, first by shooting Chub Moore and later being shot at himself. . . . Passing himself off as an U.S. Marshal [he] took possession of four horses which he claimed had been stolen by Dick Glass or the Wade brothers. The Wade brothers followed and waylaid him, shooting his horse and leaving him lying supposedly dead."[27]

About this time, the *Fort Smith Weekly Elevator* published the startling news that "Bass Reeves, one of the most successful of the marshals . . . has been discharged from the force by United States Marshal [Thomas] Boles." The paper intimated that the cause of the dismissal was Reeves's "habit of letting a prisoner escape," but it could hardly be coincidental that the firing came on the heels of revelations about the real character of his former posse member Frank Pierce. In any event, whatever problems Marshal Boles had with his black deputy were quickly resolved, and by December Reeves was reinstated.[28]

As for Frank Pierce, for a few months he was still alive and stealing, but according to a news dispatch from Gainesville in April 1885, his nefarious career evidently came to an abrupt end when officers in Texas shot him dead. In relaying that information to his readers, a Fort Smith editor could not resist tying the name of Bass Reeves to that of the notorious thief:

A Gainesville, Texas, dispatch reports a fight between Texas officers and cattle thieves from the nation a few days ago in which Frank Pierce, alias Roberts, was killed. Pierce is the man who was serving as posse for Deputy Marshal Bass Reeves some time since, and shot Chubb M, who was brought to this place and died of his wound in the U.S. jail. It has been frequently charged by correspondents to the Indian papers that Pierce was a thief and that Bass Reeves was in with him, although Marshal Boles has been unable to get evidence here to substantiate the charges against Reeves. The above indicates that the reports about Pierce must have been correct.[29]

Although Bass Reeves would have a long and eventful career as a deputy marshal working the Indian Territory, he would always remember the year 1884 as one of the best—and one of the worst. It was the year that he was praised for dispatching two dangerous criminals—James Webb, with that remarkable rifle shot, and Frank Buck, with a quick shot from his pistol—but it was also the year that he was relieved of duty for a spell and suspected of chicanery with Frank Pierce, a crooked posse member. Worst of all, it was the year he was charged with allowing his well-known violent temper to erupt again, leading to the murder of a member of his own posse.

In early February 1884 Reeves, with a handful of warrants, departed Fort Smith with a three-man posse, including Deputy Marshal Floyd Wilson,[30] a cook named William Leach, and wagon driver Johnnie Brady, who was Reeves's fourteen-year-old nephew. He was headed out on the first leg of a three-hundred-mile, several-month-long round-trip through the Creek, Chickasaw, and Seminole Nations. Two months later, having completed his sweep of the first two nations, he had five prisoners in custody: four Indians and a Creek freedman, James Grayson. On April 9 he set up camp near the Canadian River to spend the night before crossing that stream to enter the Seminole Nation the next morning. Grayson had been ill, and his wife and children, who were concerned about him, had followed the posse in another wagon and were camped nearby.

After consuming a meal that Leach had prepared, he, Reeves, Brady, and James and Mary Grayson were seated around the fire. Deputy Marshal Wilson was not present, having been detained on some matter, and was trailing about thirty miles behind.[31] The other prisoners, being Indians, were not welcome at the campfire and remained, chained together, in the tent. At first, the atmosphere around that campfire seemed congenial enough, considering the odd assortment gathered there, but suddenly an argument arose, harsh words were spoken, a shot rang out, and William

Leach toppled over with a bullet through his neck, severing an artery. Despite all attempts to stop the bleeding, William Leach died from loss of blood the next day.[32] When Reeves got back to Fort Smith on April 24, he explained the death of his cook as an accident. He had been trying to extract a jammed shell in his Winchester rifle, he said, when the weapon went off and a bullet struck Leach. Although his boss, U.S. Marshal Boles, accepted this account, and Reeves kept on working as before, other versions of what transpired that night of April 9 went the rounds, stories much more critical of Bass Reeves.

These accounts were long-lived, being repeated as late as a quarter-century later. In 1911, at a meeting of veteran deputy marshals in Guthrie, Oklahoma—which included celebrated lawmen Chris Madsen and Heck Thomas—one of them repeated the story of Leach's death as he remembered it:

> Bass was coming back into Fort Smith with a string of prisoners and a Negro cook that he allowed to carry a gun. Now Bass had a little dog that he was mighty fond of . . . and he had taught the dog to beg for something to eat by standing up on his hind legs. [The] cook got a grudge against Bass . . . and took it out on the dog. . . . One night, when the prisoners were lying by the campfire chained together, and Bass was back on his elbows with his Winchester by his side, that little dog got up on his hind feet and danced up to the cook begging with his front paws, and [the] cook didn't do anything but empty a skillet of boiling grease down the dog's throat and grabbed for his pistol. Bass slipped his Winchester forward quicker and it went off right in that cook's face, and he pitched forward into the fire. . . . Bass saw the dog die and then turned round to finish the nigger cook, but found his bullet had hit him right in the neck and shot his head so nearly off that when Bass kicked the body it rolled into the fire.[33]

Marshal Boles evidently believed what Deputy Reeves had told him and ignored these other accounts, but in November 1884 an event of national importance transpired that ultimately had a great effect on the lives of both Boles and Reeves. Democrat Grover Cleveland was elected president, and after moving into the White House in March 1885, he began purging appointees of the opposition party and replacing them with appointees of his own party, as was the long-standing practice followed by all former presidents. In October 1885 Republican Thomas Boles was removed as United States marshal for the western district of Arkansas and replaced by Democrat John Carroll. Early in his tenure, Marshal Carroll called G. J. B. Fair, one of his newly appointed deputies, into his office and directed him to pursue an investigation into the violent death of William Leach a year and a half before.

It is impossible to determine whether Carroll was simply reacting to the rumors still swirling regarding that shooting, or whether he had an ulterior motive based on an animosity toward Bass Reeves because of his race, but the backgrounds of Boles and Carroll could be significant. Republican Thomas Boles, a native of the Confederate state of Arkansas, had been a captain in the Third Arkansas Cavalry of the Union army during the Civil War, indicating that he harbored strong feelings regarding slavery and may well have been prone to overlook possible transgressions by his black deputy, who was a former slave. Democrat John Carroll, on the other hand, had been a colonel in the Confederate army in the war and quite possibly embraced a bias of the exact opposite nature regarding to race.

At any rate, Deputy Marshal Fair conducted his investigation, and on January 18, 1886, obtained a warrant charging Bass Reeves, his fellow officer, with murder.[34] After Reeves's immediate dismissal from the marshal's service, he was arrested at his home in Van Buren and placed behind bars at Fort Smith.

The news created a sensation in Arkansas. In announcing the arrest, a newspaper published in Little Rock, the state capital, leaped to the conclusion that the famous deputy marshal was guilty with the headline, CAUGHT UP WITH: AN EX-MARSHAL'S MISDEEDS BROUGHT TO LIGHT. The story stated as a fact that "Leach was cooking at Reeves' camp when the murderous official shot him dead for some trivial offense." It went on to say, "Rumors [are] reached here frequently that [Reeves] was in league with some of the worst cutthroats and outlaws in the Indian country [but he] managed to cover up his tracks so effectually as to retain his commission. . . . During his long service as an official he has stained his hands with the blood of several of his fellow-beings, and now languishes in jail with many others whom he has been instrumental in placing there."[35]

The following day Reeves's hometown newspaper printed a dispatch taken from the *Fort Smith Times* reporting that Reeves was "in the clutches of the law, charged with murder." In case anyone was unaware or had forgotten, this editor reminded readers that the former officer was "colored." Some of the details of the killing, "committed in pure wantonness," apparently uncovered by Fair's investigation, were given, including, for the first time in print, the role that a dog was said to have played in the affair, although the ownership of the animal was opposite of what was related in other accounts: "Leach was cooking supper when a dog belonging to him came up and stuck its nose into one of the cooking vessels. Reeves kicked the dog and threatened to kill it, when the cook interfered, saying it was his dog. Reeves replied, 'G—dd—n you, I'll kill you then,' and drew his revolver and shot the negro in the head, blowing his brains out."

Allegations having nothing to do with the death of Leach, but derogatory to Reeves's character, were gratuitously added in this publication also. Bass Reeves was said to be

in the habit of holding "kangaroo court" in camp and extorting small sums of money from prisoners by fining them for small imaginary offences. . . . It is charged that at one time he made an insulting proposal to a white woman . . . and his conduct was investigated by the grand jury and his dismissal [from] the force recommended by that body, but for some reason he was not dismissed but let go on making history, all of which will come to light in due time. Bass is in the toils at last and will find that the Territory is full of people who will interest themselves in his case. We have heard it stated that there are about one hundred men in the [Indian Territory] to whom he is indebted in sums ranging from $3 to $15 for provisions and feed furnished him while he was riding over the country looking (?) for criminals.[36]

Reeves remained in the Fort Smith hoosegow for six months before finally gaining his release on bond of $3,000 on June 15, 1886.[37] The case went to trial at the October 1887 term of court presided over by Judge Parker. The Grayson couple were the chief witnesses for the prosecution. (James Grayson had recently been released from the Detroit House of

Corrections,[38] where he had served his time for assault and attempted murder, the crime for which Reeves had arrested him.) Both Graysons testified that an argument had arisen between Leach and Reeves over the cook's dog and that Reeves had threatened to shoot the pet.

Mary Grayson said that Reeves "took cartridges out of his coat pocket and shoved [them] into his gun and worked the level and loaded it . . . and the dog run off among the horses and then Reese shot Leach with his Winchester." Under skillful cross-examination by defense lawyer William M. Cravens, she admitted that the deputy marshal and his cook had always been on friendly terms, that they appeared to be in good humor just prior to the shooting, and that she did see Reeves picking cartridges out of his rifle with a pocketknife.

James Grayson was no stranger to Judge Parker's court, having appeared there at least three times previously after being arrested in Indian Territory for various offenses: larceny, illegal whiskey sale, theft, assault, and attempted murder. His story was much the same as his wife's. He claimed that Reeves said he was going to kill Leach's dog, and when the cook objected, he loaded cartridges into his rifle and shot him: "He had his gun cocked and his finger on the trigger. . . . It looked like the gun was right against [Leach] as it burnt his face. [Reeves] put his gun down and his nephew [Brady] told him not to shoot anymore."

The testimony of prosecution witness Tobe Hill, one of Reeves's Indian prisoners that fateful night, had to be taken through an interpreter, since Hill understood no English. He corroborated the Grayson account, saying he saw Reeves put a cartridge in his rifle before it went off. Under cross-examination he admitted that Reeves and Leach seemed to be friendly before the shooting and that Reeves ministered to the wounded man afterward.

The defense called several witnesses who testified to the sterling character of Bass Reeves before the defendant himself took the stand. Asked to explain the shooting of Leach, he said, "Before I would start anywhere when I was out on a trip, I would always examine my cartridges and gun and that night in examining my gun I found I had a .45 cartridge in the magazine and I couldn't throw it up into the barrel. . . . I reached my hand in my coat pocket and got my knife and put my hand back . . . and either my knife or hand struck the trigger and the gun went off . . . and the boy [Johnnie Brady] hallooed and said, 'Lordy, you have shot Leach.'"

After a four-day trial, on October 15 the jury brought in a verdict of not guilty.[39] The *Fort Smith Elevator* of October 21, 1887, reported, "Bass Reeves was the best pleased man in Arkansas last Sunday when a verdict was announced pronouncing him innocent of the charge of murder. . . . His broad smiles attested his inward delight and in addition to shaking hands with the entire jury he worked Judge Parker's arm like a pump handle and assured him that he believed the trial would make him a better man."

In an analysis of this trial, Professor Nudie E. Williams of the University of Arkansas concludes that several facts persuaded the jury members to reach the decision that the death of William Leach was indeed an accident:

> There had not been any friction or argument between the deputy and the cook before the shooting incident. Most of the prosecutor's witnesses could not be considered impartial in their testimony against Reeves because he had arrested most of them at one time or another for criminal offenses. The deputy's reputation with a rifle was well known; if he had intended to kill Leach there is little doubt he would have died instantly. Reeves made every effort to provide prompt medical attention for his wounded employee. . . . And finally, Reeves made no attempt to leave the country in the two years after the indictment and continued to perform assigned duties with his usual efficiency.[40]

Other established facts could lead to an alternative conclusion. Bass Reeves was known to have a violent temper, a character flaw he had demonstrated on previous occasions, once when he struck his superior officer, and again when he was arrested on an assault with intent to kill charge. It is possible that in the dispute over the mongrel dog he may have been seized with one of those violent temper fits and shot his cook, an act that was certainly unpremeditated, for in his instant ministrations to Leach he showed complete remorse. As familiar as he was with firearms, it is difficult to believe he could have been so careless as to work on a loaded rifle pointed directly at a friend. The jammed cartridge defense could have simply been a made-up excuse to explain "an accident." In any event, if the killing of Leach resulted from his volatile temper, it apparently shocked Bass Reeves into thereafter controlling his anger, for no similar incident can be found in his remaining years.

Upon his exoneration for the Leach killing, Reeves was reinstated as a deputy marshal, but having incurred heavy legal expenses during his long period of unemployment, he found it necessary in 1887 to sell his home in Van Buren and move his family to a humbler abode in Fort Smith. According to his biographer, the trial depleted most of his savings, and he never rebounded financially despite his sizeable earnings. While the average annual salary for deputies working out of the Fort Smith court in the 1880s was $500, Reeves averaged $3,000 to $4,000 a year with the fees and expenses he collected during that period, even after paying 25 percent to the U.S. marshal. "He was one of the top grossing deputy marshals of the Fort Smith court."[41]

On June 14, 1889, a deputy marshal named Joseph Lundy, working out of the U.S. marshal's office in Kansas, was killed by horse thieves in the Unassigned Lands and Pottawatomie Nation of Indian Territory. Jacob Yoes, who had replaced John Carroll as U.S. marshal at Fort Smith, sent Bass Reeves to investigate the murder and arrest the culprits. Arriving at the area with a posse, Reeves found evidence implicating three Seminole Indians—Nocus Harjo, Billy Wolf, and one Prince—as Lundy's killers, and on June 20, only six days after the murder, warrants were issued for the suspects. The three made themselves scarce for several months, but in December, while rounding up miscreants in the area, Reeves got word from one of his informants that Lundy's killers were back in their old haunts. On December 30 he notified Marshal Yoes from Eufaula that he had eight prisoners in tow, including "the three men who killed Deputy Marshal Lundy."[42]

Reeves became involved in the story of Ned Christie, the notorious Indian outlaw. A native of the Cherokee Nation, Christie was born 1852 and trained as a blacksmith and gunsmith, and in 1885 he was elected to the Cherokee National Council. On May 4, 1887, Deputy U.S. Marshal Daniel Maples was killed, and Christie was accused of the murder. Claiming innocence, the feisty Cherokee refused to submit to arrest and holed up in a fortified cabin with friendly supporters. For years he fought off efforts by officers, including the legendary lawman Heck Thomas, to capture him.[43] In 1890 Bass Reeves was one of those officers. As reported in the *Vinita Indian Chieftain*,

On Tuesday last U.S. Deputy Marshal Bass Reeves, of Fort Smith, with his posse, made an attack on the home of Ned Christie in the

Flint district, who is perhaps the most notorious outlaw and desperado in the Indian Territory, and the outlaw's stronghold was burned to the ground. Supposing that the owner had been killed or wounded and was consumed in the building, the news went out that he had met a violent death. But Christie has turned up alive, and . . . is said to be on the war path fiercer than ever and vows revenge on the marshal and his posse. . . . A dead shot, [he] has eluded the officers of the law for about four years and says he will not be taken alive.[44]

In January 1891 the region's newspapers carried stories that Christie had exacted his revenge on Bass Reeves, but the reports of the lawman's passing, like Mark Twain's, were "greatly exaggerated." The *Muskogee Phoenix* reported, "Word reached here tonight of the killing of Deputy United States Marshal Bass Reeves, near Tahlequah, I. T., by Ned Christie . . . , one of the toughest characters in the Territory."[45] According to the *Van Buren Press*, "Deputy Marshal Bass Reeves was killed yesterday by Ned Christie near Tahlequah. . . . His death was not unexpected to those who knew him."[46] And the *Indian Journal* (Eufaula) cited yet more sources for its announcement: "It is reported in the *Republic* from Tahlequah and in the *Dallas News* from Muskogee that Bass Reeves was killed Saturday near Tahlequah, while attempting to make an arrest."[47]

The retractions were not long in coming. The *Muskogee Phoenix* admitted that Reeves was not even in the vicinity: "The report that Bass Reeves had been killed by Ned Christie . . . last week, was without foundation. Reeves was 150 miles away from the reported place of the killing at the time of the alleged killing."[48] The *Van Buren Press* stated, "Last week the *Press* contained the announcement of the killing of Deputy Marshal Bass Reeves. . . . It has been definitely ascertained that the statement was a hoax."[49] And on February 21, 1891, the *Indian Journal* published a resounding disclaimer of its earlier report of Reeves's death: "Deputy Marshal Bass Reeves lacks lots of being dead as we reported recently. . . . He turned up Saturday from [the] west with two wagons of prisoners going to Fort Smith. He had twelve prisoners in all, eight for whiskey vending, three for larceny and one for murder."

In May 1890 the United States Congress created Oklahoma Territory, a partial segment of the former Indian Territory, with its capital at Guthrie. It was the beginning of the gradual process of converting this part of America, with its unique history as a haven for displaced Indians and former black slaves, into new lands open to settlement by all races, and to eventual statehood in 1907. The changes made dramatic adjustments in court jurisdiction and law enforcement. Large areas formerly administered by Judge Parker's court and his federal officers now became the responsibility of courts and officers working out of Kansas and Texas.

Whiskey, a commodity once banned throughout Indian Territory, became legal in the new Territory of Oklahoma, and saloon towns sprang up, harboring some of the worst characters on the frontier. Three of these towns, Keokuk Falls, Violet Springs, and Corner in Pottawatomie County, just west of the Seminole Nation, were particularly notorious. One resident of the territory during this period later described these towns as "inhabited by Negroes, whites, Indians, half-bloods, gamblers, bootleggers, killers, and any kind of an outcast." Lacing his recollection with a great deal of hyperbole, he said, "Bass Reeves, a coal-black Negro was a U.S. Marshal during [this] time and he was the most feared U.S. marshal that was ever heard of in that country. To any man or any criminal . . . subject to arrest he did his full duty according to the law. He brought men before the court to be tried fairly but many times he never brought in all the criminals but would kill some of them. [If] he didn't want to spend [time chasing an arrest resister he] would shoot him down in his tracks."[50]

Charles W. Mooney, raised in Pottawatomie County in the '90s, was lavish in his praise of Reeves, who, he said, "worked closely with the early day Sheriffs before the turn of the century, as Sheriffs then could not pursue across county lines, but Marshals could." Mooney remembered Reeves as being quiet and soft-spoken, but one who "had proved his mettle and prowess with his two big .45 caliber six-shooters which materially enlarged his stature. He wore them butts forward for a cross-handed draw. This gave him quicker access to the deadly weapons—a split second edge meant life or death. He used the pistols with deadly accuracy. A remarkable man, he was a credit not only to the federal court but to his race."[51] Mooney said Reeves often used disguises and aliases. "When not in disguise, he rode a big red stallion with a white blazed face. He was always neatly dressed, and was noted for his politeness and courteous manner." To avoid offending the sensibilities of racially biased whites who might not like a black man drinking from their tin well cup, he carried a dipper tied to his saddle bag which he used when stopping at farmhouses for a drink."[52]

An account in which Reeves refrained from the use of weapons in an arrest is described in a history of early Tulsa authored by J. M. Hall (brother of H. C. Hall, the town's founder). Hall said he was in his brother's store one night when "Bass Reeves, a negro deputy marshal . . . , one of the most noted officers of the early days," came in, followed by a white man packing a brace of pistols who had "the appearance of an outlaw." When Bass asked him to give up his guns, the man's hands dropped to his weapons, but he refused to hand them over. It was a tense standoff, the kind of confrontation often leading to bloodshed, but Reeves resolved it quietly. "You are a white man and I am a negro," he said. "White men do not like to give up to a negro. You give your guns to Mr. Hall and when you are ready to leave town he will give them back to you." The white man complied.[53]

Despite some testimonials by old-timers in later years that Bass Reeves frequently unlimbered his guns in blood-and-thunder shootings and killings, it appears from the available records that in tracking down and arresting thousands of dangerous criminals throughout his long career as a lawman, he rarely resorted to gunplay. The shootings of Webb and Hamilton were exceptions. Another was his battle with Tom Barnett and Ben Billy, alias Ben Williams, who were whiskey peddlers operating in the Creek Nation.

Reeves coolly related details of this affair in a dictated letter to Marshal Yoes on November 11, 1891. After reporting his arrival at Okmulgee with six prisoners and his expectation to be back at Fort Smith within a week, he began:

> I had a writ for Ben Billy and when I demanded him to surrender he and Tom Barnett fired on me and we had a fight in which I shot Ben Billy twice. When we got down off our horses Tom Barnett fired and put [a] ball in a tree just by [Deputy U.S. Marshal Milo] Creekmore's head. He fired two shots at Creekmore while Ben Billy was firing at me. [After] Tom Barnett fired 2 shots he threw his gun down and ran in the house. Ben Billy fought until I shot him down. Please send a writ at once for Tom Barnett."[54]

Like many legendary frontier figures, Bass Reeves was "credited" with numerous killings. Most contemporary Oklahoma newspapers put the total at fourteen, a figure that has often been quoted in later publications,[55] but the *Daily Oklahoman* of Oklahoma City upped the figure, saying he had "at least 20 notches on his gun."[56] The *Herald* of Washington, D.C., in reporting Reeves's passing did not put a figure on his total, saying only that he was "credited with having more notches on his gun than he had fingers and toes."[57]

Reeves may have dispatched more than a dozen outlaws; he undoubtedly ran up against numerous hard cases who resisted arrest. He was a dead shot with six-shooter or rifle, and it is evident from those few shootings for which there is substantiation that he was not hesitant in using deadly force when he felt it necessary. He certainly killed Jim Webb and perhaps his criminal cohort Hamilton. Ben Billy fell before his gun. According to Reeves family tradition, he also did away with Bob Dosier and Tom Story. Dosier was "a master criminal whose illegal activities included cattle and horse theft, land swindles and murder," and Tom Story was "an expert horse thief and murderer."[58]

After a long and tedious tracking of Dosier and an accomplice, so went the tale, Reeves, at the head of a posse, closed in on his quarry in the forests of the Cherokee Hills. When a sudden thunderstorm prevented further pursuit, Reeves began looking for a likely location to camp for the night. Suddenly a shot rang out, a bullet just missed his head, and he and his posse sought cover. Spotting a man dodging from tree to tree, Reeves caught him between trees and dropped him with a pair of well-aimed shots. This eliminated one outlaw, and the other one revealed his position by pouring lead in Bass's direction.

Reeves then pulled off a brilliant maneuver. Immediately following a shot from the outlaw, he jerked upright, reeled away from his tree cover, fell to the ground, and waited, gun cocked and ready in his hand. After several moments, his assailant, believing that Reeves was dead or dying and that his posse had fled, emerged from behind a tree and approached, laughing. A bolt of lightning struck, illuminating his face, and Reeves recognized Bob Dosier, the man he sought. "Bass waited until he was only a few yards away before he raised up and ordered him to stop and drop his gun. Dozier stopped laughing, his eyes wide with surprise. He hesitated for a moment, then dropped into a crouch and attempted to shoot once again. . . . Before he could level his gun, Bass shot first, hitting him in the neck and killing him instantly."[59]

Tom Story, the captain of a horse stealing gang headquartered in the Chickasaw Nation, worked a lucrative enterprise from 1884 to 1889, driving stolen Indian Territory ponies across the Red River for sale in Texas. Seeing an opportunity to increase his nefarious earnings, Story reversed his operation in 1889. He and his cohorts stole the horse herd of North Texas rancher George Delaney and drove the animals into Indian Territory. Certain that Story was the culprit, Delaney went to the U.S. marshal's office in Paris, Texas, and secured a warrant for his arrest as well as the assistance of Bass Reeves, who was then working out of the Paris office, to serve it. After obtaining information that Story was about to return to Texas by way of the Delaware Bend crossing of the Red River, Reeves and Delaney set up an ambush there. On the fifth day of their wait, Story appeared, leading two of Delaney's finest mules. Reeves stepped out in front of him and announced he had a warrant for Story's arrest. "Right then and there," ran the account, "Tom Story committed suicide. Tom attempted to draw his gun on Bass, thinking he had an even chance to beat him as Bass still had his gun in its holster, But Story's gun hadn't even begun to clear leather before Reeves had already drawn and fired his Colt pistol. Story was dead before he hit the ground."[60]

In relating the Tom Story account, Judge Paul L. Brady, Bass Reeves's great-nephew, points out, "Although Bass was not a killer by nature, his job was that of a man hunter. He was fascinated by the hunt which was so unpredictable that it drew on his every skill and sometimes his intuition. This meant that at times it was necessary to spend days dogging the trail of his quarry, but it could also mean waiting in comfort for an outlaw to come to him. This was the method used to apprehend Tom Story."[61] Old West man-hunters called this method the "still hunt."

To date, no contemporary newspaper reports supporting either the Bob Dosier or the Tom Story killings has been found, but there were occasional bare-boned references to Reeves's lethal dispatch of outlaws as an item in the *Muskogee Phoenix*. Its Local Paragraphs column of June 18, 1896, read, "Deputy Marshal Bass Reeves killed a horse thief whom he was trying to arrest in the Seminole country Thursday of last week."

Reeves also killed William Leach, a member of his posse, but that unfortunate affair would certainly not deserve a notch on his gun, if Reeves did indeed keep track of his killings with gun notches.

Despite his many violent clashes with wanted men, Reeves was apparently only wounded once, late in his career, receiving a bullet in his leg, which was never removed and which bothered him a great deal until the end of his life.[62] As an early Oklahoma historian has recorded, Reeves received the leg wound in a shootout in one of the notorious Corner, Pottawatomie County, saloons. When the smoke cleared, someone went after medical help. Doctor Jesse Mooney arrived to find "Bass Reeves half-standing and half-sitting on a barroom table. He had been shot in the left leg, above the knee. Still lying on the floor in a pool of blood was a young gunslinger with his drawn pistol still in his hand, dead." When the doctor, who had known Reeves for years, asked what happened, Bass is said to have replied, "Just another young gunslinger who doubted my ability with these six-guns. He was real fast, but like a lot of them, they couldn't shoot both fast and straight."[63]

Though only shot once, Bass Reeves did survive several assassination attempts. In one of his dictated reports to Marshal Boles in 1885, he mentioned that someone had fired a round into his camp one midnight, "but I turned the duel on him and he left."[64]

Wybark, a community near Muskogee, proved to be a particularly dangerous locale for the deputy marshal. As reported in the *Muskogee Daily Phoenix* of November 14, 1906:

> An attempt was made to assassinate Deputy Marshal Bass Reeves near Wybark Tuesday night while the marshal was scouring the country after criminals, for whom he had warrants. Reeves was driving under a railroad trestle . . . when he was fired on by an unknown foe. Reeves turned in the seat and fired several shots in the direction of the would-be assassin. Reeves was not hit but the bullet splintered the wood in the trestle directly above his head.

Alice Spahn related another assassination story that she heard from her father. While riding back to Muskogee from Wybark in a buggy with two handcuffed prisoners he had arrested, Reeves was attacked by a pair of gunmen who fired shots at him. He fell backward in the buggy, at the same time pulling and cocking his pistol. "A shooter stepped out in the open and Reeves shot him in the stomach. The shooter and his confederate gave up on the spot and Reeves brought four men into Muskogee."[65]

The family life of Bass Reeves was in many respects as turbulent as his professional career. His wife Jennie bore him eleven children, five girls and six boys. All the troubles, it seems, began in July 1893, when Robert, the oldest son, was killed in a railway accident.[66] The next year Jennie was diagnosed with cancer. She lived on for two years but succumbed to peritonitis on March 19, 1896. In those latter years of the nineteenth century, with their mother dying and their father gone for long periods pursuing felons, the children were pretty much on their own. The older girls may have tried their best to take their mother's place, nurturing the younger children, but with that large brood, it was almost an impossible job.

In 1895 two of the teenaged Reeves boys found themselves on the other side of the law, which their father had devoted his life to defending. A Van Buren paper reported in June that Newland Reeves had been convicted and sentenced to five years in prison for perjury, and his brother Edgar had received a one-year sentence for the same offense.[67]

The century turned, and the run of devastating events for the Reeves family continued. On October 19, 1901, Bass Jr., the youngest of the Reeves clan, died of pneumonia. On December 28, 1903, Homer, the next youngest son, died of fever.

Sandwiched between these melancholy events, Bass's twenty-two-year-old son, Benjamin "Bennie" Reeves exhibited the loss of control followed by violence that was seemingly passed down in the blood of some of the Reeves family. On June 7, 1902, Bennie, believing that his wife was cheating on him with another man, exploded in a fit of rage and shot his wife to death. Under the headline MURDERED HIS WIFE; BEN REEVES SHOOTS DOWN THE WOMAN IN COLD BLOOD, the *Muskogee Daily Phoenix* reported the story in a torrent of immoderate prose:

> Consumed with jealousy, crazed beyond endurance because the wife he married had told him she did not love him, a monomaniac [who] lived in the lights and shadows of his imaginary wrongs, angered until his blood became a furnace heated with all the fires of unrequited love, Ben Reeves yesterday at 11 o'clock in the morning sent a bullet from a .45 Colt revolver crushing through the brain of the wife he had sworn to cherish and protect.[68]

Clearly Bennie Reeves shot and killed Cassie, his wife, on that June day in 1902, but like many important events in the life of Bass Reeves, there are several versions of how that came about and what happened after. According to the Muskogee news report, Bennie had long suspected his wife of infidelity, and when he found her at a friend's house together with another man, who was "whispering terms of endearment into her not unwilling ears . . . , he drew forth the deadly revolver and fired, the first ball striking his wife fairly in the face and going through her brain, the second a flesh wound. She died instantly. He then turned the gun on himself, but the ball only grazed his forehead." Meeting his father shortly thereafter, he told him what he had done, and Bass took him to jail.

In an interview more than a half-century later, Alice Spahn, Bennie's sister and Bass Reeve's last living child, related the story differently. She said that when Bennie first suspected that his wife was seeing other men, he had it out with her and they reconciled. When Bennie related his marital problems to their father and asked his advice, Bass responded, "I'd have shot hell out of the man and whipped the living God out of her." Shortly thereafter, according to Alice, Bennie caught Cassie with the other man, a fistic battle ensued from which the man "escaped, bloody and beaten, but otherwise unharmed." Still in a murderous rage, Bennie killed his wife and ran off to Indian Territory. A warrant was issued for his arrest and Bass, "visibly shaken" and perhaps feeling that his advice to his son made him responsible to some degree for what had happened, went after his son and brought him in.[69]

An entirely different version of the affair comes from the pen of Reeves's biographer Paul L. Brady. He names the "other man" as Jimmy Long, a "fancy Dan" gambler.[70] Learning that Cassie was with him at another house, Bennie "stuck an old pistol in his belt and went to confront Long." There the gambler admitted that he and Cassie were "romantically involved," and that he planned to take her to Kansas. He was armed, and if Ben did not like it, he could get a gun and try to settle the matter. "Whereupon Ben opened his coat and drew. As the two men exchanged shots, Cassie somehow got caught in the crossfire and was slain. . . . Long fled." Ben, with a head wound, turned himself in, but later had seized an opportunity to escape, and ran off. Bass followed him all the way to Texas, where he made the arrest without incident.[71]

Still another account of the arrest was related in a 1973 television documentary by Reverend Charles Davis, who had been a resident of Muskogee at the time of the affair. Bennie, he said, went to his house after the shooting and threatened to kill anyone who tried to arrest him. Bass urged the marshal not to send any of his other deputies, as they might be killed, and asked for the warrant himself. When he received it, he marched to Bennie's house, followed by a crowd, many imploring him not to go in as he might be shot. "But he went on, Bass did. Got to the house and yelled to his boy. . . . 'Now, Bennie,' he said, 'you are no more my son, you committed a crime. And I have a warrant in my pocket for you, a bench warrant, to bring you in either dead or alive. And I'm going to take you in today, one way or the other. You can come out with your hands up or else your whole body will be down.' Bennie came out."[72]

However he made the arrest, Bass Reeves did perform the unpleasant task of taking his own son into custody and jailing him for murder, an act adding to his legend.[73]

Tried for first-degree murder in January 1903 at Muskogee, Benjamin Reeves was convicted and sentenced by Judge C. W. Raymond to life in prison. Received at the Fort Leavenworth, Kansas, penitentiary, he was asked to describe the crime for which he was being incarcerated. His response should clarify once and for all how and why the shooting occurred:

> On the morning of June 7th, 1902, at 11 A.M. I called upon my wife at her cousin's house in Muskogee [and] asked her if it was true she was having or did have improper relations with John Wadly, [and] she answered me that she thought more of his little finger than she did of my whole body. By constant worry over her actions and breaking up of my home, and receiving such an answer, I lost all control and shot her.[74]

Judge Isaac Charles Parker died at the age of fifty-eight on November 17, 1896. In his twenty-one years on the bench at Fort Smith, he had presided over 13,490 cases of which 9,459 had resulted in convictions. Many of those cases resulted from captures of suspects by Deputy Marshal Bass Reeves, who is credited with more than three thousand arrests while working as a federal officer. Capital offenses accounted for 344 of the trials, and Judge Parker during his tenure sentenced 156 men and four women to death by hanging. Seventy-nine of those death sentences were actually carried out, the rest of the condemned died before execution, successfully appealed the sentence, or were pardoned. Upon his passing Judge Parker was replaced by John Henry Rogers, who held the office until his death in 1911.[75]

The change of legal jurisdiction for parts of Indian Territory, as mandated by the U.S. Congress in the 1890s, had an important effect on the life and career of Bass Reeves. He first worked out of the Paris, Texas, courts, and then, about 1895, was assigned to the northern district of Indian Territory and the office of newly appointed U.S. marshal Samuel Rutherford and later Leo E. Bennett, who took over from Rutherford in 1897. The district court and U.S. marshal's office was in Muskogee, and that was where Reeves moved his family. He married again and called Muskogee home for the rest of his life.

On Sunday, January 14, 1900, Bass married Winnie J. Sumner, a "thirty-or-forty-something," formerly married mother of two teenage sons and a twelve-year-old daughter.[76] To the census taker that year he gave his occupation as "retired deputy marshal." The *Muskogee Phoenix* of November 14, 1901, praised Reeves for his twenty-seven years of service, saying that in that time he had arrested more than three thousand men and women and killed twelve.

But the old law dog was not through sniffing out miscreants. On January 10, 1902, Bass came out of retirement to accept reappointment as a deputy marshal for the northern district of Indian Territory.[77] Once back in the harness, it did not take him long to set a new personal record for collars. Completing a swing through the Territory on May 20, 1902, he and Deputy Marshal David Adams reported in with a wagon stuffed with twenty-four prisoners, a haul that caught the attention of newspaper editors in both Indian Territory and Texas.[78]

In 1903 Bass, who had never been baptized, underwent the rite, probably at the insistence of his new wife. The service was performed by a black Baptist preacher named William Hobson. Three years later, in August 1907, Reeves arrested Reverend Hobson for the illegal sale of liquor.[79] Like the arrest of his own son for murder, this was another demonstration of Bass placing enforcement of the law above personal considerations.

Reeves's return to the U.S. marshal's service lasted only five years, for on November 16, 1907, Oklahoma achieved its long-sought statehood. With this achievement, the new state's need for federal law enforcement was greatly diminished, and together with many other deputy marshals, he was released.

Even though he was pushing seventy years in age, Reeves was not ready to give up police work. In January 1908 he joined the Muskogee police force under his old friend in the marshal's service, J. F. "Bud" Ledbetter, who was now the chief of police. On January 10, 1908, *Western Age*, a newspaper of the black town of Langston, Oklahoma, announced Reeves's appointment, describing him as "a giant negro . . . [who is] now over 70 years old [*sic*] and walks with a cane. A bullet in his leg, received while in the government service, gives him considerable trouble. He is as quick of trigger, however, as in the days when gun men were in demand."

Reeves served only a short time on the Muskogee force; his health began to fail, and by the fall of 1909 he was bedridden and not expected to live much longer. The *Muskogee Times-Democrat* reported on November 19 that Chief Ledbetter daily called on the man he termed "one of the bravest men this country has ever known."

Bass Reeves fought off the grim reaper for two more months, but on January 12, 1910, he departed this world. His death was caused, according to news reports, by Bright's disease "and complications."[80] Obituaries in the Muskogee papers repeated the remarkable statistics he had compiled in his life: thirty-two years of service in law enforcement under seven U.S. marshals, more than three thousand arrests, fourteen notches on his gun for outlaws' lives he had snuffed out while cheating death by desperadoes a hundred times.[81] Writers for more distant periodicals could not resist increasing his gun-notch total to twenty or more.[82]

The *Muskogee Phoenix* of January 15 reported that his funeral was attended by many white people, men who had known him in earlier days and who admired and respected him. "Black-skinned, illiterate, offspring of slaves whose ancestors were savages . . . , Bass Reeves was a unique character. Absolutely fearless and knowing no master but duty, the placing of a writ in his hands meant that the letter of the law would be fulfilled though his life paid the penalty. . . . The arrest of his own son for wife-murder . . . is best illustration of the old deputy's Spartan character. He performed that duty as he did all others entrusted to him."

Reeves never acquired monetary wealth; when his son-in-law, A. C. Spahn, handled probate proceedings for his estate in July 1913, it did not exceed five hundred dollars.[83] Even his more lasting legacy, widespread recognition of his extraordinary career, was long in coming.

Throughout the twentieth century western frontier law enforcement officers like Wyatt Earp, Wild Bill Hickok, and Bat Masterson became widely recognized household names through books, magazine articles, motion pictures, and television. The exploits of Bass Reeves, whose career as a man-hunter and law enforcement officer outshone them all, were ignored. The only explanation for this deplorable omission could be that because of his color a predominantly white audience would not accept him as a heroic figure.

It was not until a black history professor began writing and publishing books about the important roles people of color played in the remarkable story of establishing law on the American frontier that the name Bass Reeves came to notice for followers of that history. In 1991 Arthur T. "Art" Burton, an African-American professor of history, published *Black, Red and Deadly*, the first scholarly book concentrating on the part played by men of color, both black and red, both outlaw and lawman, in that violent history. It necessarily included information on Bass Reeves. Burton followed this up in 2005, almost a century after the death of Reeves, with a thoroughly researched biography of the man entitled *Black Gun, Silver Star: The Life and Legend of Frontier Marshal Bass Reeves*. Coincidentally, that same year Paul L. Brady, the grandson of Reeves's sister Jane and John Brady, who had also been studying Bass's outstanding career, published *The Black Badge: Deputy United States Marshal Bass Reeves, from Slave to Heroic Lawman*. Following that, in 2006, Gary Paulsen released *The Legend of Bass Reeves*, a largely fictional book for children. Another children's book, *Bad News for Outlaws: The Remarkable Life of Bass Reeves, Deputy U.S. Marshal*, by Vaunda Micheaux Nelson and R. Gregory Christie, appeared in 2013, which was followed by *Frontier Marshal: The Story of Bass Reeves, Deputy U.S. Marshal*, a work of historical fiction by Charles Ray in 2014.

Awakened by these books to Reeves's extraordinary story, producers of television documentaries finally joined the rush to enlighten the public. News commentator and best-selling author Bill O'Reilly's *Legends and Lies* series, purporting to tell the "real truth" about legendary western frontier figures, featured Reeves in its ending segment in 2014. It was followed closely in 2015 by a Bass Reeves segment on the *Gunslinger* series on the American Heroes Channel.[84]

Finally the remarkable and long-ignored career of this extraordinary man-hunter was receiving national attention.

— *6* —

PATRICK FLOYD JARVIS "PAT" GARRETT
1850–1908

> Garrett has never ceased to dog the footsteps of the "Kid." He said soon after the escape of the criminal that he would "follow him to the end," and he has done so with persistency, determination, and bravery through long and anxious months, finally to meet with a success which entitles him to the gratitude and respect of the people of the territory.
>
> London *Times*, August 18, 1881

Like the brutal killer Joaquin Murrieta, hunted down and beheaded by Harry Love in California; the Bloody Espinosas, trailed and killed by Tom Tobin in Colorado; the rustling gangs of Montana, wiped out by Granville Stuart's Stranglers; Black Bart, the West's most famous and successful stagecoach bandit, traced and ensnared by Californian Harry Morse; and the hundreds of killers and thieves arrested (or sometimes killed) by Bass Reeves in Indian Territory—like all of those outlaws, Henry McCarty, alias "Billy the Kid" Bonney, murderer and cattle thief, was twice hunted down and was finally killed by Pat Garrett in New Mexico. And like Murrieta and Black Bart, the Kid is better remembered today than the man who ended his criminal career. It is truly remarkable that a juvenile delinquent–turned–rustler and murderer, shot dead at twenty-one, should become a legendary figure, admired by many, while the sheriff who destroyed the Kid's criminal gang, captured him, and ended his misspent life with a bullet should be a secondary character in the sanguinary story.

Patrick Floyd Jarvis Garrett, the man-hunter who twice hunted down the most notorious criminal in New Mexico history, was born on June 5, 1850, in Chambers County, Alabama, one of the eight children of John L. and Elizabeth Ann (Jarvis) Garrett. He was three when the family moved to a plantation in Claiborne Parish, Louisiana, and there he reached manhood. Growing like a weed, he finally reached a height of six feet, five

Patrick Floyd Jarvis "Pat" Garrett. Courtesy of Wikimedia Commons.

inches, standing fully a foot taller than most men of the period. The recipient of only a few years of rudimentary education, he could read and write, but it was while roaming Louisiana's fields and woods with a gun in hand that he sharpened the tracking and shooting skills that would so benefit him in his chosen profession.[1]

Pat Garrett might have spent the rest of his life as a Louisiana planter but for the death of his father in February 1868 and the ensuing family discord over the estate. When a brother-in-law named Larkin Lay tried to take control of the family's fortunes, Pat vehemently objected. The battle grew so heated that at one point Pat threatened to kill Lay, but refrained in consideration of his sister. In January 1869, disgusted by the family's financial discord, he turned his back on them all and headed west. He was eighteen years old. As far as is known, he never saw his family again.[2]

In Texas he tried for a time to follow his father's occupation, but a single season partnered with a farmer convinced him that it was not his forte. He tried his hand at cow punching but soon realized that his hunting and shooting skills could be better utilized harvesting bison hides in the great buffalo slaughter that was then in progress. In 1876 he teamed up with Willis Skelton Glenn,[3] a Confederate army veteran from Georgia, a few years his elder, who had similar ideas. As buffalo-hunting partners, they headed for Fort Griffin, a center for the hide-hunting industry recently sprung up in North Texas. There they outfitted and hired Luther Duke, Joe Briscoe, and Nick Buck as skinners and Grundy Burns as cook. The Garrett-Glenn enterprise did well in the hide-hunting business for a time, but things turned sour after a fatal event in November 1876.

The buffalo herds had thinned out, and with winter approaching, the weather was bad. The crew was not in the best of moods one morning after Glenn had gone off to Camp Reynolds to get a rifle repaired.[4] When Garrett mumbled something derogatory about the Irish, Joe Briscoe immediately took umbrage and rushed at him. Garrett knocked the smaller man down. Two or three times, the scene was repeated. In a homicidal rage, Briscoe grabbed an ax and came at Garrett with the weapon raised to strike. Garrett stretched his long legs in a retreat around the wagon. When Briscoe continued his murderous assault, Garrett snatched up a rifle, whirled, and fired, and Briscoe tumbled over, dead.

Glenn returned later that day to find his partner suffering great anguish over the affair and uncertain what to do next. Following Glenn's advice to go into Fort Griffin and explain the circumstances of the killing to the authorities, Garrett rode off. Law officials there, reluctant to become involved in a shooting so far from their jurisdiction, declined to pursue the matter. Briscoe was buried near where he fell, and his death was forgotten, except by Pat Garrett, who always regretted having slain the young man, and Skelton Glenn, who wrote about it some years later.[5]

The once-immense buffalo herds were rapidly being decimated by the hide hunters, but Garrett and Glenn stayed at it. In February 1877 a band of Comanche Indians on the warpath against the white men who were steadily killing off the buffalo, the source of the Indians' very existence, struck the Garrett-Glenn camp, destroyed eight hundred drying hides, and stole the tethered horses. Fortunately the entire crew was out on the prairie at the time and escaped almost-certain death.[6]

Despite this calamity Garrett and Glenn continued on. But in May a Comanche war party struck their camp again. This time Glenn and a new skinner named Dofflin were there. Glenn was wounded in the leg, and Dofflin dragged him to a hiding place from which the two men watched in dismay as their hides and equipment were systematically destroyed.[7]

The partners salvaged the few hides the Indians had missed and their remaining equipment and disposed of the lot at Fort Griffin. The proceeds were barely enough to finance round-trip fares to Saint Louis, where the two, with the exuberance of youth, went to enjoy themselves after their months in the wilds and spent what little money was left.[8]

Talking over their future plans back in Texas, the two decided they would not let the unfortunate death of a crew member and a couple of raids by Indians prevent them from cashing in on what might still be a profitable and exciting business enterprise. Garrett was broke and could not contribute to another expedition, but Glenn had enough bank funds to cover initial expenses and, feeling that Garrett's exceptional skill with a rifle was essential to the project's success, agreed to hire him as a shooter at sixty dollars a month. Glenn purchased a new outfit, and with Nick Buck as a skinner, they headed out in November 1877. This operation lasted only a couple months, however. The great buffalo herds were so depleted and the few animals left were so scattered that further hunting seemed unprofitable, and in January 1878 they gave it up.[9]

Hearing that prospects for ambitious young men were better in New Mexico, Garrett rode off to that territory. Landing at Fort Sumner, he found the country densely populated with Hispanics, for Mexicans had settled there long before Anglo arrival. He immediately took a liking to these people, and the feeling was reciprocated. Awed by his great height, the locals began calling him Juan Largo (Long John).[10] Garrett tried a new business, hog raising, and took on a new partner, Thomas C. "Kip" McKinney, with whom he was destined to share many future adventures. Among the Hispanics to whom he was particularly attracted was twenty-six-year-old Apolinaria Gutierrez, the daughter of a prosperous freighter. He wooed her, and on January 14, 1880, the two were married in Anton Chico, New Mexico.[11]

The year 1880 would be momentous for Pat Garrett. He not only became a husband that year but also found his life's work. Enumerated in June by the U.S. census taker for Lincoln County, New Mexico, he gave his occupation as farmer, but not surprisingly, it wasn't as a hog raiser that Garrett would achieve fame; a few months later he would be elected sheriff of Lincoln County and embark on his remarkable man-hunting career.

Although he had been a resident of Lincoln County only a short time, he had quickly gained a reputation for bravery and determination in the West's ongoing war against human predators. When a band of renegade Indians stole a herd of horses from a ranch near Roswell, Garrett had taken quick and decisive action, organizing a posse to pursue the marauders. Slowed in their flight by difficulty in managing the purloined ponies, the Indians found the posse closing in on them and took out their frustration on the stolen horses; they brutally stabbed twenty-seven of the animals in the neck, killing fourteen of them. When the posse came on this bloody scene, many members, unwilling to continue a long chase, turned back, but Garrett and a few others stuck to the trail and were gone for days. They returned a week later, bedraggled and exhausted, but had with them some of the stolen stock and also a sack filled with moccasins, mute evidence that many thieving Indians lay dead in their wake.[12]

After this action, Garrett's admirers, including prominent citizens John Chisum and Joseph C. Lea, urged him to run for Lincoln County sheriff at the coming election. Garrett accepted the challenge, ran as a Democrat for the office on November 2, 1880, and defeated the incumbent sheriff, George Kimbrell, by a vote of 320 to 179. Although Kimbrell's term would not expire until the end of the year, the lame-duck sheriff acquiesced to the demands of many constituents and deputized Pat Garrett to assist in the search for outlaws who were then terrorizing Lincoln County. Garrett wore a deputy's badge during the last months of 1880 before replacing it with the sheriff's badge on January 1, 1881.[13]

For several years peace-loving residents of New Mexico had watched with growing trepidation the increasingly violent conflict raging in Lincoln County. Spawned by competing commercial interests, the Lincoln County War, as it came to be known, involved the leading businessmen and cattle ranchers of the county as well as county and territorial political figures, U.S. Army personnel, and murderous gunmen and criminals on both sides of the battle. Before its conclusion there was a succession of territorial governors and county sheriffs, as well as rampant thievery and bloodshed. One of Garrett's attributes was that, unlike predecessors in the sheriff's office, he had no dog in that fight, as the expression went.

By the time he took office, one criminal gang, led by a charismatic figure, had emerged from the multitude of outlaws operating in the county as a major contributor to the trouble. Pat Garrett focused his attention on this gang and its leader, Billy the Kid Bonney, as his first order of business.

In his short career the young desperado heading this gang had been known by several names: Henry McCarty, William "Kid" Antrim, and William Bonney, but he is best remembered simply as Billy the Kid. Despite intensive study by researchers, the details of the Kid's early life are still cloudy. Most believe he was born in New York City about 1860 and christened Henry McCarty, and then his mother took him and an older brother, Joseph, to Santa Fe, New Mexico, where she married William H. Antrim in 1873.

Soon after his mother died in 1874 in Silver City, New Mexico, Kid Antrim, as he was then known, committed his first crime, stealing a tub of butter. Quickly apprehended by Grant County sheriff Harvey Whitehill, he received a wayward child's punishment, a scolding and a paddling, but this youngster was incorrigible. In September 1875 he assisted a small-time thief named George "Sombrero Jack" Shaffer in the heist of a Chinese laundry, a felony punishable by a prison sentence. Sheriff Whitehill nabbed him again and slapped him in the Silver City hoosegow from which he first displayed his greatest talent, that of an escape artist. He exited the jail by way of the chimney, slithering up its length like a snake.[14]

Turning up next at Camp Grant, Arizona, as a member of a horse stealing gang, he was apprehended, but as he proved time and again, he could be caught but was hard to keep caged. He escaped, was rearrested, and escaped again.[15] Not surprisingly, the young hoodlum's escalating criminal career soon led to violence. In an August 1877 altercation he mortally wounded Frank P. Cahill, who thus became the first victim of the serial killer destined to become famous—or infamous—as Billy the Kid.[16]

Now wanted for murder as well as horse theft, the Kid skipped out of Arizona Territory and made tracks for the town of Mesilla in neighboring New Mexico, where he had learned through the criminal grapevine that a large gang of horse and cattle thieves known as "the Boys" was headquartered. His notoriety had preceded him and, despite his youth, he was welcomed into the gang by its leader, a tough Texan named Jessie Evans. Masterminded by John W. Kinney, known as "King of the Rustlers," and led by Evans, the gang was stealing stock throughout West Texas and southeastern New Mexico. Their criminality contributed greatly to the turbulence that reached its peak in the Lincoln County War.[17]

Aligned on one side of this bloody conflict was a group, collectively known as "the House," consisting of a greedy cabal of Lincoln businessmen, Lawrence G. Murphy, James J. Dolan, and John Riley, who were backed by Governor Samuel B. Axtell and New Mexico power broker Thomas B. Catron in the territorial capital of Santa Fe.[18] Opposing them were Alexander McSween, a hardheaded former Presbyterian minister turned lawyer, and his business partner, John Henry Tunstall, an entrepreneur from England who held investments in a Lincoln store and a cattle ranch.[19]

Unwilling to take orders from anyone he did not respect, including Jessie Evans and John Kinney, Kid Antrim cut loose from the Boys and punched cattle on the ranch of John Tunstall, who treated him like a gentleman, which of course, he was not. William Bonney, as the Kid was now calling himself, held an admiration for the Englishman that bordered on reverence. When on February 18, 1878, gunmen hired by the House shot and killed Tunstall, Bonney swore allegiance to the McSween faction in the increasingly violent war. The next day he joined Dick Brewer, another staunch McSween supporter, in naming Dolan, Evans, and several other gunmen as Tunstall's slayers in affidavits.[20]

Warrants were issued for those identified, and Brewer, appointed as a special constable, formed a fifteen-man posse, which included Bonney, to arrest the suspects. "The Regulators," as the posse of McSween adherents was called, captured two, Frank Baker and Buck Morton, but on the way back to Lincoln the pair made a desperate escape attempt resulting in the death of Regulator William McCloskey and both suspects.[21]

April 1878 was an eventful month in the Lincoln County War saga. On the first day of that month, April Fool's Day, Billy the Kid played what he must have thought was a great joke on Sheriff William Brady.[22] Learning that Brady was going to arrest McSween that day, the Kid assembled a six-man assassination squad and set up an ambush behind the adobe wall of the Tunstall store corral. When Brady and four of his deputies, Billy Mathews, George Hindman, George Peppin, and John Long, came down the street, they were met with a hail of lead. Brady, struck with three rifle bullets, died instantly. Hindman and Long were both wounded, Hindman fatally. Mathews and Peppin sought the cover of a neighboring house and returned fire, managing to inflict a minor wound on the leg of Jim French, one of the assassination squad, before the Kid and his cohorts mounted up and galloped off.[23]

On April 4 Bonney was one of fourteen Regulators attacking Andrew L. "Buckshot" Roberts, whom they believed was one of Tunstall's killers, but Roberts proved to be a tough nut to crack; before he was mortally wounded, he killed Dick Brewer and wounded George Coe and John Middleton during a full day of fighting.[24]

On April 8 John Copeland replaced Brady as Lincoln County sheriff. A grand jury completed its investigation into the deaths of Tunstall, Brady, Hindman, and Roberts in mid-April. Indictments were brought against Evans and three others as principals for the murder of Tunstall, "an act of brutality and malice . . . without a shadow of justification," and Dolan and Mathews were charged as accessories. Indicted for "the most brutal murder" of Brady and Hindman were Bonney, John Middleton, Fred Waite,[25] and Henry Brown.[26] The Kid, Middleton, Waite, and Brown, together with five others, were also indicted for the Roberts killing.[27]

That violent April ended in a daylong pitched battle between the Regulators and a gaggle of gunfighters calling themselves "the Seven Rivers Warriors." About thirty-five Warriors led by William Harrison Johnson, a former Brady deputy, rode more than one hundred miles from the Seven Rivers country for the avowed purpose of aiding Sheriff John Copeland in arresting those indicted for the Brady and Hindman murders. George Coe, a McSween supporter, believed their real intent was to "clean up Billy the Kid's gang."[28]

The morning after a skirmish, which took place eight miles outside of Lincoln on April 29, in which the invaders killed Francis MacNab and wounded Ab Saunders, the Seven Rivers Warriors entered Lincoln and were met with armed resistance by the Regulators. A battle raged for hours until it was finally halted by troopers from Fort Stanton, who escorted all surviving Seven Rivers Warriors to the fort. According to a correspondent for the *Cimarron News & Press*, six of the invaders were "seriously, perhaps fatally, injured [making] this is the grandest victory yet won by the people."[29] Regulator casualties were not disclosed.

In late May, Governor Axtell dismissed Sheriff John Copeland on a technicality and to replace him appointed George Peppin,[30] a tool of Dolan's. On June 18 Peppin secured warrants for the arrest of those indicted for the Brady, Hindman, and Roberts killings and deputized four trusted fighting men associated with the House to assist him in making the arrests.[31] But McSween and the Regulators had taken to the hills, and even with an additional dozen or more gunmen employed as posse members, Peppin could not collar his suspects.

The return to Lincoln of McSween, Bonney, and other staunch supporters in July precipitated what would become famous as the Five Days Battle. In preparation for the onslaught they knew their foes would launch, the Regulators took up positions in the McSween home and surrounding buildings. With McSween in his home were his wife, Susan, as well as her sister Elizabeth, Elizabeth's children, and a law student named Harvey Morris. Defending the stronghold were Billy the Kid and ten other fighters.

The battle raged from July 15 to 19. Finally, Colonel Nathan A. Dudley, in command at Fort Stanton, led his troops into the town, purportedly to protect the women and children. McSween distrusted Dudley, however, believing he was in league with the sheriff, and became convinced of the fact when troopers leveled a cannon at his house. Dolan's forces set fire to the home, and the women and children fled to the safety of a wagon that the troopers had pulled up outside. Those remaining in the house fought the flames until they realized they were losing that battle as well as the one with the enemy outside. Braving rifle fire, they ran for their lives. Several fell in that frantic dash, but Billy the Kid, Tom O'Folliard, and Jim French escaped. Alexander McSween, Harvey Morris, three other McSween supporters, and a House adherent perished in the Five Days Battle. Several on either side were wounded. Two noncombatants, including a fifteen-year-old boy, were caught in the crossfire and were also hit.

Having lost the Five Days Battle, and with the men they had championed—Tunstall and McSween—both dead, the remaining Regulators began to disperse. Charlie Bowdre and "Doc" Scurlock,[32] two older men with families, moved to Fort Sumner. Fred Waite returned to his former home in Indian Territory, Henry Brown hired on to a Texas ranch, and John Middleton joined a cattle drive to Kansas.

But Billy the Kid could not give up the fight without taking a spot of revenge. In August he and some former Regulators paid a call on Morris J. Bernstein, a bookkeeper at the Mescalero Indian Agency. Bernstein had kept books for J. J. Dolan, and in the Kid's eyes that made him an enemy. He and his gunmen riddled the inoffensive bookkeeper with bullets.[33]

In September 1878 President Rutherford B. Hayes, reacting to the wave of lawlessness in New Mexico, replaced Governor Samuel Axtell with Lewis Wallace, a veteran officer of the Mexican and Civil Wars as well as a lawyer, politician, and historical novelist, who was just completing his epic *Ben Hur*. Wallace was still being briefed on the turmoil in the territory he was to govern when President Hayes issued a proclamation giving those committing lawless acts until noon on October 13 "to disperse and return peaceably to their respective abodes."[34] In November, Governor Wallace released a document announcing that, since the disorders in Lincoln County had ended, he was issuing "a general pardon for misdemeanors and offenses" committed in that county between February 1 and the date of the proclamation.[35]

For the Lincoln County War gunmen, this was great news, but one of them, Billy the Kid, did not learn of it for some time. He had resumed his old practice of horse theft, stealing ponies in New Mexico and driving them to ranches in the Texas Panhandle then selling them there and returning with a stolen Texas herd. When Wallace issued his pardon, the Kid was in Tascosa, Texas, charming folks such as Dr. Henry Hoyt and Texas cowboy Charles Siringo who would both write favorably of the young outlaw later.[36]

On January 1, 1879, Lincoln County got another new sheriff when George Kimbrell was appointed to replace Peppin, who had resigned.

In early 1879 Governor Lew Wallace and Billy the Kid Bonney exchanged letters. Frederick Nolan, the best chronicler of the Lincoln County War, has called this correspondence—letters between an eminent political and literary figure and a youthful thief and cold-blooded murderer—"unique in the annals of outlawry."[37] Both correspondents were wily characters, each trying to use the other to achieve his own goals. Wallace, now aware that the amnesty announcement had not resolved the Lincoln County crime problem, needed a knowledgeable snitch to help him put away the bad actors and was willing to promise anything to achieve that end. Billy, on the other hand, was agreeable to providing information about his felonious enemies, but he would not betray his friends.

On March 17, 1879, Wallace and Bonney had a secret face-to-face meeting in Lincoln in which Wallace made a proposal. If the Kid identified the murderers of Huston I. Chapman (a lawyer who had been hired by the widow McSween), submitted to arrest, and remained in jail until he provided that testimony at a grand jury hearing, Wallace would release him with a pardon for his former crimes. The Kid agreed and named Dolan, Evans, and William Campbell—all his own sworn enemies—as Chapman's killers. Four days later, with Tom O'Folliard now his constant companion, he surrendered to Sheriff Kimbrell. After his grand jury testimony in April, Dolan and Campbell were indicted and Evans was named an accessory in the Chapman murder. Confined as "special prisoners" in an empty building across from the jail, Bonney and O'Folliard waited impatiently for the promised release and pardon, but hearing nothing from the governor, escaped on June 17. Billy the Kid returned to the trade he knew best, horse stealing. Lew Wallace, who had never intended to pardon a killer like Bonney, responded by issuing a $500 reward notice for his capture.[38] In January 1880 a man named Joe Grant, reputed to be a bounty hunter, became the latest in the Kid's list of murder victims, shot dead in a Fort Sumner saloon.[39]

Pat Garrett was elected Lincoln County sheriff in 1880. He knew from the outset that his success would be measured by how he handled the problem of the young desperado called Billy the Kid, who was still terrorizing Lincoln County. In the fall of 1880 counterfeit bills began showing up in Lincoln County. The U.S. Treasury Service took notice, and secret service agent Azariah F. Wild was sent to investigate. Wild soon determined that the phony currency originated somewhere in the East but was being passed in New Mexico by Billy Bonney and Billie Wilson. Since Bonney's reputation as a killer was so fearsome, Wild asked U.S. Marshal John Sherman for help in running the pair down, but he was met with a refusal. Concluding that the Kid had Sherman scared to death, Wild formed his own posse of men who were undaunted by young punks like Bonney and Wilson—Sheriff George Kimbrell, sheriff-elect Pat Garrett, John Hurley,[40] Frank Stewart,[41] Joseph C. Lea, and Ben Ellis—and obtained commissions for all of them as deputy U.S. marshals. However, Wild's elaborate plan to capture the wanted men had to be scrapped when his reports to Washington, including his capture plans, were taken from a stagecoach that was held up by outlaws.[42]

Exasperated by this debacle and certain that good old-fashioned man-hunting techniques rather than complicated schemes were needed, Garrett took over. To Wild's seven-man posse he added a number of others, including Barney Mason and Robert "Bob" Olinger,[43] and led them in a sweep of the country between Roswell and Fort Sumner, checking out all of the places Billy the Kid had been known to frequent in his travels. The net he spread did not encircle the big fish he sought, but it did land lesser prey: two wanted horse thieves and a real prize, John J. Webb, a convicted murderer who had recently escaped from the Las Vegas jail, gunning down three men in the process.[44] Garrett took his prisoners in chains to Las Vegas and turned them over to the authorities. Although he was still a deputy who would not assume office as sheriff for several weeks, it was obvious by mid-December that Pat Garrett had taken over control of the manhunt for Billy the Kid and his gang. The *Las Vegas Morning Gazette* plainly stated, "Deputy Sheriff Pat Garrett of Lincoln County sent in yesterday for a large supply of ammunition to be poured into the gang of desperadoes should they be foolish enough to resist his posse of determined men. . . . He has telegraphed the sheriff of Fort Griffin, Texas, that he has the man he is after, and claims the $1,500 reward offered for him, for his party. . . . The worst members of 'the Kid's' band are still at large but their capture is merely a question of time."[45]

During this period a posse from Texas joined Garrett's man-hunting force. The Kid had expanded his horse theft operation to include cattle rustling in Texas, thus incensing William "Outlaw Bill" Moore, manager of the LX Texas Panhandle spread. Moore dispatched a crew of gun-handy cowboys under the leadership of Charlie Siringo to the neighboring territory to kill or capture the notorious outlaw. He was met there by Frank Stewart, who as a former stock detective for the Texas Panhandle ranchers was well acquainted with Siringo and most of his men. He directed them to the Garrett posse.[46]

MAN-HUNTERS OF THE OLD WEST

From the combined posse members assembled at White Oaks, Garrett selected nine he wanted to back him in what he hoped would be his last hard, dangerous search for the Kid's gang. After choosing two of his own, Frank Stewart and Barney Mason, he picked seven of Siringo's crew: Lon Chambers, Lee Hall, Jim East, Tom Emory, Louis Bousman, Bob Williams, and Cal Polk.

On December 15, in freezing temperatures, he led these men some forty-five miles, camped for the night, and rode the next morning into Puerto de Luna, where he added four more to his posse—Juan and Jose Roibal, Charles Rudolph, and George Wilson—and pushed on to the Gayheart ranch, twenty-five miles from Fort Sumner. Well aware that the saloons and cantinas of Fort Sumner, where the Kid and his gang would likely be carousing, were patronized mostly by Hispanics, Garrett sent Jose Roibal ahead to mingle with the crowds and see if the Kid was there, and if he was, which followers might be with him. Jose returned to report that the Kid was there together with gang members Billie Wilson, Charlie Bowdre, and Tom Pickett. Another notorious outlaw, Dave Rudabaugh,[47] was reveling with them.

Early the next day Garrett and the posse rode into Fort Sumner as a bad snowstorm threatened. Positioning his men on the town's outskirts, Garrett and Mason slipped in to reconnoiter and learned that the Kid, having gotten wind of the posse's approach, had departed with his gang for the Wilcox-Brazil ranch about twenty miles away. Rather than leading his tired posse members on jaded horses through heavy snow drifts to a likely gun battle against deadly marksmen in fortified ranch positions, Garrett came up with a clever scheme to have his quarry come to him. Garret reasoned that if the Kid thought the disappointed posse had returned to Roswell, he would bring his cohorts back to Fort Sumner to celebrate, so he had a young Hispanic named Jose Valdez write a note indicating the posse's departure and sent him off to take it to Bonney at the ranch. Valdez rode off and Garrett set his trap. He and his posse moved into some empty buildings on the edge of town and waited.

The storm had dropped a foot of snow, but skies had cleared, and now the night was bright with reflected moonlight. Lon Chambers was standing guard and several others were playing poker when all came alive as it became clear the plan had worked perfectly. Posse member Cal Polk, in his imaginative grammar, syntax, and spelling style, would later write an account of what happened: "Lon come to the door and said he [saw] well armed men coming. We grabed up our guns and stept out in the shade of a high doby wall. They come on up until about 10 yards of us." Garrett ordered them to throw up their hands, but "they jerked their guns out," and the shooting started. "They was about 40 shots fired." The gang galloped off through the heavy gun smoke, but as it lifted, one rider came back, and Polk heard him say, "Don't shoot me for I am killed."[48] It was Tom O'Folliard. He lived about ten minutes more.

Choosing not to pursue the gang through the snow at night, Garrett waited to see what the morrow would bring. In the morning rancher Emanuel Brazil rode in and informed Garrett that the gang was at his ranch. The Kid had sent him into town to find out what the posse was planning and report back to him, but his sympathies were with the lawmen and not the outlaws, he said, and he sought advice on how to proceed. Garrett sent him back to his ranch with instructions to stay there if the gang remained, but to return to Fort Sumner and inform him if they had gone. About midnight Brazil was back. The gang was gone, he said, he knew not where.

By dawn the next morning Garrett's men were circling the Wilcox-Brazil ranch, looking for tracks in the snow. Finding a trail heading due east, Garrett concluded that the outlaws' destination was Stinking Springs, an overnight way station for cattle drivers and sheep herders, and had everyone saddle up.

Darkness had fallen when the posse approached the rude structure. Garrett sent Stewart and a few others around to cover the opposite side while he and the rest worked their way up an arroyo close to the front of the hut. All wrapped blankets around themselves against the cold and, in Cal Polk's words, "lay there until day lite half froze."

Shortly after dawn Charlie Bowdre emerged and put a feedbag on his horse. Then, said Polk, the posse "drew a beede on him with our winchesters," and Garrett again ordered him to raise his hands. Again Bowdre disobeyed; he "jerked out 2 pistols and fired at us and at the same time we fired." Mortally wounded, Bowdre "droped his pistols and come realing to worge [toward] us. He said something like I wish, I wish," and died.

Billy the Kid called from the hut, "Is that you Pat out there?" to which Garrett answered yes. Bonney said, "Why dont you come up like a man and give us a fair fite."

Garrett replied, "I dont aim to," and Bonney retorted, "That is what I thought of you, you old long logged S—— B——."

The outlaws began reaching out the door and leading their horses inside. They had two in when the posse fired and dropped the third in the doorway. The frightened horses inside became unruly and were turned loose. When Garrett's men built a fire to warm up, Garrett and the Kid had another exchange of pleasantries, which was later relayed by Polk. Bonney asked, "Pat have you got anything out there to eat?" to which Garrett said yes. Bonney offered, "We have got some in here if you will let us come and get wood to cook it with."

Garrett replied, "All rite you can all come out after wood if you want too," to which Bonney said, "You go to H—— you cowardly S—— B——."

Knowing he held all the cards, Garrett simply waited. It took an entire day, but at sundown Polk saw "a little white rag stuck out the winder on a stick." Then, Polk said, "Ruderbay [Rudabaugh] come out with his hands up [and] told Pat that Billy wanted to surrender . . . and wanted to know where Pat would carry them. Pat says to Las Vegas. Ruderbay says if we hafto go to Las Vegas, we will die rite here for the Mexacans will mob us there. Pat says we will carry you to [Santa Fe]." An agreement was struck. On Garrett's assurance that they would be taken to Santa Fe and not Las Vegas, the outlaws came out with their hands up and then sat by the fire and had supper.[49]

Pat Garrett, like many lawmen before, during, and after his time— even to this day—held the strong conviction that promises made to dishonorable felons were not binding on the arresting officer, as the person he was promising, being notoriously dishonest, was not worthy of mutual trust. He had every intention of taking his prisoners to Las Vegas, the nearest railroad point, but he would also defend his wards to the death from any attempt by the Mexicans there to mob them.

After escorting Billy Bonney, Dave Rudabaugh, Billie Wilson, and Tom Pickett in manacles back to the Wilcox-Brazil ranch, he sent someone to Stinking Springs to fetch Bowdre's body before prairie scavengers found it. He then led the party on to Fort Sumner, where he had the unpleasant duty of informing Mrs. Bowdre that she was a widow. He also told the sobbing woman that he would personally pay for a burial suit for her husband. The officers and their prisoners then left for Las Vegas.

They reached their destination the day after Christmas and, since the news of their feat had preceded them, were met by a large crowd. Threats were shouted, especially at Rudabaugh, who was particularly hated by the local residents for killing a Hispanic jailor in a failed attempt to break J. J. Webb out of the town's calaboose back in April. But at this juncture there was no mob action.

Writers for both local papers, the *Optic* and the *Gazette*, rushed to the jail to interview Billy the Kid, who had garnered so much attention in recent months. The *Optic* reporter described the young outlaw as having "a bold and yet pleasant cast of countenance," and said that he "laughed heartily" when told that New Mexico newspapers claimed that his societal threat was exceeded only by Apache war chief Victorio.[50]

The *Gazette* writer expanded more on Bonney's appearance, saying that at about five feet eight and 140 pounds, he was "slightly built and lithe [with] a frank and open countenance, looking like a schoolboy, with the traditional silky fuzz on his upper lip." His "clear blue eyes [had] a 'roughish snap' about them." With light hair and complexion, he was "quite a handsome looking fellow, the only imperfection being two prominent front teeth, slightly protruding like a squirrel's teeth."[51]

Pat Garrett had been too busy to take note of the passing of Christmas Day, but he had good reason to feel proud of himself that yuletide season. In less than two months after he was elected sheriff, he had led a posse that killed two of Billy the Kid's gang, he had captured and jailed its feared and elusive leader and its remaining members as well as two dangerous murderers, Webb and Rudabaugh, and he had accomplished all of this even before actually taking office. It was a remarkable achievement that he could be justifiably proud of.

He had one last chore to do before returning to Lincoln and taking the oath of office on New Year's Day of 1881. He had to board a train for Santa Fe with his prisoners and turn them over to the authorities there. Believing that with the assistance of Frank Stewart and Barney Mason he could handle that job without additional help, on the morning of December 27 he dismissed the other posse members and, together with his two deputies, headed for the jail to gather up his charges.

There he ran into his first problem of the day. The jailor was willing to release Bonney and Wilson to Garrett, but refused to turn over Pickett and Rudabaugh, saying both were wanted for local offenses. Garrett replied that he had no warrant for Pickett and that Las Vegas could have him, but that federal charges pending against Rudabaugh took precedence over municipal or territorial charges, and as a deputy U.S. marshal, he demanded his prisoner. After a lengthy heated argument, the jailor finally released Rudabaugh, and Garrett and his two deputies marched the three prisoners to the depot, where an even more dangerous difficulty awaited.

The station was packed with a crowd of armed and angry Mexicans who seemed intent on taking Rudabaugh from the officers and administering hempen justice. The officers pushed through the mob and got their prisoners onboard a private car assigned to them, only to find that the Mexicans had dragged the engineer from the locomotive to prevent its moving. A local deputy sheriff, backed by five others, forced his way into the private car and demanded Rudabaugh. But faced with Garrett's drawn pistol and stern command to back off, the group retreated. They "slid to the ground," as Garrett (or his ghostwriter) later put it, "like a covey of hardback turtles off the banks of the Pecos."[52]

Bonney and Wilson, knowing they were not the cause of the uproar, stayed calm throughout these tense moments, and the Kid even seemed to be enjoying it, but Rudabaugh was white-faced and panicky. Garrett pushed him into a seat and promised that he would protect the prisoners as best he could, and if it came to a fight, he would arm them so they could defend themselves.

At this critical moment help arrived from two directions in the form of Garrett's discharged posse members and Deputy U.S. Marshal J. F. Morley. When word of the railroad station disturbance had reached the saloon where Garrett's posse was celebrating, they quickly got their handguns and ran to the depot, where about three hundred Mexicans were gathered.

He and the others, according to Polk, "held our guns drawn by our legs and worked our way thrue the crowd as if we were passengers and when we jumped up on the steps . . . turned and threw down on the Mexicans." Garrett, pistol in hand, said, "Come inside boys and get at a winder . . . , dont burn powder for nothing. When the first shot is fired, all of you kill a man every shot and we will unchain the prisners and arm them." It was then that Deputy Marshal Morley climbed into the engineer's station and got the train moving. Said Polk, "The engine spun on track . . . and then it run out from under the greezers. So [we] went to Santefee with the boys."[53]

After turning their prisoners over to federal officers in Santa Fe, Garrett and his men returned to Las Vegas while newspapers throughout the territory applauded their achievement. "Every law-abiding man will be delighted to hear that [the Kid and his followers] were landed safely . . . in jail," gushed editor Charles W. Greene of the *Santa Fe New Mexican* in his December 28 edition. "Sheriff Pat Garrett and his posse of brave men are to be thanked."

But Garrett and his posse were expecting more than expressions of gratitude; they were interested in the reward money for the capture of Bonney that had been publicly announced. But Governor Wallace was not in the capital—his just-published novel *Ben Hur*, an instant success, had sold out its initial five thousand copies, and he had gone east to arrange additional printings—so Garrett and Stewart called on acting governor William G. Ritch to ask about the reward.

Ritch refused to pay the money, saying Governor Wallace had personally issued the reward notice, so he, as acting governor, was not responsible and could not draw the money from the treasury. Additionally, the reward notice had specified capture and delivery of the Kid to "any sheriff of New Mexico," but in December 1880 Pat Garrett was not yet officially a sheriff, and he had not delivered Bonney to any other sheriff; therefore he had not strictly complied with the terms of the offer.[54]

Garrett and his men, stunned by this obvious obfuscation, were joined in their outrage by several territorial newspapers. Remarking that the reward was "very small," the *Santa Fe New Mexican* editor thought it "should be promptly and cheerfully paid over to the men who had done New Mexico such a great service."[55] Citizens stepped into the breach. Marcus Brunswick and W. T. Thornton of Las Vegas personally gave Garrett $500 and began a subscription campaign in the town for more. By New Year's Day $900 had been raised, prompting J. H. Koogler, editor of the *Gazette*, to remark that his only regret was that the amount wasn't $1,000, "for their expenses have been great, while the risks they ran cannot be estimated in a monetary point of view."[56] Koogler, as well as Garrett and his posse, must have been relieved when he was able to report two weeks later that Governor Wallace had ordered payment of the $500 reward.[57]

With his share of the reward money plus the four dollars daily per diem and the six and one-half cents per mile that the county granted him for his stalking of the Billy the Kid gang, Pat Garrett, in his first months as sheriff, was financially better off than he had been for some time. By August of 1881 he was able to purchase a small ranch and a modest hotel in Lincoln.[58]

Lew Wallace, basking in his *Ben Hur* fame and no doubt weary of the turmoil in New Mexico, tendered his resignation as governor on March 9, 1881. President Garfield named Lionel A. Sheldon to replace him.

Meanwhile the felons Garrett had corralled were still making headlines. In January, Rudabaugh was tried and convicted of robbing the U.S. mail and sentenced to a ninety-nine-year prison term, but the sentence was stayed so that he could be tried in Las Vegas for the murder of the jailer. Before his transfer to Las Vegas, however, he conspired with Bonney and other inmates of the Santa Fe jail to break out. But the plot was thwarted by Sheriff Romulo Martinez and Deputy U.S. Marshal Tony Neis, who discovered the escape tunnel the inmates had begun, and after that kept the most desperate prisoners separated.[59]

In March the Kid and Billie Wilson, under heavy guard, were taken by train to Las Cruces, and from there by wagon to Mesilla, where they were to stand trial. Under indictment for two crimes, Bonney was tried twice, first for the killing of Buckshot Roberts, and second for the murder of Sheriff Brady and Deputy Hindman. On April 6, 1881, the first indictment was quashed by Judge Warren H. Bristol on a technicality.[60] However, a jury convicted Bonney for the Brady and Hindman murders, and Judge Bristol sentenced him to be hanged May 13.[61]

To prevent any untoward occurrence—an escape, rescue, or assassination attempt—during the transport of the prisoner to Lincoln, where Sheriff Garrett was to perform the execution, a formidable force of fighting men was assembled at Mesilla on April 21. Garrett had assigned Deputy Sheriffs Dave Woods and Bob Olinger to the task, but to insure their success, they enlisted the aid of five others: Billy Mathews, John Kinney, D. M. Reade, Tom Williams, and W. A. Lockhart.[62]

The seven guards and their single prisoner arrived without incident in Lincoln, where Bonney was incarcerated on the second floor of the empty Murphy-Dolan store, recently purchased by the county for use as a courthouse. The doors and windows were not barred, and the Kid, restrained by heavy ankle chains, was placed in what had been Murphy's bedroom. Another small room, once the bedroom of Murphy's housekeeper, contained several other prisoners who had been arrested for minor crimes and were not considered dangerous or likely to escape. Across from the stairwell, the former bedroom of Jimmy Dolan and John Riley now served as Sheriff Garrett's armory behind a locked door. In these quarters Billy the Kid was to remain for the next three weeks, guarded by Deputies Olinger and James W. Bell,[63] with only occasional trips to the outhouse behind the building, until that fateful day when Sheriff Garrett would march him to the gallows.

On April 27 Garrett departed Lincoln to purchase timber for the scaffold to hang the Kid, and to perform another onerous duty of a county sheriff, the collection of taxes. About noon the following day, Olinger led the other inmates to the Wortley Hotel for their midday meal, leaving Deputy Bell alone with Bonney. What happened then has been a topic of conjecture and speculation by western historians ever since. What is known for certain is that somehow Bonney got hold of a pistol—perhaps Bell's, perhaps one hidden for him in the outhouse by a friend—and shot and killed Bell. Olinger, returning to the courthouse, was frozen in his tracks by the sight of Bonney in an upstairs window, grinning at him over the twin barrels of Olinger's own shotgun. The Kid triggered off both barrels, and Bob Olinger, blasted with thirty-six buckshot, was dead when he hit the ground. Assisted by the courthouse caretaker, an elderly and terrified German immigrant named Gottfried Gauss, Bonney freed his legs of the shackles, saddled a horse, and armed with two revolvers and a Winchester rifle, galloped off, leaving two dead men in his wake. No one in Lincoln lifted a hand to stop him. The escape artist had done it again. This desperate escape became the basis for Billy the Kid's apotheosis, this young killer's elevation to legendary status.

News of the Kid's remarkable escape caused a sensation in New Mexico. Editor Koogler of the *Las Vegas Morning Gazette* reported that "intense excitement" prevailed in his city, but many found the news hard to believe until confirmation came in a Santa Fe dispatch. He added that the Kid, having "a few old scores to settle [might be] foolish enough to hang around awaiting an opportunity to kill his men." Anyone hunting for him should know "he will make a hard fight, and it will be risky work attempting to take him in, and several are likely to go under in the fight."[64]

The *Santa Fe New Mexican*'s editor opined that the feat Bonney had pulled off rivaled any in the annals of crime.

It surpasses anything of which the Kid had been guilty. . . . His past offenses lose much of their heinousness in comparison with it, and it effectually settles the question of whether the Kid is a cowardly cutthroat or a thoroughly reckless and fearless man. Never before has he faced death boldly or run any great risk in the perpetration of his bloody deeds. Bob Olinger used to say that he was a cur, and that every man he had killed had been murdered in cold blood and without the slightest chance of defending himself. The Kid displayed no disposition to correct this until this last act of his when he taught Olinger by bitter experience that his theory was anything but correct.[65]

Rumors abounded in the days following, suggesting that the Kid had departed New Mexico. The *Gazette* stated flatly, "Billy the Kid has made his escape to Texas."[66] But the rumors were wrong. Bonney remained in southeastern New Mexico, and Sheriff Pat Garrett once again had to take up the hunt for the elusive outlaw.[67]

Governor Ritch, perhaps chagrinned that he had delayed payment of the original reward for Bonney's capture, wasted no time when given another opportunity. On April 30, only two days after the escape, he posted another $500 reward for the capture of the notorious killer.[68]

Garrett knew that if Bonney had remained in the region for the purpose of gunning down his enemies, as many believed, his own name was undoubtedly high on the Kid's death list. He prepared for this manhunt with no intention of taking his quarry alive; this was a case of kill or be killed. To back him up in the hunt, he enlisted two deputies he held in high regard, John W. Poe,[69] and Thomas "Kip" McKinney.[70]

After riding out of Lincoln, the Kid had disappeared into the Capitan Mountains, slipping into the house of a trusted friend, Yginio Salazar, at night for food. When the horse he had ridden from Lincoln broke loose and made its way back home, he stole another mount from a Rio Feliz cow camp, rode to Conejos Springs, camped out, and then continued on to Fort Sumner, where he had many friends (and lovers) and felt he would be safe. Garrett later pieced this itinerary together, but for several weeks, fairly convinced that the Kid was long gone to old Mexico, he and his deputies kept their eyes and ears open for any lead to his whereabouts.

The tip leading to the Kid's demise originated from Pete Maxwell, brother of Paulita, the young girl Bonney was romancing in Fort Sumner.

Although he was considered Billy's good friend, Pete had become increasingly concerned about his young sister's dalliance with a notorious outlaw and deadly killer. He finally sent a messenger into White Oaks informing John Poe that Bonney was in Fort Sumner. Poe relayed this information to Garrett, who was dubious but agreed to go to the town with Poe and McKinney and check it out.

On the night of July 13 the three lawmen camped outside Fort Sumner. The next morning Garrett sent Poe, a stranger to the townsfolk whom they would not recognize as a law officer, to see what additional information he could pick up. Poe reported back that he had learned nothing definite, but casual inquiries about Billy had been met with closed mouths and suspicious glances.

Still dubious about Pete Maxwell's story, Garrett decided to talk to him. Although he believed it unlikely that the Kid was actually somewhere about the Maxwell home, he waited until late that night to be on the safe side. Leaving their horses tethered, he and his deputies walked into town. It was almost midnight when they got to the Maxwell house, a former officer's quarters in the abandoned fort. Poe and McKinney remained out on the veranda as Garrett slipped through an open doorway into the room he knew Pete used as his bedroom and found Maxwell asleep in his bed. Garrett woke him and in whispered tones began questioning him about Bonney.

Outside Poe and McKinney saw a young man emerging from the darkness and walking briskly toward them. He was very close when, obviously startled to discern two strangers lounging on Maxwell's porch, he pulled a pistol and demanded, "*Quién es?*" ("Who is it?"). Whirling, he stepped through the doorway and demanded in Spanish, "Pedro, who are those men outside?" The words were hardly out of his mouth before he saw in the darkened room the figure of a man at Maxwell's bedside and blurted again, "*Quién es?*"

"*Él es!*" Maxwell whispered to Garrett. "It's him!"

In the swift, long-practiced motion of the experienced western gunfighter, Pat Garrett pulled his single-action .45, cocked the hammer as the barrel centered on the figure framed in the backlit doorway, and pulled the trigger. Half-blinded by the flash, Garrett rolled away from the bed and triggered another ineffective shot before bolting out the door just ahead of the terrified Pete Maxwell.

In the little room that was still reverberating from the roar of the gunshots and filled with smoke from the black powder charge, Billy the Kid Bonney lay dead with Garrett's first bullet just above his heart.

Not surprisingly, the news of Garrett's extermination of Billy the Kid, following closely on Bonney's sensational escape from custody, made headlines throughout New Mexico, and Garrett was widely acclaimed. The *Las Vegas Gazette* reported that upon hearing the news, "prominent citizens of Roswell and the lower Pecos [wrote] expressing satisfaction at the brave deed." J. C. Lea suggested "a liberal contribution" be taken up for "Sheriff Garrett as part compensation for the dangers, hardships and risks he has taken in capturing and bringing to justice this noted desperado." A. H. Whetstone of Roswell wrote that shouts "of rejoicing will go up in this country at the death of this shrewd thief and desperate murderer. The words, 'God bless Pat Garrett for his good work' will escape from many a lip, and people will never cease to love him for his great achievements. He has already accomplished wonders during his short administration."[71]

Not limited to New Mexico, the exuberance was expressed in journals across the nation. Newspapers like the Saint Louis *Globe Democrat* ran lengthy front-page stories about the Kid and his criminal career and heaped praise on the man who had brought it to an abrupt end. These accounts were picked up and reprinted as far east as New York City.[72] The editor of a Texas paper extolled "the hero of the hour in New Mexico . . . , the king lion in the Territorial menagerie . . . , PATSEY GARRETT."[73]

The news even crossed the Atlantic and was featured in the August 18, 1881 edition of the staid *Times* of London, which excerpted accounts from the *Santa Fe New Mexican*:

> William Bonney, *alias* "the Kid," is dead. No report could have caused a more general feeling of gratification than this, and when it was further announced that the faithful and brave Pat Garrett, he who has been the mainstay of law and order in Lincoln county, the chief reliance of the people in the dark days, when danger lurked on every hand, has accomplished the crowning feat of his life by bringing down the fierce and implacable foe single-handed, the sense of satisfaction was heightened to one of delight. . . .
>
> All possible honours are being paid to Sheriff Garrett, his slayer, for his brave pursuit of the outlaw. . . . Garrett has never ceased

to dog the footsteps. He said soon after the escape of the criminal that he would "follow him to the end," and he has done so with persistency, determination, and bravery through long and anxious months, finally to meet with a success which entitles him to the gratitude and respect of the people of the territory.

As with his earlier attempt to collect reward money for his first capture of Bonney, Garrett had difficulty collecting the second reward. Newly appointed Governor Lionel Sheldon, unfamiliar with the proceedings from before he took office, left it up to Ritch, the acting governor who had posted the reward notice, to handle Garrett's payment request. Ritch, as before, withheld payment, questioning again whether Garrett had abided by the specific provisions of the notice. Seven months would pass before the reward was finally paid. Happily for Garrett, later in 1882 he received an unexpected windfall, a purse of more than $1,150 in donations from private citizens raised by D. M. Easton and James J. Dolan, two of his ardent political supporters.[74]

Canes were in fashion as part of a well-dressed gentleman's attire in these years, and the residents of Silver City, New Mexico, where Bonney began his criminal career, honored Garrett with the presentation of a walking stick made of wood taken from the Kid's home, topped with a golden head and "appropriate inscriptions."[75]

Pat Garrett's remaining time as Lincoln County sheriff went smoothly. There were, of course, a few dangerous felons to collar. Late in 1881 Garrett nabbed a desperado named Tom Quillan who was wanted for the murder of a Texas deputy sheriff and held him in Las Vegas awaiting the arrival of Texas authorities.[76]

Back in December 1880 at Puerto de Luna, a troublesome character named Mariano Leigo had attempted to shoot Garrett, but according to a news account, Pat "was too quick for him and broke his shoulder blade by a well-aimed shot." Tried for assault with intent to kill at Las Vegas in September 1881, Leigo got off with a small fine. According to the *Gazette*, folks at Puerto de Luna were "incensed at the verdict" and would certainly lynch Leigo if he ever returned to that town.[77]

Another who might have been inclined to take Garrett's life was Billy the Kid's brother, Joe Antrim, who had become a professional gambler in Colorado following the death of their mother. Newspapers reported a rumor that Antrim was gunning for Garrett. *Las Vegas Gazette* editor Koogler noted that although Antrim was not "a desperate character [he was] a hard one. It is said that he has a desire for the life of but one man, our sheriff, Pat Garrett, who killed 'the Kid.'"[78] Garrett may have kept an eye out for Bonney's brother, but he evidently never saw him until August 1882, when the two met in a Trinidad, Colorado, hotel and conversed for several hours, mostly about the Kid and his killing. At the end of this discussion they shook hands and went separate ways, never to meet again. Interviewed later by news reporters, Antrim said that after that talk he had a better understanding of Garrett's difficult position at the time of the killing and of his absolute need to shoot first. He said he carried no ill will against the sheriff.[79]

Reacting to the great spurt of newspaper publicity about Bonney and Garrett in 1881, pulp writers, hoping to profit from the widespread interest, slapped together books purporting to tell the Kid's life story. No less than eight of these had appeared when a former New York City newspaper reporter named Marshall Ashman "Ash" Upson put pen to paper to, as he claimed, "correct the thousand false statements which have appeared in the public newspapers and in yellow-covered cheap novels" with a thoroughly factual Billy the Kid biography. To accomplish this feat, he was aided by Billy's slayer, Pat Garrett; to add an even greater appearance of absolute verisimilitude, Garrett's name would appear as the author of the work.[80]

A self-described "rolling stone," Upson had lived and worked all over the country before settling down, more or less, in Lincoln County in 1872. He was enumerated in the 1880 U.S. census living next door to (if not with) Rebecca Stafford, the mother of the Olinger brothers, and became acquainted with Pat Garrett around this time. By August 1881 he was so chummy with the sheriff that he moved in with the Garretts, in the new Roswell home that Pat had purchased, and began work on the book. After "a two-month blaze of work," it was published in March 1882 by editor Charles W. Greene of the *Santa Fe New Mexican* under the seemingly interminable title: *The Authentic Life of Billy, the Kid: The Noted Desperado of the Southwest, Whose Deeds of Daring and Blood Made His Name a Terror in New Mexico Arizona and Northern Mexico, By Pat F. Garrett, Sheriff of Lincoln County, N.M., by Whom He*

Was Finally Hunted down and Captured by Killing Him, A Faithful and Interesting Narrative.[81]

Since Pat Garrett, the supposed author of the work, had no personal knowledge of the Kid's early life, the first few chapters were, in author Frederick Nolan's words, "full of Upson's grandiloquence and fabrications," but the account starting with Bonney's appearance in Lincoln County came from Garrett and had the ring of the authenticity it claimed.[82]

After reading the book, *Gazette* editor Koogler recognized the disparity in the two parts but still praised it highly. The first chapters, he admitted, were "slightly imaginary, [but] from the beginning of the Lincoln county war until the final death of Bonney . . . , the narrative is as true as it can be written. Bonney killed every man there charged to him and in just about the manner alleged." The Lincoln County War "was just the kind of strife which the Kid would enjoy and in which he would become noted. He took advantage of an enemy whenever he could and murdered without compassion or remorse." Koogler thought the book was valuable as history and that it would "meet with a large sale."[83]

Koogler was prescient in his prediction that the Lincoln County War, and particularly the part Billy the Kid played in it, would be studied meticulously and written about by historians for many years and that *The Authentic Life* would be a primary source of information. However, he missed the mark with his final line. Sales of the book were abysmal, in large part because of its cheap production quality and poor editing. Koogler's competition, the *Las Vegas Optic*, in a scathing comment was quick to point this out: "Pat Garrett is sick at Roswell. Probably 'The Life of Billy the Kid' in print as executed by the *New Mexican* gave him gangrene of the bowels."[84]

Upson accepted no blame for the book's financial failure, but pointed the finger at Greene and Garrett, saying Garrett insisted on giving the book to a publisher who "swindled badly in his contract" and did not know how to market a book. Upson went on to claim that although Garrett's name appeared as the author, he himself "wrote every word of it."[85]

For reasons never explained, Garrett did not run for reelection as sheriff in 1882. To reciprocate for James Dolan's political support in 1880, he backed the former House leader for the job, although his friend and fellow officer, John Poe, was also running. By 1882 Dolan and the House were in disrepute, however, and Poe won handily.

The political battles of New Mexico had always been only a half-step away from violence. When Garrett allowed his name to be entered as a candidate for election to the territorial council in 1882, he found himself in a mud-slinging battle that culminated with an incident in which he lost his temper and almost killed an adversary. Newspaper editors routinely took sides in these political disputes, and the editor of the *Rio Grande Republican* of Las Cruces was no exception. He attacked Garrett vehemently, calling him "illiterate" and suggesting that the fame he received by killing Billy the Kid had "upset his brain."[86] In its September 16, 1882, issue the *Republican* published a letter, signed only "X," castigating Garrett as being unfit for election to the council because of his lack of education, adding, "The praise of the newspapers, together with the toadying flattery of those surrounding him, has made him egotistic to a superlative degree." Suspecting Lincoln attorney W. M. Roberts of being X, Garrett confronted him three days later, called him a "God damned liar," pulled his revolver, and slammed the barrel over the man's head at least twice, leaving him unconscious and bleeding in the street.[87] Surprisingly, no charges were filed against the sheriff for this assault, and when Garrett was defeated for a council seat shortly thereafter, the matter was forgotten.

Garrett had a ranch in Lincoln County, but raising cattle was not exciting enough for him. When offered a leadership job chasing down cattle rustlers in the Texas Panhandle in 1884 he leaped at the chance.

For more than a year panhandle ranchers had been having labor trouble. In 1883 some of their cowhands, led by LS Ranch foreman Tom Harris, had gone on strike, demanding higher wages. The ranchers refused the demands and blacklisted the strike organizers. The work stoppage was of short duration, but as dissension mounted in the strikers' ranks by the spring of 1884, it was clear to ranch management that Tom Harris and other disgruntled cowboys, organized as the Get Even Cattle Company, had turned to rustling the cattle of their former employers.

In retaliation the ranchers employed Garrett to put together a force of range riders, tough fighting men, to put an end to the practice. The outfit Pat created came to be called the Home Rangers.[88] He brought along his old Lincoln County compadre, Barney Mason, as well as George Jones, a veteran New Mexico cowboy. From the LS Ranch he signed up Lon Chambers, who had backed him in his memorable Billy the Kid gang roundup; Ed King, a gunman of note;[89] former buffalo hunter G. H. "Kid"

Dobbs; Charlie Reason; Bill Anderson; John Land; and Albert E. Perry, a former stock detective, whom he enlisted as his sergeant.[90]

Throughout the summer of 1884 Garrett's rangers roamed the rangeland rounding up cattle with defaced brands and driving them into Tascosa for sale or butchering. Especially plentiful were animals carrying the tabletop brand, a rectangle with four extended legs, which was considered a classic mavericking brand by reputable ranchers.

The tabletop was a registered brand of Bill Gatlin, a particularly unsavory character who had been a leader in the strike,[91] and his partner, Wade Woods. When the Home Rangers confiscated thirty-three cows bearing the tabletop brand, Gatlin, a career outlaw, used the law to his advantage. Aided by a Tascosa attorney, he demanded reparations, threatened Oldham County officials with a $15,000 lawsuit, and hinted at bringing criminal action against the commissioners. In a settlement $800 was paid to Gatlin.[92]

Garrett's employers had not been idle, however. Presented with the evidence he had uncovered, a grand jury brought in 159 indictments in the fall of 1884, mainly for cattle theft. Garrett's rangers, armed with arrest warrants, swept the Canadian River valley for the accused. A general exodus of rustlers ensued, but three wanted men—Gatlin, Woods, and Charlie Thompson—refused to be driven out.

When Garrett learned in February 1885 that the three obstinate hard cases were holed up in a range rockhouse about forty miles west of Tascosa, he led his Home Rangers there accompanied by Oldham County sheriff Jim East. Guided by Kid Dobbs, who had hunted buffalo in that section, they made a night ride through a howling blizzard to the site, reaching it about dawn. (For Garrett, East, and Chambers the scene when they arrived must have been highly reminiscent of that bitter cold morning four years before when they had been in the posse that cornered Billy the Kid's gang at Stinking Springs.)

They found the rockhouse occupied by almost a dozen cowboys who had converged there to escape the wintry blasts. Tom Harris emerged to demand an explanation as to why Garrett had surrounded the house with a bunch of armed men. When Garrett informed him that he had warrants for Gatlin, Woods, and Thompson but had no problem with any of the others, Harris led nine men out of the rude structure. Woods was gone, he said, but Gatlin and Thompson remained inside, ready to fight.

Jim East, who had worked cattle with both recalcitrants, did not believe they would fire on him and volunteered to parley with them. After a lengthy confab, he talked Thompson into surrendering, but Gatlin held out, yelling defiantly. Waving a six-shooter, he said he would fight to the death and take Garrett and a bunch of his men along with him. East stayed cool and continued his cajolery until Gatlin finally agreed to give up, on East's assurance that he and Garrett would protect him from any mob action.

Tascosa had no jail, so Gatlin and Thompson were chained to the floor of an adobe hut and guarded by Constable Jim Moore, but their incarceration was of short duration. That very night they freed themselves from their irons with files smuggled in by friends and rode off on horses that had also been prudently provided.[93]

This last bit of business, the inability of local authorities to hold miscreants he and his men had labored hard to collar, finished the Home Ranger episode for Pat Garrett. He had long suspected that he had been hired to kill rustlers, not to arrest them and bring them in for trial, and that was not his way. Garrett resigned his captaincy of the organization, and it was disbanded.

Garrett returned to his family and concentrated on his little spread. For a time the New Mexico press took little notice of the man whose exploits had filled their pages a few years before.[94] However, in early 1886 a small item in a Lincoln paper showed that the veteran lawman's eye for lawbreakers was still as sharp as ever:

> Pat Garrett met a Mexican [on] horseback a few days ago, and remarked to a gentleman riding with him that he believed the Mexican was a horse thief. That very night Mr. Garrett received a card from Colfax county, N.M., offering $100 reward for the arrest of a horse thief answering the description of the man he met earlier in the day, to a dot. Garrett and Mr. [Lucius] Dills took in the gentleman, landing him here in the jail last week. The thief got away with a horse, saddle, bridle, pair of field glasses and a six-shooter.[95]

In the late 1880s Garrett invested in several business concerns including a livery stable and a stage line. In an endeavor to turn the arid Pecos Valley of New Mexico into lush farmland, he partnered in irrigation projects but met with little success. In 1890 he ran unsuccessfully as an independent for sheriff of newly formed Chaves County. Disenchanted with the territory whose residents had once hailed him as a hero but now seemed to ignore him, in April 1891 he moved his family to Uvalde, Texas, where he bred racehorses and explored possibilities for other irrigation projects.[96]

At Uvalde he renewed acquaintanceship with two important figures from his Lincoln County sheriff days: the hard drinking, womanizing Ash Upson, who had not mended his ways, and Billie Wilson, whom Garrett had collared along with Bonney and Rudabaugh at Stinking Springs. After his conviction, Wilson had escaped to Texas, reformed, married, and started a family, and now he was a customs inspector at Langtry. Seeing the transformation in the man, Garrett worked to get him a full pardon and was eventually successful. Amazingly, Wilson, who had ridden with one of the most famous outlaws in Old West history, later became sheriff of Terrell County, Texas, and on June 14, 1918, he died heroically in the line of duty, shot down by a man he was trying to arrest.[97]

In February 1896 the mysterious disappearance of Albert J. Fountain and his small son drew Garrett back to the territory where he had first gained fame. Adventurer, war veteran, military officer, duelist, newspaper publisher, politician, and attorney, Albert Jennings Fountain was one of the most colorful and best-known men in New Mexico. Married to a Hispanic woman—like Pat Garrett and many southwestern pioneers—he fathered six children. On February 1, 1896, Fountain, with his nine-year-old son Henry, was returning from Lincoln, where he had gone to secure rustling indictments against rancher Oliver M. Lee, and his henchman, William "Bill" McNew, both noted gunmen as well as accused cattle thieves. Fountain felt he had an ironclad case against the pair, and the prospect of their incarceration was particularly sweet because Lee was the right-hand man of attorney and longtime Fountain adversary, Albert Bacon Fall.

At the hearing Fountain had been handed a piece of paper threatening his life if he continued the prosecution, so he must have felt some twinges of apprehension as he departed for his Las Cruces home with his small boy beside him on the seat of his buggy. But Fountain, a man of steely nerves who had often faced death before, was not one to be intimidated by anonymous warnings. This, however, was no idle threat, and while crossing the desolate white sands of southern New Mexico, he and his son disappeared forever.

Fountain's family members were concerned when father and son failed to reach home as expected. That concern escalated after a mail carrier told them he had met Fountain on the road and that he had been watching three suspicious-looking horsemen who seemed to be trailing him. Hearing this report, Fountain's wife fainted.

News of the strange disappearance "spread like wild-fire and a party was immediately organized, headed by Albert and Jack Fountain, sons of Colonel Fountain, to search for Colonel Fountain, if alive, or find his body if dead."[98] Shortly afterward another party, led by Fountain's close friend, political associate, and noted man-hunter Major H. W. W. Llewellyn, joined in the search.

The area where the buggy had left the road was identified, and later, several miles away, the buggy itself was found, but there was no sign of the occupants, and blood stains, scattered belongings, and nearby empty cartridges gave a strong indication of foul play. When additional searches provided no clue to the whereabouts of Fountain and his boy, dead or alive, political friends and enemies of Fountain traded accusations and insults. As the situation in southern New Mexico became increasingly volatile, Governor William T. Thornton decided a tough, hardheaded man with exceptional badge-wearing experience was needed to take charge. Pat Garrett came immediately to mind. Although Garrett was no longer a resident of New Mexico, Thornton thought that might be an advantage, for the celebrated man-hunter who had wiped out Billy the Kid and his gang was now a Texan with no tight political ties to either side of Fountain's cattle rustling case.

Coincident to the uproar in New Mexico over the Fountain disappearance, the city of El Paso, Texas, adjacent to the territory's southeastern border, was in a different state of excitement in February 1896. Boxing promoter Dan Stuart had scheduled a heavyweight title bout between champion Bob Fitzsimmons and challenger Peter Maher to be held there that month, and sportsmen from all over the country, including Pat Garrett, were flocking there to see the big fight.[99] Anxious to talk to Garrett about the Fountain investigation (and perhaps take in the bout himself), Thornton went to El Paso and checked into a hotel. Needing the agreement of the politicians from Doña Ana County (where the Fountain disappearance occurred) before offering Garrett the job, he called them to a meeting in his hotel room. Garrett was in attendance, but only as an observer. The governor gained the attendees' close attention by citing the unresolved Fountain case as an impediment to attaining New Mexico statehood, which was an aim of all present. Then he announced his proposal, the employment of Garrett as a special deputy sheriff with full authority to investigate the Fountain case at a salary of $500 a month. Two men in attendance were engaged in a bitterly fought battle for the office of Doña Ana sheriff and vigorously opposed the idea. Another attendee, Albert Fall, the political boss behind Lee—and a prime suspect in the Fountain disappearance—was noncommittal, and the proposal was rejected.

Undismayed, Thornton convened a second meeting a few days later that was attended by men at a higher level of governmental power. Although their identities were never disclosed, Garrett described them as "the most prominent men of New Mexico." To these big shots the governor proposed hiring Garrett as a private detective to work on the Fountain case at territorial expense, with an expenditure allowance of $150 a month and a flat payment of $8,000 if he was successful in finding and convicting the murderers. To sweeten the offer for Garrett, he reminded him that success in this endeavor would almost certainly ensure his election as sheriff of Doña Ana County.[100] The "prominent men" approved Thornton's plan, and Garrett reluctantly did also. He much preferred the governor's original idea, giving him better command of the situation and freedom of action, but in poor economic straits due to gambling losses and unwise investments, he could not pass up an opportunity to escape his financial dilemma. He moved his family to Las Cruces and began work on the case.

From the first, Oliver Lee and his cohorts, Jim Gililland, Bill McNew, and Bill Carr, had been the only real suspects in the disappearance—and very likely the murder—of Fountain and his boy, but with the political discord in Doña Ana County and the unresolved sheriff's election, no real evidence had been developed to get them indicted.

Thornton realized that Garrett was a man of action, but he was inexperienced as an investigator. He wanted him to be available for the sheriff's job when the dispute was settled, though, and his involvement in the Fountain case assured that. Meanwhile, he called on the Pinkerton Detective Agency to provide the necessary investigative expertise. On March 10 Pinkerton operative J. C. Fraser arrived in Las Cruces.

Garrett and Fraser worked together on the case, but being of entirely different temperaments and law enforcement experience, they did not get along well, and Fraser soon departed to be replaced by operative W. B. Sayers.[101] When, two months later, Numa Reymond finally won the legal battle over the sheriff s office and proved even more difficult to work with than Garrett, the Pinkerton Agency withdrew from the case.

Sheriff Reymond appointed a pal named Oscar Lohman as chief deputy, his second in command. He also offered Garrett a job as an ordinary deputy, but Pat, knowing he could not operate successfully with two unco-operative superiors, refused.

For Garrett the situation seemed hopeless, but forces were at work that changed everything within a few weeks. Exactly how it all came about was never disclosed, but evidently Major Llewellyn and other prominent Las Cruces figures, realizing that the only hope for bringing the Foun-tain murderers to trial was establishing Pat Garrett as Doña Ana County sheriff, came up with $1,000 in bribery money, which convinced Rey-mond and Lohman to tender their resignations. They were gone in April, and Garrett was appointed sheriff. In July he also was appointed a deputy U.S. marshal, and a few months later he ran for re-election as sheriff on the independent ticket and won easily.[102]

For the next two years Garrett worked diligently on the case but always seemed thwarted by Albert Fall's legal maneuvering. Finally, in April 1898 he obtained bench warrants for the arrest of Lee, Gililland, McNew, and Carr for the Fountain murders. He quickly collared McNew and Carr, but the other two were not to be found. Well aware that his evidence against the accused was sketchy and that what he needed was a confes-sion, Garrett relentlessly grilled the pair in custody, but it was to no avail, and at a hearing, Albert Fall destroyed the testimony of Jack Maxwell, the prosecution's chief witness. Carr was released, but even Garrett was surprised when McNew was held and denied bond. Far-distant events then changed the game. On February 15, 1898, the U.S. battleship *Maine* was sunk off the coast of Cuba, and Spain was blamed for the catastrophe. On April 25, as the Fountain case was playing out in New Mexico, the United States declared war on Spain. War fever swept America, and Albert Fall, caught up in it, left his home and job to join the revenge attack on Spanish forces in Cuba. He never got to Cuba, being assigned to the mili-tary's legal department, but nevertheless he was gone for months.

Garrett continued to work on McNew, with promises of a reduced sentence for a confession involving Oliver Lee and others, but he got nowhere when the gunman proved a tough nut to crack. Meanwhile, without their lawyer to protect them from Garrett's clutches, Lee and Gililland hid out in the desert and mountains. It was July before a couple of Garrett's deputies, Jose Espalin and Clinton Llewellyn (a son of the major), learned that the fugitives were holed up in a house at a watering hole called Wildy Well and informed Garrett. Garrett enlisted another deputy, Ben Williams, to join him and the other two to go after the fugitives, and Kent Kearney, a likable young former schoolteacher, implored Garrett to let him come along. Although Kearney was untested in what might well become a gun battle, he was eager and persuasive, and Garrett nodded his approval, a decision he would always regret.

As in his fugitive hunting days of yore, Garrett chose to attack his quarries in the early morning when they were most vulnerable. After a thirty-eight-mile night ride to within a mile of Wildy Well, the posse tethered their horses and proceeded on foot.

Dawn's first light disclosed an adobe house, several outbuildings, a pumphouse, a big water tank mounted on a platform, and a corral holding several horses. Garrett led them stealthily forward to the door of the house. Hearing snoring within, he burst through the doorway with gun drawn, only to find that the occupants were not his quarries, but were the well manager and his family. Lee and Gililland, it turned out, were sleeping on the flat roof of the adobe to escape the midsummer heat. This changed everything for Garrett's plan. The element of surprise was lost, for the commotion below had awakened the fugitives on the roof, and positioned as they were, looking down from behind the low adobe wall surrounding the roof edges, they had a distinct advantage in any gunfight.

A furious gun battle began at once. The young rookie, Kent Kearney, was badly wounded in the first fire. No one else was hit, but it was soon apparent to Garrett that he was in a no-win situation. He called to Lee, asking him to lay down his arms and give himself up, but not unexpectedly, he received a negative response. "I don't think I will," snorted Lee. "I've heard that you intend to kill me."

Garrett assured him the reports were false and again asked him to surrender. Lee was no fool. "Who do you think has the best of it?" he retorted. "You have got yourself into a hell of a close place."

"I know it," Garrett admitted. "How are we going to get out of here?"

"If you pull off, we won't shoot you," said Lee.[103] Taking him at his word, Garrett came out to where Kearney lay, but Lee and Gililland yelled down to let him lie there and move on.

So ended the most humiliating debacle of Pat Garrett's career, walking away under the gunsights of the fugitives he had come to arrest, leaving a wounded posse member behind. Reaching their horses, Garrett and his deputies rode hard to a railroad siding and sent some section hands back for Kearney, who was taken by train to Alamogordo and then to La Luz, where he died the next day.

Within a month of the ignominious Wildy Well battle, America's war with Spain was over and Albert Fall was back working his machinations on behalf of his friend Oliver Lee. Garrett, despite the embarrassing defeat at Wildy Well, had won reelection to the sheriff's office that fall and now held warrants for the arrest of Lee and Gililland for the Kearney killing.[104] Fall knew Garrett would be unrelenting in his search for them, but he also knew Lee would be just as determined not to submit to arrest by Garrett. If they met, one or both would surely end up dead.

The wily attorney concocted a scheme to take the matter out of Garrett's hands. He pressured the territorial legislature to create a new county, carved out of Doña Ana County, which included Lee's landholdings. When accomplished, this would require a transfer of the charges against his clients from Doña Ana to the new county and remove Sheriff Garrett from the picture. It was a brilliant scheme, but when Fall had difficulty getting Governor Miguel Otero's support of the new county idea, he demonstrated how really clever he was. He proposed naming the new county Otero and soon had the governor's approval.

On January 30, 1899, the new county of Otero was formed with Alamogordo the capital and George Curry appointed sheriff. Lee's friend, celebrated author Eugene Manlove Rhodes, engineered the fugitives' surrender after getting Curry's agreement that the fugitives would not be turned over to Garrett to be locked up in the Doña Ana County hoosegow while they were awaiting construction of jail facilities at Alamogordo. The jailing problem was resolved by arrangement with Socorro County sheriff C. F. "Doc" Blackington and called for the detention of the pair in the jail at Socorro until the trial. While Fall had skillfully engineered the removal of his clients' trial from Doña Ana to Otero County, a dispute over the site of the trial began when prosecution lawyers claimed that an impartial jury could not be empaneled in Otero County, where Lee had so many supporters. After much haggling, the decision was made to hold the trial in supposedly neutral Hillsboro in Sierra County.

This sensational case was much more than a murder trial, having become a battle to determine which political party would control the future of New Mexico Territory, with opposing counsels Albert Fall (powerful leader of the Democratic Party) representing the defense and Tom Catron (political boss of the territory's Republican Party) as special counsel for the prosecution. If the accused murderer of a well-known and popular Republican like Fountain and his child were convicted, it would be seen as a serious blow to the Democratic Party and a great Republican victory.

The prosecution chose to try the defendants for the murder of the young boy, leaving trials for the murders of Fountain and Kearney for the future. After jury selection, the trial began on May 29, 1899, and lasted almost a month. Pat Garrett, of course, was an important witness for the prosecution. Much to his disappointment, as well as that of Fountain's family and friends, the jury, perhaps swayed by Fall's remarkable oratorical skills, returned a not guilty verdict, and Lee and Gililland went free. The prosecution, unable to win this, their best case, never pursued the Fountain or Kearney deaths or brought McNew and Carr to trial.

Although the Fountain murder case was the centerpiece of Pat Garrett's term as sheriff of Doña Ana County, there were, of course, other law enforcement responsibilities. When Sheriff George Blalock of Greer County, Oklahoma, traced murder suspect Norman Newman, alias Reed, to the Doña Ana County ranch of W. W. Cox, he called on Sheriff Garrett to assist him in the arrest. Blalock and Garrett, accompanied by his deputy Jose Espalin, drove a buckboard out to the Cox ranch, stopped a short distance away, and Garrett had Blalock hold the horses while he and Espalin approached the building. Entering, they found a man washing dishes at a sink who answered the fugitive's description. Garrett, pistol in hand, asked if his name was Reed, and receiving an affirmative answer, advised him that they had a warrant for his arrest. The man said nothing, but began wiping his wet hands on an apron as Garrett slid his gun back into the scabbard and pulled out his handcuffs. Suddenly the man struck out with a fist and hit Garrett full in the face. The sheriff retaliated, striking him on the head with the handcuffs and knocking him to the floor. As Garrett and Espalin worked to cuff the struggling suspect, another participant entered the fray. A bulldog leaped into the room and began snapping at all the men. With the officers' attention distracted by this intrusion, the fugitive got loose, ran to a nearby meathouse, and pulled a pistol off a shelf. Before he could fire, two pistols roared, and a bullet tore into his heart, killing him instantly.[105]

This affair only acerbated the animosity already existing between Pat Garrett and the forces supporting Oliver Lee. The deadly shooting had occurred at the home of W. W. Cox, Lee's brother-in-law, while Cox's wife (Lee's sister-in-law), pregnant at the time, sat terrified in an adjoining room. A. P. "Print" Rhode, her brother, was most demonstrably angered by the shooting, and publicly threatened Garrett's life.[106]

On February 12, 1900, a Las Cruces bank was robbed of $15,000, and Garrett worked hard to catch the culprits, but a posse led by his deputy, Ben Williams, actually nabbed the suspects.[107]

Later that year a rumor spread throughout the Southwest that Garrett, one of the most famous personalities in those parts, had been killed. Spotting Garrett in an El Paso hotel, a newsman questioned him about it and reported that the "well-known sheriff [was] very much alive and laughed good naturedly at the scare which had caused his friends such uneasiness. He did not know how the report gained credence as it was without foundation."[108]

Somehow, after failing to get convictions in the Fountain murders, Garrett lost his desire for the office of Doña Ana sheriff he had once coveted. There were irritating distractions, like having to defend Charles Telles, one of his deputies, from false charges of a killing.[109] The year 1900, the beginning of a new century, was a year of change for Pat Garrett. At the age of fifty and no longer comfortable on long saddle rides, he entertained the idea of pursuing a political career. In September of that year he threw his hat into the ring as a candidate for delegate to Congress, but that went nowhere.

In May 1901, when President William McKinley came to El Paso on a vacation trip, Garrett led a delegation from Las Cruces to meet and talk about New Mexico statehood with him. While he had the President's ear, Pat may have mentioned that he was now a good Republican and open to political appointment. (He certainly didn't mention that he had been a life-long Democrat before receiving Republican backing for sheriff.)

Nothing came of that, but when McKinley was assassinated five months later, Theodore Roosevelt became president. Here was a man who, having cowboyed, ranched, and worn a lawman's badge in the West, was a great admirer of gunfighting western peace officers, and during his presidency he would appoint several of them to important federal positions. As the *Houston Post* pointed out, "Roosevelt dearly loves a man who can shoot and will shoot."[110]

When the prestigious post of El Paso customs collector came up for appointment in December 1901, Roosevelt nominated Pat Garrett for the Senate's confirmation. The selection was not without controversy. Although Garrett was supported by former New Mexico governor Lew Wallace and powerful politico of the territory Albert Fall, there were strong objectors. A former Republican convention delegate wrote the president, saying that appointment of a man "who had made a record for himself as a 'killer'" would reflect badly on his administration. Others advised Roosevelt that Garrett was illiterate and a confirmed drunkard.

Garrett certainly wanted the job and went all the way to Washington to plead his case to the president. According to a story related by Henry Hoyt, one of Garrett's admirers, at their meeting Roosevelt handed Garrett a document and asked him to read it aloud and sign it if he agreed with its contents. Garrett read: "If I am appointed Collector of Customs at El Paso, Texas, I will totally abstain from the use of intoxicating liquors during my term of office."

"Mr. Roosevelt, it suits me exactly," Garrett said, affixing his signature. In one fell swoop three of his supposed faults had been demolished. He proved that he could read and write, and no habitual sot could possibly take such an oath.[111] Confirmation of the appointment quickly passed the Senate, and Garrett returned happily to El Paso.[112]

The position called for two-year terms, and he served two of them from 1901 to 1905. As with every endeavor Pat Garrett tackled, this one was laden with controversy. His enemies, personal and political, publicly charged him with all manner of faults, most of which he shrugged off, but in May 1903 he lost his temper and engaged one of his critics in a fistfight on an El Paso street, which had to be broken up by the county attorney and chief of police.[113]

One criticism leveled at Garrett was his choice of friends, some of whom were considered to be on the shady side of El Paso citizenry.

MAN-HUNTERS OF THE OLD WEST

Foremost of these was a one-eyed saloonkeeper and professional gambler named Tom Powers. Garrett and Powers had long been pals, and Pat spent many hours in the Coney Island Saloon, which was owned by Powers. One of Garrett's prized possessions, the pistol he used to kill Billy the Kid, was mounted in a place of honor on the walls of the Coney Island.[114] Garrett had his faults like everyone, but rock-solid loyalty to friends was one of his admirable qualities. He ignored the criticisms and maintained his controversial relationships, but the Powers association would ultimately cost him his position.

In 1905 President Roosevelt was the principal speaker at the annual convention of his Spanish-American War Rough Riders held that year in San Antonio. Garrett and Tom Powers were not Rough Riders, but they attended. When a photograph taken at the event showing Garrett and Powers in pleasant conversation with the president appeared in newspapers, Roosevelt's political foes leaped on it as an example of his consorting with nefarious types like the notorious El Paso saloon gambler and his gun-wielding pal. Aware that these reports might endanger his position, Garrett took Powers with him to Washington, hoping to prove to the president that his friend was a decent chap. Roosevelt, however, angered by the criticism, refused to see either visitor, and Garrett was not reappointed.[115]

After losing his El Paso job, Garrett returned to his New Mexico ranch and concerned himself mainly with the breeding and raising of racehorses. With his limited funds he dabbled in mining ventures, none of them lucrative. Although devoid of legal education beyond that acquired in law enforcement, he acted as counsel for a man charged with murder in Mexico, but this also ended in failure. The defendant was sentenced to life in prison.[116]

Although he was skillful as a man-hunter, Garrett seemed to lack aptitude for anything that could improve his financial situation. In a February 9, 1907, letter to his friend author Emerson Hough, he admitted: "Everything seems to go wrong with me. I was sold out last fall by the sheriff [for nonpayment of property taxes over many years]. I went on a note with a friend [George Curry] and a bank got judgment against me."[117]

The constant stress imposed by his financial straits affected Garrett's behavior. He became increasingly quarrelsome and drank heavily, leading to several brawls in 1907 and 1908. His only hope for escape from this downward spiral was the expected appointment of George Curry as the next governor of New Mexico by President Roosevelt and the fulfillment of Curry's promise to appoint him superintendent of the territorial prison.[118]

While waiting for this ray of hope to break through the dark clouds, he moved his family to Las Cruces, where his small children could attend school more easily, leaving his grown son, Dudley Poe, to manage the ranch. Taking a job with a real estate firm in El Paso, his disreputable behavior became even more blatant; he began consorting with a Mrs. Brown, a notorious prostitute.

On March 11, 1907, he signed a document, leasing part of his ranch property to a young cowboy named Jesse Wayne Brazel, an act that would profoundly affect the Pat Garrett story. Brazel, employed on W. W. Cox's ranch, resided in the home of Print Rhode, Cox's brother-in-law, where he met and became betrothed to an eighteen-year-old schoolteacher. Seeking other income in preparation for marriage, he partnered with Rhode in a goat-raising venture, and he coveted land owned by Pat Garrett called Bear Canyon Ranch. Knowing that cattleman Garrett hated goats, and that Rhode and Garrett detested each other, Brazel mentioned neither his partner nor his stock when approaching Garrett with an offer to lease the Bear Canyon property. The lease as finalized and signed by both parties specified that for use of the land, Brazel would turn over to Dudley Poe Garrett ten heifer calves and one mare colt each July for the next five years.[119]

When Garrett learned that Brazel planned on bringing a goat herd onto the Bear Canyon property and that his partner in the enterprise was Print Rhode, he tried to stop them legally, claiming that the goat herders would be in violation of an old New Mexican law prohibiting the herding of livestock near a household because there was a rockhouse in Bear Canyon that his family sometimes used. Arbitration of the dispute was scheduled before a justice of the peace, but when the two parties met, hostility was so intense that the matter was postponed for months.

Appearing on the scene next were two men who were destined to become important actors in the forthcoming drama. Carl Adamson and Jim Miller, related by marriage, approached Garrett and said they had a thousand head of cattle in Mexico that they wanted to move into New Mexico for fattening before being driven to Oklahoma. They wanted to know if Garrett's Bear Canyon Ranch was available. Garrett explained that an arrangement could be reached if a "goat man" and his animals were first moved off the property. Miller asked to see this "goat man," and Brazel was summoned. He refused to cancel his lease unless someone would buy his goat herd at $3.50 a head. Miller said he and Adamson would take them off his hands until they found a buyer, and the two signed a contract.[120]

Certainly Pat Garrett was aware that Jim Miller, the man with whom he was dealing, was one of the most notorious murderers in the West. Related by marriage to the violent Clements clan and the deadly gunman John Wesley Hardin,[121] he had posed as a church deacon while killing for hire. He had slain men in Texas for years without a single conviction. Garrett, in his zeal to eliminate Brazel, Rhode, and the horrid goats, didn't seem to care. In addition to resolving Pat's goat problem, Miller seemed to accommodate Pat's every wish, suggesting he sell the Bear Canyon Ranch to him for $3,000 and take a job driving the cattle up from Mexico at a dollar a head. Garrett was elated, seeing an end to his debt-ridden financial situation.

But Brazel threw a monkey wrench into this rosy scenario, informing Garrett that he had miscalculated the size of his goat herd. Instead of the twelve hundred Miller had agreed to buy, there were eighteen hundred. Miller balked at that and the entire deal might have been dropped.

At this juncture Adamson arrived at the Garrett home in a two-horse buggy, saying he wanted Garrett to accompany him to Las Cruces for a meeting with Brazel the next day to resolve the problem. The following morning, Saturday, February 29, Garrett and Adamson set out in the buggy for the four-hour trip to Las Cruces. Perhaps hoping to bag some game during the trip, Garrett took along his Burgess folding shotgun loaded with birdshot.

On the way they encountered Wayne Brazel, mounted on a horse and headed for the meeting. He rode along beside the buggy as they continued. There was little conversation, but at one point Garrett asked Brazel why his original goat herd estimate was twelve hundred when he now believed it was eighteen hundred. Brazel responded that he had simply miscalculated. To this Adamson snapped, "The facts are that I do not want even twelve hundred goats, but I bought them to get possession of the ranch."

"If I don't sell the whole bunch, I won't sell none," Brazel retorted.[122]

Shortly after that exchange, Adamson stopped the horses, handed the reins to Garrett, and stepped to the front of the buggy to urinate. Garrett, taking advantage of the break, picked up his shotgun, got down and walked to the rear of the buggy. Turning his back to Brazel on his horse, he cradled the shotgun in his left arm and removed his left glove to unbutton his pants. That was his position when a shot rang out and he went down with a bullet through the back of his head. He fell, and as he lay prone on the ground, another bullet struck him in the midsection and ranged upward into his shoulder.

Adamson later testified that he heard shots, saw Garrett fall, ran to him, and heard him groan once before dying. Brazel, he said, was still mounted with a six-shooter in his hand. Adamson covered the body and hurried on to Las Cruces with Brazel. There, as Deputy Sheriff Felipe Lucero would testify, Brazel burst into the sheriff's office, blurted, "Lock me up. I've just killed Pat Garrett," and pointing to Adamson, said, "He saw the whole thing and knows I shot in self-defense."[123]

Brazel was formally charged with murder, and because of the celebrity of the deceased, heavyweight legal figures for both prosecution and defense were on hand at a hearing before justice of the peace Manuel Lopez on March 3. Mark Thompson, prosecuting attorney for Doña Ana County, assisted by New Mexico attorney general James M. Hervey, represented the territory. Attorneys Herbert B. Holt, William A. Sutherland, and Edward C. Wade, assisted by Albert Fall, appeared for Brazel's defense and entered on his behalf a plea of not guilty by reason of self-defense. Adamson, the only eyewitness to the shooting other than the defendant, provided information that seemed to support Brazel's self-defense plea. After getting out of the buggy, he said he heard Garrett say, evidently in response to Brazel's earlier remark that he would sell all the goats or none, "Well, damn you. If I don't get you off one way, I will another." Adamson added, "Or something like that."[124]

Brazel was released on a bond of $10,000 quickly raised by W. W. Cox. His trial for the murder of Pat Garrett on April 19, 1909, more than a year later, was conducted by the prosecution, in the words of Garrett biographer Leon Metz, "with appalling indifference and incompetence." On the stand the defendant claimed self-defense, saying he believed his own life was in danger when he heard Garrett's last remark and saw him with a shotgun, so he pulled his revolver and shot him in the head. The second shot, he said was reflexive, only fired because he was so excited.

Prosecutor Thompson did not call the lone eyewitness, Adamson. In neither his opening statement nor his summation did he remind the jury that a man well versed in lethal gun work like Garrett, if planning to kill an enemy, would have loaded his shotgun with buckshot, not birdshot. And he did not emphasize the plain fact that a plea of self-defense for a man admitting he shot a man in the back while urinating was ridiculous on its face. The jury took only fifteen minutes to reach a not guilty verdict.[125]

Whether Jesse Wayne Brazel actually killed Pat Garrett has been debated by western historians for more than a century. Without question, Garrett's unbending and irascible temperament was responsible for creating many of his enemies, men who hated him enough to kill him. Prime murder suspects, in addition to Brazel, have been W. W. Cox and Print Rhode, both of whom openly detested Garrett, and hired assassin Jim Miller and his partner Carl Adamson.

After studying the case for many years, New Mexico attorney W. T. Moyers named Cox as the killer.[126] Prolific author and western historian Glenn Shirley believed Miller, with the assistance of Adamson, murdered Garrett.[127] In a more recent review of the case, an author makes the case for Rhodes being the assassin.[128] After careful consideration of all the suspects, biographer Leon Metz concluded that Brazel was, in fact, the killer.[129]

The undertaker administering to Pat Garrett's remains was unable to find a casket in Las Cruces long enough to handle the elongated corpse and had to stretch the body over five chairs while he waited for a special coffin ordered from El Paso. Long an agnostic, Garrett had requested no religious services be held for him, and when on March 5, 1908, he was interred in the Odd Fellows Cemetery in Las Cruces, his old friend Tom Powers, at the family's request, read with his one eye the eulogy the noted agnostic Robert G. Ingersoll had delivered at his brother's grave.[130]

Garrett will always be remembered as the man who hunted down and killed the legendary Billy the Kid, but as the Kid's fame has grown over the years, Garrett has become, in the eyes of many, a villain for his dastardly assassination of a mischievous youngster. Walter Noble Burns, author of the 1926 book *The Saga of Billy the Kid*, was one of those responsible for Bonney's rise to fame, but he recognized Garrett's demonization early on. In a 1928 letter to Maurice Garland Fulton, another student of New Mexico's violent history, Burns wrote, "I have heard Garrett damned up and down . . . as a coward and a cold-blooded murderer [but he] carried out the job he undertook with courage and determination. . . . Garrett was a brave man—he must have been a brave man to do what he did—and what he did, it seems to me, resulted in a new era of law and order for New Mexico."[131]

Another renowned author, Eugene Manlove Rhodes, while always supportive of the McSween faction for which Bonney fought in the Lincoln County War, also strongly defended Garrett. Burns's book, he said, gave the reader "the impression that Billy got shabby treatment all along the line; that it was inconsiderate of the sheriff to molest him; that it was unsportsmanlike to search for him in his own country . . . , among his devoted adherents; and that it was positively discourteous and unfair that Garrett did not let Billy the Kid kill him at the last."[132]

When Garrett was killed, Theodore Roosevelt, evidently recovered from his displeasure with his former political appointee over the Tom Powers incident, was quoted as calling Pat Garrett "the greatest New Mexican," who "was not the man who upheld the arm of law and order in New Mexico, [rather] he was the first man to introduce law and order."[133]

However one views the men's characters, Billy the Kid Bonney remains the most famous outlaw and Pat Garrett the most famous man-hunter of New Mexico. Garrett also has the distinction of being a central figure in the three most intriguing criminal cases in the state's history: the hunt for and dispatch of Billy the Kid, the investigation into the disappearance of Albert J. Fountain and his son and the prosecution of their accused murderers, and his own mysterious assassination.

— 7 —

JOHN REYNOLDS HUGHES
1855–1947

For several years I did not expect to live to the age that I have. I expected to be killed by criminals. . . . I have never lost a battle . . . , never let a prisoner escape . . . , never took a human life unless it was a case of kill or be killed.

John R. Hughes

No law enforcement agency in the United States, with the possible exception of the FBI, ever attained greater man-hunting respect with the public than the Texas Rangers, and no ranger stands higher in popular regard than Captain John Reynolds Hughes. Together with John H. Rogers, James A. Brooks, and William J. McDonald, he has long been acclaimed as one of the Four Great Ranger Captains, but because of his lengthy service and outstanding work in hunting down felons for the organization, Hughes could well be considered the greatest of the great.

Born on February 1, 1855, in Henry County, Illinois, the future ranger captain was one of seven children of farmer and hotel owner Thomas Hughes and his wife, Jane Augusta Bond Hughes. Originally Ohioans, the Hughes couple became part of that great westward movement of the mid- and late nineteenth century, stopping for a time in Illinois, then moving on to Linn County, Kansas.[1]

Their son John, large for his age (when fully grown he stood just an inch under six feet) and adventurous by nature,[2] was only about fifteen when he left to find excitement on the wild frontier. He probably ran away; years later he told a reporter that "if he neglected to obtain the consent of his parents, it was only because he deemed himself capable of making his own decisions," a remark made only partly in jest, perhaps.[3]

John Reynolds Hughes. Courtesy of C. L. Sonnichsen Special Collections, University of Texas at El Paso Library (PH074-608S).

The powerful magnet pulling him away from home and hearth, evidently, was the great buffalo hunt, centered in Kansas and just gaining momentum. Hughes quickly signed on with an outfit. He told a newspaper reporter many years later, "In 1871 when I returned to civilization from my first buffalo hunt I heard of the Chicago fire," the disaster that struck the city in October of that year.[4] Since he indicated that this was his initial buffalo hunt, there were probably others, but he soon quit the bloody hide-hunting business to take up life in Indian Territory, or the Nations, as it was called, where he lived for a time with the several Indian tribes. From these people he first acquired "invaluable knowledge on tracking down horse thieves, outlaws and other enemies of society," a knowledge that proved so beneficial in his career as a Texas Ranger.[5]

He was only seventeen in 1872 when he received the only serious wound ever suffered in a lifetime of dangerous work. Accounts of this episode provide few details, focusing instead on how he reacted to the crippling injury. As related by a nephew, Emery H. Hughes, John was working as a cowhand in Indian Territory for an outfit supplying cattle to the reservation when

> a feared breed rustler Big Nig Goombi tried to run off the stock [he] was herding. The tenderfoot puncher killed the dangerous thief, but was himself maimed by wounds in the right arm which permanently slowed his draw from that side. He quickly taught himself to fire from the left side with such speed and accuracy that few subsequent acquaintances suspected that he had not been born left-handed.[6]

Following a 1938 interview with Hughes, the great war correspondent Ernie Pyle wrote, "He was shot . . . by an Indian when he was 17, and he suffers from the wound to this day. His right arm was shattered and is weak and smaller than his left. He had to learn to do everything with his left hand, even shoot."[7] According to a 1923 newspaper article, Hughes's injury was "an accident" making "his right arm stiff and [which] caused him to shoot with his left hand, but he developed a direct fire that made him a terror to all the bad men."[8]

Hughes's first book-length biographer, Jack Martin, relates how an unnamed Indian maimed Hughes's right arm, but in his version it was by a tomahawk and not a bullet. When his trail boss and the Indian got into a fracas and the tribesman raised his tomahawk to strike, Hughes jumped into the fray. He "threw up his arm to deflect the blow. The weapon shattered the bones in his arm, but he thus saved himself from more critical injuries."[9]

First as a cowboy and later as a trader, Hughes often visited Fort Sill, headquarters of the Indian reservations, where he formed lasting friendships with Comanche chief Quanah Parker, celebrated scout Simpson E. "Jack" Stilwell, and other frontier notables.[10]

Years later, in a letter to his friend Roy Aldrich, Hughes explained how he became a trail driver. He was working at Fort Sill in the spring of 1877, delivering cattle to the Indians "to keep them from going out on buffalo hunts." When his employers lost their contract, he was one of those hired to drive the remaining herd to Kansas for sale. He remembered that the trail boss was Mike Dalton and that other drovers were Charley Nebo, Jim French, John Middleton, and an ex-soldier named Steele. They pushed the herd to Ellis, Kansas, where they sold the cattle that November. About that time, a man from New Mexico hired French and Middleton to go and fight in the Lincoln County War.[11]

In 1878 Hughes went up the trail again, driving a herd for part-owner Andrew Drumm.[12] Returning in the fall, he joined his brother Emery in the horse-raising business in Travis County, Texas. They spent $100 for the purchase of seven horses for their Long Hollow Ranch, including a mare sired by the famous quarter horse Steel Dust, but they had terrible luck with this acquisition. In April a stud stallion killed the mare, and in May two other mares were lost, one in breaking and the other from a fistula. Later, wolves killed a one-day-old foal.[13]

But the partners soldiered on, and by 1883 they oversaw a fine herd of horses. Then a disaster occurred, one that proved to be what turned John Hughes toward a career for which he was eminently fitted: man-hunting. In August a gang of horse thieves made a wholesale sweep of ranches in Williamson and Travis Counties, running off seventy-five horses, including sixteen from the Long Hollow Ranch. But members of this criminal outfit came to learn that they had picked the wrong target when they stole horses from the Hughes brothers.[14] It would be an understatement to say that John R. Hughes was angry. He later said that what most enraged him was "the very daring of the nefarious enterprise,"[15] but among the stolen horses was one called Moscow, his favorite mount and the sire of four others. Hughes packed up his necessities, loaded them on a pack mule, mounted his best long-distance horse, and rejecting any assistance, rode out alone to hunt down the thieves and take back his horses as well as any other stolen steeds he could round up.

Others may have thought him crazy to attempt such a feat, but John Reynolds Hughes was not crazy; he was a fearless, determined man. Aware that as many as a half-dozen men would be driving a horse herd of this size, he was prepared to face them alone if he caught up with them. Before he ever became a Texas Ranger or met ranger captain William J. McDonald, he already subscribed to McDonald's famous dictum, "No man in the wrong can stand up against a man that's in the right and just keeps a-comin.'"

The July 11, 1884, edition of the *Black Range* (published weekly during this period in Chloride, Sierra County, New Mexico), featured an interview in which Hughes explained what happened next. He said that when he set out from his ranch in August 1883, he already suspected that the leaders of the horse-theft gang were brothers John and James Craven, Williamson County residents who were constantly in trouble. After John had been arrested in 1879 for stealing a saddle and was released on bond provided by Ki Kirk, a rancher from New Mexico, he skipped out with his brother. Kirk partnered with John Craven in a Silver City, New Mexico, corral for about a year before returning to his ranch. The Craven brothers changed their name to Johnson about this time, an indication that they were turning to outlawry as a profession.

Then, Hughes related with a note of contempt, the brothers went back to Williamson County in 1883 to "purchase" stock with a borrowed ten dollars, "but came back with sixty head of horses and sixty cents of the ten dollars remaining."

Hughes, in pursuit, trailed the thieves throughout the remaining summer and fall months of 1883 without success. Then, luckily, he stopped at Kirk's Cisco ranch, where a cowboy told him that the Cravens had driven sixty horses there months before, and they had held them there for a time before taking them northward.

With winter setting in, Hughes returned home, but started out again on May 15, 1884, with "a pair of mules, a saddle horse, and a companion." He went directly to Cisco, but stories about outlaws so terrorized his companion that Hughes sent him back with the mules.

Following a lead that John Craven was back at Silver City, Hughes went there only to find that his quarry had left. But the trip was not entirely worthless, as he learned that the Kirk ranch hand who had provided valuable information before was currently working a roundup on the Gila River. Hughes headed there and came across two horses he recognized as stolen Williamson County steeds. Convinced that this was good country in which to gain information, he took work on a farm "and kept his ears open."

Soon the cowboy he sought rode in astride a horse from the stolen herd. "After much persuasion," the ranch hand told Hughes that the thieving brothers had the stolen horses on a ranch north of Fairview. Acting on this information, Hughes went to Hillsboro, where he learned that the thieves had been captured and jailed at Chloride, and their stolen stock was being held there.

He hurried to Chloride, examined the horses taken from the "Johnson" brothers, and found ten of his own horses (with young colts following three) as well as several belonging to his neighbors. Hughes told his *Black Range* interviewer that he would be returning to the range in search of the other stolen steeds.

The reporter concluded, "Mr. Hughes' identification of his stock is so complete and positive that no doubt exists in the minds of the people here of his ownership." An editorial comment followed: "Such is a short sketch of the Cravens alias Johnson brothers and the chase of Mr. Hughes after his property as told by himself. His manner is straightforward, his story is given unhesitatingly and nobody here doubts its truth. If the Johnsons were not in a close box heretofore they certainly are now. There is no doubt that the law will do its duty by them."

In an issue more than a month later *Black Range* mentioned Hughes's ongoing quest: "John R. Hughes, whose horses were stolen from Texas by John and Jim Johnson, has found the last but one of his animals among the wild horse herd that now occupies the Johnson range. Mr. Hughes has been exceedingly fortunate in his search."[16]

The roundup of outlaws that summer resulted in trials and convictions. In November 1884 "Toppy" Johnson, the leader of the gang who stole Hughes's stock, and a number of other outlaws, including the Craven brothers (who had evidently taken the Johnson alias out of admiration for Toppy),[17] went on trial in Sierra County. Albert Fountain, the eminent attorney, militia commander, and editor, assisted in the prosecution, a fact that indicates the importance of the cases. The defendants were convicted and given prison terms.[18] Hughes did not testify in the trials, having headed back home with his reclaimed horses in late August. Although later accounts claim he drove the herd back alone, that is most unlikely; he probably hired some out-of-work cowhands to help him.

In his response to the theft of his horses John R. Hughes demonstrated that he possessed all the attributes of the born man-hunter: determination, persistence, and courage. He also had the physical and mental toughness to spend long periods in the saddle and long, lonely nights in camp; he could shake off the disappointment of fruitless leads, follow up on new ones, and extract valuable information from often-recalcitrant informants. These were all qualities that he used to great advantage in the career that lay before him.

An atrocious murder that took place about the time Hughes returned from New Mexico led Hughes to join the rangers, a move that would prove to be truly momentous for him. On September 3, 1884, ruffians broke into a Fredericksburg, Texas, store, stripped the place of wanted items, and killed the proprietor. Wesley Collier, Ed Janes, Jackson Beam, and James Fannin were indicted for the crime. In November, Sheriff John Walton collared Collier, Janes, and Beam, but Fannin had disappeared. Because the Fredericksburg jail was unreliable for the detention of dangerous felons like these, the trio was held in the Bexar County lockup in San Antonio. This jail proved no more secure than the one in Fredericksburg, for within months all three had broken out.

Collier and Beam were recaptured and locked up, this time in the Mason County jail. Like the neighboring county calabooses, this one was also escape-prone rather than escape-proof, and on September 12, 1885, the two accused killers broke out again.

Up to this point the arrest and incarceration of the suspects had been entirely in the hands of county officers, but when the accused murderers were still loose in the spring of 1886, Texas governor John Ireland and adjutant general Wilburn Hill King thought it high time to involve the Texas Rangers. Accordingly, the governor called ranger sergeant Ira Aten into his office and gave him explicit orders to bring in the jail jumpers "dead or alive."[19]

Being handed what he felt was sole responsibility for catching the wanted men, Aten was overwhelmed. He knew he needed help for the job. Since all fellow rangers in his company were busy with other assignments, he turned to a Williamson County rancher he had heard was smart, had guts, and could be counted on when the chips were down. As he later recalled:

I had never seen Hughes before and don't think he had ever seen me. He had the usual cowman's frankness and hospitality. . . . I liked his looks and it seemed I could see a spark of sympathy in his eyes, so I just opened up and told him my whole story. After I had finished, Hughes said in his quiet, mild, sympathetic manner, "I will go with you and help you."[20]

Aten deputized Hughes, and the two began with a search for Wesley Collier. After several weeks of running down false leads, they got a hot one; an informant told them their man was holed up in the home of Williamson County rancher Nicholas Dayton. Stealthily approaching the Dayton house, they kept it under observation a whole day and night, trying to decide how to take their man without precipitating a gunfight and endangering Dayton's family members. They finally decided to make a dawn assault, when the occupants were deep in slumber. As they entered the house by separate doors, Collier, with the alert senses of animals and hunted fugitives, sprang from his bed. Spotting him in the dim light, Aten barked: "Hold up, Wesley!" But instead of raising his hands, Collier reached under a pillow for his pistol. Aten fired once and the fugitive fell back on the bed, a dead man.[21]

This was John R. Hughes's introduction to the operation of the Texas Rangers. He liked what he saw: steady, unrelenting work to locate a wanted felon; once found, a clear order to give up; and if ignored, decisive action to terminate the affair.

The Collier incident was, according to Ira Aten, "the beginning of a life of service to Texas given by Captain Hughes."[22] On August 10, 1887, Hughes stood before the Williamson county clerk and took the Texas Ranger oath of enlistment. He was assigned to Company D of the Frontier Battalion, commanded by Captain Frank L. Jones. As a ranger private he would earn the munificent sum of a dollar a day. With the exception of a six-and-a-half-month interruption two years later, when he left to take a higher paying job, Hughes spent the next twenty-seven years in the service of the Texas Rangers, most of it as a captain in command of a company. During those eventful years, he would pursue and capture hundreds of felons, and following his retirement in 1915 he would be honored as one of the Four Great Ranger Captains.

To begin with, as a greenhorn in the service, he was given mundane assignments by Captain Jones while he learned how the rangers operated.

He spent much time in the early years investigating ranchers' claims of fence cutting. For decades cattle owned by both large and small ranchers had roamed the range freely, often mixing, and had to be separated during twice-a-year roundups. With the introduction of barbed wire, some large ranchers began fencing off their land, often blocking access to watering holes for other ranchers' cattle. Open-range advocates retaliated with a campaign of fence cutting, triggering skirmishes that threatened to develop into all-out war, and the rangers were called upon to calm things. Most rangers detested taking sides in a disagreement between honest ranchers, and Hughes was no exception. His disgust was evident in his activity report of June 18, 1888: "Failed to accomplish anything, out 34 days. Marched 1000 miles."[23]

When in February 1889 Maverick County residents found four bodies, their heads brutally crushed, floating in the Rio Grande, and they could not identify the victims, a call went out for a Texas Ranger investigation. Captain Jones assigned Sergeant Aten and Private Hughes to the case with orders to "ferret out the murderer of these four people." Now this was more to John Hughes's liking. He welcomed a chance to work again with his friend Aten and to pursue and collar a brutal murderer (or murderers). As for Aten, he said, "Whenever I had a bad case I always took Hughes with me."[24]

Working the case in Maverick County, where the bodies had been found, the two rangers were able to identify the victims as members of the Williamson family of San Saba County, a sixty-year-old widowed mother, a twenty-two-year-old son, and two daughters who were thirty and fifteen. A month's investigation provided the rangers with enough evidence to suspect the recent buyer of the Williamson farm, Richard H. "Dick" Duncan, as well as his brother, George T. "Tap" Duncan, and a third man, H. W. Landers, as perpetrators of the atrocious murders. They wired San Saba County sheriff Samuel B. Howard to arrest the suspects, and the Duncan brothers were soon locked up, but Landers could not be located. At a trial in Maverick County, where the murders had taken place, Richard Duncan was convicted of murder and sentenced to death by hanging. His brother Tap was released for lack of incriminating evidence, and Landers was never found.[25]

In April 1889 Hughes helped resolve a problem for a former well-respected ranger captain. J. T. Gillespie, who had commanded Company

E, Frontier Battalion, and left the rangers to become the first sheriff of newly organized Brewster County, was chagrined when a prisoner escaped from his jail, and he requested the rangers' help. Hughes and another private trailed Spencer Morris, the escapee, to Kerr County, arrested him, and returned him to Sheriff Gillespie's tender care.[26]

Private Hughes's work had impressed his company commander, and when Captain Jones received an appeal from his brother-in-law, John G. O'Grady, proprietor of a mining operation in Coahuila, Mexico, for tough, dependable guards to be employed at his operation, he suggested Hughes and two others from his company, Privates Baz L. "Bass" Outlaw and Joseph Walter Durbin. Enticed by a great pay increase, all three tendered their resignations in May 1889 and became guards at O'Grady's northern Mexico mines, protecting silver bullion transport from predatory bandits en route from the mines to the railroad. The very presence of these former Texas Rangers seemed to act as a deterrent to outlaw activity, and as weeks passed without action, the three grew bored and restless. Outlaw was the first to go back to ranger duty, followed soon after by Durbin. Enjoying the higher pay, Hughes stayed on until the mines closed down for the winter. He then returned to Texas and reenlisted in Company D on December 1, 1889.[27]

Soon he was dispatched, together with Bass Outlaw and Calvin Aten (younger brother of Ira), to assist Edwards County officers in the apprehension of the Odle brothers, who were charged with murder and cattle theft. The rangers were members of a posse that ambushed the Odles on Christmas Day 1889. Ignoring orders to surrender, the brothers pulled guns and began shooting. Return fire killed them both. Unable to determine whose bullets downed the fugitives in that hail of fire, Hughes simply wrote in his report, "They resisted arrest and made a hard fight and we had to kill them in self defense. Also killed one horse and shot another through the neck."[28]

In his report to assistant adjutant general L. P. Sieker a few days later, Captain Jones wrote: "I guess you have seen in the papers where some of my men celebrated Christmas Day by killing the two Odles in Edwards County. It is a great strain off that country and the good people are rejoicing. John Hughes, Outlaw and young Aten and some citizens did the work."[29]

On April 8, 1890, John Hughes received his first promotion as a Texas Ranger when he was made first corporal of Company D, replacing his squad leader, Sergeant Charles Fusselman, who had been killed by outlaws in El Paso County.[30] From the company camp near Marfa in Presidio County, Hughes, at the head of a detachment, spent many days in the saddle scouting for felons in Presidio, Brewster, and Pecos Counties throughout the summer of 1890. During this period he was able to collar two suspected smugglers and another pair of suspected horse thieves and turn them over to local authorities for prosecution, but many of his long stretches on the trail proved fruitless.[31]

The remainder of 1890 and all of 1891 were much the same, with lengthy scouts, long days in the saddle, and occasional suspect arrests. It was the kind of work that could become boring, leading to carelessness and possible disaster. Well aware of that, Hughes was careful to remain constantly alert and cautioned his men, Privates Ernest "Diamond Dick" St. Leon and Alonzo Van Oden, to follow his example. His policy paid dividends when St. Leon wormed his way into a Mexican ore-stealing crowd at the Shafter mines and was enlisted to take part in a big theft planned for the night of January 12, 1892. He passed this information on to Hughes, who told St. Leon to hang back when the thieves emerged from the mine entrance; he and Ranger Van Oden would be waiting to challenge them. When three Hispanics came out into the open, their burros laden with stolen ore, Hughes ordered them to surrender because they were under arrest, but the thieves reached for their guns instead of the sky and were immediately shot down with blasts from by Hughes's and Van Oden's shotguns. Two expired at once, but another, although badly wounded, struggled to continue the fight. A bullet from Diamond Dick's six-shooter finished him.[32]

Six months later Corporal Hughes and his men engaged in another similar gunfight. In June 1892 Hughes and Privates James Putman and Alonzo Van Oden left the Marfa encampment for a Mexican settlement on the Rio Grande to arrest wanted fugitive Desidario Duran. They made the capture without incident, but stopped at a store to get supplies before returning. Van Oden wrote an account of what then transpired:

We saw three Mexican men trying get a fourth man, who was drunk, on his horse. . . . A farmer said that one of the men was Florencio Carrasco. We had orders to arrest Carrasco, as he had a bad record— everything from horse stealing to murder. [Leaving Putnam in charge of prisoner Duran,] Hughes and I got on our horses and started toward them. They quickly mounted and started firing on us, all except Carrasco [who] deliberately set about getting his rifle out of his scabbard. One of us killed him. My horse was shot and killed by the fleeing bandits.[33]

Aware that Duran and Carrasco had numerous friends and relatives in the area and that groups of angry-looking men were already gathering, Hughes thought a quick departure was wise, so he left the burial of Carrasco to them, and the three rangers set out with their prisoner for Marfa. A few miles from town, in order to thwart any ambush along the way, he led them off the Marfa road and came back by a circuitous route, which took longer but was safer.[34]

In August Company D was notified to watch for a man who was wanted for murder in Crockett County and who was reportedly coming that way, headed for the Mexican border. The fugitive, William D. "Pecos Bill" Barbee, had been the foreman at the Sierra County, New Mexico, ranch where Hughes had worked when he was chasing horse thieves in 1884. He had liked Barbee, and rather than making the arrest of a man he considered an old friend, Hughes sent Privates Van Oden and Putnam to do the chore. The two rangers collared Barbee without trouble and jailed him at Shafter, so Hughes never saw him.[35]

Hughes had worked with Baz L. Outlaw both on ranger assignments and as a guard at the Mexican mines. He knew him as tough and fearless, a good man to have with you in a fight, but he was also aware of the man's great weakness: he had a fondness for alcohol and became belligerent when drunk. Despite this flaw in his character, Captain Jones had promoted Outlaw to sergeant, probably in the hope that greater authority might straighten him out. But when that did not happen, the captain was obliged to discharge his hard-fighting, hard-drinking sergeant on September 18, 1892. The next day he promoted John R. Hughes to first sergeant.[36]

On January 17, 1893, Captain Jones penned a letter to adjutant general W. H. Mabry in which he praised his new sergeant as "a fine officer . . . in full accord with the best people in the country . . . , very familiar with the entire section for several counties along the Rio Grande. . . . Hughes knows the people and country and can do better service than any one I can think of."[37]

By June of that year, recognition of Sergeant Hughes's outstanding service had reached the Texas legislative chambers in Austin. When state senator John M. Dean learned that the rangers planned to transfer Hughes from Presidio County to Ysleta—a trouble spot near El Paso—he wrote Mabry, voicing his concern: "John R. Hughes is a splendid officer and he has had an excellent detachment with him at Shafter and I hope that if he is ordered elsewhere that you will replace him at Shafter with an equally efficient officer and detachment."[38]

Causing much of the trouble along the upper reaches of the Rio Grande that induced Hughes to relocate were the Olguins, a family of lawbreakers widely known as the Bosque Gang, named after their various hideouts in bosques or marshy stretches of the river. After receiving complaints about them from many residents of El Paso County, adjutant general Mabry ordered Captain Jones to move his company to the troubled zone and deal decisively with the Olguins. Company D broke camp and moved upriver to Ysleta "for the avowed purpose of ridding the island below and the bosque above of the desperate characters that have for years infested them."[39]

Wasting no time, on June 29 Captain Jones took Corporal Carl Kirchner and three of his squad, together with El Paso County deputy sheriff R. E. "Ed" Bryant who was carrying arrest warrants, and rode into the bosques in search of Olguins. Friendly informants had warned the gang of the rangers' approach, however, and as Jones and Kirchner, in the lead, approached four adobe houses on a stretch of dry land known as Pirate Island, they were met with gunfire. The first volley missed both men, but one slug hit Kirchner's Winchester, partially disabling it. Quickly dismounting and returning fire, the officers were joined by the other posse members, and a hot gun battle ensued between the lawmen in the open and the outlaws positioned in and behind the adobe: "The Mexicans would open the door and fire and two Mexicans on the right & left of the house would rise from behind the adobe wall & fire also. The door would then close. . . . Every time the door was opened, and a volley be fired, Capt. Jones and the men would return it."[40]

A bullet slammed into Captain Jones's leg, breaking the femur. Although in great pain, he somehow remained on his feet and continued to fight until another slug knocked him down. Still, he managed to pour lead from his pistol until, struck by a third bullet, he gasped, "Boys, I am killed," and died.[41]

In all the excitement the posse members had not realized that they had crossed an invisible line separating the United States from Mexico, but as they reassembled to take stock of their situation, the realization set in that they were in a precarious position. Their commander was dead, reinforcements would probably soon arrive to aid their adversaries, and that might include Mexican authorities to arrest the posse. Reluctantly they left their captain's body where it lay and retreated to San Elizario, where Kirchner wired the sad news to A. G. Mabry: "Have just had fight with Mexicans near line of Mexico. Capt. Jones killed. We were overpowered and have just come in for reinforcements. Only had six men." A second telegram requested Sergeant Hughes's help: "I expect trouble here. Can you send sergeant Hughes and outfit up tonight? The railway company will furnish transportation free."[42]

Kirchner also wired George W. Baylor, father-in-law of Captain Jones and a former ranger captain, and Baylor in turn asked the adjutant general to hurry Hughes and his rangers to the scene.[43]

Assistance was forthcoming from both Alpine, where Hughes departed with his men as soon as he could catch a train, and El Paso, where Sheriff Frank B. Simmons organized a posse of deputies, other officers, and civilian volunteers to go to Kirchner's aid. But the corporal was anxious to recover his fallen captain's body. Taking the rest of his men, he returned to Pirate Island and secured the Captain Jones's body without interference. Back at San Elizario he quickly informed Mabry and Baylor that he had Jones's body as well as the Mexican authorities' assurance that the captain's rifle, pistol, watch, money, and horse would be returned.[44]

Confronted with the immediate task of selecting a replacement for Captain Jones, Governor J. S. Hogg and A. G. Mabry received a number of telegrams from prominent Texans endorsing John Hughes, including missives from state senator John M. Dean,[45] state representative A. J. "Jeff" McLemore,[46] El Paso mayor W. H. Austin,[47] and El Paso County sheriff Frank B. Simmons.[48] Attorney T. T. Teel, honored veteran of both the Mexican and Civil Wars, joined in, lauding Hughes as being "sober, capable, honest and brave," and assuring the governor that his appointment would be the best that could be made.[49] Prominent businessmen like William Noyes, superintendent of the Presidio Mining Company, and J. H. Faubion, who had known Hughes since Williamson County days and currently ran a large marketing firm near Austin, also wired Mabry urging Hughes's appointment.[50]

There was at least one other active aspirant for the position, however. Bass Outlaw, former Company D sergeant, whose shameful behavior after drinking had caused Captain Jones to dismiss him and install Hughes in his place, had vowed to forego his alcoholic thirst and obtained appointment as a special ranger. Now, ironically, he coveted the job formerly held by the man who fired him, and which seemed to be going to the man who replaced him. On July 5 he wrote Mabry, making his pitch for the captaincy with the assurance that he was pursuing "temperate habits" and would "faithfully discharge all duties incumbent upon [him]."[51]

Mabry had to consider one other possible replacement for Jones: George W. Baylor, the former ranger captain who had been a colonel of the Texas Cavalry during the Civil War. Baylor, however, at sixty-one years of age, did not wish to take on such a stressful position again. He so informed Mabry, adding, "I wish to say that Sergt. Jno. R. Hughes had the entire confidence of Capt. Jones and my daughter heard him say in case he resigned he would use all his influence in the Sergt's behalf & I believe in regular line of promotion he should have the position & trust you will give it to him."[52]

John Hughes also notified Mabry that he wanted to be considered "to fill the vacancy caused by the sad death of our Brave and Beloved Captain Frank Jones."[53] But as it turned out, these endorsements and applications had no effect on Hogg and Mabry's decision regarding Captain Jones's replacement, for by July 4 the governor and his adjutant general had already agreed to appoint John Hughes as captain of Company D.

Evidently the first order of business for the new captain was to exact revenge for the killing of his predecessor. Within days of his appointment, a newspaper reported that a man, identified only as "Jaso," was found hanging from a tree on Pirate Island. Area residents claimed that the man was a Mexican and that Texans had hanged him. Although not spelled out by the paper, the implication was clear: Jaso was one of the outlaws responsible for the death of Jones, and others were on the rangers' extermination list.[54]

In a newspaper interview forty-five years later, John Hughes would vouchsafe that nineteen members of the Bosque Gang whom the rangers blamed for the death of Jones were found "where they committed suicide by hanging with Rangers' ropes around their necks."[55] About that same time, he told Texas historian C. L. Sonnichsen that Jones's killing had caused him "great grief," and he "saw to it personally that the eighteen men involved were run down and brought to justice in one way or another."[56] One of the ways, evidently, was lynching. Captain Jones was avenged, and as some saw it, justice was carried out in the manner of the frontier West.

As company captain, Hughes was much more involved in administrative duties, including camp maintenance, duty assignments, personnel management, and required paperwork, but he was still able to lead his men after particularly dangerous fugitives, working often with another celebrated man-hunter, former Jones County sheriff and current deputy U.S. marshal George A. Scarborough.[57]

Hughes was often called to potential trouble spots to maintain the peace. One of these was an explosive situation in Reeves County, where a feud had developed between former sheriff George A. Frazer and Jim Miller, a notorious killer-for-hire. Frazer had twice attempted to gun down his enemy, but a steel breastplate that Miller wore saved his life. When hearings into the case were scheduled for March 1895 in Pecos City, Sheriff Daniel Murphy, Frazer's successor, admitted his own inability to prevent trouble and requested ranger help.[58] Frazer, hiding from Miller in Eddy, New Mexico, also pleaded for ranger protection, saying his life would be in danger when he attended the hearings.[59]

Hughes arrived in Pecos City with three men on March 3, where he met with Miller and placed him under arrest to assure his safety. When court opened, he had rangers disarm all who entered, excepting only Sheriff Murphy and one deputy. Order was maintained until the case was transferred to El Paso County.[60]

Captain Hughes may have found crackpots more troubling than the thieves and murderers with whom he was familiar. One example is J. L. McAleer, who wrote the adjutant general claiming that El Paso County, where Company D was stationed, was "the most demoralized section of the state [overrun with] gamblers, drunkards, thieves & notorious libertines [and] a lot of the ranger company can most always be found loafing at the drinking & gambling saloon." McAleer saved his most shocking charge for last, asserting that a "respectable old citizen," unable to pay a fine, had been held in the ranger camp "under ball & chain" until bailed out by friends.[61] Hughes was busy with important matters when he received an extract of this diatribe from Mabry, and his initial, understated response was that McAleer "did not confine his statements to the truth,"[62] but in a long letter he later defended his rangers on every point raised, including a denial that there was a ball and chain in camp.[63]

A few months after disposing of the foolish McAleer, the captain had to deal with two others, who initially appeared to be just strange eccentrics, but whose activity led to bloodshed. A number of Mexicans whom Hughes called "a band of fanatics" came across the border to the El Paso area following Teresita Urea, a young woman they were calling "Saint Teresa," who claimed to have mystical healing powers, and Incarnacion Lorez, who was called "the Hunchback." Hughes saw the two as fraudulent hucksters, peddling bogus medicine, but after a clash between the pair's frenzied followers and Mexican police, in which five were killed and a number wounded, he moved his company into El Paso to chase them back across the border without further loss of life.[64]

Problems other than crazies also plagued Captain Hughes during this difficult period. He had to discharge two of his best men, Private Wood Saunders and Special Ranger Ernest St. Leon, for public drunkenness, and he lost dependable Private Thalis Cook a few months later, when he resigned to take a job as a railroad detective.[65]

In letters written to friends in 1895 Hughes indicated his displeasure with state officials. When they reduced a ranger company's size to one captain, one sergeant, and six privates, he wrote that the cut was hard to take, for there was work enough in that region for twenty-five Rangers, "but such is life in the far west."[66] Salary payments were often belated, also, which posed a hardship for thirty-dollar-a-month privates. As captain, Hughes was paid $100 a month, but when his men were not paid on time, they often appealed to him for loans. Hughes wrote a friend, saying that he hoped payment that month would be prompt, for lending so much money had cost him about five percent.[67]

In August 1893 two masked men held up a store in Valentine, Presidio County, which triggered a gunfight with aroused citizenry in which Richard Ellsberry, an elderly night watchman, was shot and killed. A criminal investigation followed, and Captain Hughes, ranger private Joe Sitter, Sheriff D. G. Knight, and Deputy Marshal Scarborough were soon on the trail of the killers. When a heavy rain wiped out the outlaws' tracks, they had to give up the chase. Hughes continued his investigation, however, and uncovered evidence implicating brothers Thomas and Samuel Holland.

In testimony before a grand jury in September, he presented that evidence, and the brothers were indicted.[68]

In the mid-1890s, El Paso, Texas, harbored more gunfighters of note than Dodge City, Kansas; Deadwood, Dakota; Tombstone, Arizona; or any other western town or city before or after. Numbered among those gunmen on either side of the law—and sometimes both—residing in or frequenting El Paso in those years were Emanuel "Mannie" Clements Jr., Pat Garrett, John Wesley Hardin, Jeff Milton, Bass Outlaw, George Scarborough, John Selman, and a host of other lesser lights. Outlaw, Hardin, and Selman would all die in El Paso, shot to death by other gunfighters during this period. Others would meet violent deaths later. Clements was killed in an El Paso saloon in December 1908 by an unknown assassin; Scarborough and Garrett survived the El Paso bloodbath only to be killed later in New Mexico, Scarborough by outlaws in an April 1900 gunfight and Garrett by an assassin in March 1908. Of this gunfighter hierarchy only Jeff Milton died of natural causes, passing on at the age of eighty-five in 1947.

At the very apex of this violent period in El Paso, excitement gripped the city, not over another gunfighter shooting, but ironically over the prospect of a boxing match to be held there. After the retirement of former heavyweight champion James J. Corbett, fistic promoter Dan Stuart planned to stage a bout between Bob Fitzsimmons and Peter Maher, two aspirants for the title. When he announced that the bout would take place in El Paso or its environs, sportsmen from all over the country flocked in.

But Governor Charles A. Culberson, a political enemy of Stuart's, threw a bucket of cold water on the plan by calling a special session of the state legislature for the sole purpose of blocking Stuart by enacting a law that would make prizefighting a felony in Texas. The measure was passed and signed by the governor on October 3, 1895. When rumors spread that Stuart would defy the law and hold the match anyway, Culberson ordered A. G. Mabry to mount a ranger force of sufficient size in the city to prevent that happening. Mabry responded by calling into El Paso the companies of the four men later to be exalted as the Four Great Ranger Captains: John R. Hughes, James A. Brooks, William J. McDonald, and John H. Rogers. Arriving to stop the fight were about two dozen rangers, many of whom were gun-wielders of demonstrated ability, so El Paso undoubtedly reached its high-water mark for gunfighters during this period.

At the invitation of legendary frontier character Roy Bean, who had ordained himself the "Law West of the Pecos," Stuart eventually moved his fighters, their handlers, and the entire sporting entourage by train to Bean's bailiwick at Langtry, Texas. The rangers, of course, tagged along. The fight was held on an island in the Rio Grande, presumably in Mexico, beyond the jurisdiction of the rangers. While hundreds watched the fight from inside a hastily constructed enclosure, hundreds more, including the rangers, watched from bluffs above the river. There wasn't much to see; Fitzsimmons knocked out Maher in the first round.[69]

Following the almost farcical prizefight affair, Captain Hughes returned to his more traditional role of man-hunter. In late September 1896 Brewster County sheriff James B. Gillett notified him that five men had stolen horses and guns from a ranch, and he had information indicating that their intention was to use the stolen property in a train robbery. Hughes moved quickly to hunt the culprits. Accompanied by the only two available privates, Thalis Cook and Ed Bryant, he loaded mounts and a pack mule on a train bound for Alpine. Along the way his party of rangers was joined by Deputy Sheriff Jim Pool of Presidio County as well as W. C. Combs and Jim Stroud, civilians who had lost fine horses to the thieves. Stroud proved to be an especially valuable addition to the posse, as he was an experienced trailer.

That trail led into the rugged Glass Mountains and was difficult to follow due to heavy rains and confusion deliberately caused by the outlaws, who had driven their horses back and forth over great stretches of terrain. But the keen tracking eyes of Stroud and Hughes kept the posse on the heels of their quarry. Arriving at the McCutcheon Brothers' ranch near the foot of the Davis Mountains, they found an empty sack that the outlaws had discarded. Hughes concluded that the bandits, low on supplies, would hide in the mountains, watch the valley ranch houses, and when the owners left to work, raid them for replenishments. When rancher McCutcheon offered his own service and that of his cowboys to assist in the hunt, Hughes sent Deputy Pool and Tip Franklin, one of the ranch hands, to scout one mountain pass, while Cook, Stroud, and McCutcheon went up another. Cook's party found a trail and was following it into the mountains when two men rose from concealment with leveled guns and threatened to shoot if they did not turn back. Ranger Cook wanted to charge the outlaws, but the civilians with him declined, saying they were not heavily armed enough to tackle desperate men in a gun battle. They pulled out and returned to the ranch, but Cook remained, trading shots with the outlaws for almost an hour before departing.

Hughes then reorganized his posse and followed Cook's directions back to the outlaws' location. Ascending the steep mountain, they were within three hundred yards of their objective when fired upon by hidden marksmen from above. No one was hit, but Hughes could see that in this battle, those holding the height had every advantage, so he determined, as he put it, "to take the mountain away from them. We could not see anyone on the mountain but the bullets kept coming by us. We ran on our horses almost to the top of the mountain when the fight was so hot that we left our horses." The only posse member hit in that exchange was Combs, who took a bullet through his left ear.

Once the posse got above their adversaries, they could pour effective fire down upon them, and one outlaw was quickly killed. Whose bullet hit him was never determined. Another fugitive yelled that he had had enough, but when he was ordered out with his hands high, he foolishly raised his rifle and triggered another shot. This brought on a volley from the posse, which finished him. A third man ran for his horse and successfully made his escape.

A search of the bodies of the dead outlaws and their camp produced a number of stolen weapons and five horses. One belonged to Combs, another to Stroud, and the others to neighbors. With a buckboard borrowed from the ranch, Hughes took the bodies into Fort Davis for burial. There they were identified as brothers, Jubus C. and Arthur S. Frier, the latter only seventeen years old.[70]

Not mentioned in Captain Hughes's report of the chase was the valuable property recovered by his posse. A newspaper reported that the posse returned to their owners many stolen articles, including rifles, pistols, razors, and blankets as well as seven stolen horses, several of them highly prized, including one racehorse valued at $500.[71]

Later ranger investigations determined that the man escaping the Frier shootout was Burke Humphreys, "a general hard character" who was wanted for murder near San Antonio. Within a few weeks Hughes located Humphreys. He was being held in the El Paso calaboose, awaiting officers from Tom Green County, where he was under indictment for horse theft. Hughes went to El Paso and assisted Sheriff Gerome W. Shield in transporting the prisoner to San Angelo. At his December trial Captain Hughes and Private Cook appeared as "attached witnesses" to testify regarding the role of the defendant in thefts and gunfights. Humphreys was convicted of horse theft and sentenced to six years in prison.[72]

Interviewed by Texas historian and publisher J. Marvin Hunter in 1944, retired ranger captain John Hughes, almost ninety years old, said he regarded the Glass Mountain gun battle as the toughest and perhaps most dangerous fight he had experienced during his long ranger career.[73]

Certainly some outlaw pursuits by Captain Hughes were unsuccessful. The chase after bandits who stopped and robbed a train near Lozier, Texas, on May 14, 1897, was long and arduous but unproductive. Coming up empty after trailing the robbers more than eighty miles over two weeks, Hughes confessed to Mabry that he considered the gang leader "the hardest man to catch that we have had in Texas for many years."[74]

Heading that gang, as Hughes correctly guessed, was Thomas "Black Jack" Ketchum. Wanted in Tom Green County, Texas, for a murder he committed in 1895, Ketchum had fled with his brother Sam to New Mexico to continue his criminal career. The Ketchums stayed out of Texas and the reach of the rangers until both met inglorious deaths. Apprehended with a badly shot-up arm in 1894 by New Mexico lawmen, Sam suffered the amputation of his arm before dying in a prison cell. Tom's fate was similar. Captured with a badly wounded arm after a botched train robbery in 1899, he also had an arm amputated before trial, conviction, and a 1901 hanging in which his head was snapped off.

Another killer who fled to New Mexico to escape the Texas Rangers and continue his life of crime was Geronimo Parra, who was believed to be the murderer of Sergeant Charles Fusselman back in 1890. Pursued by lawmen in the neighboring territory, Parra, using the alias Jose Nunez, was twice captured but escaped both times. In 1894 Doña Ana County deputy sheriff Ben Williams wounded him in a gunfight, and Parra was tried, convicted, and sent to prison for seven years.

Western lawmen were well aware of Captain Hughes's long-held desire to get his hands on the killer of his good friend, Sergeant Fusselman, so Williams, suspecting that Nunez was actually Parra, notified Hughes of the man's incarceration in the New Mexico penitentiary. Hughes went there, identified Nunez as Parra, and began working to get him extradited to Texas. Negotiations between state and territory officials took time and patience, so it was not until March 1899 that New Mexico turned Parra over to the custody of Hughes, who took him to Texas, where he was tried for the Fusselman murder. He was convicted and then hanged on January 5, 1900, together with Antonio Flores, another murderer. Hughes could sleep better after that, for finally the murders of his two ranger superiors and close friends, Sergeant Fusselman and Captain Jones, had been avenged. Always aware that their deaths had resulted in his own advance to command of Company D, he considered that his way of squaring things.[75]

On March 13, 1901, Hughes received his second gunshot wound. The only one in his long service as a ranger, it was not received in a battle with outlaws, but was an accident. Embarrassed, he provided few details when he notified the new adjutant general, Thomas Scurry, that he would be out of commission for a few days.[76] His embarrassment was warranted because, as he explained in a follow-up letter, the accident was caused by his own negligence: "I had bought me a new pistol 38 cal Smith & Wesson that has a safety notch in the hammer and I thought it was perfectly safe to carry all six chambers loaded—but last night I went to buckle it on and it slipped out of the scabbard and the hammer hit the floor and shot me through the right foot from the inside."[77]

The year 1901 was significant for the Texas Rangers, for that was when the Frontier Battalion was dissolved, replaced by what was called the Ranger Force, composed of four companies commanded by the Four Great Ranger Captains, J. A. Brooks, W. J. McDonald, J. H. Rogers, and J. R. Hughes.[78]

In 1902 Hughes was ordered to move his company to Alice in Nueces County. The site was chosen because of its proximity to railroad and telegraph lines and because it was "within easy reach of the various trails or routes usually traveled by outlaws, especially stock thieves making their way to Mexico or from that country to the interior of Texas."[79] In subsequent years Hughes moved his company frequently, as troubles arose in various areas.

At the request of local officials, in February 1903 Hughes took his current sergeant, Tom M. Ross, and three privates to Fredericksburg, Gillespie County, to assist in the preservation of order and decorum during a volatile, possibly explosive trial. At its completion the district judge, county sheriff, and district attorney posted a notice expressing their gratitude:

"Captain John R. Hughes [and his rangers were] of great assistance . . . throughout the entire term [of the district court]. They were at all times prompt and attentive to business, polite and courteous . . . , and it affords us much pleasure to tender to them our thanks for their service. [They] command the respect of the entire people as well as the officers with whom they are associated."[80]

John Hughes had never been married, nor shown any interest in marrying. He had said, "For several years I did not expect to live to the age that I have. I expected to be killed by criminals. An officer who hunts desperate criminals has no business having a wife and family, and I have remained single."[81] But as he approached the age of fifty, the great man-hunting ranger captain did find a woman he loved and planned to marry. He often visited and was photographed together with seventeen-year-old Elfreda G. Wuerschmidt of El Paso, and they were to be married in June 1904, but Elfreda died suddenly, and the wedding never took place.[82]

When newly reelected President Theodore Roosevelt came to San Antonio in April 1905 for a reunion of his Spanish-American War Rough Riders, Captain Hughes and four men of his company were the only rangers on special duty as part of his entourage, presumably as bodyguards.[83]

The sheriff of Wood County, Texas, feared mob violence in January 1906 when a man accused of murdering a particularly popular victim was brought to trial in Quitman, the county seat. When he requested help, Captain Hughes and three rangers went to Quitman and, as they had done in Fredericksburg, put a lid on any disorder. Robert W. Simpson, the district judge, much like his counterpart in Gillespie County, was most appreciative, thanking Governor S. W. T. Lanham for his prompt action in sending the rangers. "I feel sure that the presence of Capt. Hughes and his efficient force had a very desirable effect," he wrote, adding that since the rangers were "more efficient" than the local militia, the governor should increase the ranger force "as long as mob violence is threatened in this state."[84]

The last years of John Hughes's notable career as a Texas Ranger were spent in similar manner, taking his men to various trouble spots and pre-venting an outbreak of violence by the very presence of the storied ranger captain and his stern-faced enlisted men. Gone were long days in the saddle, following fugitive trails through the wilds of Texas. And it was a good thing, for although he may not have admitted it, Hughes, nearing sixty, was probably physically unable to do the work on which he thrived as a younger man.

In 1914 he toyed with the idea of running for sheriff of Cameron County, at the extreme southern tip of Texas, where the Rio Grande flows into the Gulf of Mexico. Rumor had it that the incumbent sheriff, former ranger Carl T. Ryan, was about to retire, and when Hughes stopped in Brownsville in June of that year, he hinted in an interview that he might be interested in the job, but election would necessitate his retirement from the rangers.[85] Later he changed his mind and did not actively pursue the position, but the word was out—Captain John R. Hughes, after twenty-seven meritorious years, most of them as a company commander, was about to retire.

Politically, 1914 was particularly momentous for the state of Texas, for in November of that year James E. "Pa" Ferguson was elected governor, leading to turmoil within the state, especially for the rangers. One of Ferguson's first acts after assuming office in January 1915 was to drop Hughes from the list of ranger captains, thus removing him from the force he had served so well for almost three decades. This was done without a word of explanation to the man he was deposing. During his time in office Pa Ferguson almost ruined the Texas Rangers by filling vacancies with political cronies rather than well-qualified, experienced members of the law enforcement community. He did not last long as governor, for in August 1917 he was impeached, convicted, removed from office, and denied the ability to hold public office again.

Texas was not done with Ferguson, however. Seven years later his wife, Miriam "Ma" Ferguson, was elected the first female governor of the state, and claiming that Texans had gotten two executives for the price of one, ran the state with her husband. During one term in office, she pardoned more than one hundred convicted felons every month. Shocked by this and by allegations that she and her husband were granting pardons in exchange for cash, the voters did not reelect her. But in 1932 she emerged under the slogan "Me for Ma and I ain't got a durned thing against Pa," and was elected governor again. Forty Texas Rangers resigned in protest.[86] Carrying on her pardoning campaign during her second term, she issued almost four thousand pardons while governor of the state. She was not reelected, and to prevent a future governor from similar excesses, in 1936 the voters of Texas passed an amendment to the state constitution, removing that power from the chief executive.

When it became known that Hughes was retired from the ranger service, however clumsily the termination had been performed by Governor Ferguson, articles appeared in many papers praising the man and recounting some of his adventures during his long tenure, when, as the *El Paso Herald* put it in a lengthy article, his name "was a terror to evil doers."[87]

Over the years several articles had recounted Hughes's legendary manhunt after horse thieves in 1883–84. The only contemporary reference that historians have found regarding Hughes's expedition and its culmination is a letter dated January 3, 1885, to the editor of the *Texas Farm and Ranch* publication in which the author mentioned the theft of sixty horses by "the Craven brothers," who were trailed by "a brave citizen" and caught and jailed in [New] Mexico."[88]

Twenty-two years passed before another paper referred to Hughes's remarkable pursuit, but details were scant in this 1907 article.[89] Four years after that, in 1911, a writer named G. W. Ogden interviewed Hughes, who related the story to him, and readers of *Everybody's Magazine* became aware of his remarkable exploit.

Starting from his ranch, Hughes told Ogden, he had followed the trail westward across the state into the Texas Panhandle, on through the desolate Staked Plains, and into New Mexico Territory. Weeks of dogged pursuit turned into months. Trail evidence indicated that originally there had been three thieves, but along the way one dropped out, so when he finally caught up with them, he faced only a pair of desperadoes. They resisted, and a gunfight ensued. Hughes said he downed one and the other fled, abandoning the horse herd. He went back with his sixteen horses and as many others as he could manage. When he got back, he had been gone for almost a year and had traveled three thousand miles.[90]

Following his long tour of duty with the Texas Rangers, Hughes was often interviewed by newsmen. When questioned by a reporter in 1914 about this memorable early chase, his reticence in discussing the affair was evident. He summed up the entire yearlong experience in a few words: "A band of thieves stole about seventy-five head of horses from my range. Among them were sixteen head of mine. I followed them to New Mexico, got all my horses back and a lot of my neighbors' horses. The band of men was all broken up. Two of them were convicted for stealing my horses, and went to the New Mexico penitentiary."[91]

In another interview, less than a month later, Hughes was either more expansive in providing significant details of what the scribe called "the most remarkable criminal chase that was probably ever made," or the reporter erred in his notes. The chase was said to have taken place not in 1883 but in 1885, and the final gun battle was not a one-against-two affair, but "one man against a desperate gang of *six* cut-throats." According to this story, Hughes killed four of the six and delivered the remaining two to the New Mexican authorities. They were tried, convicted, and imprisoned.[92]

This version of the culminating gun battle was reiterated in a 1961 magazine article by a writer who presumably got the story from John's nephew, Emery H. Hughes. According to this account, when he finally caught up to the six thieves after his long pursuit, "the furious young rancher attacked without hesitation." Following the roar of gunfire, "four rustlers lay dead and two wounded survivors [were] turned . . . over to the nearest sheriff."[93]

In a 1915 newspaper interview Hughes was apparently reluctant to discuss the chase, for the writer had to resort to repeating, word for word, that modest, bare-bones account that Hughes had provided the year before.[94]

During the Great Depression of the 1930s, the Works Progress Administration hired people to record old-timers' stories, and John R. Hughes was one of those interviewed. Again, he was reticent in providing details of his historic hunt and its denouement, saying only that "he followed the thieves month after month, overtook them and recovered his property. This led to his enlistment in the Texas Rangers."[95]

Well, that is not exactly the whole story.

There is no question that by spending almost a year (350 days, by his account) in the pursuit of horse thieves and successfully recovering many stolen animals, John Hughes performed a remarkable feat, one perhaps unequaled in frontier history. And much of the story is no doubt true, for Hughes was justifiably proud of it. But when it came to relating how he managed, alone and unaided, to take the stolen horses from the thieves, the story varies greatly in detail from time to time and becomes questionable.

The first published account of the affair was written by a correspondent called Farmer from Williamson County in 1885—Hughes's biographer Chuck Parsons suggests that Farmer was Hughes himself, or perhaps his more literate brother and partner, Emery—but the story certainly originated with the intrepid man-hunter. In this account there is no mention of a gunfight, only that the thieves were caught and jailed.

For the 1907 interview, Hughes was apparently evasive, for he provided his interrogator no details of his capture. However, by his 1911 interview with Ogden he was more forthcoming, and for the first time, twenty-seven years after its happening, he described a gunfight in which he engaged two felons, after which "one lay dead and the other fleeing, riding for his life."[96] In the interview four years later, mention of a gunfight is again omitted, and Hughes says only that the outlaw gang "was all broken up" and that two went to a New Mexico prison. Then, in another interview only weeks later, he told of finding the camp of the thieves, described as "a desperate gang of six cutthroats," and claimed he made his "attack upon the outlaws with such vehemence and boldness that they were able to offer but little resistance."[97] When it was over, according to that story, four felons lay dead and he was able to turn the other two wounded rustlers over to the law for trial, conviction, and imprisonment.

Two decades later, when he related the story once again for recording by a Works Progress Administration interviewer, he simply said that he overtook the thieves after a long chase and recovered his property without mentioning a gunfight.

The conflicting statements in these articles raise a number of questions. Was there a gunfight or was there not? And if there was, how many outlaws did he face, two or six? And if six, how could one man defeat so many without receiving a scratch himself? And if it required at least six men to drive the stolen herd to New Mexico, as Hughes himself estimated, how was it possible for him to drive most of the herd back by himself?

Much of New Mexico Territory was still pretty wild in the 1880s, but it seems unlikely that such an occurrence as a lone Texas rancher gunning down and killing or capturing as a many as a half-dozen tough outlaws could have completely escaped everyone's notice. Perusal of the extant New Mexico newspapers for the 1884 period provides answers to many of these questions.

The only mention of a gunfight with the outlaws during the summer of 1884 appeared in an edition of the *White Oaks Golden Era*:

A band of rustlers, seven in number, were discovered in the Pinos Altes Mountains last Sunday. The man who came upon them saw that they had forty or fifty head of horses and mules, and returning, reported the facts to Georgetown men who had recently lost such stock. The result was that John Bragraw, Mike Hughes, and some fifteen others took the trail, recaptured their stock, and drove the thieves to the rocks. At last accounts a sharp fight was in progress, and the rustlers stood but little show. They are in the hands of determined men.[98]

The Hughes cited in this account was not John R. Hughes. The White Oaks paper picked up the story from the *Southwest Sentinel* of Silver City, New Mexico, and Mike Hughes was a well-known "old-time miner" frequently mentioned in the Silver City papers.[99] And so the bloody gunfight described in later accounts of John Hughes's hunt were apparently fictitious, added by Hughes or the writers to embellish the story.

Many details of the Hughes 1883–84 man- and horse-hunting adventure that were published in later years were erroneous. He actually made *two* trips, not one, as was always stated. He was actually back at his home ranch during the winter months of 1883–84, but he was gone in total for almost a year.[100] Although there was no dramatic gun-fighting showdown with the men who stole his cattle, he did aid New Mexican lawmen and ranchmen in the apprehension of those culprits and other outlaws, and he did manage to recover his stock and some of his neighbors' stock. And to accomplish this, with two round-trips to New Mexico and chasing many dead-end leads, he probably did cover at least the three thousand horseback miles he claimed.

It was not his remarkable excursion into New Mexico that led to John Hughes's enrollment in the Texas Rangers, as was inferred by some of those later articles. He was not sworn into the rangers' Frontier Battalion until August 10, 1887, three years after that event.[101] Things happened fast for the rangers in the 1880s, and the decision to add a promising new rookie to the ranks would not have taken three years.

Hughes implied in the *El Paso Herald* interview after his retirement that he joined Ranger Aten in the search for Wes Collier because Collier was associated with the horse-stealing Craven brothers he had hunted down in New Mexico, and that Collier had tried to kill him in retaliation. As a "horseback Ranger [working] every county on the Rio Grande from El Paso to Brownsville," he said he had been in several engagements in which criminals were killed, but he had never lost a battle and let a prisoner escape.[102]

He had been approached by writers wanting to relate his experiences in a book, but he declined. "I do not crave notoriety [and] I do not need the money."[103] His remarkable career was not enshrined in a book at that time, but Zane Grey, the popular western novelist, after long hours listening to his accounts of man-hunting adventures, wrote *Lone Star Ranger*, a novel published in 1915 that drew heavily on the stories Hughes had related, and which concluded with a dedication to the rangers:

> Gentlemen,——I have the honor to dedicate this book to you, and the hope that it shall fall to my lot to tell the world the truth about a strange, unique and misunderstood body of men—the Texas Rangers—who made the great Lone Star State habitable, who never knew rest and sleep, who are passing, who surely will not be forgotten and will some day come into their own.

After retirement Hughes lived quietly on his ranch, but with the passing years he was not forgotten by the people of Southwest Texas. As part of the celebration of the state's centennial year in 1936, folks in El Paso planned a parade on New Year's Day and wanted Hughes to lead it as grand marshal. Twice he declined appeals via telegraph and telephone, but after old friends, Sheriff Chris B. Fox and county clerk W. D. Greer, personally visited his ranch, he finally agreed.

Hughes also led the Ranger Division in the parade opening the Texas Centennial Exposition in Dallas that June. Seated on a special $1,500 saddle atop a "gentle horse," wearing a big sombrero, his old six-shooter on his left hip and Winchester in a scabbard, Hughes, even white-bearded and eighty-one years old, personified the old-time horseback Texas Ranger and was the hit of the parade.

For many years Hughes owned a 1924 Model T Ford he had purchased off the sale-room floor, an automobile he claimed to have driven twice to the Pacific Ocean and back, about six times to the Gulf of Mexico, and several times to hot-spring spas in Arkansas and New Mexico.[104]

When a nephew expressed interest in this vehicle as a valuable antique, Hughes gave it to him and purchased Ford's latest, a "streamlined 85-horse power" V-8.[105]

Even as he aged, Hughes gained greater recognition of his achievements, both in Texas and nationally. In 1934 author Eugene Cunningham devoted a chapter to Hughes in his popular book *Triggernometry*, which first acquainted many readers of Old West history with the remarkable career of the longtime Texas Ranger captain. In 1938 the Texas Department of Public Safety issued a declaration appointing Hughes honorary captain of the Texas Ranger Force, bestowing on him "all the rights, privileges, and emoluments appertaining to said appointment."[106]

Then in 1940 *True Detective Magazine* ran a four-part series entitled "Border Boss: The Saga of Captain John R. Hughes, Texas Ranger." Written by Paul Havens (a pen name of author Jack Martin), this series, while inaccurate in many historical details, made Hughes better known beyond Texas. After reading the first installment, an executive of Republic Pictures contacted Hughes, saying his company was interested in making a movie of his career and inquiring if he was agreeable. Receiving an affirmative response, the executive approached the magazine with the idea, but negotiations evidently broke down, for the picture was never produced.[107]

Bernarr MacFadden, publisher of *True Detective*, unable to capitalize on the magazine articles with a motion picture deal, exploited them by announcing the company's award of the first Certificate of Valor to John R. Hughes. Others involved in the selection of the honoree, he said, were New York City police commissioner Lewis J. Valentine; director of the Texas Department of Public Safety Homer Garrison Jr.; and Duluth, Minnesota, chief of police Edward B. Hansen.[108] MacFadden invited Hughes to New York City for the award presentation, but he declined, saying he thought it "unwise" for a man of eighty-five with old wounds "suffered years ago" to travel so far.[109]

Jack Martin, alias Paul Havens, undoubtedly disappointed that his magazine articles had not resulted in a lucrative film contract, wasted no time in expanding his story into book form, however; his biography, entitled *Border Boss: Captain John R. Hughes—Texas Ranger*, was published by the Naylor Company of San Antonio in 1940.[110]

As he grew older, Hughes was no longer able to manage his ranch. He sold it and moved to Austin to live with a niece, Joanna Hughes.

Throughout his declining years Hughes maintained a lively correspondence with former rangers, friends, and admirers. One of the latter was Lyndon B. Johnson, then a member of the Texas State House of Representatives, and later, president. Hughes also kept a journal and a scrapbook. When he reached his nineties in 1945, his thoughts turned increasingly to death and all his friends who had passed on. At the top of one page of his journal he wrote, "My old companions killed," and listed former Rangers Charles Fusselman, John F. Gravis, Frank Jones, Joe McKindrict, Baz Outlaw, Ernest St. Leon, Joe Sitter, and Herff Carnes, as well as non-rangers but great lawmen, Horace L. Roberson, Pat Garrett, and George Scarborough. All had died from gunshot wounds, most while enforcing the law.[111]

In May 1947 the Texas State House and Senate passed similar measures honoring the "patriarch of Texas Rangers," John Reynolds Hughes, who at the age of ninety-two was still "hale and hearty under the weight of years [and was] the pride of the Texas people."[112]

Two weeks later, on June 3, 1947, John Hughes went into the garage of his Austin home, cocked the hammer of his old, pearl-handled Colt .45 six-shooter, put the muzzle in his mouth, and pulled the trigger. Racked with the various ailments of old age, the old lawman had apparently decided to end his life as decisively as he had conducted it.

After hearing testimony from Austin police officer S. H. Rosen, called to the scene by a nurse who discovered the body, and doctor J. J. Brady, who examined the deceased in the garage, justice of the peace Mace Thurman, who was also personally at the scene, determined that John R. Hughes died by his own hand.

Despite all the confirming evidence, some could not accept a suicide verdict, since Hughes left no note explaining why he was about to end his life. Among them was Emery H. Hughes, a nephew of the famous ranger, who told an inquiring historian as late as thirty-four years after the old man's death, "I just don't believe it. . . . They said he was despondent and they didn't make any further investigation. I guess they figured a 93-year-old [sic] man ought to be dead anyway."[113] The remains of John Reynolds Hughes were interred at the Texas State Cemetery at Austin, beside governors, senators, and other Texas notables.

Hughes has been honored in Texas as one of the Four Great Ranger Captains, a distinction well deserved, but he should also be remembered for the remarkable recovery of his stolen horses and the significant role he played in the apprehension of the thieves back in 1883–84. The tracking skills he had been taught by the Indians of the Nations served him well in that endeavor and throughout his long career with the Texas Rangers. He was truly one of the great man-hunters of the Old West.

— *8* —

JAMES FRANKLIN "FRANK" NORFLEET
1865–1967

Norfleet is a short, quiet appearing, gray haired man. . . . There is nothing about him to suggest the detective, amateur or otherwise.

Big Spring Daily Herald, September 28, 1937

Born and raised on a Texas ranch a decade or more after his western frontier man-hunting predecessors, J. Frank Norfleet did not achieve fame as a stalker of criminals until well into the twentieth century, but he was definitely a product of the frontier man-hunting tradition. He hunted buffalo and punched cattle in his early years and retained a frontier cowboy mentality throughout his long and eventful life.

Much of his strong character and deeply imbedded sense of right and wrong were drawn from his father, Jasper Holmes Benton Norfleet, a Virginian who came with his family to Gonzales County, Texas, in 1854 and in his teens fought Indians as a Texas Ranger. After marrying Mary Ann Shaw, he homesteaded a ranch in Williamson County. During the Civil War he served in the Confederate army until, suffering from severe rheumatism, he was discharged in 1864.

The first of six children born to Mary Ann Norfleet on February 23, 1865, James Franklin was named after Jasper's brother.[1] Formal education for Frank, as he was always called, did not extend beyond the sixth grade,[2] but by doing ranch work from an early age, he gained cattle-working skills without acquiring any of the cowboy habits frowned upon by many. He shunned tobacco, hard liquor, and gambling, and he was never known to curse.[3] He was a straight shooter, both literally and figuratively; relatives remembered that even in old age he could knock off jackrabbits

James Franklin "Frank" Norfleet. Courtesy of Library of Congress, Prints and Photographs Division, Washington, D.C. (LC-DIG-hec-32208)

on the run with his single-action six-shooter. Although "quick on the draw and a dead shot with a pistol, he never killed a man, but instead always sought to 'bring 'em in alive for the courts to handle.'"[4]

After Norfleet achieved fame as a man-hunter, he met a prolific writer of pulp fiction in the 1920s and early '30s, who described him as

> a small, slightly stocky man, about five feet four, I should judge, of late middle age, with a stubby white mustache and cold light blue eyes, the pupils of which are like pinpoints. . . . His hands are not of the type usually found in men who are quick with weapons—his hands being very short and blocky in shape. . . . His nerves are in perfect control but in his quick movements he reminds me of a cat, and like all gunfighters, he keeps his hands in constant motion and never very far from his gun.[5]

In his teens Norfleet worked longhorns for his father and later was employed as a ranch hand and drover for various outfits. In 1879 he hunted buffalo on the Staked Plains. Ranching brothers Dudley H. and John W. Snyder hired him in 1886 to help drive five thousand cattle from central Texas to new high-plains rangeland near present-day Muleshoe. After the drive the other drovers, unwilling to remain in that desolate country, headed back home, but Norfleet volunteered to remain and tend the cattle on the new range. On June 22, 1886, the twenty-one-year-old was left alone with full responsibility for the care of five thousand longhorns and fourteen horses. He remembered the date because it was the longest day of the year, and for him the loneliest. Later, other cowboys hired on to help him, but for three years the young man ran the ranch alone. In 1889 the Snyders sold out to barbed wire manufacturer Isaac A. Ellwood, who made the land part of his huge Spade Ranch. Norfleet "went along with the deal almost like a chattel."[6] Still in his early twenties, Norfleet obviously had Ellwood's trust and confidence, just as he had the Snyders', for he remained as the Spade's foreman for seventeen years, and never once in the first fifteen of those years did he meet his employer face to face. Ellwood kept expanding the Spade Ranch, and by the time Norfleet left his employ, he had fenced 246,000 acres of rangeland in barbed wire. He was aided in this task by his younger brother, William Robert "Bob," who joined him on the ranch in 1890.

Norfleet claimed that for two and a half years, while managing the Spade Ranch, he never visited the nearest town, Colorado City, which was 115 miles away, "or looked upon the face of a woman."[7] But in early 1894 he had business in Plainview, Hale County, and there he met twenty-three-year-old Mattie Eliza Hudgins and was immediately smitten. Mattie also fell for the dashing young cowman, and a few months later, on June 13, 1894, they tied the knot. When Norfleet would brag that his wife was the prettiest woman in four counties, she would always counter, "I was the *only* woman in four counties."[8] Frank and Mattie were the first couple to make their home on the Spade Ranch. Four children were born to the union, but tragically, two of them died at an early age. The firstborn, a daughter named Mary, died of diphtheria at the age of seven, and a son, Robert Lee, was only three when he drowned. Surviving were a daughter, Ruth, born in 1908, and a son, Frank Ellwood, born in 1899, who was named for his father and his father's employer but was always called Pete.

Norfleet left the Spade in 1906 to start his own ranch on two thousand acres of rangeland in western Hale County. When a railroad surveyed a route through his property in 1907, he platted a town nineteen miles west of Hale Center, which he called Norfleet. A few buildings were erected there, but the financial panic later that year prevented the railroad officials from carrying out their plans, and the place became a ghost town. Undaunted, Norfleet built a new home on Catfish Draw and gathered wild game and exotic birds into a game preserve that became an attraction for Texas Panhandle visitors. Breeding racehorses, he made famous a line he called the "Five Dollar Strain," made up of descendants of a scraggly pony he had purchased for that amount.

Norfleet continued ranching well into middle age, but in 1919 his life changed abruptly when he made a disastrous mistake, which led to his extraordinary career as a man-hunter. At age fifty-four, flush with cash, having just sold a carload of mules, he stepped off a train in Dallas in early November and went straight to the St. George Hotel to await the return of his friend Dick Slaughter from an out-of-town trip. Finding that Slaughter was not expected back for a day or two, he was disappointed, for he was anxious to complete negotiations with Slaughter for the purchase of ten thousand acres of rangeland to expand his ranch. The mules he had sold had provided the funds to close the deal.

Norfleet had spent his entire life on the Texas plains, far from the hustle and bustle of the city, and was not comfortable in Dallas. He therefore welcomed a casual conversation struck up with a man in the hotel lobby who, with his tanned face, calloused hands, and countrified dress, appeared to be a kindred soul. The man said his name was Miller and that he was from Hill County, Texas. Coincidentally, he also often dealt in mules. Norfleet, who had a wonderfully developed eye and memory for detail, would later describe his acquaintance as being of average size, "built like a burro, [with] black hair streaked with gray, scrutinizing brown eyes with overhanging eye-lids, flaring eye-brows, a deep furrowed, weather-beaten neck and a close-cropped black mustache."[9]

The two engaged in ranch and mule talk for a time, but when Norfleet mentioned that he planned on selling some improved ranchland, Miller's face brightened. It just so happened, he said, that a friend named Charles Harris, a land company representative, was looking to buy ranchland and might be interested in purchasing Norfleet's property. In due course Norfleet was introduced to Harris, a man in his early thirties, who immediately impressed him with his "keenness, alertness, a wide-awakeness and up-to-dateness," his handsome face marred only by a "crooked nose bent slightly to the right." He had blue eyes with "a suggestion of an oriental slant," blond hair, and was undersized.[10]

After discussing possible business transactions, Harris suggested Norfleet check out of the St. George and join him in his double room at the Jefferson Hotel, where he could exhibit his credentials and incidentally save Norfleet a bundle in hotel bills. Norfleet, pleasantly surprised that he had stumbled on such friendly, generous folks in the big city, accepted the offer.

Thus was the country bumpkin drawn like the proverbial fly; he was drawn into the well-spun web of one of the most successful con gangs of the period by "Miller," whose real name was Reno Hamlin, and "Charles Harris," actually W. B. Spencer. Both were steerers for a confidence gang led by Joseph Furey, who was variously called "the cleverest bunco man in the country,"[11] the "internationally known confidence man,"[12] "one of the smartest confidence men ever to operate in this country,"[13] and "one of the most dangerous confidence men in America."[14]

Norfleet had been selected as a mark, a prospect who was financially successful and open to opportunities to acquire more wealth but naïve enough to be taken in by the con men's spiel. At the appropriate times he would be introduced to the top man himself and other gang members who would play their roles. As the play progressed and Norfleet readily accepted each new act, the crooks must have felt they had found the ideal sucker. What they found out too late was that the innocent sheep they were about to fleece, once awakened to his folly, would become a vindictive, implacable foe, who, with incredible determination and tenacity, would hunt them all down to recover his money and bring them to justice.

Will Rogers, another western cowboy cut from the same cloth as Frank Norfleet, famously said, "I never yet met a man I didn't like." Norfleet might have said, before that fateful day in 1919, that he never met a man he didn't trust. He would later frankly admit to his gullibility in allowing himself to be conned by the gang, but said it was because of how he was raised. "With us in the plains country," said the man who had worked fifteen years for an employer without ever meeting him,

> a man's word was his bond. Our cattle deals, our land sales—transactions running into many thousands, frequently—were often completed "sight unseen," the whole agreements being based on verbal representations and verbal understandings. We never doubted each other; in fact, no graver insult could have been passed upon a neighbor than to demand legal formalities in dealing with him. . . . I was simply following the reasoning habits I had acquired in my lifetime of experience.[15]

Over the next days and weeks the gang carried out an artfully planned, carefully programed drama in nine acts known as the Big Con. It was designed to gain the mark's complete confidence, appeal to the grain of cupidity that everyone possesses, and convince him that his newfound friends, experienced in the world of financial markets, were willing to share investment secrets with him that would yield large, quick profits. Then, after squeezing every possible dollar out of him, they would vanish.

The men involved in this Big Con played distinctive roles in the performance. The first act, "putting the mark up," was enacted by steerers Hamlin and Spencer, who selected Norfleet and made the initial approach. The second act, "playing the con," began in the lobby of the Adolphus Hotel, where Spencer, as Harris, had taken him to meet his boss, who was due to arrive in the city, to discuss the purchase of Norfleet's acreage.

Of course, the boss never arrived, as Spencer had no boss, nor a land company job. Sale of Norfleet's acreage was no longer mentioned, for it was time for the third act, "roping the mark," in which steerer Spencer, turned Norfleet over to ace con artist Joe Furey, the "spieler," to continue the operation.

Then was enacted what is called in con parlance the "wallet drop." While waiting in the Adolphus lobby, Norfleet felt a lump behind his seat cushion, and reaching back, pulled out a man's billfold (furtively placed there a moment before by Spencer). Examining it, he found $240 in cash, a Masonic card, a copy of a $100,000 bond payable to McLean & Company, a cipher code card, a United Brokers membership card, and several other documents under the name J. B. Stetson. Norfleet, an honest man, immediately told Spencer they must find Stetson and return the wallet to him. The venerable wallet ploy achieved several important goals for the con men: it established in Norfleet's mind the desired persona of a man of means called Stetson who dealt in large financial transactions, it afforded the necessary motivation for a meeting between Norfleet and Stetson, and it provided evidence of Norfleet's basic honesty so that the presumably cautious financier, Stetson, would deign to involve Norfleet in the big investment opportunity to follow.

A check at the desk confirmed that J. B. Stetson was a guest at the hotel. Norfleet and Spencer went to his room, and there Norfleet first laid eyes on Joseph Furey. He would later describe the man introduced as Stetson as being large, with a "manly, swinging carriage." He had "chestnut hair" and a "round, smooth face" with "greenish blue eyes" that had a "magnetic pull."[16]

Act four of this drama, "the tale," began with Stetson thanking Norfleet and Spencer profusely for returning his wallet and offering them each a hundred-dollar reward, which was politely refused by both. Stetson then explained that his firm, United Brokers, working on behalf of a clandestine syndicate of Wall Street firms to control the stock market, had just directed him by secret code to make certain company investments for a lucrative quick return. He asked Norfleet and Spencer if they would like him to invest the hundred dollars they had declined. A little baffled by the financial finagling he was witnessing, Norfleet saw nothing wrong in venturing money he never really possessed and nodded. Spencer also agreed, of course.

Saying he had to hurry to the stock exchange, Stetson departed, leaving Norfleet and Spencer to discuss this bewildering world of high finance. Soon returning, Stetson jubilantly announced that he had made $20,000 for his employers in that short time and handed each of his two new friends $800, the return on their hundred-dollar investments.[17]

Norfleet, awestruck by this whole episode, accepted the bills, and in doing so, albeit unknowingly, he played his role in act five of the play, "the convincer." For the first time in his life, he was the recipient of funds not honestly earned, obtained by questionable, if not illegal, methods. Before his visitors left, Stetson invited them back to his rooms the next day, as he had some further business he wanted to discuss with them.

Riding high on the euphoria of meeting such fascinating new acquaintances and feeling the warmth of a totally unexpected $800 in his pocket, Norfleet quickly closed the land deal with Dick Slaughter for $95,000 (paying $5,000 in cash and signing a forty-five-day promissory note for the remainder). The transaction was reported in a Dallas paper with the admiring comment that Norfleet had begun "as a $30-a-month 'cow-puncher' and has amassed large holdings."[18]

Act six, "the breakdown," opened the next day with Stetson, the virtuoso spieler, assuring Norfleet and Spencer that he was convinced they were honest, trustworthy men with whom he could confide. Despite his apparent opulence, he admitted to being deeply in debt. He explained that he could amass thousands for his employers through secretly obtained stock market information, but he could not ethically use this information in his own name for personal gain. However, another man could, and he said he had once circumvented this problem by involving an old friend, Chief Justice Charles Evans Hughes of the New York Supreme Court, who had allowed Stetson to use his name and Stetson's money in a tipped stock purchase. The ploy had rewarded the justice with a cool $200,000.[19]

Now desperate to meet the payment of a large personal debt, Stetson asked Norfleet and Spencer if, like the eminent Justice Hughes, they would visit the stock exchange and, using their own names, invest his money in a secretly tipped investment. They would be rewarded with half the profits. Spencer enthusiastically agreed, and Norfleet, after receiving assurances that the plan was perfectly legal, also acquiesced.

The next morning Stetson took Norfleet to the offices where the transaction was ostensibly to take place. Supposedly it was the facility where

Stetson conducted business, but it was actually the Dallas Cotton Exchange, which handled cotton futures contracts. To Norfleet, however, it was everything it was purported to be. Stetson introduced Norfleet to a man he said was the secretary of the exchange, Edward McDorney, who was, in fact, E. J. Ward, another gang member. Described later by Norfleet, Ward had a square face and greenish-blue eyes, hair that was "roached straight up and close-cropped, [a nose] slightly inclined to crookedness," eyebrows "arched into half-moons over his eyes and a loose bag of flesh hung from his chin." A big man, he was now "inclined to pouchiness and flabbiness."[20]

In his exchange secretary role, Ward advised Norfleet that only members were allowed on the premises and, over Stetson's strong objections, asked him to leave. Ward was adamant, and Norfleet returned to Stetson's hotel rooms. Stetson rejoined Norfleet and Spencer later, apologized for Norfleet's rejection at the exchange, but said it was of little consequence as he could place the spurious investments for him and Spencer. Excusing himself, he went to another room to perform what he called his daily chore, decoding secret purchase orders from his employers. Later emerging, he prepared two separate order forms, one for United Brokers and another in the names of Norfleet and Spencer. With their agreement, he added the $800 each had received from him the day before to the money he purportedly committed, and he left to place the orders at the exchange.

He returned with bundles of cash that he ceremoniously dumped on the bed. When the eye-popping, mouth-watering display of cash—which con men called the "boodle"—was divided up, Norfleet's share from his $800 investment and his cut from Stetson's purchase totaled $28,000.[21] He pocketed this wonderful windfall and was about to leave when Ward, the phony exchange secretary, burst in to announce excitedly that the transaction had been improper because Norfleet and Spencer were not exchange members and had not established their financial viability and their ability to pay up if their bid had been lost. He demanded return of the money.

Even as Norfleet envisioned his bonanza taking flight, Stetson provided a solution to the problem. He pointed out that exchange rules called for settlement on the first and fifteenth of each month, and since the fifteenth of that month fell on a Saturday, he, as a member of the exchange, would guarantee confirmation until Monday, the seventeenth, the last day of the period, giving Norfleet and Spencer time to prove their financial capability. Ward agreed to that arrangement but said he would be obliged to return the money to the exchange until confirmation was completed. Before departing with the entire boodle, he made out a bill for the total amount, $68,000, which, if Norfleet and Spencer so desired, could meanwhile be used as credit for further exchange dealings.

Stetson, Norfleet, and Spencer then discussed the next procedure, including the delicate question of available personal finances. Spencer said he would wire his family in Kansas for $35,000. Norfleet could contribute $20,000, he said, but would have to return home to get it. Stetson agreed to provide the balance.

The play now advanced to act seven, "the send." Claiming continuing interest in the purchase of Norfleet's property, but actually merely keeping close tabs on the mark, Spencer accompanied Norfleet to Hale County and stayed three days at the Norfleet home, using his considerable charm to ingratiate himself with the family. After walking the acreage, he said he would recommend purchase of the land to his boss, who surely would pay more than $100,000 for it. Norfleet was elated, as this would more than cover his indebtedness in the Slaughter deal. The two men stopped at Norfleet's Plainview bank to borrow the needed $20,000 before returning to Dallas.

With $20,000 in cash to turn over to his new friends, the mark was primed for the eighth act of the con play, "the touch," when his money would vanish along with all those friends. But Spencer, convinced that Norfleet had more assets at his disposal than previously believed, had persuaded Stetson by phone that the udder of this dairy cow had not been drained dry and could be milked again. When Norfleet and Spencer arrived in Dallas, they were handed a telegram from Stetson, asking them to join him in Fort Worth at the Terminal Hotel, where they could post their pooled money and communicate with the Dallas exchange by phone.

In the neighboring city, Norfleet was given a repetition of the Dallas performance: a brief glimpse of a building purported to house the local stock exchange (but which was in actuality was the Fort Worth Cotton Exchange), a fevered code-deciphering session back at the hotel, Stetson's assurance of another safe United Brokers investment, followed by his suggestion that the three of them "climb aboard that tip," before posting their $68,000 pool of money with the Dallas exchange. Thoroughly convinced of the infallibility of coded instructions from Stetson's employers, Norfleet agreed, and of course, Spencer went along. Stetson said his instructions were to sell his employers' shares of Mexican Petroleum that day on a two-point margin. He made out a bid slip to that affect and sent Spencer to the exchange with it, together with the bill for the money owed and the $68,000.[22]

Returning a short time later, Spencer was beaming. Everything had gone smoothly, he said, although in the crowded room he had lost the bid slip and he had had to make out a replacement for the Mexican Petroleum buy offer.

Norfleet, stunned, stared at him in disbelief, certain that Stetson's instructions were to sell, not buy, the stock, while Stetson flew into a rage, berating Spencer for his stupidity. Cooling down, the gang chief spent a few moments in deep thought. Then, grabbing his hat, he told the others to wait while he rushed to the exchange and tried to hedge by placing a selling order. He returned later to report that just before the market closed he had been able to place an order to sell $80,000 worth of Mexican Petroleum at a two-point margin.[23]

Later that evening Charles Gerber, supposedly the secretary of the Fort Worth Exchange, but actually another gang member, called on them. Norfleet described Gerber as dark haired, with black "bullet eyes," a nose "thick at root and end," and a mouth that looked "like a slit cut in a smooth surface." He would later learn that the man was a killer, "the death-dealer of the organization."[24]

Gerber said their sell bid had earned $160,000, but then recited a familiar tale. The bid had been placed in the names of Norfleet and Spencer, who were not members of the exchange, and it was therefore necessary for them to deposit $80,000 in one of the city's banks to prove they could have paid their debt had they lost. Spencer said he would go to Kansas, and mortgage a farm there for his $30,000 requirement. Norfleet left at once to raise $25,000, his share of the needed $80,000. As before, Stetson agreed to cover the balance.

Back in Hale County, Norfleet had great difficulty explaining to his wife, Mattie, why he needed another $25,000 to save the loss of his initial $20,000 investment, but finally was able to borrow the amount from his brother-in-law. Now beginning to feel the first twinges of doubt about his partners and their convoluted financial ventures, Norfleet carried a

.32-calibre automatic pistol in his coat pocket when he returned to Fort Worth.[25]

When they got his $25,000, the gang was now ready for the ninth and final act of the drama they had so carefully performed, the "blow-off," in which they would vanish with the mark's money, leaving him to ponder just how he had suddenly become poorer. But when Norfleet checked into Fort Worth's Westbrook Hotel, two things happened to disrupt the blow-off temporarily and confirm Norfleet's growing suspicions.

First, his overcoat and automatic pistol mysteriously disappeared from his room. Then, he learned that only $70,000 of the required $80,000 had been raised. Spencer immediately offered to make up the deficit by cashing $10,000 in Liberty Bonds he had in an Austin bank. Stetson said he would go to Dallas, deposit the $70,000 with the exchange there against the due bill, and pay off the remainder when Spencer wired it from Austin.

Suspicious that Stetson and/or Spencer had discovered the gun in his coat and taken it to disarm him, Norfleet's hackles were now raised. Saying he needed to take a walk to mull things over, he went out for a while. When he returned he packed a double-action Smith and Wesson revolver in his hip pocket. Back in the room, he objected strongly to Stetson leaving town with the $70,000. He wanted to retain his portion until the full amount had been raised and final payment could be made. Stetson laughed at this suggestion, rolled the money up in a newspaper, and headed for the elevator. Still voicing his objections, Norfleet followed him. As Stetson pushed the elevator button, he suddenly felt a pistol muzzle jammed against his ribs. "You are going back to the room and settle this matter," growled Norfleet, "or I'll settle it right here and now."[26]

Stetson was visibly shaken by this display of bravado from his heretofore-complacent mark, but back in the room his fertile criminal mind quickly came up with a compromise to solve the problem. He asked Spencer to have his boss wire $30,000 as a down payment for his purchase of Norfleet's farm, which could act as earnest money until Norfleet's title to the land could be certified. Spencer would then hurry to Austin to cash his Liberty Bonds while Stetson and Norfleet met in Dallas the following morning to redeem most of the due bill with the $70,000. This plan satisfied Norfleet's qualms, and he and Spencer headed for the express office while Stetson went his way, toting the money-laden satchel.

Spencer exited the express office carrying a small suitcase. Opening it back in the hotel room, he counted out $30,000 as Norfleet watched.

He put the currency back in the case, together with a signed sales contract, and took it to a bank, where he placed it in a safe deposit box to await confirmation of the land title abstract. He then entrained for Austin.

Norfleet went to Dallas later that day, spent a comfortable night, and then sat down in the lobby of the Cadillac Hotel to await Stetson's arrival. When time passed with no sign of him, he checked with the desk and found that no one named Stetson was registered there. Thinking he might have mistaken which hotel had been set for the meeting, Norfleet canvassed the other guesthouses that he knew the man frequented. Stetson was checked into none of them.

Then the enormity of his situation began to set in, and with cold fear, it struck him that he may have been swindled out of his life savings. In a daze, he went to the offices of the Pinkerton National Detective Agency, explained the situation, and requested their help in locating the missing men. One of their operatives accompanied him to Fort Worth, where Norfleet repeated his woeful tale to the chief of police and the county sheriff. He then went to the bank in which Spencer had placed the $30,000 earnest money. The box was empty.

He now realized with certainty that he had been swindled. "Forty-five thousand dollars gone! Ninety thousand dollars in debt! Fifty-four years old! The three facts crashed on my brain. . . . The knowledge paralyzed, then shook me like an earthquake, crumbling my castles into ashes about my feet."[27]

Sleepless in his hotel room that night, Norfleet fought off the deep depression into which he was falling and steeled himself with a single resolve: He would hunt down the crooks who had stolen his money, recover it if possible, and put every one of them behind bars. It would take him years, but this strong-minded Texas rancher was up to a task that others of less determination and grit would deem impossible. In the end he succeeded, and the experience would transform his life completely. Remarkable man-hunting success would change him from a bucolic West Texas unknown to a national celebrity, acclaimed in the press as the nemesis of confidence men and criminals of all types.[28] His man-hunting feats would be recounted in two popular books, serialized in newspapers from coast to coast, and depicted in a motion picture in which he starred.

But now, back in Hale County, he had to go to the Plainview bank and recount his tale of woe. Dead broke and unable to pay his debts, he told the bank managers he intended to hunt down those who had fleeced him and recover his losses. It is a testament to the high regard they had for the man that they agreed to finance his mission.

The quest began with the flimsiest of leads. From his remarkably retentive memory, he came up with a name he had once seen in Stetson's address book, S. N. Cathey of Corpus Christi. On a hunch that Cathey might have been on the gang's sucker list, Norfleet entrained for the South Texas town only to find Cathey had recently departed for California on a prospecting venture.

Returning home, Norfleet stopped in San Antonio, a sporting town that he knew might be fertile grounds for con men. Checking hotel registers, he found at the St. Anthony that "J. Harrison" had signed in with the same distinctive flourish in the letter J that he remembered the gang leader used when signing "J. B. Stetson." The desk clerk's description of J. Harrison fit Stetson perfectly, but the man had gone, leaving no forwarding address. The dates of his hotel stay convinced Norfleet that Stetson had gone to San Antonio immediately after his flight from Dallas, and he was heartened by this first investigative success.

Before returning home, Norfleet swallowed his pride and gave a full account of his fleecing to the local newspapers. The story was picked up and spread nationally by the Associated Press, a fortuitous circumstance that would prove crucial to his ultimate success.

Back home, his wife gave him his second lead by remarking that Spencer, in bragging about all the states he had visited during his stay at their place, never once mentioned California. Norfleet considered that for a few moments and then shouted that she had hit it. California had not been mentioned because, after his fleecing, they planned on picking up their next victim, Cathey, and heading for that state.[29]

Norfleet was soon on a westbound train. He got off in San Bernardino, for no particular reason other than the fact that he had decided to start his search in southern California and work his way north. The next day, which he remembered as being Christmas,[30] he stopped in the office of county sheriff Walter A. Shay, told his story, and asked if Shay had any helpful information. With a sly grin, Shay replied that he did not make a practice of bestowing Christmas gifts on strangers, but he believed he had one for Norfleet.[31] He led Norfleet to his cellblock where, to his utter amazement, he saw Ward and Gerber, the two fake secretaries of the Dallas and Fort Worth "stock exchanges," behind bars.

The story of Norfleet's successful hunt for his swindlers was so replete with serendipity and incredible coincidence that when it appeared in print, skeptics scoffed and the devout proclaimed that his quest was blessed with divine intervention. This discovery of Ward and Gerber was the first of several incredible happenstances.

Struck speechless by surprise, Norfleet returned with Shay to the office, where the sheriff explained that a Texan named Cathey had come in a few days earlier with a newspaper clipping containing a full account of Norfleet's swindling and a description of the crooks who had pulled it off. Cathey said he was about to close a big deal with a group of purported stock brokers when he read the story, realized the stock brokers answered the con men's descriptions, and rushed to the sheriff's office. "He wanted them pinched," said Shay, "so I took a chance and staged a little raid. I only succeeded in landing these two. The others got away." He had notified Sheriff Sterling Clark at Fort Worth of the arrest, and one of Clark's deputies was on his way to take the two suspects back to Texas for trial.[32]

After he had recovered from the shock of this unexpected but welcome Christmas present, Norfleet looked up Cathey, who told him that the methods the gang employed on him approximated those used on Norfleet. Some of the same names were even used. Like Norfleet, he had been hooked with the lost-wallet gimmick.

Miraculously, it seemed, within only a few weeks following Norfleet's vow to hunt down the five swindlers who had robbed him, two were in custody. When Ward and Gerber fought extradition to Texas, Norfleet testified at a grand jury hearing in Fort Worth to get them returned. He was the star witness at a trial the next year, when both were convicted of swindling and sentenced to ten years in prison.[33]

While Ward and Gerber awaited trial, Norfleet made repeated efforts to get information from them about the other gang members. Finally, Gerber, hoping to avoid conviction by some kind of legal loophole, squealed on Reno Hamlin, saying he was living in Cleburne, Texas. When lawmen failed to find Hamlin there, Norfleet suspected this was some kind of lawyer's trick. But he and the Fort Worth prosecutors showed that they could be clever and deceptive also. They publicly announced that Hamlin's indictment had been quashed, and when he showed up, thinking he was in the clear, they had him arrested on a new indictment.[34]

With three of the gang behind bars, Norfleet concentrated on hunting down the remaining two, Spencer and the man he knew only as Stetson, who was the top prize. He roamed southern California cities, calling on police stations and perusing hotel registers as well as telephone and telegraph records, looking for a lead. While examining a book of suspects' mug shots in a Los Angeles police station, he recognized Stetson and learned for the first time that the real name of the outfit's chieftain was Joseph Furey.

He was on a train returning to Texas when another of those incredible strokes of luck that seemed to bless his quest occurred. In a conversation with a woman from Georgia, he learned that before her marriage she had been a detective, so he related his story, including detailed descriptions of the men he sought. The woman, listening with rapt interest, requested his address and promised to keep her eyes open and notify him if she turned up any leads in her travels. A few days later he received a letter from the lady saying that a man closely matching Furey's description had boarded her train at Houston. Moving closer to the seat where he was talking with an associate, she heard him say he was en route to Miami "to play the game," but would stop off a few days in Jacksonville as, he said, "so many of the boys are down there, and I like to keep up with the gang and find out who the new suckers are."

That information started Norfleet off again, this time eastward to Florida. Stopping first in Tallahassee, he called on Governor Cary A. Hardee and obtained a requisition warrant allowing him to remove suspects he found out of state.[35] Continuing on to Jacksonville and Saint Augustine, he questioned city and county law enforcement officers and pored over rogue's-gallery photos. When no leads turned up, he crossed over to Tampa and Saint Petersburg and did the same thing. Learning that there was a confidence gang at work in Sanford, which was called Celery City for the abundant crop raised in its surrounding fields, he went there and set a trap with himself as bait. Using the name Parkinson, and properly dressed for the part, he played the role of a hick from the sticks looking to invest some money in celery-producing acreage.

The first nibble came within a day. A man giving his name as Johnson struck up a conversation and invited him to go to Daytona Beach with him, where land investment opportunities were better. Familiar with the procedure, Norfleet (as Parkinson) went along with the game, and at

Daytona Beach he recognized the next step. Johnson introduced him to a man named Steel, who, Johnson confided, had taken $125,000 out of a stock exchange in a single day. Norfleet was not surprised when Steel's wonderful ability to multiply money was demonstrated. Steel excused himself for a quick visit to the exchange, taking with him twenty dollars of Johnson's cash, and returned shortly afterward to announce that Johnson's twenty had miraculously become eighty.

Apparently warming to his newfound friends, Steel invited them to join him at a private exchange. Hoping this would lead him to Furey, Norfleet assented and, together with Steel and Johnson, rode in Steel's chauffeur-driven car to a clubhouse on the beach. All the phony exchange accouterments were there: telephones and tickertape, telegraph operator with green eye shade, and a man feverishly chalking and erasing stock figures on a blackboard. Two armed guards flanked a money-laden table.

Norfleet became apprehensive. This scene did not fit the scenario with which he was familiar. Perhaps these crooks enticed wealthy marks to this location and rolled them for the cash they carried. As he edged toward the door, a motorboat pulled up at the dock. A man leaped out, ran into the clubhouse, and handed Steel a slip of paper. Steel's face turned malevolent after he read it, and he grasped Norfleet's arm.

Knowing the time had come for action, Norfleet pulled a gun, jammed it into Steel's ribs, and ordered everyone in the room to get their hands high. Johnson started toward him, but froze when Norfleet covered him with a second pistol. Keeping his guns trained on Steel and Johnson, he directed them to Steel's car and ordered the driver to take them back to Daytona Beach.

There, having no evidence of a crime with which to charge them, he turned them loose after retrieving the note from Steel's pocket. It read: "That is Norfleet himself. Don't get him started. If you do, he'll kill every dam one of you. Don't let him get away, boys. Don't let him get away!" and was signed, "Joe." Norfleet was convinced that it was penned by Joseph Furey, now heading a new, more murderous gang, and that he was nearby.

Undaunted by his close call, Norfleet continued his search, following reported sightings of Furey and other leads, and eventually he worked his way far down the eastern Florida coast to Key West, where he spotted Furey. He called on the local police for help in nabbing him, but officers assigned to the job fled with the crook in a motorboat, confirming Norfleet's growing conviction that many local law enforcement officials worked in league with the confidence gangs. Believing Furey was headed for Cuba to escape his clutches, Norfleet chartered a hydroplane and had the pilot fly over the coral islands and along the Cuban coast while he scanned the area with binoculars for the motorboat carrying the three men, but they had vanished.

Disappointed, Norfleet returned home and pondered his next move. Reviewing the events of the past few months, he recalled talking to a shoplifter in the San Antonio police station who told him that she had sold a stolen Hudson seal coat to a man answering Furey's description, who was staying in room 113 of the St. Anthony Hotel.

Chasing this slim lead, Norfleet returned to San Antonio, accompanied by Jesse Brown, the Fort Worth district attorney who, after prosecuting Ward and Gerber, had taken a personal interest in the Norfleet manhunt. There, St. Anthony Hotel registries confirmed that "J. Harrison," who was certainly Joe Furey, had stayed three days in room 113 during December 1920.

Believing that Furey might have shipped the purchased coat from San Antonio before leaving, Norfleet chased that possibility. District attorney Brown used his official clout to gain access to parcel post records, generally unavailable to the general public, and learned that during the period Furey was in San Antonio, an uninsured three-pound package, without sender's or recipient's name, had been sent from San Antonio to 506 Stanford Court Apartments in San Francisco.

Norfleet and Brown were on the next train to California. Stopping in San Bernardino for an overnight stay, Brown accepted an invitation to dine with Sheriff Shay while Norfleet continued his detective work at the Stewart Hotel, where Furey had stayed under the name Peck during the Cathey swindle. A review of the phone records revealed that he had made a long-distance call to Glendale 684-J in Los Angeles. To Norfleet this was of great significance; it meant that Furey knew someone in Glendale, and he hoped that person could lead him to his prey.

Leaving a note for Brown, Norfleet caught the next train to Los Angeles, where he checked into the Alhambra Hotel and placed a call to Glendale 684-J. When a woman answered, he asked who was speaking. "This is Mrs. Furey," she responded. "To whom did you wish to speak?"

Blurting that he had the wrong number, Norfleet slammed down the receiver, let out a whoop of triumph, and danced in a fit of elation. He had traced his quarry to his lair!

The next day he headed for Glendale, specifically 412 Piedmont Park, the address he had obtained by cross-referencing the phone number. He found the residence, a large manor house surrounded by an orange grove, a vineyard, and a verdant garden. For three days, posing as a landscape gardener puttering around a park across the street, he kept an eye on the house, hoping Furey might appear. One day a little boy came out and began playing in the yard. Engaging him in conversation, Norfleet learned that the boy's "papa" was coming home for Christmas.[36]

Norfleet hurried to the sheriff's office, told his story to Undersheriff Al Manning, and requested help in surveillance of the house until Furey could be captured. Deputies Walter Lips and William Anderson, who were assigned to the job, assured Norfleet they could handle Furey without his help and warned him to stay away from the house. Seeing and recognizing him, they said, Furey might panic, begin shooting, and "plug one of us."[37]

Believing he had left the Furey house in the care of trustworthy officers, Norfleet rejoined Jesse Brown and Sheriff Shay, who had arrived from San Bernardino, and together the three went on to San Francisco to investigate the Stanford Court apartments, the destination of Furey's sealskin coat.

Stanford Court, like Furey's Glendale manor house, was a vision of opulence. An enormous residential hotel, it occupied almost a full block atop Nob Hill. When Norfleet asked about the resident of apartment 506 at the front desk, he was told that such information was not given out, and furthermore, outsiders were not permitted within the building without written permission. Norfleet left, but outside he chatted up a genial-appearing Irish doorman who looked like he might enjoy a wee off-duty drop. After careful questions in a nearby pub, the doorman revealed that a mother, a daughter, and two sons lived in apartment 506.

The next day Norfleet ignored the admonitions of the desk clerk, crossed the spacious lobby, entered an elevator, and requested the fifth floor. But when he could not produce written permission requested by the elevator operator, he was escorted out by two uniformed guards.

Deciding a new tack was necessary, Norfleet thought a female might overcome the formidable Stanford Court roadblocks easier than a man.

While in town, Jesse Brown was visiting with friends, Mrs. Jesse Carson and Lucille, her eighteen-year-old daughter, and Norfleet, having met them, was particularly impressed by the vivacious Lucille. He asked her if she would like to play detective, and she readily agreed.

He showed her Furey's photo and said he wanted to know if that man lived at the Stanford Court address, and if not, who did. He hoped she could gain entrance to the apartment and look for a displayed photo of Furey or a Hudson seal coat. Her excuse for calling at 506 was to be the sale of a puppy. When told that no one there was buying a puppy, she was to produce an address slip Norfleet had prepared with the apartment number crudely written so Lucille could apologize, saying she must have misread the number. He gave her another slip containing her own telephone number and asked her to flirt with the young elevator operator, and then pass him the slip and ask him to call her when the male resident of 506 returned.

Lucille, dressed in a little-girl smock that made her look years younger than her actual age, followed instructions implicitly, gained access to 506 without challenge, and while speaking with the woman occupant, had an opportunity to scan the living room. Rejoining Norfleet, she provided him with much vital information. The occupant of 506 was Mabel H. Harrison. Lucille saw no pictures of Furey, but did note a black derby hat on the coat rack and a Hudson seal coat draped over a living room chair. Her flirtation with the elevator operator elicited the additional information that the apartment's male occupant, "a big, husky rich stockbroker from New York," was expected to arrive for Christmas.[38]

Norfleet was delighted that his seal coat clue was paying off. Harrison was one of Furey's aliases, and it now became evident that the slick crook was maintaining two homes and families, a wife and children in a magnificent Glendale manor house and a mistress and more children in a luxurious apartment in San Francisco. Both women expected to see him at Christmas. Surely he could be nabbed at one home or the other.

Returning to his hotel, Norfleet found a message from one of his contacts that made him think capture might be made even before Christmas. Furey, it said, was currently staying at a San Diego hotel. Norfleet hurried southward, only to find that his quarry was not registered at any hotel in the city and that the report was false.

Arriving back in Los Angeles late at night, he went straight to the sheriff's office and was appalled to find Deputies Lips and Anderson in huddled conference with Undersheriff Manning instead of keeping watch on Furey's home. He knew at once that he had been double-crossed.[39]

Double-crossed indeed! Norfleet would later learn that when Furey showed up at his Glendale home, the deputies had nabbed him, but instead of taking him to headquarters, they hid him out in a hotel, where they demanded payment of $20,000 for his release. Furey called his wife, who was able to raise $12,000, cleaning out their son's bank account in the process. Furey said he and his captors would have to go to San Francisco for the balance, so off the three went. After arranging for the bogus lead sending Norfleet to San Diego, they checked into the very room he had just vacated. Furey called his mistress, Mabel Harrison, and had her bring $8,000. When the money was turned over to the crooked cops, they released Furey and returned to Los Angeles with their $20,000.

They had little time to enjoy their ill-gotten cash, however. Two months later they were arrested and charged with extortion and bribery. At a trial they were convicted and sentenced to terms of one to fifteen years in San Quentin Penitentiary.[40] Of course, Lips and Anderson might have gotten away with their duplicity had not Joe Furey spilled the beans about the bribery when he was finally apprehended.

After his release by the crooked cops, California was too hot for Furey, so he crossed the continent again. Norfleet got a lead on that move when a confidante he had cultivated in the Los Angeles telegraph office tipped him off that Furey had wired a large sum of money to his wife in Glendale as a Christmas present. The telegram originated in Jacksonville, Florida, and Norfleet immediately entrained for another cross-continent trip, with a short stopover in Texas to spend Christmas with his family. His son Pete accompanied him when he resumed his journey. After stopping in Tallahassee to get the governor's signature on a requisition warrant for Furey, father and son arrived in Jacksonville and split up to canvass the hotels. When Pete reported that he had seen a man answering Furey's description in the lobby of the Mason Hotel, Norfleet went there in disguise, confirmed the recognition, and finally had the man he had hunted all over the country in his sights.

The Norfleets tailed Furey from his hotel to the Hilton Café. Pete waited outside as his father entered. Frank gestured that he would like a table near Furey, but the headwaiter, misinterpreting the move, seated him at the same table. For one tense moment the two men stared at each other. Then Furey, seeing through Norfleet's disguise to the pure hatred burning in the eyes of the man he had conned, leaped to his feet. Norfleet also arose, pulled a pistol, and announced that Furey was his prisoner.

The crafty con man began shouting that he was being robbed at gunpoint. Pandemonium ensued as the café's patrons panicked. Women screamed, tables were overturned, and china and glassware crashed to the floor as Furey's cries continued.

A man surged through the doorway, plowed past the frightened diners, grabbed Norfleet from behind, and twisted his gun hand down. It was Steel, Furey's Florida confederate. He shoved a knee into Norfleet's back and wrapped an arm around his neck, cutting off his air. With Norfleet's gun no longer pointed at him, Furey tried to escape, but Norfleet grasped his coat in a viselike grip, and the three men were locked in a deadly tableau.

Like a trapped animal, Furey sank his teeth into Norfleet's hand. Even in pain and gasping for breath, Norfleet retained his clutch on Furey's coat. "He'd have to cut that hand off before I'd loosen my grip," he recalled. "I'd waited too long to get my hands on him. Between his frantic squalls for help he would snarl and snap at my hand like a captive wolf."[41]

At this critical moment Pete Norfleet, with guns in both hands, burst through the door, followed quickly by several policemen responding to the ruckus inside. The officers accepted Furey's claim that he was being robbed by the two gunmen until Norfleet, freed of Steel's clutches, produced police mug shots of Furey and the requisition warrant, recently signed and dated by the Florida governor, and they turned the gang leader over to him. At police headquarters Norfleet explained that before entraining with his prisoner, he wanted to hold him at a secluded location where he could not contact lawyers and start habeas corpus or other stalling procedures. He was provided a Cadillac limousine and driver from a rental agency as well as a recommendation to take the prisoner to a particular flag station outside of Jacksonville to catch the train. Following these directions, the Norfleets took Furey to the location and awaited a westbound train. The con artist meanwhile employed his usual tactic to gain freedom and plied his captor with monetary offers. In addition to the $45,000 he had lost to the con men, Norfleet had incurred heavy debts in his pursuits and he was tempted. He fervently wanted to put Furey behind bars, but the recovery of some of his lost cash was enticing. Perhaps planning to get some money back and then renege on his release promise,

MAN-HUNTERS OF THE OLD WEST

he agreed to accept $20,000 in cash and sent Pete back to present Furey's underlings in the city with his signed order.

After Pete's departure two carloads of gunmen pulled up, and Norfleet, finding himself surrounded by shotgun-toting toughs, realized he had been double-crossed by the Jacksonville lawmen. He kept the gunmen at bay by pressing a pistol to Furey's head and threatening to blow out his brains if they advanced closer. Furey believed him and screamed at his men to stay back. The Mexican standoff continued until Pete returned, not surprisingly without the money. Aware that he had been hoodwinked by both the Jacksonville constabulary and Furey, Norfleet was not surprised when the train he wanted to flag down flew right on by; the villainous cops had directed him to a station no longer in use.

Things looked bleak, but in this perilous game of wits he still held an ace in the hole, his pistol at Furey's head. Well aware that a twitch of Norfleet's finger meant his own instant death, Furey commanded his gunmen to back off as Norfleet and Pete steered their prisoner to the limousine and directed the driver to take them to the city.

The Cadillac moved down the road, flanked on either side by the gunmen's cars with shotguns protruding from the windows. Norfleet ordered his driver to floor it, and the big, powerful car leaped ahead, leaving the other automobiles in its dust. Seeing his last chance at freedom thwarted, Furey made a desperate grab for the steering wheel and the car swerved precariously before a blow from the barrel of Norfleet's pistol knocked him cold.[42]

Back in town Norfleet fired off a telegram to District Attorney Jesse Brown: "Have Joe Furey. On way to Texas. Have good man meet me in New Orleans at police station."[43] Then father and son, exhausted from the day's adventures, booked a drawing room on a train and boarded with their prisoner.

Although equally fatigued from that day's arduous events, Furey, with manacled hands and a throbbing head, was unwilling to concede victory to his tenacious adversary. The Norfleets allowed him to nervously pace the limited confines of the drawing room as the train moved slowly through the outskirts of Jacksonville. Suddenly, Furey raised his arms to protect his face and threw his copious bulk headfirst through the window. Norfleet glanced up in time to see his feet disappearing. Without hesitation

Pete dove through the broken window in pursuit of the escaping felon. The conductor, who witnessed this remarkable scene, immediately pulled the emergency brake cord, stopping the train. Racing through the Pullmans to the baggage car at the rear, Norfleet leaped to the ground while a quick-thinking porter found his baggage and tossed it after him.

When father and son were reunited minutes later, Pete reported that he had seen Furey board a switch engine headed back to Jacksonville. Norfleet shouted to a man in a nearby switch tower that they were officers in pursuit of a dangerous criminal and instructed him to telegraph a man he could trust, Jacksonville detective W. B. Cahoon, informing him of Furey's escape attempt and requesting to have reliable officers meet the switch engine at the station to hold the fugitive for Norfleet's arrival. An obliging engineer on another locomotive agreed to take the Norfleets after the fleeing felon, and when the two switch engines arrived at the Jacksonville station almost simultaneously, an officer took Furey into custody and Norfleet relieved him of his charge.

With his head battered by Norfleet's pistol and legs injured from his bold leap from the train, Furey needed medical treatment. Norfleet fired off another wire to Brown: "Furey jumped through train window. Badly injured. Do not know when we can leave with him."[44]

For several days the captors shuttled their prisoner around Jacksonville, avoiding the duplicitous police and lawyers with habeas corpus papers, before setting out on a succession of trains, and on the way, locking Furey up overnight in various holding cells. On arrival in Fort Worth on January 24, 1921, he faced swindling charges filed by a Tarrant County grand jury and was jailed.

In a *Fort Worth Star-Telegram* interview, Norfleet related for the first time the account of his determined quest for the men who had fleeced him, a tale he would repeat many times in the future. The story was picked up by newspapers across the country, and the name Frank Norfleet became nationally known. The man the press began touting as the "Nemesis of Crookdom" claimed that searching eighteen states and Mexico for the con gang had cost him $18,000 in addition to the $45,000 stolen from him. He said he had never fired his pistol, and the only blood spilled by either hunter or quarry resulted from minor injuries to his hand when Furey bit him, and the gang leader's sore head and injured legs.[45]

MAN-HUNTERS OF THE OLD WEST

Tried and convicted on two counts of swindling Norfleet, Furey received ten-year sentences on each count, to be served consecutively, and went off to Huntsville State Prison facing twenty years imprisonment.[46]

After tracking down and playing the preeminent role in the conviction and incarceration of four of the five men who had swindled him, Norfleet attended to some long-neglected affairs at home. But the fifth crook, W. B. Spencer, was still on the loose, and the man-hunter could not rest until he also was put away. Postponing retirement plans, he spent the latter months of 1921, all of 1922, and much of 1923 crisscrossing North America in search of Spencer.

In Montreal, Canada, he had Spencer in his grip—literally—but lost him. Spotting him on a busy street, Norfleet got his hands on him and pushed him out of the crowd into a theater, but an excited manager pulled him off his catch, and Spencer got away.[47]

In August 1922, acting on a tip that Spencer might now be working out of Denver, Norfleet went there and stepped squarely into a huge super-secret undercover operation conducted by Philip S. Van Cise, an energetic district attorney. Van Cise was determined to bring down the swindling syndicate overseen by Lou Blonger, who had dominated crooked work in the Colorado capital for more than twenty years. For eighteen months Van Cise had been building his case against Blonger as well as his right-hand man, Adolph "Kid" Duff, and their cohorts, and he feared the appearance of lone-wolf man-hunter Norfleet might alarm Denver criminals and disrupt his carefully prepared plans. Like all newspaper readers, Van Cise knew Norfleet by his "Nemesis of Crookdom" renown, but on meeting the man, he was surprised by how little he resembled fictional heroes:

> Instead of the steely gray eyes of fiction, he had watery blue ones. Instead of the powerful, crushing grip of the man-killer, he had a soft and flaccid paw. Instead of being tall and broad-shouldered, he was a little fellow about five feet six inches tall, weighing about one hundred and twenty-five pounds, [with] a soft, drawling Texas voice.
>
> He was . . . one whom you would pass on the street without noticing, and yet he was as brave and fearless a man as ever rode the Western plains. He toted one gun in a shoulder holster under his left arm; he had another one stuck under his trousers in front, and he carried a pair of handcuffs in his right hand hip pocket. He was

quick on the draw, a dead shot. . . . Hated and feared by the con-men, he would have been instantly murdered by any of them at the least possible opportunity, and [when he went] after them he took his life in his hands.[48]

Van Cise realized that such a man could aid rather than impede his campaign against the Blonger gang. Learning that Norfleet planned to nab Spencer with his own sting operation by playing the part of a well-heeled mark, ripe for fleecing, he reached an agreement with the Texan. Norfleet would continue his charade, and Van Cise, hopefully, would ensnare Spencer when he lowered his widespread net.

In disguise and passing himself off as a big cotton raiser from Texas named L. A. Mulligan, Norfleet checked into Denver's prestigious Brown Palace Hotel. He was soon approached by a steerer who drew him into the multi-act con game with which he was quite familiar. After a tortuous period playing his part, which included being held and guarded day and night in a hotel room by gang members while waiting for supposed fund transfers, Norfleet feigned a toothache, reached a dentist's office, and was able to phone Van Cise and inform him of his plight. This triggered the district attorney's roundup.

Early on the morning of August 24, 1922, a force of trustworthy city and county police officers and detectives, augmented by Colorado Rangers and reliable World War combat veterans, fanned out to roust Blonger and his cohorts from their various dens, arrest and cuff them, and herd them into a temporary holding area in a church. As ordered by Van Cise, the first taken into custody were Norfleet's guards. When a Denver detective and a ranger, guns in hand, burst into the room, Norfleet breathed a sigh of relief, but his captors, of course, had entirely opposite reactions.

Lou Blonger, Kid Duff, and thirty-two of their underlings were collared that day, but Spencer, Norfleet's target, was not among them. Of those arrested, only Blonger and Duff managed to raise the $25,000 bail and gained their release the next day.[49] Norfleet was waiting when Duff emerged from the jail, and he was accompanied by Patrick "Red" Galla-gher, who was "well-known in sporting circles" and had pledged half his interest in a Denver hotel as security for the bail bonds.[50] Confronting Duff, Norfleet demanded to know if he thought Spencer was worth all this trouble for the gang, to which Duff responded that if he had known it was just Spencer who was wanted, he would have gladly turned him over to Norfleet. Pressed further, he denied any knowledge of Spencer's current location, but said he had been staying at the Empire Hotel.[51]

When questioned by Norfleet, the Empire's proprietor confirmed that Spencer had been a guest, but had checked out that morning, leaving his suitcase with a note instructing her to forward it to an address in Salinas, Kansas. Searching the grip, Norfleet found the usual assortment of con-game gear and, surprisingly, the pistol stolen from him three years before.[52] Norfleet boarded a train for Salinas that same day, but on arrival found no trace of Spencer and concluded sadly that he had followed a false trail prepared for him by the slick con man. Following up on other leads, he traveled through Colorado, Wyoming, Utah, and Montana before going to Kingston, Ontario, Canada, Spencer's original hometown, where he enlisted the Royal Canadian Mounted Police to aid him in the search. Although he came close to apprehending Spencer several times, all efforts proved fruitless.

His search was interrupted by a summons to appear in Denver and testify in a Blonger gang case hearing. After his testimony, rumors spread that he had been marked for death by the criminal gang. Van Cise gave these reports sufficient credence to assign two armed guards to Norfleet, providing twenty-four hour protection while he was in the city. The *Denver Post* cautioned possible assassins that Norfleet was also well armed, packing three pistols.[53] Norfleet took the rumors seriously; boarding a train after the hearing, he was accompanied by two bodyguards, his son Pete, and a hired private detective. Over the next few months he pursued other dead-end leads in Colorado, New Mexico, and Texas before returning home to attend to affairs and get some much-needed rest.

On February 5, 1923, the trial in Denver got underway for the bunko charges against Lou Blonger, Kid Duff, and eighteen of their cohorts, and Norfleet was called back to provide his damning prosecution testimony. As he related details of his "vendetta against the facile-tongued parasites of society," spectators sat entranced and defendants squirmed, according to the *Denver Post*.[54] The prosecution rested its case on March 23, and to everyone's amazement, the defense also rested without calling a single witness. This maneuver, followed by almost a week of waiting for a verdict, triggered speculation that the jury had been fixed. But finally the jury reached a unanimous verdict, finding all twenty defendants guilty as charged. Blonger, Duff, and nine others received prison terms of seven to ten years; eight others got three-to-ten-year stretches, and one, deemed insane, went to an asylum instead of prison.[55]

Resuming his hunt for Spencer, Norfleet, accompanied by his fifteen-year-old daughter Ruth, went by car following recent information that his quarry now traveled by automobile rather than railroad. Receiving word in September 1923 that a man calling himself A. P. Hunt but answering Spencer's description had been arrested in Salt Lake City, he wired authorities there to hold the suspect until he arrived and caught a train for Utah. The moment he confronted the suspect, he knew his relentless four-year manhunt was finally over, for he was looking at the last member of the gang that had fleeced him.

"How are you, Spencer?" he asked, as quietly and courteously as if greeting an old friend.

"Don't you call me Spencer!" was the defiant response. "I am A. P. Hunt."

A woman ran up, crying, "Spencer isn't our name. Our name is Harris! His name is Charlie and I'm Mildred." Norfleet could only grin and nod, for it was as Charles Harris that the man standing before him had introduced himself when this saga began four years earlier.

Mildred's outburst convinced her husband that the jig was up, and he confessed to being Norfleet's long-sought culprit,[56] but now that the hunt and capture were over, he vented venomously about his pursuer to other officers. Norfleet, he growled, "always comes along at the right minute for himself and the wrong minute for me. . . . I'd rather die and go to hell tonight than live as I have since I met Norfleet. Every knock on the door, every telephone bell, every stranger in the night has raised hell with my nerves. . . . I'm through now, but I can draw a free breath at last!"[57]

Utah authorities refused to release Spencer to Norfleet's custody until he was prosecuted for charges against him there. But after serving jail time in Salt Lake City, the veteran con man was convicted in Texas of two counts of fleecing Norfleet, and in March 1924 he was sentenced to eight years in the penitentiary.[58]

The completion of Norfleet's self-appointed task—hunting down and jailing the last of the swindlers who had victimized him—was disseminated by the Associated Press to newspapers across the country, activating another round of editorials lauding the exploits of the Texas man-hunter. Typical was this comment in a New Hampshire paper:

The amateur detective is usually a joke. Likewise the fleeced farmer. But J. Frank Norfleet is very far from being a joke. A few days ago he finished off one of the most remarkable chapters in American criminology with the capture . . . of the last of six [*sic*] crooks who beat him out of $42,000 [*sic*] . . . in 1919.

Norfleet, a rancher, who stands five feet two [*sic*], decided promptly to bring the crooks to justice. [Armed with] two six-shooters [he] started to round them up [and has] arrested not less than 75 crooks [*sic*], most of who [*sic*] have been convicted. He is going back now to his ranch, much poorer in money than when he started, but thoroughly satisfied.

There is a lesson in persistency, courage and resourcefulness for any officer of the law. There is a lesson, too, for victimized citizens who let crooks get away with their boodle and thus encourage the bunko business. Half a dozen men like Norfleet might rid the country of such bands and save honest people many millions a year.[59]

A Michigan editor opined that Norfleet "did not pursue the bunko men merely because they had taken his money, but because they had violated his confidence and trust [and] to do that on the Texas plains is a fatal mistake."[60]

Although he achieved his goal of bringing the men who had fleeced him to justice, Norfleet never recovered the funds they stole from him nor the money he spent in his four-year-long search. Returning home after the Spencer apprehension, he faced a grim financial situation. He was deeply in debt, with farm mortgage payments long in arrears and the banks pressuring him for repayment of the loans they had advanced to finance his man-hunting. He almost lost his farm when a bank began foreclosure proceedings, but he was rescued by a friend who purchased a five-thousand-acre parcel of his land for $153,000, enough to cover his immediate financial needs, and then rented it back to him.[61]

Recognizing that his amazing story had the potential for monetary gain, Norfleet spent the next several years exploiting his four-year experience in the pursuit of profit. First was a Texas lecture tour. Advertised as cautionary addresses, his talks warned listeners to avoid falling for the get-rich-quick schemes of professional con men as he had done. But they soon became enlivened, according to a newspaper report, by "frequent illustrations of quick drawing [and] shooting from the hip," punctuating his discourses "with an enthusiastic vigor that twangs an excitable cord along the spinal column."[62]

In his talks Norfleet stressed the complicity of some law enforcement officers in the crimes committed by the swindling gangs, saying he could have gotten the whole gang in four months instead of four years if he hadn't been double-crossed by crooked officers, who had been bought off. He claimed to have fought them as hard as the men he chased.[63]

Turning to the publication industry, Norfleet, with the help of ghost-writers, spent the latter months of 1923 and early 1924 writing a book that recounted his experiences as a con game mark turned con artist nemesis. In the fall of 1924 a small Fort Worth publishing house brought out his work under the title *Norfleet: The Actual Experiences of a Texas Rancher's 30,000-Mile Transcontinental Chase after Five Confidence Men*. Due to the publisher's lack of national advertising and marketing capability, sales of this edition were meager, limited mostly to Texas.

Reviewers in that state, however, were almost unanimous in their praise. "English literature," gushed the *Lubbock Morning Avalanche*, "has been enriched by a most gripping, startling compilation of thrills, laughter and pathos, held together by a thread of stupendous human endeavor, tempered by tolerance and compassion. . . . The plot of this true account is as perfectly constructed as any work of a master fiction writer."[64] The *Mexia Daily News* found that this native Texan's "true story" was full of "thrilling experiences and hair-breadth escapes [that would] satisfy even the most exacting lover of excitement and adventure."[65]

A *Dallas Morning News* reviewer praised the book as "our own indigenous detective story—of, by and for Texas." While critical of the writing style as "cheap and crudely sensational . . . , modeled on the dime novel of a generation ago," this reviewer admitted that possibly Norfleet himself might someday become a legendary hero like Jesse James or Robin Hood.[66]

Despite scant financial returns from his initial lecture tour and book sales, Norfleet plunged ahead. In 1925 he joined a touring vaudeville circuit, relating his adventures to audiences for "a liberal weekly stipend," according to the *Dallas Morning News*.[67] The following year he embarked on a more ambitious lecture tour, concentrating on those cities across the country where important events in his man-hunting campaign occurred.[68] Then, in 1927, the Imperial Press of Sugar Land, Texas, published a second edition of his story. Entitled *Norfleet: The Amazing Experiences of an Intrepid Texas Rancher with an International Swindling Ring*, and coauthored by Gordon Hines,[69] it followed the earlier volume closely but added additional details. With better advertising and wider distribution than its predecessor, this edition received excellent reviews and better sales. The *Port Arthur News* quoted a cross-section of reviews from around the nation: "Twenty such men [as Norfleet] would stop the more serious phase of any crime wave"; "Norfleet's story is perhaps the most dramatic single-handed [crook] haul in American criminal history"; "[Norfleet is] one of the most amazing amateur detectives in history"; and "[His story] has more thrills than a good mystery yarn."[70] Under various titles, the book was serialized in newspapers and magazines of large circulation, including *McClure's*, Henry Ford's *Dearborn Independent*, and *Holland's*.

While involved in all these efforts to capitalize on his fame and recoup some of the money the adventure had cost him, Norfleet, now a bounty-hunter, continued to search for and apprehend wanted criminals.

In April 1927 he provided Fort Smith, Arkansas, authorities information leading to the arrest of a fugitive who had been wanted for two years in Texas, and personally escorted him back for trial.[71]

His son Pete, after helping his father in the pursuit of Furey, in subsequent years followed closely in his father's footsteps, maintaining a ranch while chasing crooks. He wore the badge of a Hale County deputy sheriff and, like his dad, was commissioned a special Texas Ranger.[72] (His father also received a commission as an officer of the Royal Canadian Mounted Police,[73] and later was awarded a special certificate from the FBI in recognition of his work.[74]) In November 1927 Pete tracked a confidence man from Panhandle City to Austin, but missed his quarry by only a day.[75] In an interview a month later he said he and his dad would rather be home than chasing around the country, but they could not see folks robbed, as they had been, and not try to nab the crooks. Widespread publicity of the father and son's man-hunting prowess, he said, had brought a flood of letters from other con game victims, asking them to run down swindlers. He intimated that financial rewards had been substantial, "giving us a chance to get on our feet again [and] we are gradually paying off our debts."[76]

Newspaper readers across the nation were transfixed in December 1927 by the atrocious kidnapping, murder, and dismemberment of the twelve-year-old daughter of a prominent Los Angeles banker. Suspicion fell on William E. Hickman, a former bank employee. His picture was spread nationally, and a huge $50,000 reward was offered for his capture. Norfleet immediately joined the twenty thousand law enforcement officers and American Legion volunteers converging on southern California in a search for Hickman. When Hickman was captured a week later, Norfleet returned and told a newsman, "Like hundreds of other officers I was just out there trying to do everything I could in the case."[77]

In May 1928 Norfleet was in California again, where newspaper headlines extolling him as the "Champ Crook Catcher" announced he had captured his seventy-ninth felon, one A. J. Sharrard, who was wanted for fleecing an Amarillo widow. An Associated Press report quoted him as saying he had trailed Sharrard for a week and "captured him through the latter's fondness for women."[78] A photo of the intrepid man-hunter, his hand firmly gripping the arm of his handcuffed prey, enhanced one press account. "I dunno that I'll quit after I get No. 80," Norfleet said. "It seems that catching fellows like this will be my life's work. I don't war much on other crooks, but I'll never rest till all the rings are busted up, I guess."[79] Another paper said his goal was the arrest of one swindler for each thousand of the $45,000 stolen from him. When asked how many notches were on his gun, he replied to what he obviously thought was a ridiculous question with an equally ridiculous answer: "I only put notches on when I miss a shot."[80]

Norfleet's claim to have personally captured seventy-nine criminals, seventy-six of whom were convicted, was clearly exaggerated, but newspaper editors, perhaps awed by his proven record as a man-hunter, accepted the figure. "Norfleet's most recent capture was his seventy-ninth, and he seems to be getting only a fair start on his chosen life work," ran one editorial. "More power to him."[81]

The celebrated detective and nemesis of dangerous criminals suffered extreme embarrassment when he himself was arrested in 1928. He was emerging from a leather goods store in San Antonio when a pistol slipped out of his pocket, struck the sidewalk, and discharged. The sound of the gunshot brought a patrolman who arrested Norfleet and escorted him to the police station, where he was recognized and released. But the incident was reported in the local paper, much to Norfleet's chagrin.[82]

Pulling out all the stops in his attempt to make the name Frank "Nemesis" Norfleet recognizable in every household, he turned to the new media outlets, radio and cinema. In New York City he was interviewed in several radio broadcasts, and in 1929 he even started a motion picture company to produce a film depicting his adventures.[83] Shooting for the silent movie, entitled *Norfleet* like his books, began in July 1929. Edward H. Griffith (no relation to the celebrated director D. W. Griffith) directed; Norfleet played himself in the leading role. Several minor-league actors filled out the cast, including a dancer named Jackie Dola in one of the few female roles. It soon became apparent that 1929 was the wrong year to produce a silent film. Al Jolson's *Jazz Singer* exploded on the screen with sound that year and talkies were about to transform the motion picture business. Norfleet tried to convert his movie to sound, but the money ran out, and he had to drop the project. Topping off the disaster, Jackie Dola sued him for nonpayment of the $125 weekly salary she had been promised.[84]

Back to man-hunting after the movie debacle, Norfleet again became a prime subject for newspapers during the 1930s. Under the headline NORFLEET ON TRAIL AGAIN, a 1930 Associated Press dispatch called the sixty-five-year-old rancher, with his big hat and trouser legs tucked inside his knee-length boots, a "crook catcher extraordinary." When interviewed, he said he was now engaged in "private detective work" and was after a man wanted for the brutal slaying of a schoolteacher several years earlier. The number of crooks he claimed to have captured now stood at eighty-three, eighty of whom had been tried, convicted, and jailed, according to Norfleet. "The other three are in jail but have not been tried yet."[85]

In the summer of 1934 he nabbed four men in California who allegedly conned several elderly El Paso, Texas, couples out of $117,000. This brought his total captures to ninety-one, Norfleet said, with eighty-five convictions.[86]

Still going strong at the age of seventy-one in 1936, Norfleet showed an Abilene, Texas, newspaper reporter the contents of his briefcase. It contained mug shots and detailed information about underworld "big shots" obtained from innumerable police sources. He said a half-dozen of these felons were on his personal wanted list, and he assured the newsman he would get them before he was through.[87]

In another interview Norfleet claimed he had gone into the detective business as a "sort of hobby,"[88] but according to this report, Norfleet's man-hunting avocation had improved his financial situation considerably:

> In between chasing criminals Norfleet retires for brief rests to one of his four farms in Hale County. They are all paid out, along with a fine brick home, all from his fees as a detective. Once he was ruined

financially—and in his mid-fifties—victim of a [swindling] gang, but he ran the gang to earth, one by one, [and] reestablished himself financially. [He has] nothing to worry about, not even his health. He is a fast-mover, strong, wiry, still able to give as good account of himself in pursuit and battle as in the days when his campaign of vengeance was keeping his name on the front pages.[89]

Despite that glowing account, only a few months later another wire service report announced the old man's imminent retirement from the man-hunting business. "I'm getting old and deaf," he admitted, "and the work is too dangerous. I'm going to quit while I'm still alive."[90]

In 1937 residents of Hale County, Texas, began laying plans to honor J. Frank Norfleet, their most prominent citizen, with construction of a gymnasium named for him and erected on the site of the original Norfleet ranch.[91]

Although he had indicated two years earlier that he was about to retire, a headline in 1939 announced, NORFLEET AT 78 STILL SLEUTHING. While not currently working on a case, the aged man-hunter assured an interviewer that before long he would add another felon to the string of ninety-three he had captured.[92]

No doubt Norfleet drew the long bow regarding his exploits. Certainly, the always-mounting personal arrest record was greatly exaggerated, but it awed reporters for years.[93] Included in that total, for instance, were the Blonger gang members, although he personally made no arrests in that case. Phillip Van Cise, the man mainly responsible for ending Blonger's crime reign in Denver, really liked and admired Norfleet and evidently took no offense when the old codger claimed credit for the gang's demise, for the two kept in touch for years. A letter Norfleet penned on July 4, 1957, when he was ninety-two is a good example of his truth stretching (as well as his sense of humor):

> I am not too Frisky. I have been Shot Down 5 times, Stabbed Down Twice. Been in 4 accidents When I was the only Survivor in Each Accident. The Last one June 20th '54 I got my Left Hip and Knee Badly Crushed. Have been in Doctors Shops ever since. Can walk some by using 2 canes but cannot Dance a Step. But wife says I still make a Full Hand at the Dining Table.[94]

Norfleet had remained remarkably healthy over his long span of years, but the injuries he sustained in the automobile accident of June 1954 laid him up for some time. He was ninety-one when he finally announced his retirement in 1956.[95]

His hearing gradually diminished, and in his final years he was almost deaf. But he never lost his determination, and his small body remained remarkably strong and agile. He was ninety-eight when at a family gathering someone, certainly as a joke, dared him to do a headstand on the front lawn. Norfleet rose from his chair, grabbed his cane, and headed for the front door. Before anyone could stop him, there he was, in the grass, standing on his head.[96]

Norfleet often said he wanted to live to be one hundred, and his extraordinary determination was in evidence when he reached that goal and beyond. On his 102nd birthday President Lynden Johnson, a fellow Texan who was well aware of the man-hunter's remarkable career, sent his personal congratulations.

Death finally took him eight months later. On October 15, 1967, J. Frank Norfleet, man-hunter extraordinaire, passed on quietly in his own home.[97] "With his death," eulogized publisher Tom Rambo of the *Hale Center American*, "Hale Center lost some of its luster and color gained for his community through his spectacular episodes. . . . Physically he was never impressive, yet his flashing blue eyes and frosty bark of a voice showed he could mean business when he hit the trail in search of the criminals he succeeded in catching. . . . Fast on the draw and a deadly sharpshooter, he seldom drew his gun on a human being. He succeeded in outwitting some of the best criminal minds in the country."[98]

A Texas historical marker honoring Frank Norfleet, erected in Hale Center in 1978, encapsulates the man's eventful life and alleges that his determined manhunts earned for him the nickname "Little Tiger."

AFTERWORD

Considering the relatively short life span of Americans in the nineteenth century and the extreme dangers inherent in the lives they led, the long lives of these eight men are remarkable. The shortest-lived among them were Love and Garrett, both dying at fifty-eight, victims of gunshot wounds. Reeves lived to be seventy-two, Morse seventy-seven. Tobin and Stuart survived into their eighties; the former died at eighty-one, the latter at eighty-four. Hughes committed suicide at the age of ninety-two. And Norfleet defied all the actuarial tables by living to 102.

Also surprising is how few injuries these men suffered in their long careers. Half of the eight, Love, Stuart, Morse, and Garrett, apparently never suffered a disabling wound, but Love and Garrett, of course, died after being shot in their later years, when their man-hunting days were over. Tobin and Reeves both received gunshot wounds, Tobin in a domestic dispute and Reeves in the performance of his law enforcement duties. Norfleet's only injury, evidently, was a bite on his hand inflicted by the gang-leader he had run down. With three bullets into his body, Texas Ranger captain Hughes took the record for most gunshot wounds; one crippled his right arm, a second came from his own, accidentally dropped pistol, and the third was a self-inflicted shot ending his long life.

As for the number of criminals this gallery of man-hunters dispatched to the cemetery, most killed many outlaws, but since most killings resulted from vigilante or posse action involving others, few could be attributed to a particular individual. The major exceptions, of course, were Pat Garrett, who single-handedly eliminated Billy the Kid, and Frank Norfleet, who captured many felons without firing a shot.

In stature these eight ranged from Norfleet's diminutive five feet, four inches to Garrett's towering six feet, five. Love, at six foot, three, Reeves, at six, foot two, and Hughes, just under six feet, were also imposing physical figures, while Stuart and Morse were about the size of Tobin, who was five feet, seven inches tall and weighed about 140 pounds, average for an American male in the nineteenth century.

The institution of marriage had a wide range of success or failure for the eight. Hughes, of course, never wed, though he came quite close. Norfleet, on the other hand, enjoyed seventy-three years of happily married life, with his wife supporting him consistently throughout his long campaign to hunt down confidence men. Morse experienced fifty-two years of happily married life, marred only by the antics of his wayward son. Garrett's marriage of twenty-eight years, terminated abruptly by his assassination, was also a happy one by all accounts. The union of Love and the woman he wed was strife-ridden from the outset, however, and led directly to his violent death. Three of the eight were married twice. After Tobin's first wife of forty-two years died, he remarried, and this union lasted sixteen years until his death. Reeves's first wife bore eleven of his children before passing on after thirty-two years of marriage. This union, like that of Morse, was troubled greatly by the actions of a violence-prone son. Reeves's second marriage lasted ten years until his death. Stuart's first wife of twenty-six years also gave birth to eleven children before her death. Stuart was fifty-five when he remarried a twenty-six-year-old woman, and they lived happily for the next twenty-eight years until he passed on. Interestingly, four of the eight man-hunters married nonwhite women. Since Reeves was black, his choice of a black wife was not surprising, but both Tobin and Garrett married Hispanic women, and Stuart married a full-blooded Indian.

All eight have been the subject of biographies; those of Stuart and Norfleet were self-written. Norfleet also attempted to memorialize his man-hunting feats in a motion picture, but that was a failure, and to date the diminutive man-hunter's remarkable story has never been committed to film. Because of his association with the legendary Billy the Kid,

Garrett has undoubtedly been depicted most frequently in movies, most ludicrously in Howard Hughes's *The Outlaw*, when the slim, gangling, six foot five inch Garrett was played by short, stocky veteran actor Thomas Mitchell. As explained in the Reeves chapter, the exploits of the black man-hunter, after being ignored for almost a century, have been celebrated in recent years by several television shows. It has even been contended that Reeves was the inspiration for the fictional Lone Ranger, but if that character of fiction had a real life counterpart, it was John R. Hughes.

Although only fifty-five years separated the birth of Tobin, firstborn of the eight, and Norfleet, the last born, the methods they used to pursue their quarries were greatly different, thanks to advanced technology.

The earliest western man-hunters, Love and Tobin, constrained by the lack of any mechanized transportation and the limitations of their authority beyond California and Colorado, respectively, carried on their manhunts in the 1850s and '60s entirely on horseback. Also, the absence of photographic or communication devices necessitated the beheading of their quarries.

Harry Morse's long career spanned four decades, and he was able to graduate from the 1860s practice of chasing felons entirely from the saddle or buckboard to the use of trains in the 1890s. The career of Bass Reeves was also lengthy, from the 1870s to the 1900s, but he worked in Indian Territory, where the railroad, the telegraph, the telephone, and other modern conveniences were late in coming, and he had little benefit from them.

These new services were available in many parts of the country by the 1880s when Granville Stuart conducted his short man-hunting activity, but the ranges of Montana, where he attacked the felons, was still so remote that he and his cowboys carried out their campaign on horseback like Love and Tobin decades earlier, and it was weeks before the news was reported.

Pat Garrett, who hunted felons in the 1880s and '90s, was one of the first to use the railroad to transport his prisoners. The career of ranger captain Hughes, like Morse and Reeves, was lengthy, covering almost three decades from the 1880s to the 1900s, and he was able utilize the inventions of the time as they became available in the Texas counties along the Rio Grande, his bailiwick.

But it was Frank Norfleet, who didn't hunt criminals until the 1920s and '30s, who really used modern technology to his full advantage. As an independent man-hunter, he was, like those he hunted, undeterred by jurisdictional restrictions, and he used the railroad to chase confidence operators from one end of the country to the other. The telegraph, the telephone, and photographic images were also extremely useful instruments in his quest. When those he sought fled Florida for Cuba, he even hired a pilot and airplane to pursue them. Of all the man-hunters of the Old West, he was the most successful in making that huge change from horseback tracker to modern-day pursuer.

Notes

Chapter 1. Henry "Harry" Love

1. Love's gravestone gives his date of birth as 1809, but according to census records and historians, this is in error.

2. The family name evidently originated in the French *le Loup* (the Wolf) and evolved through the centuries into Lou, Louf, Luff, Luef, Luv, Lov, and finally Love. William B. Secrest, *Man from the Rio Grande: A Biography of Harry Love, Leader of the California Rangers Who Tracked Down Joaquin Murrieta* (Spokane, WA: Arthur H. Clark, 2005), 20.

3. Ibid.

4. Ibid., 22; Teresa Griffin Viele, *Following the Drum* (New York: Rudd & Carleton, 1858), 227.

5. Secrest, *Man from the Rio Grande*, 22; Margaret Koch, *Santa Cruz County* (Fresno, CA: Valley Publishers, 1973), 227; "Harry Love (lawman)," *Wikipedia*, https://en.wikipedia.org/wiki/Harry_Love_(lawman).

6. William B. Secrest, "Hell for Leather Rangers," *True West* (March–April 1968): 20; Dan L. Thrapp, *Encyclopedia of Frontier Biography* (Glendale, CA: Arthur H. Clark, 1988), 2:879.

7. Love used his first visit to California in 1839 as credentials for admittance into the Society of California Pioneers in 1866. Secrest, *Man from the Rio Grande*, 23.

8. *New Orleans Picayune*, May 5, 1846.

9. Secrest, *Man from the Rio Grande*, 32.

10. Ibid., 28.

11. Viele, *Following the Drum*, 228–29.

12. *New Orleans Picayune*, August 2, 1846.

13. The war with Mexico officially ended on February 2, 1848, with the signing of the Treaty of Guadalupe Hidalgo, which provided for the United States to pay $15 million to Mexico and for American citizens to resolve claims against the Mexican government up to $3.25 million. The boundary between the two countries was set at the Rio Grande. Mexico relinquished its claim to the land that would become Texas, New Mexico, Arizona, Nevada, Utah, California, and parts of Wyoming and Colorado. Mexican residents of this vast area could

relocate to within the new borders of Mexico or stay and be granted full U.S. citizenship. "The Treaty of Guadalupe Hidalgo," *Wikipedia*, https://en.wikipedia .org/wiki/Treaty_of_Guadalupe_Hidalgo.

14. *Matamoros Flag*, October 9, 1848.

15. Caleb Coker, ed., *The News from Brownsville, Helen Chapman's Letters from the Texas Military Frontier, 1848–1852* (Austin: Texas State Historical Association, 1992), 145.

16. Ibid., 146. Helen Chapman mentioned Harry Love often in her letters home. One might suspect from her effusive descriptions of him that this woman's feelings extended beyond simple admiration of this gallant frontiersman.

17. Keelboats were long, slim, unpowered vessels, sometimes outfitted with a cabin or sail, designed for river travel. Often called pole boats, they were moved upstream by crews with long poles and downstream simply by the river current. They were light enough to be portaged around waterfalls and rapids by the crews.

18. Viele, *Following the Drum*, 227.

19. *Sacramento Daily Union*, February 28, 1852.

20. Quoted in Secrest, *Man from the Rio Grande*, 88. The letter was reprinted in the *Sacramento Daily Union*, May 6, 1852; the *San Francisco Herald*, May 7, 1852; and the *San Joaquin Republican*, May 15, 1852.

21. Secrest, *Man from the Rio Grande*, 88.

22. The pueblo of San Buenaventura is now the city of Ventura, which is the county seat of Ventura County.

23. *Los Angeles Star*, June 19, 1852.

24. John Boessenecker, *Gold Dust and Gunsmoke: Tales of Gold Rush Outlaws, Gunfighters, Lawmen, and Vigilantes* (New York: John Wiley & Sons, 1999), 80.

25. Secrest, *Man from the Rio Grande*, 119.

26. Boessenecker, *Gold Dust and Gunsmoke*, 92.

27. *Los Angeles Star*, June 4, 1853.

28. Quoted in the *San Joaquin Republican*; Secrest, *Man From the Rio Grande*, 123.

29. In his long and successful life William Howard was a rancher, stable owner, deputy sheriff, lawyer, and district attorney. He was ninety-six when he died in Portland, Oregon. *Reno Evening Gazette*, January 4, 1924; *Fresno Morning Republican*, January 6, 1924.

30. A particularly perspicacious selection was Patrick Connor, whose leadership ability was demonstrated a decade later, when he rose to the rank of brigadier general commanding the military district of Utah and Nevada during the Civil War. Charles Bludworth had been involved in at least one gunfight, having shot and wounded a man in Stockton. Another valuable enlistee was William W. Byrnes, a former sheriff in Utah Territory and veteran of the Mexican and Indian Wars, whom knew Murrieta well, having often faced him across the gambling tables. Other privates were Lafayette Black, William H. Harvey, Philemon T. Herbert, D. S. Hollister, G. V. McGowan, a Colonel McLane, Bob

Masters, James M. Norton, George A. Nuttall, Willis Prescott, Edwin B. Van Dorn, John S. White, and Coho Young. *San Joaquin Republican*, June 8, 1853; Secrest, *Man from the Rio Grande*, 124–27; Boessenecker, *Gold Dust and Gunsmoke*, 92; William B. Secrest, *Lawmen and Desperadoes: A Compendium of Noted, Early California Peace Officers, Badmen and Outlaws, 1850–1900* (Spokane, WA: Arthur H. Clark, 1994), 70–75.

31. Frank F. Latta, *Joaquin Murrieta and His Horse Gangs* (Santa Cruz, CA: Bear State Books, 1980), 479; Secrest, *Man from the Rio Grande*, 136.

32. Boessenecker, *Gold Dust and Gunsmoke*, 95.

33. Ibid.; *San Joaquin Republican*, August 11, 1853.

34. *San Joaquin Republican*, August 11, 1853; Boessenecker, *Gold Dust and Gunsmoke*, 95–96; Secrest, *Man from the Rio Grande*, 144–48. Much of the story of Murrieta's killing is derived from an account written twenty-six years later by William Henderson and published in the *Fresno Expositor*, November 12, 1879.

35. Following the return of the rangers, the *San Joaquin Republican*, August 11, 1853, reported that they brought back five six-shooters, two holster pistols, seven horses, and five saddles and bridles.

36. *New York Daily Times*, August 24, 1853. Bill Henderson was the man who cut off Murrieta's head, according to Horace Bell, a member of the Los Angeles Rangers, a volunteer law enforcement group formed in August 1853. Long a neighbor and close friend of Bell, Henderson told him, "I never would have cut Joaquin's head off except under the excitement of the chase and the orders of Harry Love." Horace Bell, *On the Old West Coast: Being Further Reminiscences of a Ranger* (New York: Grosset & Dunlap, 1930), 36.

37. According to one historian, Love had anticipated the need for preservation of severed bandit heads by bringing along on his expedition several large tins of alcohol, but his rangers drank up the contents of the tins before the gang was located. Latta, *Joaquin Murrieta*, 595. Secrest doubts this, pointing out that "if the heads had been carried in tin containers, the flesh might have been boiled from the skulls in that 100-degree summer heat." Secrest, *Man from the Rio Grande*, 150.

38. *San Francisco Chronicle*, August 10, 1891; Secrest, *Man from the Rio Grande*, 151–53.

39. July 30, 1853.

40. Secrest, *Man from the Rio Grande*, 158.

41. Ibid., 156. Jailed at Martinez in Contra Costa County, Ochoa was taken out by vigilantes and hanged on the night of September 4, 1853.

42. *San Francisco Alta*, August 23, 1853. It took five years, but the absurdity of this report was absolutely proven when Joaquin Valenzuela, the man Love supposedly killed, beheaded, and palmed off as the real Joaquin, met the same fate as Jose Ochoa when he was lynched by vigilantes at San Luis Obispo in May 1858. Secrest, *Man from the Rio Grande*, 219.

43. *San Francisco Herald*, August 26, 1853.

44. Joaquin Murrieta Papers, California State Archives, Sacramento, quoted in Secrest, *Man from the Rio Grande*, 165.

45. *Sacramento Daily Union*, September 10, 1853.

46. Ibid.

47. *Marysville Herald*, September 17, 1853.

48. February 13, 1854.

49. *San Joaquin Republican*, November 1, 1853; *San Francisco Daily Placer Times and Transcript*, October 26, 1853. In late October, Love, Henderson, and Norton met with former ranger Pat Connor, now undersheriff of San Joaquin County, and turned over the artifacts to him to dispose of as he saw fit. The much-traveled relics found a home in a San Francisco gun shop and then in a museum of that city, where they were destroyed in the horrendous earthquake and fire of 1906. Secrest, *Man from the Rio Grande*, 170–71; Boessenecker, *Gold Dust and Gunsmoke*, 96.

50. *San Francisco Daily Placer Times and Transcript*, November 21, 1853.

51. May 20, 1854.

52. Secrest, *Man from the Rio Grande*, 243.

53. William Heath Davis, *Seventy-Five Years in California* (San Francisco: John Howell, 1929), 149.

54. Secrest, *Man from the Rio Grande*, 185–86.

55. Ibid., 191.

56. *Santa Cruz Pacific Sentinel*, January 30, 1862; Secrest, "Hell for Leather Rangers," 23.

57. *Santa Cruz Pacific Sentinel*, May 14, 1864; June 15, 1867.

58. *Santa Cruz Pacific Sentinel*, October 26, 1867.

59. The story circulated that Mary had disposed of Vardamon by means of a unique method: poisoning him by inserting a venomous spider in a dumpling she served him. Secrest, *Man from the Rio Grande*, 243.

60. Ibid., 246–47.

61. Coroner's report quoted in ibid., 252.

62. Ibid., 255–56.

63. July 8, 1868.

64. Secrest, *Man from the Rio Grande*, 260.

65. The grave of Harry Love lay unmarked and unattended for 135 years. In May 2003, through the efforts of a historical association, a memorial stone was finally placed at the site. William Secrest, Love's biographer, spoke at the event. Ibid., 259.

66. Ibid., 260–61.

Chapter 2. Thomas Tate "Tom" Tobin

Epigraph: Edgar J. Hewett, "Tom Tobin," *Colorado Magazine* 23, no. 5 (September 1946): 211.

1. "Thomas Tate Tobin," *Wikipedia*, https://en.wikipedia.org/wiki/Thomas _Tate_Tobin.

2. There is some disagreement about the day and month of Tobin's birth. Most students of his life have accepted May 1, 1823, but March 15, 1823, has been cited by Thrapp in his *Encyclopedia of Frontier Biography*, 3:1431. According to Tobin's best biographer, the date may have been in March or May of 1823, or perhaps 1824. Evidently Tobin was not positive himself, for he was illiterate and always sketchy with regard to dates. James E. Perkins, *Tom Tobin, Frontiersman* (Monte Vista, CO, Adobe Village Press, 2005), 7–8.

3. Charles Bent (1799–1847) and his brother William (1809–69) were the driving forces behind the Bent brothers' western business ventures. Brothers Robert (1816–41) and George (1814–47) died fairly young and were not as active in the business; Robert was killed and scalped by Comanche Indians; a "high fever" took George's life. Charles was twenty-nine and William nineteen when they broke into the trading business, taking a wagon train of supplies from Saint Louis to Santa Fe in 1828 and returning with a load of furs. In following years they established valuable trading contacts in Santa Fe and Taos and formed a partnership with Ceran Saint Vrain, a Saint Louis friend. Thrapp, *Encyclopedia of Frontier Biography*, 1:96–100.

4. Ceran St. Vrain (1802–70) descended from a family of affluent French aristocrats and provided badly needed financial support in the early days of the venture called Bent, St. Vrain & Company. His business acumen contributed greatly to the venture's success. Ibid., 3:1260.

5. John Charles Frémont (1813–90) earned the cognomen "the Pathfinder" by taking many exploratory trips across the West, the most famous of which was the route to Oregon he charted in 1842 with the aid of Kit Carson. Ibid., 1:519–20.

6. Christopher Houston "Kit" Carson (1809–68) was already a veteran mountain man when he met Tobin at Bent's Fort in the early1840s. Frémont employed him as a guide for his first western expedition at a hundred dollars a month, which was "the turning point" of Carson's life. Ibid., 233–340.

7. Richens Lacy "Uncle Dick" Wootton (1816–93) was twenty when he worked with Tobin at Bent's Fort. He later hunted, trapped, and scouted throughout the West. He is best remembered for the toll road he built, which ran through Raton Pass from New Mexico to Colorado. Ibid., 3:1596.

8. Kentuckian Simeon Turley (1806–47) came to Taos in 1830 and a few years later constructed his distillery, flour mill, and store at Arroyo Hondo. Crippled in one leg by a childhood accident, he was unable to pursue the physically active life of the mountain men, but he supported his Mexican wife and seven children by catering to the needs of those men with his store, and especially his distillery. The whiskey he produced has been called "Taos Lightning" by some writers, but the term is of much later origin, according to the website *Mountain Men and Life in the Rocky Mountain West*. Early travelers through that

country, such as George Frederick Ruxton and Lewis Garrard, "went to considerable efforts to record and publish the spoken language of the mountain man. If such a colorful phrase as Taos Lightning was then in use, one or both of these men would have captured the term." Michael Schaubs, "Simeon Turley—Distiller," *Mountain Men and Life in the Rocky Mountain West*, www.mman.us/turleysimeon.htm; Michael Schaubs, "Siege at Turley's Mill," *Mountain Men and Life in the Rocky Mountain West*, www.mman.us/siegeatturleysmill.htm.

9. "Charles Bent 1st Territorial Governor of New Mexico," *GENi*, www.geni.com/people/Charles-Bent-1st-Territorial-Governor-of-New-Mexico/60000000019457568552," *GENi*; "Christopher Houston 'Kit' Carson," *GENi*, www.geni.com/people/Christopher-Houston-Kit-Carson/6000000001977907751; Janet Lecompte, "Charles Autobees," *Colorado Magazine* (July 1957): 163.

10. Charles F. Price, *Season of Terror: The Espinosas in Central Colorado, March–October, 1863* (Boulder: University Press of Colorado, 2013), 242; Perkins, *Tom Tobin*, 7–8. Oddly enough, through her father, Pedro Espinosa y Bernal, Maria was related to the Espinosas who nineteen years later would be the object of Tom Tobin's memorable hunt. It is not known if Tobin was aware of this family connection. Tobin at that time was going by the name Jose Thomas Autobees and was so enumerated in the 1850 census. But according to the Taos County marriage records, Maria Pascuala Bernal was married on November 3, 1844, to one Tomas Irtivi, which was a Spanish name that Tobin was then using.

11. U.S. census, Taos, New Mexico, 1850. In the enumeration of the Tobin family in the 1860 census, the word BLIND in capital letters follows the listing of Narcisco, aged eleven.

12. Hampton Sides, *Blood and Thunder: An Epic of the American West* (New York: Random House, 2006), 176. If true, this would strongly indicate that Romero was well practiced with the unusual method of scalping by bowstring.

13. James A. Crutchfield, *Revolt at Taos: The New Mexican and Indian Insurrection of 1847* (Yardley, PA: Westholme Publishing, 2015), 73–78. Canadian-born Charles Beaubien was the recipient of a massive Maxwell Land Grant expanse. Surveyed in 1877, it covered 1,714,764 acres. "The Maxwell (Beaubien-Miranda) Land Grant and the Colfax County War," *Sangres*, www.sangres.com/history/maxwelllandgrant.htm#.WMl6LxLyuRs.

14. John David Albert (1806–99) was only six when his father was killed in the War of 1812. When his mother died shortly thereafter, he was raised by an older sister in Harrisburg, Pennsylvania. He worked on Mississippi keelboats until he went west to trap beaver. In 1837 he came to know Tom Tobin at Bent's Fort. After the turmoil of the Taos Revolt, he farmed in that country and finally settled at Walsenburg, Colorado. He survived three wives, all fully or partly Mexican, and fathered twenty-one children. He died at the age of ninety-three. Thrapp, *Encyclopedia of Frontier Biography*, 1:12; "John David Albert," *Wikipedia*, https://en.wikipedia.org/wiki/John_David_Albert.

15. The siege of Turley's Mill is described in detail in G. F. Ruxton, *Adventures in Mexico and the Rocky Mountains* (London: J. Murray, 1847), and reprinted

in Michael McNierney, ed., *Taos 1847: The Revolt in Contemporary Accounts* (Boulder, CO: Johnson Publishing, 1980), 15–21.

16. Lewis H. Garrard, *Wah-to-yah and the Taos Trail; or Prairie Travel and Scalp Dances, With a Look at Los Rancheros from Muleback and the Rocky Mountain Campfire* (Norman: University of Oklahoma Press, 1955), 214–15. Price hastily established a military court in Taos to try the insurrection leaders for murder and treason. No fair-minded person could call it impartial. Jacob Houghton and Charles Beaubien were appointed judges. Both had close ties to the victims of those charged; Houghton was a close friend of Charles Bent, and Beaubien was the grieving father of Narcisco Beaubien. George Bent, brother of Charles, was foreman of the jury that included Lucien Maxwell, brother-in-law of Beaubien, and other friends and associates of the Bent brothers. Bent's business partner Ceran St. Vrain was court interpreter.

At least one Anglo observer, Lewis Hector Garrard, was displeased by the trial: "It certainly [was] a great assumption on the part of the Americans to conquer a country, and then arraign the revolting inhabitants for treason. . . . After an absence of a few minutes, the jury returned with a verdict of 'guilty in the first degree'—five for murder, one for treason. Treason indeed! What did the poor devil know about his new allegiance? But so it was . . . and the culprits were sentenced to be hung. . . . I left the room, sick at heart." Ibid., 197–98.

17. In this treaty, certainly one of the most momentous in American history, Mexico accepted the Rio Grande as the southern boundary of the United States and gave up all claim to territory in California, Nevada, New Mexico, Utah, Wyoming, and Colorado (See note 13 in chapter 1). Younger officers who contributed to the success in the Mexican War but would achieve even greater fame in the Civil War some years later included George Meade, Ulysses S. Grant, James Longstreet, and Thomas "Stonewall" Jackson.

18. Price, *Season of Terror*, 243.

19. Quoted on the website *The Virtual Museum of Métis History and Culture*, created by the Gabriel Dumont Institute of Native Studies and Applied Research, www.metismuseum.ca/. Edward Fitzgerald Beale (1822–93) was born into a family of strong naval tradition; his father was an officer in the U.S. Navy who received the Congressional Medal of Valor for his actions in the War of 1812, and his mother was the daughter of Commodore Thomas Truxton. After attending Georgetown University and the Naval Academy, young Beale was commissioned a naval officer but made his reputation on land rather than sea. He served in General Stephen Kearny's column in the Mexican War and in 1848–49 made six transcontinental trips carrying dispatches from Washington to California. His later important posts included head of Indian affairs for California and Nevada, brigadier general of the California militia, surveyor general of California and Nevada, and ambassador to Austria-Hungary. Thrapp, *Encyclopedia of Frontier Biography*, 1:76; "Edward Fitzgerald Beale," *Legends of America*, www.legendsof america.com/we-edwardbeale.html.

20. The U.S. census of 1860 for the Costilla District, Taos Territory County, Colorado, enumerated Thomas Tobin, thirty-six; his wife, Pascuala, thirty; and their blind son, Narcisco, eleven. Two daughters aged ten and six had now joined the family. Another member of the Tobin household, listed as a "servant," was sixteen-year-old Dario Mondragon, an Indian slave, whose value was presumably part of that $3,000 personal property figure.

21. Felipe was a particularly ugly man, with a "jack-o-lantern grin, over-sized and gapped teeth—his canines pronounced and hanging lower than any other tooth." "The Bloody Espinosas," *Rocky Mountain Legends*, December 14, 2010, https://adamjamesjones.wordpress.com/2010/12/14/the-real-story/. In an April 13, 1897, letter to Tobin, a man who knew Felipe well, T. D. Burns, described him as having "a big scar on his left cheek, and his face was covered with a black, grisly beard." Price, *Season of Terror*, 132. The *Denver Daily News* of March 10, 1899, quoted a soldier as saying Felipe's face was "sloped back to the crown of the head and the forehead seems to be entirely missing." Perkins, *Tom Tobin*, 176.

22. U.S. census, 1850, Santa Ana County, New Mexico Territory. In *Season of Terror* Charles F. Price cites an 1845 Mexican census that lists nearly all these same family members. Exceptions were daughter Maria Juana, age six in the Mexican census and absent in the 1850 listing, and the nephew Jose, only three in 1850 and not yet born at the time of the earlier listing. The ages of every family member (with the exception of the mother) show a ten or eleven year span between the two enumerations, which would indicate that the Mexican census was taken in 1840 and not 1845. If this is true, Maria Juana would have been sixteen years old in 1850, probably married and living with her husband, thus accounting for her absence.

23. "Bloody Espinosas," *Legends of America*.

24. "Martinez says that the Espinozas [*sic*] were on a mission of revenge after American soldiers raped Felipe's wife and daughters, with his wife dying four days later, in the fall of 1861." Ibid. Meticulous research of the Espinosas by Charles F. Price and James E. Perkins reveals no basis for this assertion. It is clear that Maria Merijilda Segundina, Felipe's wife, did not die in 1861 as claimed, for on August 26, 1862, she gave birth to a third child. Price, *Season of Terror*, 119; Perkins, *Tom Tobin*, 128.

25. "Bloody Espinosas," *Rocky Mountain Legends*.

26. *Rocky Mountain News Weekly*, February 12, 1863.

27. Charles F. Price, "Rampage of the Espinosas," *Colorado Central Magazine* (October 2008).

28. Henry Priest, "The Story of Dead Man's Canyon and the Espinosas," *Colorado Magazine* (January 1931): 36.

29. Price, "Rampage of the Espinosas."

30. *Rocky Mountain News Weekly*, April 16, 1863.

31. In some accounts Metcalf's first name is given as Edward (Price, "Rampage of the Espinosas"), in others as Matthew ("Bloody Espinosas," *Rocky Mountain Legends*).

32. Price, "Rampage of the Espinosas"; Price, *Season of Terror*, 63–65. Interestingly, among the papers in Metcalf's breast pocket that saved his life was a copy of President Lincoln's Emancipation Proclamation.

33. Price, *Season of Terror*, 70–72, 79–85.

34. "Captain" was a title conferred on McCannon by the group he headed. He would officially attain that rank the following year, when he was commissioned a captain in the Third Colorado Volunteer Regiment. Ibid., 75.

35. *History of the Arkansas Valley, Colorado* (Chicago: O. L. Baskin, Historical Publishers, 1881), 214, 425, 575–78, 735.

36. *Weekly Commonwealth*, May 21, 1863.

37. Price, *Season of Terror*, 198; Kenneth Jessen, John Lamb, and David Sandoval, "Colorado's Worst Serial Murders: The Espinosa Story." *San Luis Valley Historian* 27, no. 4 (1995): 21; Thomas T. Tobin, "Capture of the Espinosas," *Colorado Magazine* 9, no. 2 (March 1932): 61.

38. *Rocky Mountain News Daily*, September 3, 1863.

39. *Rocky Mountain News Weekly*, October 21, 1863.

40. Tobin, "Capture of the Espinosas," 62.

41. Price, *Season of Terror*, 239–40; Perkins, *Tom Tobin*, 271–85.

42. Price, *Season of Terror*, 242. This author states that Tobin's mother was not an Indian but "a light skinned mulatto."

43. Hewett, "Tom Tobin," 211.

44. Tobin, "Capture of the Espinosas," 65.

45. Ibid., 63.

46. Ibid.

47. Price, *Season of Terror*, 252.

48. Tobin, "Capture of the Espinosas," 62.

49. *Weekly Commonwealth*, October 28, 1863.

50. Tobin, "Capture of the Espinosas," 64.

51. Ibid.

52. Ibid., 65.

53. Ibid. Since Tom Tobin was illiterate, he never was able to write of his experiences. His version of these events was dictated in a statement taken on March 23, 1895, at Fort Garland and later published as "The Capture of the Espinosas" in the March 1932 issue of the *Colorado Magazine*. Price, *Season of Terror*, 249.

54. Kit Carson III, "The Lives of Two Great Scouts," in *The Westerner's Brand Book* (Denver: Artcraft Press, 1946).

55. *Weekly Commonwealth*, October 28, 1863.

56. Tobin, "Capture of the Espinosas," 65. According to *History of the Arkansas Valley*, 576, the reward totaled only $1,500: "The Governor offered $300, Lieut. [George L.] Shoup $500, the balance made up principally by friends of those who were murdered."

57. Dominga's child was recorded as "natural," indicating an unknown father. Tom Tobin was officially the child's godfather. Price, *Season of Terror*, 243–44, 259–60, 287.

58. The 1880 U.S. census for Costilla County, Colorado, enumerated the families of Thomas T. Tobin, a farmer, and his son, Thomas W. Tobin, a stockgrower of Lower Trenchera, with residences side by side. Living with Thomas Sr. (fifty-six) were his wife, Maria Pascuala Tobin (fifty-one); his daughter, Sarah (Serefina) Tobin (nineteen); and son, Narcisco Tobin (thirty-one), a musician. In the home of Thomas Jr. (twenty-seven), a stockgrower, was his wife, Dolores Tobin (seventeen). Next to the home of Thomas Jr. was the residence of William Carson (twenty-six), with no occupation listed; his wife and Tom Jr.'s daughter, Maria Pascuala Carson (seventeen); and their one-year-old daughter as well as Carson's two sisters and one brother.

59. Although Tobin was thirty years older than William Carson, he outlived his son-in-law, who later died of an accidental, self-inflicted gunshot wound. Tobin then raised the children of the man who almost killed him, one of whom was Kit Carson III, who idolized both of his famous grandfathers. Price, *Season of Terror*, 289, 291.

60. Ibid., 290.

61. Ibid.

62. Ibid.

63. Judge Wilbur Stone of 1897 was indeed intimately familiar with the characters and events of the Espinosa drama, for in 1863 he had covered the entire story as "Dornick," the correspondent for the *Weekly Commonwealth*. Price, *Season of Terror*, 306. However, when interviewed by the *News* reporter, the judge seemed to contradict what he had previously written.

64. Ibid., 285, 290; Virginia McConnell Simmons, *The San Luis Valley: Land of the Six-Armed Cross* (Niwot: University Press of Colorado, 1999), 85.

65. Perkins, *Tom Tobin*, 249–50. In another letter to Shoup, Tobin said that he had already applied to the federal government for a pension based on his volunteer service during the Taos uprising of 1847. The amount was a mere eight dollars a month, but his request had been denied because he had not been a member of a regularly constituted military unit. Ibid., 248.

66. Ibid., 250; Price, *Season of Terror*, 287.

67. *Arizona Republican*, May 17, 1904. The Tobins are buried in the small Mac-Mullan Cemetery, about one mile northwest of Fort Garland near the site of Tom's ranch. In 1993 James A. Browning, author of *Violence Was No Stranger: A Guide to the Grave Sites of Famous Westerners* (Stillwater, OK: Barbed Wire Press, 1993), wrote that the cemetery was on property owned by Malcolm Forbes since 1988: "Entrance to the cemetery is very difficult as there are several locked gates and permission must be obtained from an employee of Forbes Enterprises" (p. 257). Tom's name is misspelled "Toben" on his tombstone, and his birthdate is given, evidently incorrectly, as March 15, 1826.

68. Kit Carson III believed his grandfather Tobin "was incommunicative [especially] in the presence of educated people as he could neither read nor write." Gerald C. Smith, "The Adventures of Three Fort Garland Heroes," *San Luis Valley Historian* 2, no. 2 (1970): 1–20.

69. Price, *Season of Terror*, 240.

70. Ibid. The 1900 U.S. census for Garland, Costilla County, Colorado, listed Thomas Tate Tobin, seventy-seven, and his wife, Rosita, fifty-five. They had been married twelve years. Enumerated with them was William Carson, eleven, a grandson and the younger brother of Kit Carson III. Living next door was Tom's blind son, Narcisco, now fifty-one, and his forty-year-old wife of twenty years, Madela Tobin.

71. Price, *Season of Terror*, 289.

Chapter 3. Granville Stuart

1. Granville Stuart, *Prospecting for Gold: From Dogtown to Virginia City, 1852–1864* (Lincoln: University of Nebraska Press, 1977), 23–82.

2. Ibid., 83–103; Victor C. Dahl, "Granville Stuart in Latin America: A Montana Pioneer's Diplomatic Career," *Montana: The Magazine of Western History* (July 1971): 18–33.

3. Granville's affliction was probably smallpox, a disease prevalent on the frontier during this period that killed many.

4. Stuart, *Prospecting for Gold*, 105.

5. Clyde A. Milner and Carol A. O'Conner, *As Big as the West: The Pioneer Life of Granville Stuart* (New York: Oxford University Press, 2009).

6. Stuart, *Prospecting for Gold*, 237–38.

7. Lew L. Callaway, *Montana's Righteous Hangmen: The Vigilantes in Action* (Norman: University of Oklahoma Press, 1982), 16–17; Thomas Josiah Dimsdale, *Vigilantes of Montana, or Popular Justice in the Rocky Mountains* (Virginia City: Montana Post Press, D. W. Tilden, 1866); Nathaniel Pitt Langford, *Vigilante Days and Ways: The Pioneers of the Rockies* (New York: A. L. Burt, 1912).

8. Langford, *Vigilante Days and Ways*, 113–14.

9. Interestingly, the town was originally called "Verina," named by the miners (most of whom were southern sympathizers) to honor Varina Howell Davis, the wife of Jefferson Davis, president of the Confederacy. When a judge from Connecticut, G. G. Bissell, took office, he changed the name to Virginia City. Dillon, *Montana Vigilantes*, 8–20.

10. Granville Stuart, *Pioneering in Montana: The Making of a State, 1864–1887* (Lincoln: University of Nebraska Press, 1977), 21. The U.S. census of 1870 found him in Deer Lodge, age thirty-six, occupation miner. His family consisted of his wife, "Audrey," now twenty, and four children, ages spanning four months to seven years. His brother James, thirty-eight, a miner, lived next door with his wife, Ellen, also twenty years old, and three sons, ages eight months to five years.

11. Thrapp, *Encyclopedia of Frontier Biography*, 3:1380–82.

12. Ibid., 3:1379–80.

13. When he died, Granville bequeathed the rifle to his grandson, Granville Stuart Abbott. *Independent Record*, January 7, 1951.

14. Kentuckian Samuel Thomas Hauser (1833–1914) was educated by his father (a judge) and a cousin (a Yale graduate). Railroads were Samuel's first interest, and he worked on rail lines in Kentucky and Missouri. Bitten by the gold bug, he went to Montana in 1862, struck it rich in silver lodes, and soon owned six mines. Partnered with Nathaniel Langford, he got into banking and over the years opened banks in Fort Benton, Butte, and Missoula. He was married in 1871 and fathered two children. Thomas A. McMullin, "David Walker," *Biographical Directory of American Territorial Governors* (Westport, CT: Meckler Publishing, 1984), 218–19; W. H. Maguire, "Samuel T. Hauser: An Early Governor of Montana," *Montana: The Magazine of Western History* (March 1991).

Andrew Jackson Davis (1819–90) of Massachusetts showed an unusual propensity for wheeling and dealing at an early age. During the Black Hawk War of 1832 he acquired from the Indians eight hundred acres of land, where he built a distillery that would become the source of his first fortune. With the advent of the Montana gold rushes, he quickly recognized the miners' great need for goods of all kinds, including liquor, and he freighted merchandise into the boom camps by the wagon trainload. Around 1866 he unloaded his entire whiskey inventory in Montana at a huge profit, which he invested in mining ventures. One of his mines yielded gross earnings of $1.6 million during his ownership. He sold it in 1881 for $1 million in cash. Considered the first millionaire in Butte, when he died his estate was valued at $7 million. He never married. *Anaconda Standard*, March 12, 1890; Joaquin Miller, *An Illustrated History of the State of Montana* (Chicago: Lewis Publishing, 1894); Frank D. Myers, "The Iowaville Roster: Andrew Jackson Davis," *Lucas Countyan*, September 19, 2008, https://lucascountyan.blogspot.com/2008/09/iowaville-roster-andrew-jackson-daivs.html.

15. Stuart, *Pioneering in Montana*, 99.

16. Ibid., 99–144. During this trip Stuart walked the site of the Battle of the Little Bighorn, where Custer had made his famous last stand four years before. "Saw just where the men and horses fell," he wrote in his journal. "Bones of men and horses are scattered all along. . . . On the point where Custer fell . . . a pyramid of cord wood with a ditch around it and inside filled with bones of horses. . . . The field is a ghastly sight" (pp. 120–21). He was still on this trip when the federal census taker at Helena enumerated him at the head of an extensive household, which included his wife, Awbonie, seven of his own children (three boys and four girls), two nephews (sons of his deceased brother whom he was raising), and a thirty-eight-year-old sister-in-law, Mary Burr. His occupation was now given as stock raising.

17. Stuart, *Pioneering in Montana*, 145.

18. Ibid., 148–49. In a footnote Stuart said he afterward learned that the white man was not a priest at all.

19. Ibid., 154.

20. Ibid., 156.

21. Ibid., 167.

22. Ibid., 176–77.

23. Ibid., 195; R. K. DeArment, "When Stuart's Stranglers Raided the Rustlers," *Wild West* (August 2007): 48–49.

24. Stuart, *Pioneering in Montana*, 195.

25. The attendance of a French nobleman and a future American president at the stockgrowers' meeting epitomizes the eclectic membership of the region's ranch owners.

26. Stuart, *Pioneering in Montana*, 196.

27. T. A. Clay, "A Call to Order: Law, Violence and the Development of Montana's Early Stockman's Organizations," *Montana: The Magazine of Western History* (Autumn 2008).

28. June 12, 1884.

29. *Mineral Argus*, July 31, 1884.

30. Stuart says there were "about fourteen" involved in his manhunt. Stuart, *Pioneering in Montana*, 209. Other estimates of participation ranged from seventeen to forty. Norman H. Hyatt, *An Uncommon Journey: The History of Old Dawson County, Montana Territory* (Helena, MT: Sweetgrass Books, 2009), 81–83, 150, 173, 180–85.

31. Hyatt, *Uncommon Journey*. DHS cowboy John Barrows describes Cantrell as "an ungainly horseman, much over six feet in height, bony, muscular, slow moving, with a bearing of combined reticence and dignity." John R. Barrows, *U-Bet: A Greenhorn in Old Montana* (Lincoln: University of Nebraska Press, 1990), 213. Two of the cowboys who worked for the DHS later wrote books about their range experiences: John R. Barrows and E. C. "Teddy Blue" Abbott. Barrows began work at the DHS ranch in August 1880 and left in 1885 to take charge of his father's herd at Buffalo, Wyoming. Barrows, *U-Bet*, 2–3. Abbott worked the DHS ranch and married Stuart's daughter Mary. E. C. Abbott and Helen Huntington Smith. *We Pointed Them North: Recollections of a Cowpuncher* (New York: Farrar & Rinehart, 1939).

32. Stuart, *Pioneering in Montana*, 198.

33. Ibid., 198–201. Although Stuart disposes of the capture and execution of McKenzie in one sentence, John Barrows remembers much more of the story. He says that three DHS hands captured McKenzie, brought him into the home ranch, and held him "in the bunk house with his arms tied behind his back. . . . His bonds were released, and he sat at table with us for the evening meal. . . . Next morning Mackenzie was not there. After the midday meal, I rode with Charley Stuart [Granville's son] over to Fort Maginnis, and . . . came upon the mortal remains of Sam MacKenzie dangling from the limb of a cottonwood tree . . . , the pinioned body, swinging and swaying at a rope's end, the center of an admiring concourse of flies." Barrows, *U-Bet*, 203–204.

34. Stuart, *Pioneering in Montana*, 201–202. Stuart would later receive a telegram from Buffalo, Wyoming, informing him that Fallon and Owen were indeed desperate characters, wanted in Wyoming for horse theft. Still later he learned

that Owen was wanted for murder in Shreveport, Louisiana, and Fallon, a native of Laredo, Texas, was a fugitive from New Mexico, where he had shot up a ranch and set fire to its buildings. Ibid., 205.

35. Ibid., 204–205.

36. Ibid., 206; DeArment, "When Stuart's Stranglers," 50.

37. Stuart, *Pioneering in Montana*, 206–207; DeArment, "When Stuart's Stranglers," 51.

38. Stuart, *Pioneering in Montana*, 197–98.

39. In a footnote Paul C. Phillips, the editor of Stuart's *Pioneering in Montana*, quotes Granville's son Sam as saying Dixie Burr was a son of the well-known F. H. Burr and also a nephew of Granville Stuart (p. 207).

40. Stuart, *Pioneering in Montana*, 207–208.

41. Ibid., 208.

42. DeArment, "When Stuart's Stranglers," 51.

43. *Daily Gazette*, August 6, 11, 1884. The *Las Vegas Daily Gazette*, August 10, 1884, reporting on the battle fought a month earlier, said that there were nine outlaws killed, but five escaped.

44. "Granville Stuart informed us last week that sixty-nine head of horses recovered from horse thieves, are held at his ranch, awaiting identification." *Mineral Argus*, August 28, 1884.

45. Stuart, *Pioneering in Montana*, 209.

46. Abbott and Smith, *We Pointed Them North*.

47. Oscar O. Mueller, "The Central Montana Vigilante Raids of 1884," *Montana: The Magazine of Western History* (January 1951).

48. Joseph Kinsey Howard, *Montana, High, Wide and Handsome* (New Haven, CT: Yale University Press, 1943).

49. Wallis Huidekoper, *The Land of the Dakotahs* (Helena, MT: The Montana Stockgrowers Association, n.d), 14–15.

50. E. Ward McRay, "Stuart's Stranglers," *True Western Adventures* (February 1961). These figures were repeated by B. Morando in his article, "Montana's Stranglers," *Real West* (July 1974). However, John Harrison, in "Montana's Horse Thief War," *Great West* (October 1973), concluded that "nineteen of the 20 men on the Vigilantes' original list were dead."

51. Barrows, *U-Bet*, 9–10.

52. *Rocky Mountain Husbandman*, August 21, 1884.

53. Ibid.

54. *Daily Yellowstone Journal*, February 17, 1885.

55. Stuart, *Pioneering in Montana*, 214; *River Press*, July 8, 1885.

56. *River Press*, October 14, 1885.

57. Ibid.

58. Stuart, *Pioneering in Montana*, 236–37.

59. David Remley, "Granville Stuart, Cowman," *Montana: The Magazine of Western History* (Summer 1981): 28–41. Stuart never got rich in the ranching

business. After he left the DHS and got out of his partnership with Hauser and Davis, he still owed Hauser $3,500 in 1895. Ibid.

60. William Kittredge and Steven M. Krauser. "'Mr. Montana' Revised: Another Look at Granville Stuart," *Montana: The Magazine of Western History* (Autumn 1986): 14–23.

61. Stuart was at the side of Juan Idiarte Borda when the Uruguayan president was assassinated at a parade in Montevideo on August 25, 1897. Victor C. Dahl, "Granville Stuart in Latin America: A Montana Pioneer's Diplomatic Career," *Montana: The Magazine of Western History* (July 1971): 18–33.

Chapter 4. Henry Nicholson "Harry" Morse

1. John Boessenecker, *Lawman: The Life and Times of Harry Morse, 1835–1912* (Norman: University of Oklahoma Press, 1998), 5.

2. Ibid.; Charles Howard Shinn, *Graphic Description of Pacific Coast Outlaws: Thrilling Exploits of Their Arch-Enemy Sheriff Harry N. Morse (for Many years the Terror of the Brigands of California—a Man of Intrepid Courage, Wonderful Skill, and Splendid Leadership); Some of his Desperate Hand-to-Hand Encounters with Bandits* (Tucson, AZ: Westernlore Press, 1990).

3. Boessenecker, *Lawman*, 7; Shinn, *Graphic Description*, 88–89.

4. Boessenecker, *Lawman*, 8–11; Shinn, *Graphic Description*, 89–94.

5. Boessenecker, *Lawman*, 15–16. Six children were born to this marriage: George B. (1856), Emma Charlotte (1858), Henry N. Jr. (1860), Anne Virginia (1863), Lincoln Philander (1869), and Charles Felton (1870). Three of the six— George, Emma, and Annie—grew to adulthood, but the other three did not. Lincoln, only two months old, and Henry, nine, died in 1869; Charles, born in 1870, survived only five weeks before he, too, passed on. Ibid., 94.

6. *San Francisco Call*, February 24, 1878, reprinted in Shinn, *Graphic Description*, 44–45.

7. Boessenecker, *Lawman*, 23.

8. *Alameda County Gazette*, September 3, 1875.

9. *Oakland Daily Transcript*, March 9, 1873.

10. *Oakland Daily News*, March 12, 1873.

11. Boessenecker, *Lawman*, 45–46.

12. Ibid., 23–24.

13. *California Police Record*, October 1, 1885, quoted in ibid., 47–48.

14. Ibid., 49.

15. February 25, 1872.

16. *Alameda County Gazette*, July 8, 1865.

17. Boessenecker, *Lawman*, 52.

18. Ibid., 52–53.

19. Quoted in ibid., 53.

20. *Oakland Daily News*, July 17, 1866; *Alameda County Gazette*, July 21, 1866; Boessenecker, *Lawman*, 54–55.

21. *California Police Record*, October 1, 1885. Morse's experience with Bojorques is quoted in full in Boessenecker, *Lawman*, 57–70.

22. Ibid. Bojorques had only a few more months to live. In a February 1867 Copperopolis cantina gunfight, his bullet creased the head of his adversary "One-Eyed Jack" Williams, but the return shot killed him.

23. Ibid.

24. *Mano a mano* translates literally as "hand to hand," but has come to mean "man to man." A more accurate term in this instance would be *pistola a pistola*.

25. Boessenecker, *Lawman*, 80.

26. *Oakland Daily News*, July 24, 1867; *Alameda County Gazette*, October 27, 1867.

27. *Oakland Daily News*, August 12, 1877.

28. *Oakland Daily News*, December 16, 1867. The story was also reported in the *Alameda County Gazette*, December 17, 1867, and the *San Francisco Chronicle*, February 25, 1872.

29. *Alameda County Gazette*, September 26, October 3, 1868.

30. Morse's account of the hunt was serialized in the November and December 1885 issues of the *California Police Record* and is quoted in Boessenecker, *Lawman*, 113–29.

31. Ibid.

32. Ibid., 130–31; *Stockton Daily Independent*, December 11, 12, 13, 14, 16, 1869.

33. Morse's account of the hunt for Tejada was published in the *California Police Record*, October 24, 31, November 7, 1885, and was reprinted in Boessenecker, *Lawman*, 131–49. Those surprised by Morse's decision to take his thirteen-year-old son along on this dangerous mission should remember that Morse himself had been on his own, often in hazardous situations, since the age of ten. He obviously felt it was time George enjoyed some of the dangerous but thrilling experiences he had known at a tender age.

34. Boessenecker, *Lawman*, 323. Sheriff Morse's daring expeditions and successful capture of Tejada served as a wake-up call to the lethargic San Joaquin County lawmen. In the ensuing months they captured Padilla and Garcia, the other participants in the Medina massacre. Padilla and Tejada were indicted, tried, convicted of murder, and sentenced to death by hanging. Their attorney, the flamboyant David S. Terry, appealed the convictions on a legal technicality to the California Supreme Court and obtained retrial orders. Tejada died of syphilis in his jail cell before his retrial, and a month later a jury acquitted Padilla. Harry Morse bitterly explained that after long delays, important witnesses could not be found, "and thus [Padilla] escaped his just and merited punishment." Ibid., 148.

35. Ibid.; *California Police Record*, October 24, 31, November 7, 1885; *San Jose Daily Independent*, January 18, 1871; *San Francisco Bulletin*, January 20, 1871.

36. Joseph Henry Jackson, *Bad Company: The Story of California's Legendary and Actual Stage-Robbers, Bandits, Highwaymen and Outlaws from the Fifties to the Eighties* (New York: Harcourt, Brace, 1949), 259.

37. Quoted in Robert Greenwood, ed., *California Outlaw* (Los Gatos, CA: Talisman Press, 1960), 172.

38. Ibid., 168–73; *San Jose Daily Patriot*, May 12, 1871; *Oakland Daily News*, May 13, 1871; *Alameda County Gazette*, May 18, 1871; Shinn, *Graphic Description*, 68–74; D. S. Richardson, "Duel to the Death," *Overland Monthly* (August 1888); Boessenecker, *Lawman*, 152–67.

39. *Alta California*, May 14, 1871.

40. *Alameda County Gazette*, September 23, 1871.

41. Boessenecker, *Lawman*, 174.

42. Ibid., 177–78; *Oakland Daily Transcript*, February 12, 1872; *Oakland Daily News*, February 12, 1872; *Alameda County Gazette*, February 15, 1872; *San Francisco Call*, February 11, 1872; *San Francisco Chronicle*, February 11, 1872; *San Francisco Bulletin*, February 12, 1872.

43. *Alameda County Gazette*, May 2, 1872.

44. *Alameda County Gazette*, March 14, 1872; *Oakland Daily News*, March 15, 1872.

45. Boessenecker, *Lawman*, 182–83.

46. Ibid., 183–84.

47. *Oakland Daily News*, July 29–August 2, 1873; July 3, 1874. The legal battle over Sepulveda's conviction continued long after he entered San Quentin. His attorneys uncovered new evidence debunking the jailhouse snitch whose testimony had done much to secure Sepulveda's conviction and found proof that their client was in a San Jose jail cell when the crime was committed. They inferred, but never proved, that Morse had committed perjury to assure the conviction. Their efforts resulted in a pardon for Sepulveda, and on January 22, 1885, after almost twelve years of incarceration for a crime he did not commit, he was freed. Evidently reformed, he was never in trouble with the law again. In his review of the case, Morse's biographer concludes, "Bartolo Sepulveda no doubt deserved punishment for other crimes. But Alameda's sheriff had come within a hair's breadth of sending an innocent man to his death on the gallows. . . . Whether [Sepulveda's trials are] a classic example of racial injustice, a case of mistaken identity, [or] a matter of over-zealous law enforcement, one fact is plain: the arrest, prosecution and conviction of Bartolo Sepulveda constitute the darkest chapter in Harry Morse's long career." Boessenecker, *Lawman*, 184–94.

48. August 6, 1874.

49. Boessenecker, *Lawman*, 197–98.

50. April 26, 1874.

51. Boessenecker, *Lawman*, 200–208.

52. *San Francisco Chronicle*, May 16, 1874. The two foremost authorities on the history of California lawmen and outlaws, John Boessenecker and William B. Secrest, have commented on the question of whether Rowland double-crossed Morse to gain the glory and reward for the capture of Vasquez. Boessenecker

states, "Having been publicly criticized and embarrassed by an interloping sheriff from a distant county, Rowland surely felt no loyalty to Morse. . . . The conclusion is inescapable that Rowland acted on Morse's information. . . . Although Sheriff Rowland and his men garnered the glory and the reward, it is clear that it was Harry Morse's painstaking and exhausting legwork that was ultimately responsible for the bandit chieftain's capture." Boessenecker, *Lawman*, 210. However, Secrest claims, "Indications are that [Rowland] took Morse's information, checked it out, then went into action. Giving Rowland the benefit of the doubt, however, he may have already had the information from another source. In either case, the Los Angeles sheriff could hardly be blamed for not wanting to share capturing the notorious bandit with some 'big city' sheriff from the San Francisco Bay area." William B. Secrest, *Showdown: Lionhearted Lawmen of Old California* (Fresno, CA: Craven Street Books, 2010), 111.

53. Greenwood, *California Outlaw*, 42–43.

54. *San Francisco Bulletin*, August 13, 1905.

55. Morse to Booth, February 10, 1875, Rhodes Collection, Huntington Library, San Marino, California.

56. Boessenecker, *Lawman*, 214–15; Secrest, *Lawmen and Desperadoes*, 86–88.

57. *California Police Record*, November 28, 1885. Today in our politically correct world, a law officer administering such punishment would be condemned for police brutality, but of course, his accusers would never have been shot at in an attempted assassination by a known murderer.

58. Boessenecker, *Lawman*, 223. Tyrel won and served two terms as sheriff of Alameda County.

59. *Oakland Times*, March 5, 1878; *Hayward Weekly Journal*, March 9, 1878.

60. *San Francisco Chronicle*, May 19, 1878; *Alta California*, May 19, 1878. The swindler, a lawyer named Wright LeRoy, got five years in San Quentin for this theft. After his release, he swindled and then murdered a wealthy merchant, for which he was hanged in 1885. Boessenecker, *Lawman*, 226.

61. Boessenecker, *Lawman*, 226–27.

62. Ibid., 229.

63. In the late nineteenth century, James Hume, Isaiah Lees, and Harry Morse, three of the most celebrated lawmen in America, were working out of San Francisco. Although each undoubtedly respected and admired the other two for their success in criminal apprehension, animosity between them was engendered by a natural competition for recognition as the greatest lawman of their time.

64. Boessenecker, *Lawman*, 231–37.

65. Ibid., 237–38; Evans to Folger, April 14, 1882, Records of the United States Customs Service, U.S. National Archives, Record Group 36.

66. Evans to Folger, September 23, 1882, Records of the United States Customs Service, U.S. National Archives, Record Group 36.

67. *San Francisco Call*, August 2, 3, 4, 7, 9, 1883.

68. *San Francisco Examiner*, November 11, 12, 15, 17, 1887.

69. The original spelling of the name was "Bowles."

70. William Collins and Bruce Levene, *Black Bart: The True Story of the West's Most Famous Stagecoach Robber* (Mendocino, CA: Pacific Transcriptions, 1992), 40–48.

71. James B. and John N. Thacker, *Wells, Fargo & Co. Stagecoach and Train Robberies, 1870–1884. The Corporate Report of 1885 with Additional Facts about the Crimes and Their Perpetrators* (Jefferson, NC: McFarland, 2010), 42–43; Boessenecker, *Lawman*, 245–46.

72. Boessenecker, *Lawman*, 246.

73. For details of James Hume's long man-hunting career, see R. K. DeArment, *Man-Hunters of the Old West*, vol. 1 (Norman: University of Oklahoma Press, 2017).

74. Jimmy Rolleri was the son of Olivia "Grandma" Rolleri, a California pioneer and proprietress of an inn, stage station, and ferry crossing of the Stanislaus River. Bart had spent a night at the inn shortly before the holdup, and Jimmy had ferried him across the river. Collins and Levene, *Black Bart*, 136.

75. Ibid., 139.

76. Ibid., 143.

77. *San Francisco Call*, November 17, 1883.

78. Ibid.

79. Ibid.

80. Boessenecker, *Lawman*, 256.

81. Collins and Levene, *Black Bart*, 169.

82. Ibid., 175. A rifle "inlaid in silver with a hand-carved stock" was presented to Jimmy Rolleri by Wells Fargo, but it exploded the first time he fired it, so the company gave him another. Ibid., 146.

83. Boessenecker, *Lawman*, 267–69; *San Francisco Bulletin*, July 15, 1889.

84. Ibid., 298–99; *San Francisco Chronicle*, July 20, 21, 1904; *Oakland Herald*, July 20, 21, 22, 1904. Despite his youth and provocation, Claude F. Hankins, who killed George Morse, was convicted and sentenced to sixteen years in San Quentin for the crime. *Oakland Tribune*, October 14, 19, 23, 26, 1904; *San Jose Evening News*, October 26, 1904.

85. When Tom Cunningham dropped dead of a heart attack in 1900, Morse wrote a lengthy tribute to his friend, which was published in the *Oakland Tribune*, November 30, 1900.

86. Boessenecker, *Lawman*, 272.

87. Ibid., 274. Returning to San Diego, Sam Black later killed a man in a gunfight and was convicted of manslaughter. He died of natural causes at San Quentin in 1902. Ibid., 275.

88. The posse was composed of "a collection of first-class frontiersmen and good shots." U.S. Marshal George Gard was a twenty-year police veteran, with experience as a detective, police chief, and sheriff. He chose for his posse three men: Morse agent Tom Burns, who was familiar with the fugitives and the terrain;

Fred Jackson, an expert marksman, so good he was barred from local shooting matches; and Fresno County deputy sheriff Hiram Rapelje, also a known locally as a crack shot. Secrest, *Showdown*, 222.

89. Hiram Rapelje, was later quoted as saying, "There was no intention of trying to capture Sontag and Evans alive. . . . It was our intention to kill them without giving them any show whatever!" Secrest, *Lawmen and Desperadoes*, 275.

90. *Fresno Morning Republican*, June 7, 1893.

91. Secrest, *Lawmen and Desperadoes*, 210.

92. Quoted in William B. Secrest, *California Desperadoes: Stories of Early California Outlaws in Their Own Words* (Clovis, CA: Word Dancer Press, 2000), 210.

93. Ibid., 211. Ironically, these two adversaries, Witty and Burns, suffered violent deaths in the same year. In 1901 Burns was killed in a personal altercation in Arizona, and Witty committed suicide.

94. Boessenecker, *Lawman*, 277.

95. Ibid., 298, 300.

96. *San Francisco Chronicle*, July 29, 1895.

97. Boessenecker, *Lawman*, 277–83.

98. Ibid., 300–302; *San Francisco Chronicle*, February 21, 1905.

99. Boessenecker, *Lawman*, 302–308.

100. Ibid., 309. In March 1911, Jules Callundan, the man Morse had trained from the age of sixteen to succeed him, died from diabetic complications at the age of forty-seven. Joint ownership and management of the detective agency was transferred to Morse's grandson, Harry de la Montanya, and Callundan's nephew, William Rowe.

101. Ibid., 309; *Oakland Tribune*, October 1, 1907; June 23, 1908.

102. Richardson, "Duel to the Death."

103. Shinn, *Graphic Description*, 97.

Chapter 5. Bass Reeves

Epigraph: Paul L. Brady, *The Black Badge: Deputy United States Marshal Bass Reeves from Slave to Heroic Lawman* (Los Angeles: Milligan Books, 2005), 137.

1. Some information about the life of Bass Reeves, most of which was intended for black readership, appeared in the latter years of the twentieth century: Daniel F. Littlefield Jr. and Lonnie E. Underhill, "Negro Marshals of the Indian Territory," *Journal of Negro History* (April 1971): 77–87; Nudie E. Williams, "Bass Reeves," *Negro History Bulletin* (April–June 1979); Paul L. Brady, *A Certain Blindness: A Black Family's Quest for the Promise of America* (Atlanta: ALP Publishing, 1990). But it wasn't until Art T. Burton published his biography, *Black Gun, Silver Star: The Life and Legend of Frontier Marshal Bass Reeves* (Lincoln: University of Nebraska Press, 2006), that most students of western frontier history became aware of this extraordinary lawman.

2. There is some disagreement about the year and place of Bass Reeves's birth. In Ron Tyler, *The New Handbook of Texas* (Austin: Texas State Historical Association, 1996), 5:907, his birth is given as 1824. In Paul L. Brady, *The Black Badge: Deputy United States Marshal Bass Reeves from Slave to Heroic Lawman* (Los Angeles: Milligan Books, 2005), Brady, a great-nephew of Reeves, says he was born "about 1839 in northeast Texas" (p. 4). But Burton's biography of Reeves, *Black Gun, Silver Star*, makes a strong case for 1838 in Arkansas, and I have accepted his conclusion. Ray Brady's account of Reeves's early life differs markedly from Burton's. Brady claims that Bass was the son of Arthur Reeves, "a former slave, now a free man," and "Paralee," the black slave companion of a Texas plantation owner's wife named Stewart. No mention is made of William S. Reeves, his son, George, or of Bass's service with Confederate troops in the Civil War. In fact, Brady asserts that Bass Reeves escaped servitude in Texas, fled to Indian Territory in 1857 (p. 21), and fought for the Union with the First Kansas Colored Volunteers (p. 28). However, in his self-published book he provides little documentation to support his claims, saying that his account is primarily based on stories handed down in the Brady family, which he heard as a child (pp. viii–ix).

3. William Steele Reeves (1794–1872) was a veteran of the 1812 war with England and the Creek Wars (1813–14), and he served in both the Tennessee and Arkansas legislatures. Burton, *Black Gun, Silver Star*, 20.

4. Ibid., 19.

5. Gideon, *Indian Territory*, 115–16.

6. Burton, *Black Gun, Silver Star*, 15–16.

7. *Chickasaw Enterprise*, November 28, 1901. George Robertson Reeves (1826–82) was a member of the Texas Legislature from 1856 to 1858. After the war he served again in the Texas Legislature from 1870 to 1882 and was Speaker of the House in his last term. He died of hydrophobia in 1882 after being bitten by a rabid dog. Burton, *Black Gun, Silver Star*, 22; Tyler, *New Handbook of Texas*, 5:507–508.

8. Burton, *Black Gun, Silver Star*, 23–24.

9. Or Jinnie, as she is consistently called by Paul L. Brady.

10. Burton, *Black Gun, Silver Star*, 26; 1870 U.S. census, Crawford County, Arkansas.

11. Burton, *Black Gun, Silver Star*, 27.

12. Isaac Charles Parker, an Ohioan, was born in 1838, the same year (presumably) as Bass Reeves. He studied law and was admitted to the bar in 1859, and during the 1860s he practiced his profession in St. Joseph, Missouri. He represented his Missouri district in Congress from 1871 until 1875, when he was offered appointment as chief justice of Utah Territory. He declined that offer to accept the Arkansas judgeship, a position he held until he died in 1896. He is buried in the National Cemetery at Fort Smith. Thrapp, *Encyclopedia of Frontier Biography*, 3:1112.

13. Burton, *Black Gun, Silver Star*, 27.

14. Ibid., 11.

15. Ibid.

16. Ibid., 34. Sadly, Mershon lost his mind eight years after retiring from the marshal's service and died in a Terrill, Texas, insane asylum in 1899. He is one of eighty-two deputy U.S. marshals interred in Oak Cemetery at Fort Smith.

17. *Fort Smith Weekly Elevator*, July 11, 1884.

18. *Oklahoma City Weekly Times-Journal*, March 8, 1907.

19. D. C. Gideon, *Indian Territory: Descriptions, Biographical, and Genealogical, Including the Landed Estates, County Seats . . . with a General History of the Territory* (New York: Lewis, 1901), 115–18. If this exchange of rifle fire was indeed at a distance of five hundred yards, as claimed by Reeves, both parties displayed excellent marksmanship.

20. Brady, *Black Badge*, 103–104. In Brady's account of the second gunfight involving Webb, Reeves's partner was Deputy Marshal John Cantrell, not Mershon; there is no mention of Hamilton as reported in the contemporary press; and Reeves did not bring Webb down with long-distance rifle shots, as Reeves himself related. After describing how Webb's bullets "shot the bridle out of his hands" and "clipped the brim of his hat," the author writes that Bass drew his pistol and "fired one shot from the hip," and then Webb started to fall. Before he struck the ground, Bass hit him with two more shots. "It was later discovered that all three bullets had hit Webb's body within a hand's width of each other." As usual, Judge Brady provides no documentation for this story.

21. Art T. Burton, *Black, Red and Deadly: Black and Indian Gunfighters of the Indian Territory* (Austin, TX: Eakin Press, 1991), 171.

22. *Oklahoma City Weekly Times-Journal*, March 8, 1907. This article was reprinted in its entirety in the *Washington Post*, March 10, 1907. Paul L. Brady repeats the Brunter brothers' story in *Black Badge*, 99–100. The portion of the newspaper account concerning the Brunter brothers may have resulted from confusion with a case in the Creek Nation not involving Reeves at all. In July 1883 a Creek Indian named Johnson Foster, on the run after a previous murder, brutally killed two brothers, Nathan and Lewis Bruner (not Brunter). Discovering the bodies, friends of the Bruners avenged their deaths by following the killer and shooting him to death. Robert Ernst, *Deadly Affrays: The Violent Deaths of the United States Marshals* (Phoenix: Scarlet Mask, 2006), 231–32.

23. *Muskogee Indian Journal*, August 28, 1884. In an article extolling Bass Reeves, the *Muskogee Phoenix*, November 14, 1901, quoted him as saying there were fifteen members of the Bruner family he knew personally, and eleven of them died with their boots on.

24. Haskell Pruett Collection Diaries, Indian-Pioneer History Collection, Oklahoma Historical Society, Oklahoma City, quoted in Brady, *Black Badge*, 94.

25. This case exemplifies the remarkably mottled racial aspect of law enforcement in Indian Territory at this time: a black officer, working out of a

white-dominated court, arresting an Indian for lynching a black man, who was suspected of raping a white woman.

26. *Fort Smith Weekly Elevator*, September 12, 1884.

27. *Muskogee Indian Journal*, October 16, 1884.

28. Burton, *Black Gun, Silver Star*, 107.

29. *Fort Smith Weekly Elevator*, April 24, 1885.

30. Floyd Alderman Wilson (1860–92), who worked with Bass Reeves on several desperado roundups, had a distinguished career as a deputy U.S. marshal, but he is best remembered today as "the one and only person killed by the famous Cherokee Indian bank robber Henry Starr." Art T. Burton, "Floyd Wilson: Fort Smith Lawman," *Art Burton's Frontier*, http://artburton.com/floyd-wilson-fort-smith-lawman/; Ernst, *Deadly Affrays*, 390–92.

31. Ernst, *Deadly Affrays*, 195.

32. Ibid., 194–95; Burton, *Black Gun, Silver Star*, 81.

33. Burton, *Black Gun, Silver Star*, 81–82.

34. The warrant issued by Stephen Wheeler, United States commissioner, charged that Bass Reeves did "feloniously, willfully, and premeditatedly and of his malice aforethought, kill and murder William Leach, a Negro." It was signed and sworn to by Fair and eleven others, including James and Mary Grayson and Reeves's nephew Johnnie Brady. Burton, *Black Gun, Silver Star*, 129–30.

35. *Arkansas Gazette*, January 22, 1886.

36. *Van Buren Press*, January 23, 1886.

37. Signing for the bond, besides Reeves himself, were his three attorneys and his good friend and fellow officer Jim Mershon. Burton, *Black Gun, Silver Star*, 133.

38. During these years most of those sentenced to serve time by the Fort Smith court were sent to the federal prison at Detroit, Michigan. In May 1881, Valentine Dell, then a U.S. marshal at Fort Smith, tapped Reeves to accompany him as a guard in the transportation of twenty-one convicts to Detroit. Other deputies assigned to the task were Jake Ayres, Tom Lacy, J. M. Caldwell, Addison Beck, and George Maledon, Judge Parker's famous hangman. Burton, *Black Gun, Silver Star*, 34. This appears to be the only time in his life that Reeves saw any part of the country beyond his Arkansas–Indian Territory–Texas bailiwick.

39. Burton, *Black Gun, Silver Star*, 139–47; Ernst, *Deadly Affrays*, 196–97.

40. Nudie E. Williams, "United States vs. Bass Reeves: Black Lawman in Trial," *Chronicles of Oklahoma* (Summer 1990): 154–67.

41. Burton, *Black Gun, Silver Star*, 147.

42. Ibid., 156–57; Ernst, *Deadly Affrays*, 204–205.

43. Burton, *Black Gun, Silver Star*, 163–64; Bonnie Stahlman Speer, *The Killing of Ned Christie* (Norman, OK: Reliance, 1990); Phillip Steele, *Last of the Cherokee Warriors* (Gretna, LA: Pelican Press, 1987); Ernst, *Deadly Affrays*, 208–13. Andrew "Heck" Thomas (1850–1912) was one of the storied three guardsmen

of Oklahoma. The others were William Matthew "Bill" Tilghman (1854–1924) and Christen "Chris" Madsen (1851–1944).

44. *Vinita Indian Chieftain*, November 17, 1890.

45. January 29, 1891.

46. January 31, 1891.

47. January 29, 1891.

48. February 5, 1891.

49. February 7, 1891.

50. Harve Lovelday interview, Indian Pioneer Papers, Oklahoma Historical Society.

51. Burton, *Black Gun, Silver Star*, 175. Alice Spahn, Reeves's daughter, who remembered her father when he later worked out of the Muskogee federal court, said he packed not two but three pistols, one in a hip scabbard, one in a shoulder holster, and one behind his belt in the small of his back. Fronterhouse, "Bass Reeves, the Forgotten Lawman," Historic Oklahoma Collection, Manuscript Division.

52. Burton, *Black Gun, Silver Star*, 175.

53. J. M. Hall, *Beginning of Tulsa* (Tulsa, OK: Scott-Rice Publishing, 1933), 39.

54. Burton, *Black Gun, Silver Star*, 183.

55. *Oklahoma City Weekly Times Journal*, March 8, 1907; *Muskogee Phoenix*, January 13, 1910; *Muskogee Times-Democrat*, January 13, 1910; Tyler, *New Handbook of Texas*, 5:507.

56. January 13, 1910.

57. January 13, 1910.

58. Tyler, *New Handbook of Texas*, 5:507. The story of the confrontation with Dosier (or Dozier) was related in dramatic detail by Alice Spahn, as she said she heard it from her father, Bass Reeves, and it was recorded by Richard Fronterhouse as part of an unpublished 1960 manuscript.

59. Fronterhouse, "Bass Reeves," 31–34; Burton, *Black Gun, Silver Star*, 149–50; Brady, *Black Badge*, 137–38; Burton, *Black, Red and Deadly*, 198–99.

60. Fronterhouse, "Bass Reeves," 35–37.

61. Brady, *Black Badge*, 137.

62. *Muskogee Daily Phoenix*, November 14, 1906.

63. Charles W. Mooney, *Doctor in Belle Starr Country* (Oklahoma City: Century Press, 1954), 115. The author said Dr. Jesse Mooney extracted the bullet, but as evidenced by the 1906 newspaper report cited above, he was evidently unable to do it.

64. Burton, *Black Gun, Silver Star*, 125.

65. Fronterhouse, "Bass Reeves," 35.

66. *Van Buren Press Argus*, July 22, 1893. Robert Reeves, a brakeman on the Central Arkansas & Houston Railway, was twenty-seven years old, married, with two small children.

67. *Van Buren Press Argus*, June 8, 1895, quoting the *Fort Smith Record*. "These are the Bass Reeves' boys," the Van Buren editor noted sadly, "and have started early on a criminal life."

68. June 8, 1902.

69. Fronterhouse, "Bass Reeves," 37–41.

70. According to Bennie, the man's name was John Wadly. Burton, *Black Gun, Silver Star*, 248.

71. Brady, *Black Badge*, 168–70. This version, like many stories in the book with no documentation, was evidently drawn entirely from stories passed down in the Reeves family.

72. Burton, *Black Gun, Silver Star*, 247–48, from *Through the Looking Glass*, a documentary produced for television station WKY, Oklahoma City, July 1973.

73. Although the arrest of his own son was certainly unusual for Bass Reeves, it was not unique in western annals. In 1909, seven years after the Reeves episode, Undersheriff Lewis Kreeger of Las Animas County, Colorado, collared his only son, William Squire "Squick" Kreeger, for participating in armed robbery. Kreeger was convicted on three counts and received concurrent sentences, but the sentence was later commuted to time served and Squick was paroled. His father, however, died six months before Squick's release. R. K. DeArment, "Kreeger's Toughest Arrest," *True West* (June 1986): 14–19.

74. Burton, *Black Gun, Silver Star*, 248. Benjamin Reeves served eleven years and ten months in prison until the commutation of his life sentence on November 13, 1914. He then returned to Muskogee, where he worked in a restaurant and apparently had no further legal difficulty. Ibid., 249.

75. Roger Tuller, *"Let No Man Escape": A Judicial Biography of Isaac C. Parker* (Norman: University of Oklahoma Press, 2001).

76. *Muskogee Phoenix*, January 18, 1900. To the U.S. census taker that year, Winnie gave her birthdate as 1869 and her age as thirty-one, but in an attempt to get on the Cherokee Freedman Rolls a year later, she said she was born "around 1858," making her "around forty-one" in 1900. Burton, *Black Gun, Silver Star*, 233.

77. Burton, *Black Gun, Silver Star*, 240.

78. *Dallas Morning News*, May 21, 1902; *Cherokee Advocate*, May 31, 1902.

79. *Van Buren Press*, August 14, 1907.

80. *Muskogee Times-Democrat*, January 13, 1910.

81. Ibid.; *Muskogee Phoenix*, January 13, 1910.

82. *Daily Oklahoman*, January 13, 1910; *Washington Herald*, January 13, 1910.

83. Burton, *Black Gun, Silver Star*, 301.

84. Unfortunately, both the *Legends and Lies* and *Gunslinger* presentations depict Bass Reeves as the inspiration for the fictional western law enforcement hero the Lone Ranger. This character, originally conceived by Fran Striker, a radio scriptwriter, debuted on a Detroit radio station in 1933 and went on to immortality in radio, television, motion pictures, novels, comic strips, books, and even a video game. To date, no one has been able to prove conclusively that Striker ever heard of Bass Reeves, let alone had him in mind when he invented the Lone Ranger. A better case can be argued that Captain John R. Hughes of the Texas Rangers was the inspiration for the fictional lawman, based on the fact that in some of the radio shows, mention is made that the Lone Ranger was a former

Texas Ranger (not a deputy U.S. marshal), and when the great western novelist Zane Grey published his novel *The Lone Star Ranger* in 1915, he dedicated it to Captain Hughes.

Chapter 6. Patrick Floyd Jarvis "Pat" Garrett

1. Leon C. Metz, *Pat Garrett: The Story of a Western Lawman* (Norman: University of Oklahoma Press, 1974), 5–9; 1850 U.S. census, Chambers County, Alabama; 1860 U.S. census, Claiborne Parish, Louisiana.

2. Metz, *Pat Garrett*, 8–9.

3. Skelton Glenn Papers, University of Texas at El Paso Archives; Leo Reminger, Miles Gilbert, and Sharon Cunningham, eds., *Encyclopedia of Buffalo Hunters* (Union City, TN: Pioneer Press, 2006), 55–63.

4. A small hide-hunter settlement, Camp Reynolds was also called Reynolds City and Rath City. Metz, *Pat Garrett*, 18.

5. Metz, *Pat Garrett*, 16–17; Robert N. Mullin, "Pat Garrett, Two Forgotten Killings," *Password* (Summer 1965): 57–63; Skelton Glenn Papers; Thrapp, *Encyclopedia of Frontier Biography*, 2:541.

6. Metz, *Pat Garrett*, 18.

7. Ibid., 18–19.

8. Ibid., 19. In 1877 Garrett reportedly married a woman named Juanita Gutierrez, who died a few months later, perhaps in childbirth. Tyler, *New Handbook of Texas*, 3:99. Garrett's biographer Leon Metz could find nothing to verify this story. Metz, *Pat Garrett*, 40.

9. Metz, *Pat Garrett*, 38.

10. Ibid., 39.

11. Ibid., 40–41.

12. Ibid., 54.

13. Ibid., 57, Frederick Nolan, *Lincoln County War: A Documentary History* (Norman: University of Oklahoma Press, 1992), 398.

14. Nolan, *Lincoln County War*, 3–9, 56–57.

15. Ibid., 58–59.

16. Ibid., 148–49.

17. Ibid., 149–50.

18. Irish-born Lawrence Gustave Murphy (c. 1831–78), a Union veteran, partnered with Emil Fritz in operating a brewery and store near Fort Stanton, which became the genesis of the business and political association called "the House." When Fritz died in 1874, James Joseph Dolan (1848–98) became Murphy's partner. Believing Pat Garrett could be a powerful tool for the House as sheriff, Dolan supported him strongly in the election of 1880. Rancher John Henry Riley (1850–1916) was a partner in the Murphy firm but carefully avoided personal involvement in the Lincoln County violence. Strong political support for the House was provided by Samuel Beach Axtell (1819–91), who was appointed

New Mexico governor in 1874, and Thomas Benton Catron (1840–1921), who made a fortune manipulating Mexican land grants and held many important posts, including mayor of Santa Fe, U.S. attorney, and United States senator. Nolan, *Lincoln County War*.

19. Alexander Anderson McSween (c. 1843–78), a bitter opponent of the House, befriended John Henry Tunstall (1853–78), an investment-seeking Englishman, and helped him establish a ranch in Lincoln County. Tunstall's murder escalated the violence of the Lincoln County War. Ibid.; Thrapp, *Encyclopedia of Frontier Biography*, 1: 411–12; 2:1035; 3: 1222, 1445–46.

20. Nolan, *Lincoln County War*, 201. Richard M. Brewer (1852–78) was "tall, somewhat heavy, green-eyed, lantern-jawed, with thick, curly hair, a handlebar mustache and bristling whiskers." When he was killed, McSween eulogized him as "a young man of irreproachable character who commanded the respect and admiration of all who knew him . . . , generous, sober, upright and noble-minded," but Tunstall once remarked that Brewer was hot-tempered and likely to "shoot first and ask afterwards, being as desperate and lawless as they come." Thrapp, *Encyclopedia of Frontier Biography*, 1:166.

21. *Mesilla Valley Independent*, March 10, 1878.

22. Irish immigrant William Brady (1829–78), after lengthy service in the U.S. Army and the New Mexico Volunteer Infantry, was the first sheriff of Lincoln County following its organization. Nolan, *Lincoln County War*, 447; Thrapp, *Encyclopedia of Frontier Biography*, 1:159; Donald Lavash, *William Brady: Tragic Hero of the Lincoln County War* (Santa Fe, NM: Sunstone Press, 1986).

23. Nolan, *Lincoln County War*, 249.

24. Cousins George Washington Coe (1856–1941) and Benjamin Franklin "Frank" Coe (1851–1931) were members of the Regulators. After the Lincoln County War they, together with other family members, were involved in the violence in the Farmington area of northern New Mexico. Ibid., 453–54; R. K. DeArment, *Deadly Dozen: Forgotten Gunfighters of the Old West* (Norman: University of Oklahoma Press, 2003), 3:162–89.

John Middleton (1854–82), a man "who feared nothing and nobody," had black hair, mustache, and eyes. Tunstall found him "about the most desperate looking man [he] ever set eyes on. . . . [Tunstall] could fancy him doing almost anything ruffianly. [In appearance] he is mild & composed as any man can be, but his arms are never out of his reach." Nolan, *Lincoln County War*, 475; Thrapp, *Encyclopedia of Frontier Biography*, 4:353–54; Phillip Rasch, *Warriors of Lincoln County* (Stillwater, OK: Western Publications, 1998), 189–90.

25. Fredrick Tecumseh Waite (1853–95), part Chickasaw, returned to Indian Territory after the Lincoln County War, where he had a distinguished political career. Nolan, *Lincoln County War*, 490; Rasch, *Warriors of Lincoln County*, 194.

26. Henry Newton Brown (1857–84) hunted buffalo in Texas and reportedly killed a man there before moving on to New Mexico. "A queer character [who] neither drank, smoked nor gambled," Brown was both an outlaw and a lawman.

When he was town marshal of Caldwell, Kansas, in 1882–83, he was described as "very quiet," with blond hair and mustache. He generally "wore a sort of business suit, colored shirt, not loud, tie and kerchief around his neck cowboy-style." Nolan, *Lincoln County War*, 449. Respected by Caldwell residents for maintaining order in that rough cow town, they rewarded him with a gold-mounted Winchester rifle, but were shocked when Brown, his deputy, and two others held up the bank of Medicine Lodge, Kansas, on April 30, 1884, killing the bank president and wounding a cashier in the process. Captured almost immediately, they were jailed, but that night vigilantes stormed the calaboose and shot-gunned Brown to death when he made a run for it. The other three were hanged. O'Neal, *Henry Brown: The Outlaw Marshal* (College Station, TX: Creative Publishing, 1980).

27. Nolan, *Lincoln County War*, 269–70.

28. Caleb Coe, ed., *Frontier Fighter* (Chicago: Lakeside Press, R. R. Donnelley & Sons, 1984), 117.

29. Quoted in Maurice G. Fulton, *History of the Lincoln County War* (Tucson: University of Arizona Press, 1975), 216–17.

30. George Warden Peppin (c. 1841–1904), a mason by trade, was later a jailer and a deputy under Sheriff George Curry at Lincoln. Nolan, *Lincoln County War*, 478–79.

31. Coincidentally, that same day, June 18, 1878, the United States Congress passed the Posse Comitatus Act, prohibiting the federal military from assisting civilian law enforcement officers in the arrest of suspected lawbreakers unless specifically authorized by the president, a measure that would hinder civilian law enforcement in Lincoln County, New Mexico, and many other western jurisdictions.

32. Charles Bowdre (1848–80) was "thin [with a] scrawny, sandy mustache. He had a high forehead [and] usually wore a fine black hat and a vest, winter or summer." Thrapp, *Encyclopedia of Frontier Biography*, 1:147.

Josiah Gordon "Doc" Scurlock (1849–1929) acquired his nickname from an early study of medicine. Fair of hair and complexion, he was "quiet spoken." His front teeth were missing, lost in a gambling table dispute, when a bullet took them out and passed through the back of his neck. Nolan, *Lincoln County War*, 484–85.

33. Ibid., 339–40.

34. Ibid., 351.

35. *Mesilla Valley Independent*, November 23, 1878.

36. Henry F. Hoyt, *A Frontier Doctor* (Chicago: Lakeside Press, R. R. Donnelley & Sons, 154–56, 1929); Charles Siringo, *A Texas Cowboy or Fifteen Years on the Hurricane Deck of a Spanish Pony* (New York: William Sloane, 1950), 110.

37. Nolan, *Lincoln County War*, 382.

38. Maurice Garland Fulton, introduction to John W. Poe, *The Death of Billy the Kid* (Boston: Houghton Mifflin, 1933), xxii.

39. Carl Hertzog, *Little Known Facts about Billy the Kid* (Santa Fe, NM: The Press of the Territorian, 1964), 10; Nolan, *Lincoln County War*, 397.

40. Emerson Hough, who knew him, said John Hurley was "brave as a lion." While he was a deputy under Sheriff John Poe, he was killed in January 1886 by escaped rustler Nicolas Aragon. Nolan, *Lincoln County War*, 468.

41. Frank Stewart (1852–1935), christened John W. Green, was arrested in 1887 for cattle theft in New Mexico. He jumped bail, escaped, changed his name to Frank Stewart, and became a stock detective. Frederick Nolan, *The West of Billy the Kid* (Norman: University of Oklahoma Press, 1998); *Amarillo Sunday News and Globe*, November 30, 1930.

42. Metz, *Pat Garrett*, 60.

43. Bernard "Barney" Mason (1848–1916), "short, stocky, red-faced, red-haired, and hot-tempered," drove cattle from Texas to Kansas and turned up later in New Mexico, where he shot and killed a cowboy at Fort Sumner, but got off on the time-honored plea of self-defense. Two weeks after the shooting he got married on the same day, at the same church, and before the same witnesses as Pat Garrett, leading to the erroneous conclusion by some writers that Mason and Garrett were brothers-in-law. After serving as a deputy for Sheriffs Garrett and Poe, he was convicted of stealing a calf and sentenced to a year in prison, but was pardoned by Governor Edmund G. Ross. Thrapp, *Encyclopedia of Frontier Biography*, 4:346; Rasch, *Warriors of Lincoln County*, 102–107.

Robert Meridith "Bob" Olinger (1850–81) was "considered the most able deputy of Garrett's posse," according to Mary Hudson Brothers, *A Pecos Pioneer* (Albuquerque: University of New Mexico Press, 1943). She describes him as "two hundred pounds of bone and muscle, six feet tall, round as a huge tree trunk, with a gorilla-like chest that bulged out so far his chin seemed to set back in his chest. He had a heavy bull neck, low-browed head, short and wide, topped with shaggy hair, bushy eyebrows, and a hat rack moustache. His arms were long and muscular, with fists like hams." Quoted in Rasch, *Warriors of Lincoln County*, 63.

44. John Joshua Webb (1847–82?), like Henry Brown, operated on both sides of the law. He was a deputy of Sheriff Bat Masterson at Dodge City, Kansas, in 1877 and later a city marshal of Las Vegas, New Mexico. In 1880 he participated in a botched robbery and killed a man. Convicted and sentenced to hang, he was saved from the noose by Governor Wallace, who commuted his sentence to life in prison. After two unsuccessful jailbreaks engineered by Dave Rudabaugh, Webb did escape, murdering three in the process. He reportedly died of smallpox in 1882 in Arizona. Leon C. Metz, *The Encyclopedia of Lawmen, Outlaws, and Gunfighters* (New York: Checkmark Books, 2003), 259; Metz, *Pat Garrett*, 62; Nolan, *Lincoln County War*, 483; Phillip Rasch, "Amende Honorable: The Life and Death of Billy Wilson," *West Texas Historical Association Year Book* (1958): 63; *Santa Fe Daily New Mexican*, December 30, 1880.

45. *Las Vegas Morning Gazette*, December 12, 1880. Editor Koogler of the *Gazette* was not enamored with Billy the Kid. In a December 22 editorial he

reminded readers that his paper had led the campaign to capture or drive out Billy and his gang, and now the Kid was threatening to make it hot for "those Gazette fellows." To this Koogler responded, "We are delighted to know that Billy has read our little obituary notice for from all accounts he is not long for this world."

46. Charles Siringo, *Riata and Spurs: The Story of a Lifetime Spent in the Saddle as Cowboy and Detective* (Boston and New York: Houghton Mifflin, 1927), 75–91.

47. David Rudabaugh (1854?–86?) has a sketchy biography. One of a gang that staged an unsuccessful train holdup at Kinsley, Kansas, in January 1878, he was hunted down and arrested by Sheriff Bat Masterson and a posse that included Josh Webb, with whom Rudabaugh would be closely associated in later years. Rudabaugh avoided prison by ratting on his train-robbing associates. As the *Kinsley Graphic* put it, he was "promised immunity if he would 'squeal,' therefore he squole." After his arrest by Pat Garrett and subsequent conviction and life sentence, Rudabaugh escaped jail and disappeared. One report of his passing had him beheaded by an angry mob at Parral, Mexico, in 1886 after he killed two men. Another has it that he hid out a year in Mexico and then went to Montana, became a top cowhand, married, fathered children, and died at the Oregon home of a daughter in 1928. Nolan, *Lincoln County War*, 482–83.

48. Polk, "Life of C. W. Polk," quoted in Nolan, *Lincoln County War*, 406–407.

49. Ibid., 407–408.

50. *Las Vegas Daily Optic*, December 18, 1880.

51. *Las Vegas Morning Gazette*, December 28, 1880.

52. Pat F. Garrett, *The Authentic Life of Billy the Kid* (Albuquerque, NM: Horn and Wallace, 1964), 116.

53. Polk, "Life of C. W. Polk," quoted in Nolan, *Lincoln County War*, 410–11.

54. Metz, *Pat Garrett*, 90.

55. December 30, 1880.

56. *Las Vegas Morning Gazette*, January 1, 1881.

57. *Las Vegas Morning Gazette*, January 13, 1881.

58. Metz, *Pat Garrett*, 90–91.

59. Nolan, *Lincoln County War*, 411.

60. Claiming the murder was committed on the Mescalero reservation, a federal facility, the prosecution was conducted by a U.S. district attorney. Mid-trial, Bonney's attorney contended that Blazer's Mill, the site of the shooting, was not on the reservation and that the United States had no jurisdiction. Judge Bristol agreed and dismissed the federal case. Ibid., 413.

61. Ibid., 414. Counterfeiter Billie Wilson was also convicted, but he escaped and fled to Texas. Cured of his criminal ways by the harrowing time spent with Billy the Kid, he reformed, married, raised a family, and became a law-abiding citizen. Years later, when Garrett learned of his conversion, he lobbied President Grover Cleveland for a full pardon for the former outlaw, which was granted.

Wilson became a lawman himself and, sadly, on June 14, 1918, was shot to death in Terrell County, Texas, while making an arrest. Metz, *Pat Garrett*, 159.

62. Nolan, *Lincoln County War*, 415. Biographer Metz has pointed out the irony of the scene: the notorious outlaw, sentenced to hang, was flanked on one side of the wagon seat by "John Kinney, one of the worst cattle rustlers and killers in the Territory," and on the other by "Billy Mathews, a deputy in the posse that killed Tunstall," while opposite sat "Bob Olinger, a locally well-known manslayer." Metz, *Pat Garrett*, 91.

63. James W. Bell (1853–81), "a tall, dark man with a livid knife scar across his left cheek," was reportedly a former Texas Ranger who came to New Mexico and prospected near White Oaks before Pat Garrett engaged him as a deputy sheriff and got him appointed a deputy U.S. marshal. Reynolds, *Trouble in New Mexico: The Outlaws, Gunmen, Desperados, Murderers and Lawmen for Fifty Turbulent Years* (Bakersfield, CA: B. Reynolds, 1994), 153–54.

64. May 3, 1881.

65. May 4, 1881.

66. *Las Vegas Morning Gazette*, June 23, 1881.

67. After his escape, Bonney stopped at the ranch of his friend, John P. Meadows, who later related how he advised the Kid to light out for Old Mexico, but Bonney was broke and wanted to get some money at Fort Sumner before heading for the border. John P. Meadows, "Reminiscences, February 26, 1931," quoted in Frazier Hunt, *Tragic Days of Billy the Kid* (New York: Hastings House, 1956), 301. The magnet pulling Bonney back to Fort Sumner was probably not money but the warm embraces of his several female admirers there, including Pete Maxwell's teenaged daughter Paulita and Celia Gutierrez, a married woman, and amazingly, Pat Garrett's sister-in-law. Nolan, *Lincoln County War*, 421.

68. This notice emulated the wordage of the one issued by Governor Wallace previously, saying the reward would be paid anyone "who captured William Bonny [*sic*], Alias Billy the Kid, and delivered him to any sheriff of New Mexico." As before, the ambiguity of the wordage would give Garrett problems.

69. John William Poe (1851–1923), was city marshal of Fort Griffin and Mobeetie, two of the toughest towns in Texas, before coming to New Mexico in 1881. Thrapp, *Encyclopedia of Frontier Biography*, 3:1153–54.

70. Only ten days after the Kid's escape, McKinney drew applause for killing notorious horse thief Bob Edwards. "Too much cannot be said in praise of Mr. McKinney for his good work. He started out almost alone, and has accomplished unlooked-for results. With such deputies as he Pat Garrett will soon bring order out of chaos in Lincoln County." *Las Vegas Gazette*, May 17, 1881.

71. *Las Vegas Gazette*, July 22, 1881.

72. *New York Sun*, August 10, 1881.

73. *Longview Democrat*, August 26, 1881.

74. Metz, *Pat Garrett*, 127; *Rio Grande Republican*, September 2, 1882.

75. Nolan, *West of Billy the Kid*, 291.

76. *Las Vegas Daily Gazette*, December 2, 1881.

77. *Las Vegas Daily Gazette*, February 27, August 12, September 7, 1881.

78. *Las Vegas Daily Gazette*, December 6, 1881.

79. Metz, *Pat Garrett*, 127; *Albuquerque Review*, August 8, 1882.

80. Nolan, *West of Billy the Kid*, 291–92.

81. Ibid., 293; Adams, *Six-Guns and Saddle Leather*, 244.

82. Nolan, *West of Billy the Kid*, 295.

83. *Las Vegas Daily Gazette*, March 28, 1882.

84. *Las Vegas Optic*, March 22, 1882.

85. James D. Shinkle, *Reminiscences of Roswell Pioneers* (Roswell, NM: Hall-Poorbaugh Press, 1966), 22. Because of its limited sales and its historic value, the book has become a highly valued collector's item in later years, with numerous reprints, but Garrett and Upson never profited financially from the book's belated popularity.

86. Metz, *Pat Garrett*, 133.

87. Ibid., 135. Garrett's temperament was not helped by his acquisition of "a full crop of mumps—that is to say—on both sides." *Lincoln County Leader*, September 28, 1882.

88. The *Las Vegas Daily Gazette* of June 25, 1884, quoting the *Springer Stockman*, reported that the Texas governor commissioned Garrett to head up this organization, but biographer Metz could find no contemporary confirmation and suggests that the governor may have given unofficial permission as long as the ranch owners assumed all cost responsibility. Ibid., 141.

89. Two years later Ed King was killed in a gunfight at Tascosa in which he and three others were shot to death and two others wounded. Metz, *Encyclopedia of Lawmen*, 240.

90. Metz, *Pat Garrett*, 142.

91. Dan Bogan (Gatlin's real name) and Dave Kemp, another tough, murdered a man in Hamilton, Texas, in 1881 and were arrested and jailed. Bogan pulled off one of the daring escapes at which he was adept and next appeared in the panhandle as Bill Gatlin. DeArment, *Deadly Dozen*, 1:152–68.

92. Metz, *Pat Garrett*, 158.

93. Ibid., 158–59.

94. Ibid., 145. The 1885 New Mexico census listed Garrett as a rancher living in Las Vegas with his wife, Apolinaria, age twenty-four, and their children. In all, Garrett fathered eight: Ida (b. 1881), Elizabeth (b. 1885), Dudley Poe (b. 1886), Annie (b. 1889), Patrick Floyd Jr. (b. 1896), Pauline (b. 1900), Oscar (b. 1904), and Jarvis Powers (b. 1905). His second-born, Elizabeth, was blind, and in adulthood she became an associate of Helen Keller's. An accomplished musician, she wrote "Oh Fair New Mexico," the official state song, and many others. Ibid., 156–57.

95. *White Oaks Golden Era*, January 28, 1886.

96. Among Garrett's many Uvalde friends was John Nance Garner, who would become vice president of the United States. In the 1950s Garner, responding to an inquiry from Pat's son Oscar about that relationship, said, "I knew your father as an honorable, honest, patriotic American. When movies slander him, they slander their betters." Metz, *Pat Garrett*, 160.

97. Ibid., 156, 159; Sammy Tise, *Texas County Sheriffs* (Albuquerque, NM: Oakwood Printing, 1989), 488.

98. *Rio Grande Republican*, February 4, 1896.

99. See chapter 7.

100. Metz, *Pat Garrett*, 178–79.

101. Pinkerton detective Charles A. Siringo, who worked with this operative on many cases, consistently called him "W. O. Sayles" in his autobiographical books, but later Pinkerton historians believe his name was W. B. Sayers.

102. *Rio Grande Republican*, October 9, 1896.

103. Metz, *Pat Garrett*, 210; *El Paso Times*, July 12, 13, 14, 16, 1898.

104. The *Western Liberal*, November 18, 1898, quoting the *El Paso Times*, opined that, since Garrett's election, lawbreakers "will have to take their medicine. While they would have taken their medicine from any [in] the sheriff's office, they do hate to take it from Pat Garrett."

105. Metz, *Pat Garrett*, 236–38.

106. Ibid., 238–39.

107. *El Paso Daily Herald*, February 13, 1900.

108. *El Paso Daily Herald*, September 6, 1900.

109. *El Paso Daily Herald*, December 24, 1900.

110. November 21, 1901. During his presidency Roosevelt appointed Ben Daniels and Bat Masterson, former gun-fighting lawmen of the wild cattle town of Dodge City, Kansas, to federal offices.

111. Hoyt, *Frontier Doctor*, 120.

112. *El Paso Herald*, December 26, 1901.

113. *El Paso Evening News*, May 8, 1903; *El Paso Herald*, May 8, 1903; *El Paso Daily Times*, May 9, 1903.

114. Metz, *Pat Garrett*, 252.

115. Ibid., 253. An interesting sidebar to the Roosevelt-Powers difficulty occurred later, when the president got over his pique. In 1911 Roosevelt visited El Paso, shook hands with Powers, and posed for a photo with him, his animosity evidently assuaged by a gift the saloon-keeper had sent him, a bear cub Powers had captured on a hunting trip. Roosevelt was "dee-lighted" with the gift, and the press, running with the story, dubbed it "Teddy's bear," thus inadvertently creating a common expression and a child gift industry that is still active a century later. Ibid., 254.

116. Ibid., 258–59.

117. Emerson Hough Collection, Iowa State Department of History and Archives, Des Moines, quoted in ibid., 281.

118. *Rio Grande Republican*, April 27, October 5, 1907.

119. Pat had evidently given the property to Dudley Poe, as his name was specified in the lease agreement. Metz, *Pat Garrett*, 286.

120. *El Paso Herald*, March 8, 1908; Metz, *Pat Garrett*, 288.

121. Both Hardin and Mannen Clements, a part-time peace officer and a killer for hire, respectively, were slain in El Paso saloons, Hardin in 1895 by John Selman in the Acme Saloon, and Clements by an unknown gunman in Tom Powers's Coney Island Saloon in 1908. Other Clements men met similar fates.

122. *El Paso Herald*, March 2, 1908; *Rio Grande Republican*, March 7, 1908; Metz, *Pat Garrett*, 291.

123. *New Mexico Sentinel*, April 23, 1939.

124. *Rio Grande Republican*, March 7, 1908.

125. Metz, *Pat Garrett*, 294–95. As late as 1908 many westerners held the firm belief that once a man threatened an enemy's life before witnesses, each was free to kill his foe at any opportunity and claim self-defense. It was called "the Code of the West," and accounted for many killings, including back-shootings, during the frontier period.

126. Ibid., 301.

127. Glenn Shirley, *Shotgun for Hire* (Norman: University of Oklahoma Press, 1970). A year after the Garrett killing, enraged residents of Ada, Oklahoma, lynched Miller and three accomplices for the murder of a popular peace officer. An example of ridiculous statements appearing in newspapers, then and now, is an account of the lynching in a Texas paper, the *Bryan Daily Eagle and Pilot*, on April 19, 1909. A description of Miller's nefarious career included the ludicrous assertion that Miller and Pat Garrett "were comrades for a long time and shared many adventures together."

128. Mark Lee Gardner, *To Hell on a Fast Horse* (New York: William Morrow, 2010).

129. Metz, *Pat Garrett*, 303.

130. Ibid., 306.

131. Burns to Fulton, January 21, 1928, Fulton Papers, University of Arizona Library.

132. Rhodes, "In Defense of Pat Garrett," quoted in W. H. Hutchison, *The Rhodes Reader* (Norman: University of Oklahoma Press, 1975), 305–16.

133. Patrick J. Hurley, secretary of war in the Herbert Hoover administration and later ambassador to China, in a letter to Pat's son Oscar Garrett, quoted by Jarvis P. Garrett in his introduction to Garrett, *Authentic Life*, 64.

Chapter 7. John Reynolds Hughes

Epigraph: Thrapp, *Encyclopedia of Frontier Biography*, 2:691.

1. Chuck Parsons, *Captain John R. Hughes: Lone Star Ranger* (Denton, TX: University of North Texas, 2011), 2–4.

2. Ibid., 32.

3. Jack Martin, *Border Boss: Captain John R. Hughes—Texas Ranger* (San Antonio: Naylor, 1942), 8.

4. *San Antonio Express*, October 11, 1925.

5. *Austin-American*, June 5, 1947.

6. Hancock, "Ranger's Ranger," 23–24.

7. *El Paso Herald-Post*, April 12, 1938. After talking with Hughes for several hours, Pyle concluded his article: "I've never spent a calmer, pleasanter half-day with anybody in my life."

8. *El Paso Herald*, January 13–14, 1923.

9. Martin, *Border Boss*, 3.

10. Parsons, *Captain John R. Hughes*, 7.

11. Quoted in ibid., 9–11.

12. Ibid., 11.

13. Hughes Brothers Horse Record, Texas Ranger Hall of Fame and Museum, Waco.

14. Parsons, *Captain John R. Hughes*, 18, 21–22. *Border Boss* author Jack Martin erroneously attributed the theft of the horses to the Butch Cassidy gang, a mistake repeated in later publications.

15. *San Antonio Daily Express*, January 17, 1915.

16. *Black Range*, August 22, 1884.

17. Outlaw Toppy Johnson was notorious in New Mexico. Others charged included J. Sullivan, A. Brady, W. McKinsie, one Fortman, and one Weatherford. *Black Range*, June 13, 1884.

18. *Black Range*, September 12, 1884. The case cost Sierra County $7,000 and the Central New Mexico Stock Raisers Association $1,500, amounts partially offset by the $3,500 bail Weatherford forfeited when he fled. *White Oaks Golden Era*, May 7, 1885.

19. Parsons, Captain John R. Hughes, 25–26; Ira Aten, "Six and One Half Years in the Ranger Service Fifty Years Ago," Briscoe Center for American History, Austin, TX, 8.

20. Aten, "Six and One Half Years," 9.

21. *Burnet Bulletin*, "43 Years Ago," May 30, 1929. Three of the four accused of the Fredericksburg murder met violent ends: Collier was killed by Ranger Aten, one burned to death in jail, and another was "shot to death near Mason." Fannin, the fourth man, escaped. Robert Peninger, *Fredericksburg, Texas. . . The First Fifty Years* (Fredericksburg, TX: Arwed Hilton, 1896), 79.

22. Aten, "Six and One Half Years," 42.

23. Record of Scouts, Frontier Battalion, Ledger 401–1084, quoted in Parsons, *Captain John R. Hughes*, 42.

24. Parsons, *Captain John R. Hughes*, 48; Bob Alexander, *Rawhide Ranger: Ira Aten* (Denton: University of North Texas Press, 2011), 172.

25. Parsons, *Captain John R. Hughes*, 47–50. On September 18, 1891, Richard Duncan was hanged. Some believed Landers was never found because Duncan had murdered him also. Ibid., 49–50.

26. April 1889 Monthly Return of Captain Frank Jones, in ibid., 50.

27. Captain Jones's monthly returns for May and December 1889, in ibid., 50–52.

28. Hughes to King, December 25, 1889, quoted in Bob Alexander, *Six-Shooters and Shifting Sands: The Wild West Life of Texas Ranger Captain Frank Jones* (Denton: University of North Texas Press, 2015), 271.

29. Jones to Sieker, December 29, 1989, Adjutant General Papers, Texas State Library and Archives, Austin.

30. Parsons, *Captain John R. Hughes*, 61. Hughes greatly admired Fusselman, calling him "one of the finest men ever to take the trail that law and order might pave the way for civilization, for progress." L. A. Wilke, "The Wide Loop of the Ranger Noose," *Real Detective* (September 1936): 24–29.

31. Parsons, *Captain John R. Hughes*, 65.

32. Ibid., 71; Captain Jones's monthly return, January 31, 1892, Texas State Library and Archives; Alexander, *Six-Shooters*, 319–20; *Chicago Daily Tribune*, July 3, 1892; *Los Angeles Times*, August 31, 1898; *El Paso Daily Times*, September 1, 1898.

33. Ann Jensen, *Texas Ranger's Diary and Scrapbook* (Dallas: Kaleidograph, 1936), 59.

34. Ibid.

35. Ibid., 36; unidentified El Paso newspaper clipping, Hughes Scrapbook, in Parsons, *Captain John R. Hughes*.

36. Captain Jones's monthly return, September 30, 1892, Texas State Library and Archives.

37. Jones to Mabry, January 17, 1893, Adjutant General Papers.

38. Dean to Mabry, June 19, 1893, Adjutant General Papers.

39. *San Antonio Daily Express*, July 1, 1893.

40. Baylor to Mabry, July 9, 1893, Adjutant General Papers. Baylor, Captain Jones's father-in-law and a former Ranger captain, got the story from other posse members.

41. Ibid.

42. Kirchner to Mabry, June 30, 1893, Adjutant General Papers.

43. Baylor to Mabry, July 1, 1893, Adjutant General Papers.

44. Baylor to Mabry, July 9, 1893, Adjutant General Papers. Eventually Captain Jones's possessions were returned and given to the Jones family. For his efforts in locating and punishing the captain's killers, the family presented Hughes with the pocket watch. Later, in appreciation for the dedicated service of the Aten brothers in his company, Hughes passed the watch on to Eddie Aten. Alexander, *Rawhide Ranger*, 317.

45. Dean to Hogg, July 2, 1893, Adjutant General Papers.

46. McLemore to Hogg, July 3, 1893, Adjutant General Papers.

47. Austin to Hogg, July 3, 1893, Adjutant General Papers.

48. Simmons to Hogg, July 3, 1893, Adjutant General Papers; Simmons to Mabry, July 3, 1893, Adjutant General Papers.

49. Teel to Hogg, July 3, 1893, Adjutant General Papers.

50. Noyes to Mabry, July 5, 1893, Adjutant General Papers; Faubion to Mabry, July 5, 1893, Adjutant General Papers.

51. Outlaw to Mabry, July 5, 1893, Adjutant General Papers. Of course, Outlaw never pursued his "temperate habits." On one of his drunken rampages only nine months later, he killed Private Joe McKidrict of Company D and wounded Constable John Selman before Selman gave him a mortal wound. Another Company D private, Frank McMahan, disarmed and arrested him and placed him on a prostitute's bed in the rear of a saloon, where Outlaw died. Parsons, *Captain John R. Hughes*, 102–104. Disgusted by the affair, Hughes's official report was succinct: "Joe McKidrict a member of Co. D was killed tonight while attempting to arrest B. L. Outlaw. Outlaw is dead also." Hughes to Mabry, April 6, 1894, Adjutant General Papers.

52. Baylor to Mabry, July 5, 1893, Adjutant General Papers.

53. Hughes to Mabry, July 5, 1893, Adjutant General Papers.

54. *San Antonio Daily Express*, July 17, 1893.

55. *El Paso Herald-Post*, May 13, 1938.

56. C. L. Sonnichsen, "Last of the Great Rangers—Captain John R. Hughes," Special Collections Department, University of Texas at El Paso Library.

57. Hughes and Scarborough were close friends, and Frank McMahan, Scarborough's brother-in-law, was a private in Company D. Scarborough was severely criticized by the El Paso press after two murder indictments, one for killing a fugitive rustler, and the other for killing John Selman. Although acquitted both times, he resigned his deputy U.S. marshal commission and sought Hughes's support for appointment as a special Texas Ranger. In a letter to Mabry, Hughes explained that although Scarborough was a good friend to him personally, it might hurt the ranger image if he were made a member, as the press might use it "against Governor Culberson and yourself." Scarborough did not receive the appointment. R. K. DeArment, *George Scarborough: The Life and Death of a Lawman on the Closing Frontier* (Norman: University of Oklahoma Press, 1992); Parsons, *Captain John R. Hughes*, 140.

58. Murphy to Mabry, February 21, 1895, Adjutant General Papers.

59. Frazer to Culberson, February 24, 1895, Adjutant General Papers.

60. Before Frazer could be tried, he was shotgunned to death in a Toyah, Texas, saloon by Miller. One trial for the murder resulted in a hung jury, and Miller was acquitted at a second trial on the time-honored plea of self-defense. The long career of "Killer Miller," consisting of calculated, cold-blooded murder, ended on April 19, 1909, at Ada, Oklahoma, when he was lynched along with three others who had hired him for an assassination.

61. McAleer to Mabry, February 1, 1895, Adjutant General Papers.

62. Hughes to Mabry, February 15, 1895, Adjutant General Papers.

63. Hughes to Mabry, February 18, 1895, Adjutant General Papers.

64. Hughes to Mabry, April 2 1895, Adjutant General Papers; *Galveston Daily News*, April 23, 1895; Parsons, *Captain John R. Hughes*, 116–18.

65. Bob Alexander, *Winchester Warriors: Texas Rangers of Company D, 1874–1901* (Denton: University of North Texas Press, 2011), 281. All three were later reinstated. Ibid., 289, 290.

66. Hughes to Ranger Quartermaster W. H. Owen, May 1, 1895, quoted in ibid., 281. The rosters were later enlarged and remained in effect until the disbanding of the Frontier Battalion in 1901.

67. Hughes to Henry Orsay, Secretary to Governor Culberson, June 11, 1895, quoted in ibid., 281.

68. Tom Holland established an alibi and was released. Sam Holland was tried, convicted, and sentenced to fifteen years in prison, but his lawyers won a reversal and change of venue. The charges were eventually dropped. Parsons, *Captain John R. Hughes*, 122–23.

69. Ibid., 124–34.

70. In a typical succinct report, Hughes said that after an eight-day hunt covering 625 miles, his posse was fired upon. "We charged on them and returned the fire killing two of them, the third man escaped." Hughes to Mabry, October 4, 1896, Adjutant General Papers.

71. *San Antonio Daily Express*, October 1, 1896.

72. Parsons, *Captain John R. Hughes*, 146–47.

73. Hunter, "The Outstanding Texas Ranger."

74. Hughes to Mabry, May 27, 1897, Adjutant General Papers.

75. By coincidence, the particular train that Hughes chose to escort Parra back to Texas contained a number of western luminaries on either side of law. Author Eugene Manlove Rhodes, self-appointed lawman, was taking Oliver Lee and Jim Gililland, charged with the murder of Albert Fountain and his son, to Las Cruces for trial. And just by chance Sheriff Pat Garrett, sworn enemy of the suspected Fountain killers, was also on the train. So passengers included three tough gunmen headed for murder trials (Parra, Lee, and Gililland) as well as two famous western man-hunters (Garrett and Hughes). The stage was set for an explosion of memorable proportions, but nothing untoward happened.

76. Hughes to Scurry, March 13, 1901, Adjutant General Papers.

77. Hughes to Scurry. March 14, 1901, Adjutant General Papers. Several experienced gun-wielders of the frontier West learned the hard way that single-action six-guns should always be kept with the hammer on an empty chamber to prevent discharge of a dropped pistol. Among them were gun-fighting lawman Wyatt Earp, famed Pinkerton detective Charlie Siringo, and renowned Texas Ranger John R. Hughes. All failed to observe that important fact and were embarrassed by the firing of an accidentally dropped six-shooter. Fortunately, no one was killed or seriously injured by their carelessness.

78. Parsons, *Captain John R. Hughes*, 172–73.

79. *Alice Echo*, January 19, 1905.

80. District Judge Clarence Martin et al. "To Whom It May Concern," February 26, 1903, quoted in Parsons, *Captain John R. Hughes*, 181–82.

81. Thrapp, *Encyclopedia of Frontier Biography*, 2:691. Hughes stated these views in an interview for the *El Paso Herald*, June 5, 1915, the year after he had almost married Elfreda G. Wuerschmidt.

82. Parsons, *Captain John R. Hughes*, 182–85.

83. Quoted in ibid., 192.

84. Simpson to Lanham, January 13, 1906, quoted in ibid., 195–96.

85. *Brownsville Daily Herald*, June 11, 1914. According to the *El Paso Herald*, April 20, 28, 1915, Hughes also declined appointment as El Paso chief of police.

86. Among the protesting rangers were famous ranger captain Frank Hamer and William W. Sterling, the latter of whom was commander of Company D after the departure of Hughes.

87. June 5, 1915.

88. Undated clipping in the Hughes Scrapbook in Special Collections at the University of Texas at El Paso, quoted in Parsons, *Captain John R. Hughes*, 22.

89. Clipping, January 17, 1907, Hughes Scrapbook, quoted in ibid.

90. G. W. Ogden, "The Watch on the Rio Grande," *Everybody's Magazine* (September 1911): 353–65.

91. *Houston Chronicle*, December 27, 1914.

92. *San Antonio Daily Express*, January 17, 1915.

93. William C. Hancock, "Ranger's Ranger," *True West* (March–April, 1961): 23–24.

94. *San Antonio Light*, May 30, 1915.

95. Transcript of the undated WPA interview, quoted in Parsons, *Captain John R. Hughes*, 21.

96. Ogden, "Watch on the Rio Grande," 353–65.

97. *Houston Chronicle*, December 27, 1914; *San Antonio Daily Express*, January 17, 1915.

98. August 21, 1884.

99. *Southwest Sentinel*, March 21, 1893; *Silver City Eagle*, January 22, 1896.

100. The Hughes Scrapbook, clipping, January 17, 1907, in Parsons, *Captain John R. Hughes*.

101. Parsons, *Captain John R. Hughes*, 31.

102. *El Paso Herald*, June 5, 1915.

103. *El Paso Herald*, June 5, 1915.

104. Undated typed note, C. L. Sonnichsen Collection, University of Texas, El Paso, quoted in Parsons, *Captain John R. Hughes*, 261.

105. Ibid.

106. Parsons, *Captain John R. Hughes*, 265.

107. Ibid., 271.

108. Ibid.

109. Hughes to MacFadden, December 14, 1940, quoted in ibid., 271.

110. Martin's book received excellent reviews but contained many factual errors, which were picked up and repeated in later publications. Not until 2011, seventy-one years later, did a well-researched, definitive biography of Hughes appear. Written by Chuck Parsons, an astute student of Texas history, it has been used as a guide throughout this chapter.

111. Parsons, *Captain John R. Hughes*, 283.

112. Ibid., 284; *Amarillo Daily News*, May 23, 1947.

113. *Houston Chronicle*, December 16, 1981.

Chapter 8. James Franklin "Frank" Norfleet

1. The usually reliable *New Handbook of Texas* gives his name as "Jasper," like his father, and the year as 1864. Tyler, *New Handbook of Texas*, 4:1032. However, U.S. census records, death certificate, and obituary notices agree he was born in 1865 and was christened James.

2. U.S. census, Hale County, Texas, 1940.

3. Norfleet may have learned abstention from the Snyder brothers for whom he worked during his formative years. "We adopted three rules for our cowboys on our first drive in 1868," said D. H. Snyder. "First: You can't drink whiskey and work for us. Second: You can't play cards and gamble and work for us. Third: You can't curse and swear in our camps or in our presence and work for us. These rules we kept inviolate as long as we were in the cattle business." Marvin J. Hunter, ed., *The Trail Drivers of Texas* (Austin: University of Texas Press, 1985), 4:1031.

4. Tyler, *New Handbook of Texas*, 4:1033.

5. Jim Cornelius, "Her Old Wild Past," *REH: Two-Gun Raconteur*, August 30, 2015, www.rehtwogunraconteur.com/?s=norfleet.

6. Amy Reading, *The Mark Inside: A Perfect Swindle, a Cunning Revenge, and a Small History of the Big Con* (New York: Vintage Books, 2012), 48.

7. Frank J. Norfleet and Gordon Hines, *Norfleet: The Amazing Experiences of an Intrepid Texas Rancher with an International Swindling Ring* (Sugar Land, TX: Imperial Press, 1927), 8. It should be noted that two books entitled *Norfleet* are cited here. One, written by Norfleet alone, was published in 1924, and the other, expanded upon with coauthor Gordon Hines, came out in 1927.

8. Reading, *Mark Inside*, 51.

9. Ibid., 19.

10. Ibid., 21.

11. *Oakland Tribune*, August 6, 1922.

12. *Fort Worth Star-Telegram*, March 14, 1921.

13. *Oakland Tribune*, March 2, 1928.

14. *San Francisco Chronicle*, February 14, 1913.

15. Norfleet and Hines, *Norfleet*, 13.

16. Frank J. Norfleet, *Norfleet: The Actual Experiences of a Texas Rancher's 30,000-mile Transcontinental Chase after Five Confidence Men* (Fort Worth, TX: White Publishing / Norfleet), 1924, 20–21.

17. Norfleet and Hines, *Norfleet*, 22.

18. *Dallas Morning News*, December 10, 1919.

19. This was a typical con-game ploy, to introduce the name of an impeccable, universally respected individual as a participant in the proposition in order to convince the mark of the con man's trustworthiness. Justice Holmes, of course, knew nothing of Furey or how his own name was being used.

20. Norfleet and Hines, *Norfleet*, 40.

21. The amount of $28,000 would be about $350,000 in today's inflated currency. Reading, *Mark Inside*, 16.

22. Norfleet and Hines, *Norfleet*, 29; Reading, *Mark Inside*, 19.

23. Norfleet and Hines, *Norfleet*, 30.

24. Norfleet, *Norfleet*, 22.

25. Reading, *Mark Inside*, 20.

26. Norfleet and Hines, *Norfleet*, 33.

27. Norfleet, *Norfleet*, 18–19.

28. "We don't know what Frank Norfleet's middle name is. It ought to be Nemesis." *Wichita Falls Daily Times*, August 27, 1922.

29. Norfleet, *Norfleet*, 34.

30. In both his books Norfleet embellishes his San Bernardino experience by saying it happened on Christmas, but court records show that the events actually occurred several days before the holiday. Reading, *Mark Inside*, 73.

31. Norfleet, *Norfleet*, 37.

32. Norfleet and Hines, *Norfleet*, 60.

33. Both convictions were appealed. While the appeals were pending, Ward was released on $25,000 bond, but he was rearrested and extradited to Washington, D.C., for trial on another swindling charge. On the day of his trial, guards found him battered and bleeding in his cell. He was treated at a hospital and returned to his cell, where he was later found dying from wounds he had inflicted on himself with a knife stolen from the hospital. Reading, *Mark Inside*, 75. Gerber evidently served his sentence without incident and disappeared from history.

34. Ibid.; *Lubbock Avalanche*, May 20, 1920. Hamlin was released on bond, and his lawyers obtained trial postponements for more than a year. In October 1921 he skipped bail. Norfleet, having learned from his swindlers that a good trick could twice entice a sucker, trapped Hamlin again by dropping the charges against him and having the move published in the papers, while he secretly got a new grand jury indictment. Aware that Hamlin had a wife living in Oklahoma City, Norfleet alerted police there to watch for him. When he showed up, they arrested him on a misdemeanor charge and notified Norfleet, who obtained a requisition and helped escort Hamlin to Fort Worth to stand trial. This time Hamlin could not raise his bond, set at $20,000, and remained in jail while his lawyers delayed

trial with one postponement after another. The case was finally dropped. Hamlin was killed in an automobile accident in 1933. Reading, *Mark Inside*, 133; *Lubbock Avalanche*, October 27, 1921; *Jefferson City Post-Tribune*, July 10, 1933.

35. Cary A. Hardee was elected governor of Florida in November 1920 and did not officially assume office until January 4, 1921, so requisition warrants he signed twice at Norfleet's request in December 1920 were probably illegitimate.

36. Norfleet and Hines, *Norfleet*, 158.

37. Ibid.,159.

38. Ibid., 176.

39. Norfleet, *Norfleet*, 154–55.

40. Reading, *Mark Inside*, 99–100.

41. Ibid.

42. A discrepancy between Norfleet's two books appears here. In the original 1924 account (p. 185) Norfleet wrote, "The barrel of my gun met [Furey's] forehead with a crashing blow and sent him senseless to the floor." The 1927 version (p. 219) has it, "Pete was in action and he crashed the barrel of his gun into Furey's head and he fell in a limp heap."

43. *Fort Worth Star-Telegram*, January 22, 1921.

44. Ibid.

45. *Fort Worth Star-Telegram*, February 6, 1921; *Reno Evening Gazette*, March 3, 1921; *Pinedale Roundup*, April 3, 1921.

46. Reading, *Mark Inside*, 127–28.

47. *Ogden Standard Examiner*, August 26, 1922.

48. Phillip S. Van Cise, *Fighting the Underworld* (Cambridge, MA: Riverside Press, 1936), 183.

49. Reading, *Mark Inside*, 195.

50. *Denver Post*, August 26, 1922. This newspaper's owners, Fred G. Bonfils and Harry H. Tammen, and its sports editor, Otto Floto, had joined Gallagher twenty years before in a vendetta against another Denver figure "well known in sporting circles," W. B. "Bat" Masterson, leading to Masterson's departure from Denver to a sports writing career in New York City R. K. DeArment, *Gunfighter in Gotham: Bat Masterson's New York City Years* (Norman: University of Oklahoma Press, 2013).

51. Norfleet and Hines, *Norfleet*, 372.

52. Reading, *Mark Inside*, 196; Van Cise, *Fighting the Underworld*, 230.

53. *Denver Post*, September 15, 1922.

54. *Denver Post*, February 21, 1923.

55. Reading, *Mark Inside*, 232.

56. *Dallas Morning News*, October 2, 1923; *Oakland Tribune*, October 2, 1923.

57. Norfleet, *Norfleet*, 333–34.

58. Reading, *Mark Inside*, 234; *Dallas Morning News*, March 9, 1924. Released on appeal, Spencer was imprisoned again, but in 1927 Texas governor Miriam "Ma" Ferguson granted him a full pardon. *Abilene Morning Reporter-News*,

January 16, 1927; Reading, *Mark Inside*, 234; *Galveston Daily News*, January 15, 1927. Norfleet, the man who had spent four years of his life and a great deal of borrowed money to hunt Spencer down and send him to prison, received the news stoically, giving the pardon one line in his 1927 book. Spencer, he said, "came as grist to Ma Ferguson's pardon mill and was released for no very good reason at all." Norfleet and Hines, *Norfleet*, 387.

59. *Portsmouth Herald*, October 30, 1923.

60. *Ironwood Daily Globe*, October 30, 1923.

61. Reading, *Mark Inside*, 236; *Dallas Morning News*, November 5, 1924.

62. *Nevada State Journal*, January 29, 1924.

63. *Port Arthur News*, August 13, 1924.

64. *Lubbock Morning Avalanche*, April 6, 1924.

65. *Mexia Daily News*, October 12, 1924.

66. *Dallas Morning News*, August 17, 1924. Frank Norfleet may have been displeased by this comparison of his exploits with those of Jesse James or Robin Hood; both were robbers, after all.

67. July 11, 1925.

68. Reading, *Mark Inside*, 237.

69. Gordon Hines may be familiar to readers of Oklahoma history. After working with Norfleet, Hines collaborated with former U.S. marshal Evett Dumas Nix in an account of the territory's outlaw period entitled *Oklahombres*. He also authored *Alfalfa Bill*, a biography of Oklahoma governor William Henry Murray, and *True Tales of the 101 Ranch and Other Tales*.

70. January 1, 1928.

71. *Galveston Daily News*, April 22, 1927.

72. *Abilene Morning Reporter-News*, December 4, 1927.

73. *San Antonio Light*, November 25, 1927; *Abilene Morning Reporter-News*, December 4, 1927.

74. Tyler, *New Handbook of Texas*, 4:1033.

75. *San Antonio Light*, November 25, 1927.

76. *Abilene Morning Reporter-News*, December 4, 1927. Pete Norfleet later became an officer in the immigration service and retired in 1965 after twenty-eight years of service. *Amarillo Globe*, January 8, 1965.

77. *Amarillo Globe*, December 28, 1927. A week after the murder, Hickman was arrested in Echo, Oregon. He was subsequently tried, convicted, and hanged for the crime.

78. *Abilene Morning Reporter-News*, May 6, 1928.

79. *Lancaster Eagle Gazette*, July 2, 1928.

80. *San Antonio Light*, May 16, 1928.

81. *Port Arthur News*, July 25, 1928.

82. *San Antonio Light*, December 28, 1928. Norfleet should have been thankful the bullet from the dropped pistol did not hit anyone. With this incident, he joined other notable man-hunters, Charlie Siringo and John Hughes, who were also embarrassed by their dropped revolvers.

83. Famous actor Wallace Beery also portrayed the man-hunter in a radio dramatization of the Norfleet story. Tyler, New *Handbook of Texas*, 4:1033.

84. *Amarillo Globe-Times*, May 24, 1976; Reading, *Mark Inside*, 237. According to Nat Segaloff, there have been several attempts to bring Norfleet's tale to the wide screen. It "plays like something out of a movie, and several people (including the author) have tried to get it going. One who almost succeeded is Oscar-winning actor Robert Duvall, who would have been the perfect Norfleet—charming, steely, obsessive. Unfortunately, the media conglomerate that was developing the film with him decided that Norfleet was too old a character to attract the 16-to-24-year-old movie audience. They put Duvall's project 'under advisement.'" Nat Segaloff, *Everything Tall Tales Legends & Other Outrageous Lies* (Holbrook, MA: Adams Media, 2001), 85.

85. *Abilene Morning Reporter-News*, October 19, 1930. In later years Norfleet's man-hunting range grew wider. According to the *Commerce Weekly Farm Journal*, November 6, 1931, his chases took him into nearly every state in the Union as well as Canada, Mexico, Cuba, and Puerto Rico.

86. *Amarillo Globe*, August 24, 1934.

87. *Abilene Morning Reporter-Mews*, July 5, 1936.

88. *Abilene Reporter News*, February 9, 1938.

89. *Abilene Morning Reporter-News*, July 5, 1936.

90. *Ada Weekly News*, February 11, 1937.

91. *Abilene Reporter News*, August 24, 1937.

92. *Big Spring Daly Herald*, June 21, 1939. While there was no record of a felon capture by Norfleet that year, he said his tally had risen to ninety-seven by December 1939. *El Paso Herald-Post*, December 13, 1939. By 1956 that figure was being quoted in the press as "more than 100." *Amarillo Globe-Times*, February 24, 1956; *Kerrville Times*, October 30, 1956.

93. In a 1960 interview Norfleet gave sixty-one as the total. *Abilene Reporter News*, April 1, 1960. Perhaps at age ninety-five he had forgotten his earlier tally.

94. From a scrapbook kept by Van Cise, quoted in Reading, *Mark Inside*, 243–44.

95. *Kerrville Times*, October 30, 1956.

96. Reading, *Mark Inside*, 244.

97. Ibid.; *Washington Post*, October 17, 1967. Mattie, his devoted wife of seventy-four years, also lived past the century mark. She died on January 18, 1972, one month shy of her 101st birthday. *Lubbock Avalanche-Journal*, April 11, 2011; "Mattie Eliza Norfleet," *Find a Grave*, www.findagrave.com/cgi-bin/fg.cgi?page=gr&GSfn=mattie&GSiman=1&GScid=6329&GRid=20457280&.

98. "James Franklin Norfleet," *Find a Grave*, www.findagrave.com/cgi-bin/fg.cgi?page=gr&GRid=20457270.

Bibliography

Government Documents

Records of the United States Customs Service. U.S. National Archives, Record Group 36.
Texas State Library and Archives, Austin.
  Adjutant General Papers.
  Texas Rangers Monthly Returns.

Manuscripts

Aten, Ira. "Six and One Half Years in the Ranger Service Fifty Years Ago." Briscoe Center for American History, Austin, TX.
Fronterhouse, Richard. "Bass Reeves, the Forgotten Lawman." Historic Oklahoma Collection, Manuscript Division.
Fulton, Maurice G., Papers. University of Arizona Library, Tucson.
Hughes Brothers Horse Record. Texas Ranger Hall of Fame and Museum, Waco.
Loveldav, Harve, Interview. Indian Pioneer Papers. Oklahoma Historical Society.
Rhodes Collection. Huntington Library, San Marino, California.
University of Texas at El Paso Library.
  Glenn, Skelton, Papers.
  Sonnichsen, C. L. "Last of the Great Rangers—Captain John R. Hughes." Special Collections Department.

U.S. Census

1850. Chambers County, Alabama.
1850. Santa Ana County, New Mexico Territory.
1850. Taos, New Mexico Territory.
1860. Claiborne Parish, Louisiana.
1860. Costilla District, Taos Territory County, Colorado.
1870. Crawford County, Arkansas; Deer Lodge, Montana.
1880. Costilla County, Colorado.

1900. Garland, Costilla County, Colorado.
1940. Hale County, Texas.

Newspapers

Abilene Morning Reporter-News, 1927–1928, 1930, 1936–1938, 1960
Ada (OK) Weekly News, 1937
Alameda County (CA) Gazette, 1865–1868, 1871–1872, 1875
Albuquerque Review, 1882
Alice (TX) Echo, 1905
Alta California (San Francisco), 1871, 1878
Amarillo Daily News, 1947
Amarillo Globe, 1927, 1934, 1965
Amarillo Globe-Times, 1956, 1976
Amarillo Sunday News and Globe, 1930
Anaconda (MT) Standard, 1890
Arizona Republican, 1904
Arkansas Gazette, 1884, 1886
Austin-American, 1947
Big Spring (TX) Daily Herald, 1937, 1939
Black Range (NM), 1884
Brownsville (TX) Daily Herald, 1914
Burnet (TX) Bulletin, 1929
California Police Record, 1885
Cherokee Advocate (Tahlequah, OK), 1902
Chicago Daily Tribune, 1892
Chickasaw Enterprise (Pauls Valley, OK), 1901
Commerce (TX) Weekly Farm Journal, 1931
Daily Gazette (Fort Wayne, IN), 1884
Daily Oklahoman, 1910
Daily Yellowstone Journal (Miles City, MT), 1885
Dallas Morning News, 1899, 1902, 1919, 1923–1925
Denver Daily News, 1899
Denver Post, 1922–1923
El Paso Evening News, 1903
El Paso Herald/Daily Herald, 1900–1901, 1903, 1908, 1915, 1923
El Paso Herald-Post, 1938–1939
El Paso Times/Daily Times, 1898, 1903
Fort Smith Weekly Elevator, 1884–1885
Fort Worth Star-Telegram, 1921
Fresno Expositor, 1879
Fresno Morning Republican, 1893, 1924
Galveston Daily News, 1895, 1927

Hayward (CA) Weekly Journal, 1878
Houston Chronicle, 1981, 1914
Houston Post, 1901
Independent Record (Helena, MT), 1951
Indian Journal (Eufaula, OK), 1891
Ironwood Daily Globe (MI), 1923
Jefferson City (MO) Post-Tribune, 1933
Kerrville (TX) Times, 1956
Lancaster (OH) Eagle Gazette, 1928
Las Vegas (NM) Daily/Morning Gazette, 1880–1881, 1884
Las Vegas (NM) Daily Optic, 1880, 1882
Lincoln County (NM) Leader, 1882
Lincoln County (NM) News, 1971
Longview (TX) Democrat, 1881
Los Angeles Star, 1852–1853
Los Angeles Times, 1898
Lubbock Avalanche, 1921, 1924
Lubbock Avalanche-Journal, 1920, 2011
Marysville (CA) Herald, 1853
Matamoros Flag, 1848
Mesilla Valley (NM) Independent, 1878
Mexia (TX) Daily News, 1924
Mineral Argus (Maiden, MT), 1884
Muskogee (OK) Indian Journal, 1884
Muskogee (OK) Phoenix/Daily Phoenix, 1891, 1896, 1900–1902, 1906, 1910
Muskogee (OK) Times-Democrat, 1909–1910
Nevada State Journal, 1924
New Mexico Sentinel, 1939
New Orleans Picayune, 1846
New York Sun, 1881
New York Times/Daily Times, 1853, 1926
Oakland Daily News, 1866–1867, 1872–1874, 1877
Oakland Daily Transcript, 1872–1873
Oakland Herald, 1904
Oakland Times, 1878
Oakland Tribune, 1874, 1900, 1904, 1907–1908, 1922–1923, 1928
Ogden (UT) Standard Examiner, 1922
Oklahoma City Weekly Times-Journal, 1907
Pinedale (WY) Roundup, 1921
Port Arthur (TX) News, 1924, 1928
Portsmouth (NH) Herald, 1923
Reno Evening Gazette, 1921, 1924
Rio Grande Republican (Las Cruces, NM), 1882, 1896, 1907–1908

River Press (Fort Benton, MT), 1885
Rocky Mountain Husbandman (Diamond City, MT), 1884
Rocky Mountain News Daily/Weekly (Denver, CO), 1863
Sacramento Daily Union, 1852–1853
San Antonio Daily Express, 1893, 1896, 1915, 1925
San Antonio Light, 1915, 1927, 1928
San Francisco Alta, 1853
San Francisco Bulletin, 1871–1872, 1889, 1905
San Francisco Call/Morning Call, 1872, 1878, 1883, 1894
San Francisco Chronicle, 1872, 1874, 1878, 1891, 1895, 1904–1905, 1913
San Francisco Daily Placer Times and Transcript, 1853
San Francisco Examiner, 1887
San Francisco Herald, 1852–1854
San Joaquin Republican, 1852–1854
San Jose Daily Independent, 1871
San Jose Daily Patriot, 1871
San Jose Evening News, 1904
Santa Cruz Pacific Sentinel, 1862, 1864, 1867
Santa Fe Daily New Mexican, 1880–1882
Silver City (NM) Eagle, 1896
Southwest Sentinel (Silver City, NM), 1893
Stockton (CA) Daily Independent, 1869
Times (London), 1881
Van Buren (AR) Press, 1886, 1891, 1907
Van Buren (AR) Press Argus, 1893, 1895
Vinita (OK) Indian Chieftain, 1890
Visalia (CA) Delta, 1868
Washington (DC) Herald, 1910
Washington (DC) Post, 1907, 1967
Weekly Commonwealth (Denver, CO), 1863
Western Age (Langston, OK), 1908
Western Liberal (Lordsburg, NM), 1898
White Oaks (NM) Golden Era, 1884–1886
Wichita Falls Daily Times, 1922

Articles

Carson, Kit, III. "The Lives of Two Great Scouts." In *The Westerner's Brand Book*. Denver: Artcraft Press, 1946.
Clay, T. A. "A Call to Order: Law, Violence and the Development of Montana's Early Stockman's Organizations." *Montana: The Magazine of Western History* (Autumn 2008).
Dahl, Victor C. "Granville Stuart in Latin America: A Montana Pioneer's

Diplomatic Career." *Montana: The Magazine of Western History* (July 1971): 18–33.

DeArment, R. K. "Kreeger's Toughest Arrest." *True West* (June 1986).

———. "When Stuart's Stranglers Raided the Rustlers." *Wild West* (August 2007): 48–49.

Hancock, William Cx. "Ranger's Ranger." *True West* (March–April 1961): 23–24.

Harrison, John. "Montana's Horse Thief War." *Great West* (October 1973).

Hewett, Edgar J. "Tom Tobin." *Colorado Magazine* 23, no. 5 (September 1946): 211.

Hunter, J. Marvin. "The Outstanding Texas Ranger." *Frontier Times* (December 1944).

Jessen, Kenneth, John Lamb, and David Sandoval. "Colorado's Worst Serial Murders: The Espinosa Story." *San Luis Valley Historian* 27, no. 4 (1995).

Kittredge, William, and Steven M. Krauser. "'Mr. Montana' Revised: Another Look at Granville Stuart." *Montana: The Magazine of Western History* (Autumn 1986): 14–23.

Lecompte, Janet. "Charles Autobees." *Colorado Magazine* (July 1957).

Littlefield, Daniel F., Jr., and Lonnie E. Underhill. "Negro Marshals of the Indian Territory." *Journal of Negro History* (April 1971).

Maguire, W. H. "Samuel T. Hauser: An Early Governor of Montana." *Montana: The Magazine of Western History* (March 1991).

McMullin, Thomas A. "David Walker." *Biographical Directory of American Territorial Governors*. Westport, CT: Meckler Publishing, 1984.

McRay, E. Ward. "Stuart's Stranglers." *True Western Adventures* (February 1961).

Morando, B. "Montana's Stranglers." *Real West* (July 1974).

Mueller, Oscar O. "The Central Montana Vigilante Raids of 1884." *Montana: The Magazine of Western History* (January 1951).

Mullin, Robert N. "Pat Garrett, Two Forgotten Killings." *Password* (Summer 1965).

Ogden, G. W. "The Watch on the Rio Grande." *Everybody's Magazine* (September 1911): 353–65.

Price, Charles F. "The Rampage of the Espinosas," *Colorado Central Magazine* (October 2008).

Priest, Henry Priest. "The Story of Dead Man's Canyon and the Espinosas." *Colorado Magazine* (January 1931).

Rasch, Philip J. "Amende Honorable: The Life and Death of Billy Wilson." *West Texas Historical Association Year Book* (1958).

———. "Garrett's Favorite Deputy." *Corral Dust: Potomac Corral of the Westerners* (Fall 1964).

———. "The Story of Jessie J. Evans." *Panhandle-Plains Historical Review* (1960).

Remley, David. "Granville Stuart, Cowman." *Montana: The Magazine of Western History* (Summer 1981): 28–41.

Richardson, D. S. "Duel to the Death." *Overland Monthly* (August 1888).

Secrest, William B. "Hell for Leather Rangers." *True West* (March–April 1968).

Smith, Gerald C. "The Adventures of Three Fort Garland Heroes." *San Luis Valley Historian* 2, no. 2 (1970): 1–20.

Tobin, Thomas T. "The Capture of the Espinosas." *Colorado Magazine* 9, no. 2 (March 1932).

Wilke, L. A. "The Wide Loop of the Ranger Noose." *Real Detective* (September 1936): 24–29.

Williams, Nudie E. "Bass Reeves." *Negro History Bulletin* (April–June 1979).

———. "United States vs. Bass Reeves: Black Lawman in Trial." *Chronicles of Oklahoma* (Summer 1990).

Books and Pamphlets

Abbott, E. C. "Teddy Blue," and Helen Huntington Smith. *We Pointed Them North: Recollections of a Cowpuncher.* New York: Farrar & Rinehart, 1939.

Adams, Ramon F. *Six-Guns and Saddle Leather: A Bibliography of Books and Pamphlets on Western Outlaws and Gunmen.* Norman; University of Oklahoma Press, 1969.

Alexander, Bob. *Rawhide Ranger: Ira Aten.* Denton: University of North Texas Press, 2011.

———. *Six-Shooters and Shifting Sands: The Wild West Life of Texas Ranger Captain Frank Jones.* Denton: University of North Texas Press, 2015.

———. *Winchester Warriors: Texas Rangers of Company D, 1874-1901.* Denton: University of North Texas Press, 2011.

Barrows, John R. *U-Bet: A Greenhorn in Old Montana.* Lincoln: University of Nebraska Press, 1990.

Bartholomew, Ed. *Jesse Evans: A Texas Hide-Burner.* Houston: Frontier Press of Texas, 1955.

Bell, Horace. *On the Old West Coast: Being Further Reminiscences of a Ranger.* New York: Grosset & Dunlap, 1930.

Boessenecker, John. *Gold Dust and Gunsmoke: Tales of Gold Rush Outlaws, Gunfighters, Lawmen, and Vigilantes.* New York: John Wiley & Sons, 1999.

———. *Lawman: The Life and Times of Harry Morse, 1835–1912.* Norman: University of Oklahoma Press, 1998.

Brady, Paul L. *The Black Badge: Deputy United States Marshal Bass Reeves from Slave to Heroic Lawman.* Los Angeles: Milligan Books, 2005.

———. *A Certain Blindness: A Black Family's Quest for the Promise of America.* Atlanta: ALP Publishing, 1990.

Brothers, Mary Hudson. *A Pecos Pioneer.* Albuquerque: University of New Mexico Press, 1943.

Browning, James A. *Violence Was No Stranger: A Guide to the Grave Sites of Famous Westerners.* Stillwater, OK: Barbed Wire Press, 1993.

Burton, Art T. *Black Gun, Silver Star: The Life and Legend of Frontier Marshal Bass Reeves.* Lincoln: University of Nebraska Press, 2006.

———. *Black, Red and Deadly: Black and Indian Gunfighters of the Indian Territory.* Austin, TX: Eakin Press, 1991.

Callaway, Lew L. *Montana's Righteous Hangmen: The Vigilantes in Action.* Norman: University of Oklahoma Press, 1982.

Coe, George. *Frontier Fighter.* Chicago: Lakeside Press/Donnelley & Sons, 1984.

Coker, Caleb, ed. *The News from Brownsville, Helen Chapman's Letters from the Texas Military Frontier, 1848–1852.* Austin: Texas State Historical Association, 1992.

Collins, William and Bruce Levene. *Black Bart: The True Story of the West's Most Famous Stagecoach Robber.* Mendocino, CA: Pacific Transcriptions, 1992.

Crutchfield, James A. *Revolt at Taos: The New Mexican and Indian Insurrection of 1847.* Yardley, PA: Westholme Publishing, 2015.

Cunningham, Eugene. *Triggernometry: A Gallery of Gunfighters.* New York: Press of the Pioneers, 1934.

Davis, William Heath. *Seventy-Five Years in California.* San Francisco: John Howell, Publishers, 1929.

DeArment, R. K. *Deadly Dozen: Forgotten Gunfighters of the Old West.* Vol. 3. Norman: University of Oklahoma Press, 2003.

———. *Deadly Dozen: Twelve Forgotten Gunfighters of the Old West.* Vol. 1. Norman: University of Oklahoma Press, 2003.

———. *George Scarborough: The Life and Death of a Lawman on the Closing Frontier.* Norman: University of Oklahoma Press, 1992.

———. *Gunfighter in Gotham: Bat Masterson's New York City Years.* Norman: University of Oklahoma Press, 2013.

———. *Man-Hunters of the Old West.* Vol. 1. Norman: University of Oklahoma Press, 2017.

Dillon, Mark C. *Montana Vigilantes 1863–1870: Gold, Guns, and Gallows.* Logan: Utah State University Press, 2013.

Dimsdale, Thomas Josiah. *Vigilantes of Montana; or, Popular Justice in the Rocky Mountains.* Virginia City: Montana Post Press/Tilden, 1866.

Ernst, Robert. *Deadly Affrays: The Violent Deaths of the United States Marshals.* Phoenix: Scarlet Mask, 2006.

Fulton, Maurice G. *History of the Lincoln County War.* Tucson: University of Arizona Press, 1975.

Gardner, Mark Lee. *To Hell on a Fast Horse.* New York: William Morrow, 2010.

Garrard, Lewis H. *Wah-to-yah and the Taos Trail; or Prairie Travel and Scalp Dances, with a Look at Los Rancheros from Muleback and the Rocky Mountain Campfire.* Norman: University of Oklahoma Press, 1955.

Garrett, Pat F. *The Authentic Life of Billy the Kid.* Albuquerque, NM: Horn and Wallace, 1964.

Gideon, D. C. *Indian Territory: Descriptions, Biographical, and Genealogical, Including the Landed Estates, County Seats . . . with a General History of the Territory.* New York: Lewis, 1901.

Greenwood, Robert, ed. *The California Outlaw*. Los Gatos, CA: Talisman Press, 1960.

Grey, Zane. *The Lone Star Ranger: A Romance of the Border*. New York: Grosset & Dunlap, 1915.

Hall, J. M. *The Beginning of Tulsa*. Tulsa, OK: Scott-Ric Publishing, 1933.

Hertzog, Carl. *Little Known Facts about Billy the Kid*. Santa Fe: The Press of the Territorian, 1964.

History of the Arkansas Valley, Colorado. Chicago: Baskin/Historical Publishers, 1881.

Howard, Joseph Kinsey. *Montana, High, Wide and Handsome*. New Haven, CT: Yale University Press, 1943.

Hoyt, Henry F. *A Frontier Doctor*. Chicago: Lakeside Press/Donnelley & Sons, 1929.

Huidekoper, Wallis. *The Land of the Dakotahs*. Helena, MT: The Montana Stockgrowers Association, n.d.

Hume, James B., and John N. Thacker. *Wells, Fargo & Co. Stagecoach and Train Robberies, 1870–1884. The Corporate Report of 1885 with Additional Facts about the Crimes and Their Perpetrators*. Reprint, edited and expanded by R. Michael Wilson. Jefferson, NC: McFarland, 2010.

Hunt, Frazier. *Tragic Days of Billy the Kid*. New York: Hastings House, 1956.

Hunter, J. Marvin, ed. *The Trail Drivers of Texas*. Austin: University of Texas Press, 1985.

Hutchison, W. H. *The Rhodes Reader*. Norman: University of Oklahoma Press, 1975.

Hyatt, Norman H. *An Uncommon Journey: The History of Old Dawson County, Montana Territory*. Helena, MT: Sweetgrass Books, 2009.

Jackson, Joseph Henry. *Bad Company: The Story of California's Legendary and Actual Stage-Robbers, Bandits, Highwaymen and Outlaws from the Fifties to the Eighties*. New York: Harcourt, Brace, 1949.

Jensen, Ann. *Texas Ranger's Diary and Scrapbook*. Dallas: Kaleidograph, 1936.

Koch, Margaret. *Santa Cruz County, Parade of the Past*. Fresno, CA: Valley Publishers, 1973.

Langford, Nathaniel Pitt. *Vigilante Days and Ways: The Pioneers of the Rockies*. New York: A. L. Burt, 1912.

Latta, Frank F. *Joaquin Murrieta and His Horse Gangs*. Santa Cruz, CA: Bear State Books, 1980.

Lavash, Donald. *William Brady: Tragic Hero of the Lincoln County War*. Santa Fe: Sunstone Press, 1986.

Martin, Jack. *Border Boss: Captain John R. Hughes—Texas Ranger*. San Antonio: Naylor, 1942.

McCright, Grady E., and James H. Powell. *Jesse Evans: Lincoln County Badman*, College Station, TX: Creative Publishing, 1983.

McNierney, Michael, ed. *Taos 1847: The Revolt in Contemporary Accounts*. Boulder, CO: Johnson, 1980.

Metz, Leon C. *The Encyclopedia of Lawmen, Outlaws, and Gunfighters*. New York: Checkmark Books, 2003.

———. *Pat Garrett: The Story of a Western Lawman*. Norman: University of Oklahoma Press, 1974.

Miller, Joaquin. *An Illustrated History of the State of Montana*. Chicago: Lewis Publishing, 1894.

Milner, Clyde A., and Carol A. O'Conner. *As Big as the West: The Pioneer Life of Granville Stuart*. New York: Oxford University Press, 2009.

Mooney, Charles W. *Doctor in Belle Starr Country*. Oklahoma City: Century Press, 1954.

Nolan, Frederick. *The Lincoln County War: A Documentary History*. Norman: University of Oklahoma Press, 1992.

———. *The West of Billy the Kid*. Norman: University of Oklahoma Press, 1998.

Norfleet, J. Frank. *Norfleet: The Actual Experiences of a Texas Rancher's 30,000-mile Transcontinental Chase after Five Confidence Men*. Fort Worth, TX: White Publishing/Norfleet, 1924.

Norfleet, J. Frank, and Gordon Hines. *Norfleet: The Amazing Experiences of an Intrepid Texas Rancher with an International Swindling Ring*. Sugar Land, TX: Imperial Press, 1927.

O'Neal, Bill. *Henry Brown: The Outlaw Marshal*. College Station, TX: Creative Publishing, 1980.

Parsons, Chuck. *Captain John R. Hughes: Lone Star Ranger*. Denton: University of North Texas Press, 2011.

Peninger, Robert. *Fredericksburg, Texas . . . the First Fifty Years*. Fredericksburg, TX: Arwed Hilton, 1896.

Perkins, James E., *Tom Tobin, Frontiersman*. Monte Vista, CO: Adobe Village Press, 2005.

Poe, John W. *The Death of Billy the Kid*. Boston: Houghton Mifflin, 1933.

Preece, Harold. *Lone Star Man: Ira Aten Last of the Old Time Rangers*. New York: Hastings House, 1960.

Price, Charles F. *Season of Terror: The Espinosas in Central Colorado. March–October, 1863*. Boulder: University Press of Colorado, 2013.

Rasch, Philip J. *Trailing Billy the Kid*. Stillwater, OK: Western Publications, 1995.

———. *Warriors of Lincoln County*. Stillwater, OK: Western Publications, 1998.

Reading, Amy. *The Mark Inside: A Perfect Swindle, a Cunning Revenge, and a Small History of the Big Con*. New York: Vintage Books, 2012.

Reminger, Leo, Miles Gilbert, and Sharon Cunningham, eds. *Encyclopedia of Buffalo Hunters*. Union City, TN: Pioneer Press, 2006.

Reynolds, Bill. *Trouble in New Mexico: The Outlaws, Gunmen, Desperados, Murderers and Lawmen for Fifty Turbulent Years*. Vol. 1. Bakersfield, CA: Reynolds, 1994.

Ruxton, G. F. *Adventures in Mexico and the Rocky Mountains*. London: Murray, 1847.

Secrest, William B. *California Desperadoes: Stories of Early California Outlaws in Their Own Words*. Clovis, CA: Word Dancer Press, 2000.

———. *Lawmen and Desperadoes: A Compendium of Noted, Early California Peace Officers, Badmen and Outlaws, 1850–1900*. Spokane, WA: Arthur H. Clark, 1994.

————. *The Man from the Rio Grande: A Biography of Harry Love, Leader of the California Rangers Who Tracked Down Joaquin Murrieta*. Spokane, WA: Arthur H. Clark, 2005.

————. *Showdown: Lionhearted Lawmen of Old California*. Fresno, CA: Craven Street Books, 2010.

Segaloff, Nat. *Everything Tall Tales Legends & Other Outrageous Lies*. Holbrook, MA: Adams Media, 2001.

Shinkle, James D. *Reminiscences of Roswell Pioneers*. Roswell, NM: Hall-Poorbaugh Press, 1966.

Shinn, Charles Howard. *Graphic Description of Pacific Coast Outlaws: Thrilling Exploits of Their Arch-Enemy Sheriff Harry N. Morse (for Many Years the Terror of the Brigands of California—a Man of Intrepid Courage, Wonderful Skill, and Splendid Leadership); Some of His Desperate Hand-to-Hand Encounters with Bandits*. Tucson, AZ: Westernlore Press, 1990.

Shirley, Glenn. *Shotgun for Hire*. Norman: University of Oklahoma Press, 1970.

Sides, Hampton. *Blood and Thunder: An Epic of the American West*. New York: Random House, 2006.

Simmons, Virginia McConnell. *The San Luis Valley: Land of the Six-Armed Cross*. Niwot: University Press of Colorado, 1999.

Siringo, Charles. *Riata and Spurs: The Story of a Lifetime Spent in the Saddle as Cowboy and Detective*. New York: Houghton Mifflin, 1927.

————. *A Texas Cowboy or Fifteen Years on the Hurricane Deck of a Spanish Pony*. New York: William Sloane, 1950.

Speer, Bonnie Stahlman. *The Killing of Ned Christie*. Norman, OK: Reliance, 1990.

Steele, Phillip. *Last of the Cherokee Warriors*. Gretna, LA: Pelican Press, 1987.

Stephens, Robert W. *Walter Durbin: Texas Ranger and Sheriff*. Clarendon, TX: Clarendon Press, 1970.

Stuart, Granville. *Pioneering in Montana: The Making of a State, 1864–1887*. Lincoln: University of Nebraska Press, 1977.

————. *Prospecting for Gold: From Dogtown to Virginia City, 1852–1864*. Lincoln: University of Nebraska Press, 1977.

Thrapp, Dan L. *Encyclopedia of Frontier Biography*. 3 vols. Glendale, CA: Arthur H. Clark, 1988.

Tise, Sammy. *Texas County Sheriffs*. Albuquerque, NM: Oakwood Printing, 1989.

Tuller, Roger. *"Let No Man Escape": A Judicial Biography of Isaac C. Parker*. Norman: University of Oklahoma Press, 2001.

Tyler, Ron, ed. *The New Handbook of Texas*. 6 vols. Austin: Texas State Historical Association, 1996.

Van Cise, Philip S. *Fighting the Underworld*. Cambridge, MA: Riverside Press, 1936.

Viele, Teresa Griffin. *Following the Drum*. New York: Rudd & Carleton, 1858.

Index

Maher, Peter, 173, 204–5
Mancella, Patricio, 85–87
Manning, Al, 237, 239
Maples, Daniel, 130
Maria, Jose, 83–85
Martin, Jack, 189, 216
Martin, T. P., 107, 108
Martinez, Marin Edward, 36
Martinez, Romulo, 161
Mason, Bernard "Barney," 154–55, 158, 169, 287n43
Masters, Bob, 260–61n30
Masterson, William Barclay "Bat," 141
Mathews, Billy, 150, 161
Maxwell, Jack, 175
Maxwell, Paulita, 163–64
Maxwell, Pete, 163–64
McAleer, J. L., 202–203
McCannon, John, 39–40, 47–48
McCarty, Henry (alias "Billy the Kid" Bonney), 143, 148–69, 172, 173, 181, 185–86, 255
McCloskey, William, 149
McClure's Military Academy, 93
McConnell, Reason E., 105, 107, 108
McCurry, Ed, 120
McCutcheon (rancher), 205
McDavid, A. J., 95
McDevitt, James, 70
McDonald, William J., 187, 191, 204, 208
McDorney, Edward. *See* Ward, E. J. (alias Edward McDorney)
McGowan, G. V., 260n30
McKindrict, Joe, 217
McKinley, William, 71, 112, 179–80
McKinney, Thomas Christopher "Kip," 147, 163–64
McLean & Company, 225
McLemore, A. J. "Jeff," 200
McNew, William "Bill," 172, 174–75, 178

McSween, Alexander Anderson, 149–52, 186
McSween, Susan Hummer, 151, 153
Medina, Frank, 83, 86
Mershon, James H. "Jim," 120
Mescalero Indian Agency, 152
Metcalf (fortunate fellow), 38
Metz, Leon, 184–85
Mexican Petroleum Company, 229
Mexico, 31, 82, 83
Mexico City, Mex., 32, 34
Middleton, John, 150, 152, 190, 285n14
military units: California Militia, 52; California National Guard, 112; Confederate Army, 38, 120, 126, 145, 192; Eleventh Texas Cavalry, 201; First Colorado Cavalry, 43, 48; Illinois Volunteer Infantry, 103; Oakland Guard, 75–76; Texas Volunteers, 12; Third Arkansas Cavalry, 126; U.S. Army, 53, 120, 148; U.S. Quartermasters, 6
Miller, Jim, 182–85, 202
Milton, Jeff, 204
Mission San Jose, Calif., 13, 78
Mitchell, Thomas, 256
Monka, Pedro, 17
Montana cities, towns, villages: Bannack, 54, 60, 61; Deer Lodge, 55, 71; Fort Benton, 57, 65, 69, 70; Helena, 58, 65; Lewistown, 56, 63; Maiden, 61; Miles City, 58, 69; Silver Bow, 71; Virginia City, 55 67
Montana counties: Chouteau, 70; Lewis and Clark, 56; Meagher, 67–68
Montana Historical Society, 55, 70
Montana Senate Council, 57
Montana Stock Growers Association, 58, 59, 66, 70
Montana Territorial Council, 55
Montana Territorial Legislature, 55, 57